Advance Praise for
Meditations on Everything
Under the Sun

"Margo Adair weaves together three disparate threads of human mental capacity
— visualization, psychic awareness, and mindfulness — and, by braiding the
resulting approach to meditation with a concern for community building and
social justice, gives us a rare tapestry of wisdom for a world in disarray."
— Chellis Glendinning, author of *Off the Map* and
My Name is Chellis and I'm in Recovery from Western Civilization

"This one volume is a master guidebook to the art and practice of meditation
in all of its applications. Margo has done an incredible job organizing this
material, explaining this process, and demonstrating the many ways meditation,
imagination and creativity can work together to promote emotional and
spiritual health in the individual, in kinship groups, and the global community.
I recommend this book as a text and a reference for artists, teachers,
guidance counselors, and spiritual seekers . . . anyone who wants to fully
develop their potential as human and spiritual beings. Amazing!"
— Yeye' Woro, Luisah Teish, Women Chief, author of
Jambalaya: The Natural Women's Book of Personal Charms
and Practical Rituals and *Jump Up: Good Times Throughout the Seasons*
with Celebrations from Around the World

"Margo Adair has written a most engaging book, in all senses of that word. It is pleasant to read, for she writes well. The mind is engaged as she offers some compelling thoughts about the nature of consciousness and the role of imagination. But mostly your whole being is engaged as Margo invites you to consult with your self and your colleagues in the gentle silence of meditation."
— Harrison Owen, author of *Open Space Technology* and *The Power of Spirit*

"There is nothing new under the sun, except your moment-to-moment awareness. This book will help you be present for your life — all of the 10,000 joys and sorrows of being human."
— Wes "Scoop" Nisker, author of *Crazy Wisdom* and *Buddha's Nature*

"I can't think of a better handbook on meditation than this one. Margo Adair has taken the profound and complex workings of Buddhism (and other traditional contemplative practices) and translated them into simple, everyday practices that seem especially focused for Westerners with our overactive rational minds. Stripped of religiosity and moralism, yet filled with the understanding that only comes with true experience, these extremely pragmatic exercises lead one directly into the presence of the sacred. . . . Eventually I found myself enjoying the book as an oracle — just letting it fall open to wherever it would, and then reading that meditation as my message for the day (or the situation or event), with excellent results."
— Vicki Noble, healer, teacher, co-creator of Motherpeace, and author of
*Shakti Woman: Feeling Our Fire and
Healing Our World — The New Female Shamanism*

"Margo Adair has written a much needed and moving book on meditation, imagery, and intuition. Its practical approach and tone will be invaluable and can open the door to a new dimension of spirituality, and healing rituals."
— Barbara Dossey, RN, MS, HNC, FAAN, author of
*Florence Nightingale: Mystic, Visionary, Healer;
Holistic Nursing: A Handbook for Practice;* and *Rituals of Healing*

"There are countless books on meditation, but what Margo Adair does so splendidly is to create a framework where a multitude of different meditative processes can be explored (breath, visualizations, affirmations, among many) in a way that connects them to every aspect of life. Adair's Applied Meditation goes way beyond the topics that are usual in such books, such as healing, spiritual growth, and relationships. Adair boldly looks at issues of community, the workplace, political health, morality, creativity and freedom. It is primarily a book to be used with friends, family, co-workers: with groups, not individuals. This sets it apart as unique: It is a use of meditation that does not flee, but embraces the world."
— Margot Adler, author of *Drawing Down the Moon* and *Heretic's Heart*

"Meditations is like having a wise and caring personal guide through the complexities of modern life. Practical and inspirational, Margo Adair's book provides clear advice for tapping our subjective consciousness and making it a powerful part of our lives. Given the increasing challenges of our world this is a wonderful guidebook that we each need to get through our days in health, good spirits, and community."
— Paul Kivel, activist, healer, and author of
Boys Will Be Men: Raising Our Sons for Courage, Caring, and Community and
Uprooting Racism: How White People Can Work for Racial Justice

"I've been using the exercises in Margo's first book, *Working Inside Out*, for years with my business school students and career clients. *Meditations on Everything Under the Sun* offers even more tools — from basic instruction to advanced practices. . . This new book offers a well-rounded guide to using applied meditation in every aspect of our lives. I'm inspired and eager to introduce these meditations into my own life and the lives of everyone I know."
— Claude Whitmyer, business consultant, career guide, and author of
Running a One-Person Business and *Mindfulness and Meaningful Work*

"In these pages Margo Adair, a masterful activist/organizer, teaches us how to weave spirituality into our vision of a better society and then struggle caringly (rather than selfishly or dogmatically) to make that vision a reality. The book heals with delicious possibilities."
— Terry A. Kupers, M.D., author of *Revisioning Men's Lives* and *Prison Madness*

"A must for anyone seriously concerned with their personal growth."
— Philip Slater, author of *Pursuit of Loneliness: American Culture at the Breaking Point*

"I loved this book! It is such a powerful tool for organizers. I found meditations to use for every kind of facilitation, training, and situation I need in working with organizations. I have used it successfully for rituals with spiritual groups and with groups who have never used meditation before. This is the kind of book that every organizer should keep close at hand. It is a user-friendly book not only for leading guided meditations, but also to use as a source for exploratory questions for social change work. These questions can get groups to think and explore in new ways in order to find solutions to the complex problems we face today as social change activists."
— Linda Stout, author of *Bridging the Class Divide and Other Lessons for Grassroots Organizing*

MEDITATIONS ON EVERYTHING UNDER THE SUN

MEDITATIONS
ON EVERYTHING
UNDER THE SUN

THE DANCE OF
IMAGINATION,
INTUITION,
AND MINDFULNESS

Margo Adair

NEW SOCIETY PUBLISHERS

Dedicated to the Web of Life

Cataloguing in Publication Data:
A catalog record for this publication is available from the National Library of
Canada.

Cover design by Diane McIntosh. Photo © Corbis Images.

Printed in Canada by Friesens Inc.

New Society Publishers acknowledges the support of the Government of Canada
through the Book Publishing Industry Development Program (BPIDP) for our
publishing activities, and the assistance of the Province of British Columbia
through the British Columbia Arts Council.

BRITISH
COLUMBIA
ARTS COUNCIL
Supported by the Province of British Columbia

Paperback ISBN: 0-86571-428-2

Inquiries regarding requests to reprint all or part of *Meditations on Everything
Under the Sun* should be addressed to New Society Publishers at the address below.

To order directly from the publishers, please add $4.50 shipping to the price of the
first copy, and $1.00 for each additional copy (plus GST in Canada). Send check
or money order to:

New Society Publishers
P.O. Box 189, Gabriola Island, BC V0R 1X0, Canada

New Society Publishers aims to publish books for fundamental social change
through nonviolent action. We are committed to building an ecologically sustainable and just society not just through education, but through action. We are
acting on our commitment to the world's remaining ancient forests by phasing
out our paper supply from ancient forests worldwide. This book is one step
towards ending global deforestation and climate change. It is printed on acid-free
paper that is **100% old growth forest-free** (100% post-consumer recycled),
processed chlorine free — supplied by New Leaf Paper — and printed with
vegetable based, low VOC inks. For further information, or to browse our full
list of books and purchase securely, visit our website at: www.newsociety.com

NEW SOCIETY PUBLISHERS   **www.newsociety.com**

Contents

PART I: *Working with Spirit*

PART II: *Applied Meditation*

PART III: *Meditations for All Occasions*

APPENDIX

Foreword

BY ANGELES ARRIEN

SILENCE and solitude are doorways for contemplation, reflection, and meditation. By quieting ourselves and moving to a still point of reflection, we touch the mystery and allow the human spirit to reveal itself to itself. As Margo Adair reminds us, "The act of meditation brings us into contact with the harmonizing forces intrinsic to life itself."

Meditating, accessing intuition, and active imagining are practices that unify internal experiences with outer action and service. Perennial wisdom of the world's spiritual traditions has long recognized that these practices increase human awareness and creativity, while promoting harmony in our daily lives.

This is a practical resource guide. You can use its numerous meditations in your personal, professional, and creative life, regardless of your current spiritual practices, personal beliefs, or age. The meditations also lend themselves to groups. Meditating in groups can amplify a collective intent to access different perspectives, ideas, and solutions from the guidance received. And they recognize the diversity of our experience; rather than directing you according to any particular tradition, the meditations invite you to call on whatever you most revere, making them accessible to all. Ultimately, these are tools for healing, designed to empower you to develop a more intimate relationship with your own nature.

Perhaps when the human nature is at peace, we may have an opportunity to experience world peace.

Acknowledgments

M EDITATIONS has been in the works for a decade. Throughout the years it has
been held in an energy field of support, without which it would have never
have come to fruition. My heartfelt gratitude goes to:

All the people in my meditation support groups and training workshops.
Many, many people trusted me enough to open their hearts and allowed me to
witness their aspirations and struggles. Both the meditation work and what I
learned as I worked with people through the difficult issues of power imbalances
and historical wounding were equally illuminating.

William Aal, my partner in life and work. There are not words to ade-
quately thank Bill or to describe all the ways in which he contributed. He read
every single draft and offered vital and insightful feedback — sometimes not so
easy to give. His presence is alive on every page; his love and belief in the importance of the work gave me much-needed fortitude. And he had the patience to
put up with all my trials and tribulations, which has been no small task.

The many Buddhists and Quakers who generously welcomed me to their
gatherings. Special thanks go to the Mindfulness Community of Puget Sound. I
also want to acknowledge the Quaker Friends meetings in both San Francisco and
Seattle. I have often appreciated sharing silence and opening to the Sacred with
them.

All the participants in my Energy Circles. They were indispensable in helping me hold clear intention and maintain faith.

The Church Street household in San Francisco, and to Melissa Young and
Mark Dworkin, who provided a refuge in Seattle. All of them generously gave me
space through years of writing.

All the people who offered critical feedback, took time to edit intrinsically
nonlinear material, or spent hours proofreading. I especially want to thank Beth
Brown, Autumn Riddle, and George Franklin, all of whom were involved in the

organizing and editing of the manuscript during the many years of its development. Additional appreciation goes to Casey Adair, Nina Allen, Disa Alemeta, Linne Cambell, Linne Gravestock, Ellie Hochman, Sharon Howell, Lynn Johnson, Paul Kivel, David Kubrin, Janet Labinski, Julia Lasage, Rae Lavine, Steve Leeds, Myra Levy, Pamela Osgood, Bruce Pardel, Ruby Phillips, Leonard Rifas, Will Roscoe, Ann Rosencranz, Robin Roth, Jill Singer, Dessida Snider, Charles Varon, and Sandy Voit. Joanna Macy and Sharda Rogell sharpened my portrayal of the Witness and Naomi Finkelstein put meat on the bones of the Meditation Use Index. To those whose names have slipped through the cracks — thank you all!

Barbara Moulton and Randy Fingald, who generously helped me navigate the publishing world. (The manuscript somersaulted through two other houses before landing in its rightful home.) Thanks go to Laura Wood and Sharon Cadwallader — the editors in the other houses, whose work bettered the manuscript.

Judith Plant and Chris Plant at New Society Publishers, who are inspiring role models in running a values-based company. Thanks also to editor Audrey Keating, who poured hours into straightening my nonlinear explanations for ease in reading.

The Earth for all the hundreds of flowers that accompanied me as I wrote and rewrote, and to Bill for growing them.

To Spirit for its great healing power and mystery.

PART I

Working with Spirit

At the Heart of Applied Meditation

APPLIED MEDITATION enlightens the spirit, brings peace to the heart, and reminds us of our intrinsic connectedness. It invites healing, creativity, and wisdom, and enables people to be more effective in the practical affairs of everyday life. If you have a spiritual practice, Applied Meditation will augment it; if you don't, it will open up the vast realm of the spirit to you. The theory and meditations in this book will enable you and those you share them with to apply the deeper resources of intelligence to the specific challenges you face.

The act of meditation brings us into contact with the harmonizing forces intrinsic to life itself. In short it does nothing less than empower us to be more alive, joyful, and caring. Most of us have lost sight of the sacred in the midst of the demands of daily living. It is ironic that when we stop and look within, it connects us to all that is around us. Meditation in a simple, yet elegant way reconnects us to our authentic selves, one another, and the world itself.

A self-organizing principle runs through All That Is. The symmetry of a snowflake and a dandelion or an atom and a solar system is awesome. It is at the heart of mystery — makes one take a deep breath. Physicist David Bohm offers us a theory of implicate order that suggests the universe is like a hologram — we are all part of the whole and the whole lives inside each of us.[1] There is no real separateness in the universe. When we meditate it is as though we sink into this implicate order where all is in accord.

We need to remember the connective tissue of culture. In a world that is coming apart at the seams, competition and greed rule; alienation cuts deep into the fabric of our psyches. We do not experience ourselves as being supported by and embedded in collectivity. Instead we think that the group is in opposition to the individual — that the group holds the individual back. Individualism is the malaise of our culture.

To heal ourselves and our culture we need to share time in deeper heart/spirit space. My purpose in writing this book is to provide tools for that healing. My intention is to empower you to develop a deeply intimate relationship with your own consciousness — that place inside that experiences your connection to All That Is. There is nothing more vital to reclaiming personal power than coming to trust your own subjective process. You will learn how to interpret what is taking place in your consciousness and to identify where and how to direct attention to increase well-being. As a result you will be able to apply inner resources to what concerns you at the moment, whether you are dealing with the usual demands of daily living, facing a major crisis, or addressing an issue that grips our society as a whole. Much of what meditation offers individuals is easily translated into processes that groups can use. Because meditation opens both the heart and the spirit, using it with groups creates the kind of cohesiveness that inspires wise choices, collaborative creativity, and community spirit.

This book presents a new theory and practice for working with consciousness. It emerges out of 25 years of my experience developing and teaching Applied Meditation for intuitive problem-solving and my ongoing work on social justice issues. As with Alice's looking glass, it is likely to turn your idea of reality inside out. The theory transforms the imagination from the generator of fantasy into the aspect of consciousness best suited to reveal reality and initiate positive change. It works with the interplay of the subjective and objective realms, inviting us all to participate in the co-creation of reality.

Applied Meditation weaves together three approaches to consciousness that rarely cross paths. I call them the Witness (pure awareness) — as in the mindfulness of Eastern forms of meditation; the Active Imagination — as in visualization, guided imagery, and self-hypnosis; and the Receptive Imagination — as in intuition, psychic awareness, and creativity. This book offers you a methodology by which to align yourself with your goals and increase the probabilities of them manifesting; to apply intuitive insight to your problems; and to develop your capacity for mindfulness, which grounds you in the reality of the present moment.

Included are 157 meditations that can be used for gaining insights, for healing, for deepening your relationships, and for connecting with your spiritual experience to bring the power of the sacred into your everyday life. The meditations do not emerge out of a particular tradition, but they do invite you to draw on your sense of the sacred. The meditations lend themselves to diverse groups because they invite people to call on whatever is revered by them. Designed for easy mixing and matching, you can use the meditations to create combinations that speak specifically to your circumstances or to those of your group.

RECLAIMING THE IMAGINATION

The imagination is profoundly powerful, yet in today's harried times it is the most underdeveloped and underutilized endowment we possess. The phrase, "You are just imagining it," reflects the prevailing mentality — the very fact that one imagines something is the reason why it is dismissed. We think of the imagination as the dwelling place of everything that is unreal. In fact, it is the dwelling of all our interpretations of what has happened and of all our assumptions of what will happen. Those interpretations and assumptions shape every single choice we make as we navigate through our lives.

We are completely loyal to our imagination, whether or not we dismiss it. There is nothing we do that we haven't imagined first. Not only does our behavior emerge out of what we imagine, our bodies continually respond to what we are imagining.[2] If you have a phobia of heights, you don't need to stand on a ledge to get your adrenaline pumping — all you need to do is imagine yourself there. Since the imagination plays such a crucial role, it behooves us to work with it.

Five hundred years of Western rationalism have established norms that alienate us from the immense capacities of consciousness. We disqualify ourselves from contributing to decision-making when we are "too involved" — in other words, when we really care. We are taught that the only perspective of any value is the objective point of view and so cut ourselves off from what is most meaningful. Life experience doesn't count; only the facts are to be taken into account. Science establishes the facts with experiments and analytic thinking, and legitimacy rests on how successfully the scientist gets himself or herself out of the context. Psychic phenomena are labeled paranormal, if not denied — the reasoning mind is incapable of understanding them. (To expect it to is like asking our taste buds to understand sound.) Our entire educational system aims to train the intellect. Arts and athletics are afterthoughts — for entertainment — and are not viewed as relevant to policy-making. The training of intuition is not even conceivable. We don't know how to pay attention to the imagination, much less work actively with its capacities.

Rationalistic processing will not provide what is needed for us to pass on the planet to the many generations to come. For the first time in history the future of life itself is in question. The daily paper brings story after story depicting evidence of our malaise: homelessness, the greenhouse effect, classroom shootings, toxic spills, and the rise of heart disease. The historical development of this state of affairs has everything to do with our fixation on reductive rationalistic thinking. The reasoning mind separates. It does not experience either the heart or the whole. When we exclude other ways of knowing we act unwisely and perpetuate our problems. (If people were operating out of a sense of connectedness would they have continued to develop nuclear power when there was no solution for nuclear waste?) As long as the rational process is the only one taken seriously we continue to fragment our world.

It is the rationalistic mind that cannot tolerate more than one view at a time. This is not to say that we should throw out rational analysis, only that it needs to be accompanied by other ways of knowing. We need to break out of binary, either/or, dualistic, linear consciousness and view reality from a holistic perspective.[3] We need to balance the receptive and active parts of ourselves. Imagine what the world would be like if we spent as much time developing our intuition as we do training the rational mind. Imagine how much less strife there would be in the world if intuition were an integral part of decision-making.

This society leaves little room for reflection — we think of it as a luxury separate from the world of activity. In fact, it is vital for making choices that do not backfire, whether in our personal lives or as we face the global issues that affect us all. We need to create a culture in which reflection is a shared and not a private activity. When we truly reflect together our wisdom and creativity become synergistic; we soften the context and make room for heart and spirit. When we reflect together we secure the future.

Not extraneous but vital, the imagination is the purveyor of our experience of the sacred. The sacred and the material are not separate. Our imaginations live upon pure awareness just as our bodies live upon the Earth. In fact, our entire reality is mediated through the imagination. Contrary to what most of us have been taught, spirit and matter, and the subjective and objective infuse one another in a perpetual dance — they are what root us to the very ground of being. When we ignore the imagination it is as though we are trees that have been ripped out of the ground — our roots dangle in the air. When we bring spirit and matter together in our everyday lives we make ourselves and our culture whole again.[4]

IMAGINATION AND MINDFULNESS

Applied Meditation works intimately with the imagination and mindfulness to bring about well-being. I use the word "imagination" to encompass the modes of consciousness other than rational processing. The rational mind is linear, logical, analytical, cause and effect oriented, abstract, critical, particular, and categorical. The imagination is the language of the soul and speaks in poetry, story, art, music, metaphor, feeling, and visceral experience. It is the meeting ground of heart and spirit. Holistic and multidimensional, it is where the dance of probabilities takes place. The imagination makes patterns out of particulars, and it communes with healing energies. It is the locale of prayer. Through the imagination we access our intuitive/psychic awareness. It is the dwelling place of beliefs (which in turn dictate expectations). And it is the agent of creativity. The imagination rests on pure awareness, which we experience when we work with the inner Witness to cultivate mindfulness.

Applied Meditation weaves together the Witness, the Active Imagination, and the Receptive Imagination. The Witness watches what transpires in the environs of your subjective landscape and is continually aware of how energy is moving or getting stuck in the river of consciousness. (I use the term "The Witness" for ease in communication, but it is not a noun. It is a verb, a process — or more to the point, a way of being.) The Witness resides in the universal intelligence that underlies all of reality. It recognizes what is true and offers knowing that has no form.

The spacious awareness of the Witness can be likened to mindfulness in Eastern forms of meditation practice. The Witness always senses the whole, notices intent, and reveals true expectations. It perceives intuitive hunches, flashes of insight, and understands metaphor. It is the Witness that recognizes the truth of the matter. The Witness, therefore, makes it evident whether we need to engage the Active or the Receptive Imagination.

The Active Imagination projects what you want as if it has already taken place. As a result, you become so thoroughly familiar with your desires that you orient toward them and act naturally in accordance with your goals. Visualizing also generates energy, which increases the likelihood that your goals will manifest. You use the Active Imagination when you know what you want — that is, when you have a vision to strive for.

The Receptive Imagination engages your story-making capacities, which invite the creative and intuitive insights that can illuminate a way out of a bind. The Receptive Imagination reveals exactly what constraints are operative and what is needed to overcome them. You use the Receptive Imagination when you are unhappy with your situation but cannot conceive how it could be otherwise — that is, when you have no vision to strive for.

All three aspects of Applied Meditation continually weave together and are not distinctly separate activities. The Active Imagination and the Receptive Imagination are interdependent; the Witness observes their interplay. To try to work solely with one is like trying to breathe without exhaling.

Applied Meditation pays attention to and works with a very familiar part of you that is always present. Great powers reside in the ordinary. Everyone possesses an inner Witness and an imagination. These aspects of consciousness move into the forefront of awareness when you are relaxed and don't have to actively think about what you are doing — when you are exercising, cleaning, walking, staring into space, or simply taking a moment to relax. Most people actually spend a lot of time in this receptive/creative state. The problem is that we are accustomed to ignoring the contents of our consciousness at the very times when our imagination is most active and the Witness is most accessible.

You don't have to go somewhere else to find the answers to your difficulties. There are no techniques that need to be mastered, no quick fixes to be found, no exotic places to be revealed. All you need to do is give yourself permission to relax into your own experience, to be with yourself completely, to be present, and then to act on the insights that emerge.

With Applied Meditation you establish new pathways for your thoughts — paths that you choose. We have all inherited conditioning that keeps us alienated from our true selves and isolated from each other. The meditations provide both a vehicle and a map for traveling through the terrain of the psyche; using them, you will be able to literally re-map your cognitive processes and reconstruct your response mechanisms. You can create ways of being that are coherent with your values and no longer be plagued with thinking one way and acting in another. Nothing less is needed if we are to genuinely create a sustainable culture.

The meditations use rhythm, repetition, and rhyme to induce a relaxed state of mind; just by reading them you awaken the deeper powers of consciousness. Metaphor, fantasy, and memory — the language of the imagination — draw out sensation, feeling, and vision, and give energy form. A gentle feeling of well-being accompanies the meditation experience as you move into alignment with the harmonizing forces of the universe. In this state of consciousness you access the healing powers flowing through the terrain of inner dimensions. It becomes self-evident what is needed to bring balance to the situation on which you are focusing. The inner and outer realms are engaged in a perpetual dance, influencing and infusing one another. Each has everything to do with what transpires in the other. When you participate with your subjective world you not only influence your ability to do well and feel good about it; you also influence what happens to you.

The decision to commit yourself to develop and maintain a deeply intimate relationship with inner consciousness may be the decision that brings the most far-reaching changes in your life — it was in mine. When communities engage in these dimensions together and share what emerges from the experience, it has an equally profound impact on community life. People can rediscover what is needed to create a just and sustainable community life. The meditations, themselves, become exponentially more powerful when used by groups. Meditative consciousness is naturally synergistic; it is about the experience of communion and, therefore, takes to groups the way a duck takes to water.

In group settings meditation is one of the most effective ways of establishing a sense of shared intention. By simply taking a few moments to meditate together and share presence in these dimensions, we experience a natural shedding of the isolating patterns that keep us alienated from one another. Since meditating moves us into alignment with the harmonizing forces of the universe, people act with more heart, and decisions tend to emerge easily — as though they just happen. In addition meditation can be the best antidote for those egotistical personalities who thwart the emergence of team spirit — not because these people necessarily like to meditate but because group meditation creates an energy field of shared resonance: when the tide rises, all of the boats are lifted.

Use the meditations in groups that are already part of your life — your family, workplace, or community. No meditation experience is necessary for either leading or listening to the meditations. Because they are written in a voice that speaks directly to deeper awareness anyone can lead them, and most everyone will be transported into their inner dimensions. Almost invariably, helpful insights emerge and the experience is a healing one. Indeed, Applied Meditation has much to offer you whether you practice it as an individual or as part of a group.

The Anatomy of Consciousness[5]

CONSCIOUSNESS IS SOMEHOW directly entwined with the stuff of which the universe is made. As discoveries in quantum physics have shown, the observer affects the observed and is a determiner of outcome. When physicists look for subatomic phenomena to behave like waves of energy, they do; look for them to behave like particles of matter, and they do. (In other words when a particle question is asked, a wave answer is never received and vice versa.)[6] The notion that there is such a thing as "objective" disappears at these subatomic levels — the levels that constitute the building blocks of matter. In his theory of the implicate order Bohm asserts that mind and matter are really separate aspects of one whole and unbroken movement.

I believe that consciousness itself is energy; in some mysterious way it is part of the mix that shapes what unfolds — not just our interpretations but what actually takes place in the world. Anticipation and our focus of attention not only determine how our body/mind experiences and responds to circumstances; they also feed probabilities. We are part of a grand cosmic dance of co-arising.

THE WITNESS
Engaging the Knowing of the Inner Witness

We each have a quality of our consciousness that simply knows — this is the Witness. The Witness does not argue or try to prove anything. It isn't fearful or pushy. It just knows. It notices what you can and cannot imagine; it also recognizes where you are out of balance and where change is possible. The Witness has no investment and, therefore, no blind spots. In its openness it simply witnesses what is so.

The Witness is the aspect of consciousness that recognizes the answers; there is a felt sense when you come across the answer to a problem you have been grappling with — it feels right. It fits. There is no conflict, no attachment, and no judgment. There is an acknowledgment, a feeling of wholeness about it that simply is. Other aspects of you may not like (or may ignore) the answer, but they cannot argue with it.

Full breath engages the Witness. (We use the term "breathtaking" to identify something so awesome that we can only comprehend it from a state of wholeness.) As with your breath the Witness is always with you. Similarly both breath and the Witness can be affected by your reactions. When you confront anything uncomfortable you tense up — a reaction that creates shallow breathing. Breathlessness narrows your attention and squeezes out knowing. You find yourself cut off from wholeness. When we get exasperated and need a fresh start or when we are about to embark on a challenging task, we naturally take a deep breath. We draw in knowing — we draw upon the fullness of being and reside in our wholeness. Full breath always invites the spacious awareness of the Witness. The Witness is what roots us in direct experience of the moment.

Drawing Out Your Wholeness

Find the knowing aspect of yourself now as you slowly read these words. Pause between each sentence. Take a moment and become aware of your body breathing. Let your breath be full and relaxed. Watch your breath fill your body; feel your breath turn around and come back out of your body. Feel the rise and fall of your belly as you breathe. Watch your body breathing. Sense every cell in your body breathing, bathed in waves of breath. Acknowledge that you have a body, yet you know that you are more than your body.

As you are breathing, notice your thoughts. Be aware of the thoughts moving through your mind. Take a moment to simply watch your thoughts as they move through your awareness like birds that fly through the sky. Just witness your thoughts. Imagine as though there is space in between your thoughts. Appreciate the fact that you have thoughts, yet you know that you are more than your thoughts.

Continue to be aware of your breathing. Extend your awareness to include all that you are feeling at the moment. Be aware of all the emotions present in you. Witness your feelings. Simply take note of the feelings that are present in you. Your feelings enrich your life, filling it with color. Appreciate that you have feelings, yet you know that you are more than your feelings.

Notice the quality of your awareness that witnesses these aspects of your being.[7] We do not experience breath — we experience breathing. Similarly we do not experience "a Witness inside" — we experience open awareness. The Witness is the act of open awareness. It always comes forth when your breath is relaxed. Remember that the Witness is not a noun but a quality of being.

THE ACTIVE IMAGINATION
The Imagination Is the Ground out of Which All Action Grows

At every moment we act out of what we are imagining; the challenge is to be consciously engaged with the contents of our imagination. You will succeed in making change more quickly and easily when you engage the Active Imagination and consciously project what you want. When we deliberately give our imagination another point of reference, we are no longer compelled to act out of past experience. When we don't, we are trapped in the past — an insight that was brought home to me in social change work.

For many years I have been attempting to unravel why the internal dynamics in social justice organizations often duplicate the very relations those selfsame organizations are working to change in society. In "Patterns of Power" workshops we do an exercise where people create dramatizations of how domination and compliance manifest in their relationships even if there is no immediate structural power relationship present (as there would be in employer/worker or landlord/tenant relationships, for example). People easily come up with scenarios depicting what happens. After they act it out, we ask them to replay the scenes so that everyone is equal. Despite people's best intent, their replays invariably regress into the same patterns. Rationally understanding the cause of the problem provides no alternative vision of what would be better. With no positive vision people are left with the problem image by default — and it continues to form the basis of their behavior.

If we don't actively work with the contents of our imagination, then our memories are the sole source of its vocabulary: we find ourselves playing out the same dramas with a different cast of characters.[8] This is why patterns of abuse repeat themselves from one generation to the next. Despite a resolve to do otherwise, people get caught in familiar ways of being and doing. Like Sisyphus we push the boulder up the mountain over and over again, only to have it roll back down.

Only the imagination can create new vision: it is simultaneously the doorway into new realities and the aspect of ourselves that can produce new keys to fit. For any given problem you need to ask yourself how you would like it to be instead. Then ask what that would actually be like? What would it feel like? Look like? None of these questions is difficult to answer. It is just that as a result of our culture's preoccupation with the question "why" (rational analysis) it usually doesn't occur to us to ask them. You can use your imagination to discover/create positive visions of what you want and then come to know them intimately. This process does not work rationally — you need not know why, when, where, or how you will accomplish your goal. Just imagine you already have and you will generate the energies that are needed. Envisioning what you want is an indispensable and unavoidable first step in bringing about personal or cultural change.

The Active Imagination As a Catalyst for Change

When you imagine what you want as though it has already occurred (positive projection), six things happen.

1. Your anticipation illuminates your path.

2. You provide yourself with an alternative point of reference, which in turn provides a new basis of behavior. You inspire yourself.

3. You familiarize yourself with a new way of being. You will find yourself having impulses that are congruent with your vision. It is as though you set up an internal compass. You so align yourself with your desires that you find yourself intuitively acting in accord with what you want.

4. Because you evoke energy that attracts circumstances that resonate with your desire, you increase the likelihood of realizing the outcomes you want. It is as though you set up a magnetic force field that both pulls you into, and pulls toward you, occurrences that have affinity with the quality of energy you project.

5. You cultivate optimism. You find yourself establishing the plausibility of your desires rather than your fears.

6. You discover (via the Witness) what doesn't take hold and (via the Receptive Imagination) what is obstructing change — information that lets you know exactly where further attention is called for.

Seeding Change: Breaking the Perpetuation of Negative Experience

How do you generate a positive vision/sense when your objective experience has been negative? You use inner consciousness as a vast storehouse of different experiences — experiences that can be rearranged. Suppose you want to feel confident speaking up in public, yet despite your desire your shyness dictates your behavior. What you can do is think of something that you are confident about: maybe for you that is playing racquetball. Take time to imagine yourself playing, and experience again the internal sensation of confidence. Then imagine feeling this way when you're speaking in public. As soon as you lose your feeling of confidence, go back to imagining racquetball, then back to imagining public speaking. This method is not a quick fix — it will take practice to be able to hold the vision/sense of yourself as confident in public speaking — but it does work. You will find that the more you change your subjective experience the more your objective experience changes.

Apply the same principles to break out of a cycle of abuse. Imagine a relationship in which mutual respect and care are always present. (It is okay if you cannot locate one in your own experience; maybe there is someone you know who embodies these qualities in their relationships. The important thing is that you locate an alternate frame of reference.) Then work toward becoming very familiar with what this way of being would actually feel like. You are giving your imagination a new resource. It doesn't matter whose experience you use nor if what you imagine is actually true. What does matter is that you imagine yourself inside the experience you conjure up and that you come to believe it is possible. This exercise — like the meditations — puts your imagination to work creating the basis of action that you want.

Your rational mind will think this exercise is crazy. That doesn't matter, because your rational mind is not at the base of behavior. (If it were then you would have already freed yourself from the limitation.) The non-critical nature of the imagination is what makes it suggestible. The rational mind has critical capacities; the imagination does not — what is "objectively" true is meaningless to it. The imagination cannot comprehend negatives either. If you read "Don't imagine a rose," or "Imagine a rose," the same thing happens: your imagination pictures a rose. In the same way the idea of stopping abuse only evokes the idea of abuse. What you need is a vision of what you want and what that would feel like. Once you have created and come to know a positive alternative, you will find that you are able to shed unwanted lifelong patterns. You will no longer act at cross-purposes with your own intent but will, instead, provide yourself with a new foundation for your behavior.[9]

Anticipation guides where the light of awareness travels: your entire being moves into alignment with whatever is in your imagination at any given moment. Rationally, it makes no difference to describe a glass as half empty or half full — it is the same glass. But to inner consciousness it does matter — we are continually looking for signals in the outer world that validate our perceptions. The quality of your life will significantly improve if you focus on what you want rather than on what you don't. Be on the lookout for desirable experiences: if you are anxious you will notice anything that threatens your well-being and are likely to miss those things that might give you pleasure. Unless you want your problems to solidify into permanence be especially vigilant in noticing when you slip into a victim mentality, and move immediately to change it. Look for signs of your competence rather than of your incompetence. Call it the placebo approach to life — you get what you expect.[10] The trick is to expect what you want.

Expectation versus Wishful Thinking: How to Avoid the Pollyanna Trap

The projection of positive outcomes is not a Pollyanna approach that compulsively and perpetually denies negativity (an approach common among proponents of The New Age who hold that we individually create our own reality.) By denying the full range of our feelings we set up control patterns, dissociate, and cut ourselves off from an authentic relationship with life. We use up our energy in avoidance. Repression increases the negative energy charge and makes learning and transformation impossible. Denial is an investment in not seeing what is — a sure invitation to trouble. It is only in wholeness that we open to the unifying, healing forces within.

It is natural for tension to arise when we are confronted with difficulty. When we experience pain our first reflex it to tense up and try to close ourselves off from the feelings it engenders. People who work with pain, however, know that the exact opposite response is what is needed — breathing into pain relieves it. Breathing releases tension in both the body and the mind. Full breath invites the presence of the Witness, which expands subjective space, creating room to discover what is needed to change the difficulty or to come to peace with it.

When you work with the Active Imagination you are invited to know what you want and to imagine what that would feel like. As you work in the presence of the Witness you sense the energy patterns that are currently operating and perceive anything that is impeding the energy flow. Then you engage the Receptive Imagination, and it will help you to work through the obstacles.

It is of the utmost importance that you witness whether you are engaged with expectation or with wishful thinking. Expectation and wishful thinking operate on different ends of the continuum of change and are qualitatively different because they anticipate opposite outcomes.[11] Expectation assumes something can and will happen: you can feel how it would be to experience what you want; your desire feels entirely plausible, and you can imagine it transpiring easily, clearly, and vividly — as clearly as you can imagine opening the door to your home. Wishful thinking assumes something can't and won't happen: you cannot feel how it would be to have what you want; while you might wish for your desire to come true, it feels unattainable. In fact, wishful thinking is usually preoccupied with feeling the emptiness of your unmet desire.

You can detect if your projection falls on the wishful thinking end of the continuum of change, because it just won't stick when you bring it to mind. The negative sense returns as soon as you move your attention elsewhere. Subsequently whenever the concern comes to mind the first sense you have is of the unsatisfactory state of affairs. (It's like trying to keep a marble from rolling down an incline — you can hold it there but as soon as you focus elsewhere, it rolls.) Rather than signaling a failure, the way your imagination depicts your concern acts as a barometer of your state of being and ought to be welcomed as useful information.

Always witness where your expectations seem to settle. When you are projecting desired results, observe the nuances of how the projection moves. Notice what is pervasive and what persists. There are always real reasons why you cannot fully imagine something (that is, fully feel what your projection would be like). It could be that an accumulation of past experience that is contrary to your desire has caused you to carry limiting beliefs (a subjective limitation). It could be that you are intuiting something external that makes your projection impossible at this time (an objective limitation). Don't get tangled in assessing whether a limitation is subjective or objective — the two are linked and continually responding to changes in the other, and either way you still need to work with the energy of the limitation. The goal is to avoid attracting circumstances that resonate with your limited expectation and to intuit where there are openings that may be receptive to change.

When a limitation is primarily subjective you will find that you hold an underlying belief that contradicts your projection. (Your beliefs are those aspects of your subjective experience that you take for granted. They are what you assume to be true, so there seems to be no need to focus attention on them.) Your beliefs are the roads upon which your projections travel: any that are contrary to what you are projecting will block you from really feeling that the desirable situation is possible.

It is not difficult to become aware of self-defeating beliefs — and you need not go to therapy for years to uncover them. To illustrate, think of something specific that is unsatisfactory in your life then simply ask what is "normal" about it. The question will reveal the particular assumptions you hold that perpetuate the unsatisfactory state of affairs. Whenever your positive projection contradicts a belief you hold, the act of projection provokes the negative or disempowering belief into the light of awareness. If you are working in the presence of the Witness, you will see the negative belief.

Once you uncover the negative beliefs that support the blockage, you can ask yourself what the opposite state of affairs would be and imagine what life would be like if that were true instead. You will find that as soon as you are able to establish the plausibility of a different belief, you will also have moved from the wishful thinking to the expectation end of the continuum in relation to your original projection. As you work your positive projection will become stronger, clearer, more fluid, and fully plausible. Your consciousness will no longer roll back into old, familiar assumptions but, instead, will trust that the situation is indeed changing. You will no longer block energy flow but will move naturally with the harmonizing forces of life.

When you apply your imagination to creating a different subjective sense through positive projections, you work through blocked energy and receive insights that reveal what is needed to bring about change. If a positive expectation continues to elude you and you have not come to a deeper understanding that enables you to feel at peace with an issue, then you need to employ your Receptive Imagination — it will help you discover what is needed to resolve your difficulty. You will find a vision with which to work.

From Victims to Visionaries: Transforming Our World

The Active Imagination is as important for cultural transformation as it is for personal transformation. Apply the principles to social change and the impact is nothing less than revolutionary. As with personal change, we need to have a vision to strive for. Wherever there are gaps between our ideals and what is taking place with issues such as fair and just relations, diversity, ecological sustainability, etc. we need to find and create points of reference that illuminate how it could be otherwise. If, as a woman, you want to get rid of sexist role expectations, then imagine how life would feel if you both saw yourself and were seen as indispensable to policy-making. When you do you will act differently and inspire others to treat you differently. Envision how the dominant culture would change if we didn't leave the particular ways we are different at the door in order to fit in. How would it feel if there truly were a diversity of approaches? How would it feel if we refrained from acting once we realized something's negative ecological impact? If we want to relate to one another and the planet in ways that are respectful and sustaining, then we have to create visions of how that would be — not just think about it but imagine and sense how it would actually be and feel.

Creating visions is not a private affair. Since the vocabulary of each of our imaginations is limited by our past experience, we all need to look to those whose experience is different if we want to stop perpetuating unwanted patterns. What if people from indigenous cultures that have been self-sustaining for more than a millennium were to sit at the table that is addressing global warming? What if people whose cultural practices emphasize sharing rather than accumulating were to sit on the boards of the World Bank? The voice of the outsider has always been on the leading edge of cultural transformation. Would their input not expand the collective imagination of those grappling with the problems? When we take on the attitude of humility and curiosity we discover what is needed. When we combine our differences we have what it takes to be whole again.

Thinking by itself is not enough. We must imagine true justice in our relations with one another, across nations, and with the Earth itself. When we create contexts in which we share our varied experiences, our horizons expand and we give the Active Imagination a rich pool of resources from which to draw. And what we can imagine, we can bring about.

THE RECEPTIVE IMAGINATION

Wanting something doesn't mean you can imagine it. You can think about what you want, but to feel what it would be like to have it and to assume that it will transpire is a different matter. Ironically, one of the first steps in the transformation process — whether personal or cultural — requires that you become acutely aware of what you have not yet been able to imagine. This is the work of the witness. Then you invite the insights you need in order to create conditions conducive to change; this is the work of the creative and intuitive/psychic aspect of the imagination that I call the Receptive Imagination. It is important that you pay careful attention to the nuances of how it depicts the situation — those nuances will mirror subjective and objective reality. When you cannot imagine something it is never due to limitations of your imagination but to limitations in yourself and/or your life.

The Imagination is the Medium of Psychic Awareness

I have come to view the imagination not as the container of all that is illusion but as a window through which we can witness reality — a statement that may turn your idea of reality inside out. In my book, *Working Inside Out*, I describe an experience that changed my life and catapulted me into working directly with consciousness.[12]

At the end of a six-day training session, each participant was asked to do a psychic case reading. While I was in a meditative state I was given only the name, age, and address of a woman and was expected to decipher what ailed her physically. To my chagrin no spirit whispered into my ear to tell me what to say. People were waiting for me to say something, and so left to my own devices I used my imagination and just made up a story. It felt as ordinary as anything that had ever gone on in my mind. Everything I described — the print on the woman's dress, her dog, the layout of her kitchen, and even the chalky substance on her spine — was accurate! The other training participants were also all successful in their case readings.

That one experience required me to completely reevaluate my understanding of the nature of reality. Everything I had been taught up to that point was woefully inadequate to explain it. I have never been a religious person — I was raised in an academic family that viewed spirituality as something people turned to because they couldn't face reality head-on. I realized I was not a separate being moving through the world: somehow, inexplicably, the world moved through me as well. That is why I appreciate the model of the universe as hologram. If you cut a hologram in half, you do not end up with two halves of a whole; instead, the whole is contained in each half. Cut it again, and the whole will be contained in each new part. Everything is part of the whole, and the whole lives in all the parts.

I remember wondering if the many hours of guided meditation exercises in the training sessions made us psychic or if they only opened us to the possibility that we were psychic all along. I gave a case to a friend who had never been involved in any spiritual or metaphysical activities. I asked him to relax and didn't even take him through a guided relaxation process — I just asked him to tell me when he was ready. When he spoke, I gave him only the name, age, and address of a man who had motor problems on his left side as the result of a gunshot wound to the head. My friend said he saw a big, circular black spot behind the man's right ear and that the left side of his body felt rubbery. I asked if there was anything else he was aware of, and he said no. (When I give this same case in my training sessions students always go into great detail.) We are all psychics, but like unused muscles our abilities have nearly atrophied. Perhaps our awareness moves to a holographic level when we engage with our psychic perception.

Rejected Awareness

Our rational selves are truly tenacious about dismissing the legitimacy of our inner perceptions. Consider the results of numerous ESP experiments in which subjects were asked in advance whether or not they believed psychic perception was possible.[13] Those who said yes scored significantly better than chance in their tests. Those who said that there was no such thing as psychic perception scored below chance — their test results had significantly more inaccuracies than mere chance would allow! Anticipation really does direct the light of our perceptions or, in the latter case, the blinders of our denial.

I have been using case readings in my Applied Meditation training sessions for over 25 years and have yet to discover a better way for people to learn that their imagination has psychic power. Participants in my workshops do not know the person whose case they will read: while they are in a meditative state, they are given only the name, age, and address of a person whom they know has a disabling physical condition. (I've guided more than 1,000 people through the process, and all those who tried succeeded in doing an accurate reading.) Although participants have no prior knowledge of the case subjects and cannot know what would or not be accurate, I have found that they usually discount the most accurate pieces of information first.

On one occasion, a case reader who was having trouble kept saying he wasn't getting anything. I encouraged him to just make it up. Eventually he said that he saw a man in a wheelchair and he didn't know why, but he thought the man couldn't walk. After this reader came out of his meditative state I informed him that he was correct — the person for whom he had read had become a paraplegic by falling off a roof. The reader's jaw dropped, and he told me that when he first heard the case subject's name he had seen the fleeting image of a man falling but had dismissed it.

Having psychic abilities is so threatening to many people's worldview that they grab at anything to dismiss the possibility. They often say, "Oh, they're just reading the mind of the person who presents the case." (As if somehow that were ordinary behavior!) But case readers frequently come up with information that the presenter doesn't have. When I did my first reading, I saw a woman wearing black "old lady" shoes with brown laces. After the reading, the presenter informed me that the only thing I had gotten wrong was the shoes — her friend always wore the latest style. I later learned that the next time the presenter saw her friend, the woman was wearing the shoes I had described.

When people do readings they often expect themselves to come up with a specific medical diagnosis: that is how we have been taught to view physical problems. When someone does a reading of a person with leukemia they are more likely to report "white stuff in the blood" than to say "leukemia." During one training session, a reader described the brain of the woman she was reading as containing a lot that could not be expressed. She went on to say that the woman could not talk or eat; she could only drink. The case subject was a woman who had had a cancerous tumor removed and was recovering from throat surgery. What the reader described would be apt for anyone who had undergone throat surgery; still this reader felt that she had failed to do the reading accurately because she hadn't actually said the words "throat cancer."

Our rational mind is incapable of understanding intuition, but it does know when we are on to something! Threatened by the direct form of knowing that is characteristic of case reading work, our rational mind goes into a frenzy of discounting. And it seems that the more attuned we are to this other way of knowing, the more the rational mind discounts it. The implications are grave if we dismiss our experience at the very moments when we are most attuned to direct knowing. At the very least our knowing gets truncated. But what's worse is that when we distrust our own awareness we effectively relinquish our personal power.

Toward Understanding the Psychic Process

I continue to be astounded by the abilities of consciousness. My current understanding of psychic readings is that the name, age, and address of the case subject act as a pointer and direct the reader's light of awareness to a specific spot in the amorphous collective unconsciousness. (Think of it as a location in the holographic universe.) Once attuned to the case subject, readers perceive how case subjects see themselves, but the information is filtered through the vocabulary of the reader's own imagination. For instance, I once did a case reading of a man whom I imagined as being in a wheelchair, though I could find nothing in his body that would explain why he needed one. As I was imagining his head I was startled by the vivid image of a hugely distorted left eye. Unsuccessful at finding out why the man was in a wheelchair, I came out of the meditative state. The case presenter told me that I had been tuning in on her brother who had had an accident that disfigured and blinded his left eye. She said that after the accident he always referred to himself as "crippled." In my mind "crippled" people use wheelchairs. This illustration demonstrates how information is revealed through the subjective language of the reader.

Consciousness is a material force. I have come to view anything and everything that takes place in the imagination as energy that influences not only the subjective world but the objective material world as well. I had a visceral experience of this principle when I did a case reading of a woman who had problems in her finger joints. My dominant imaginative mode is visual, but I wanted to develop my inner sensate (or kinesthetic) ability, so I focused on how my body felt as I described what I saw going on inside the woman's body. As I opened and closed my hands to move my fingers I felt and heard every joint crack. (The other five people in the room also heard them crack.) I had never experienced a sensation quite like it. When I was done with the reading I cleared myself and returned to my usual waking awareness. For weeks afterward I opened and closed my hands, trying to recreate that sensation but couldn't (an illustration of how thinking and imagining are not the same thing). Most readings provide insights that people find useful. Occasionally, though, a reading will seem to have dramatic objective effects. In one case, on the same day as a reading, a mute woman who did not know that her case was being read spoke for the first time in ten years.[14]

The Receptive Imagination Makes Pearls

An energy blockage underlies all problems. To find out what is needed to transform a persistent negative sense, give imaginary form to what is obstructing
your vision by making up a story. Give yourself permission, in the privacy of
your own psyche, to make-believe just as children do. The act of story-making
provides a context in which the operative energies reveal themselves. The
insights you receive will illuminate the attitudes and/or actions that can bring
about change or will help you to discover how to come to peace with what is.
You can employ your Receptive Imagination to work through anything from
mundane irritations to major crises; it can make pearls of wisdom from the most
difficult of circumstances.

Consider the example of someone endeavoring to heal herself of a cancerous tumor.[15] She wants to imagine the tumor shrinking and then disappearing
altogether. She can envision herself as being well in a general way, but it becomes
harder for her to feel a sense of wellness when her focus of attention is right in
the area of her body where the cancerous growth is. She might be able to
momentarily picture the growth disappearing, but then the sense slips away and
the more familiar reality of the tumor fills her imagination. (It's like a rubber
band that snaps back as soon as you let go. The cancer itself is much more real
to her.)

Because the tumor is obstructing her feeling of well-being, the woman
talks with it. She engages her Receptive Imagination in a story, portraying what
the tumor cares about and conversing with it to try to find another way to address
its concerns. Her imagination acts as a barometer of her state of being: she can
know in a profound way what is actually happening in her body and can directly
participate with it. If she is successful, then she will be able to imagine the tumor
shrinking. If she cannot sustain a sense of the tumor shrinking, then she can
engage her deeper experience to discover how she can be at peace with herself and
her body. The story-making she does elicits insights that illuminate what is needed
to bring about change in her approach to her circumstances.

Story-making is central to the work of the Receptive Imagination and,
many people have difficulty accepting this necessity. When people in my training
workshops are doing case readings, they always want the answers to come to
them: they feel that making up the answers is a sure sign of being wrong. Nothing
could be further from the truth. The act of "making it up" is the means by which
the energy makes itself known. Furthermore, it doesn't matter how the story
comes to be: those who feel they have "made something up" are just as accurate
with their readings as are those who feel they are reporting on something that
"came to" them. The important thing is that the story-making capacity of the
imagination creates the context in which information can reveal itself.

The characteristics of the Receptive Imagination take some getting used to.
Just as anticipation illumines where you are headed, so questions angle the direction in which the light of awareness moves. Questions, therefore, determine what

comes into view. Think of yourself as standing in an absolutely dark room, holding a flashlight. Whenever you move your hand the light illuminates a particular section of the room: the movement of your hand is the equivalent of a question.

We are used to thinking in sequential terms — when we ask a question we wait to be answered. But when you work with the Receptive Imagination, you need to shift your thinking. In inner dimensions, experience transpires in the perpetual here and now — question and answer occur simultaneously. As quickly as you formulate or hear a question, you find yourself knowing the answer. There is no time lag between the two, just as there would be no time lag between the movement of your hand and the movement of the light of a flashlight.

When you work with the Receptive Imagination your task is to develop a keen sensitivity for the moment at which the question and your instantaneous response to it become clear. It is as though you always keep an eye on the back of your mind, noticing immediately what breaks into the light of conscious awareness. Like a surfer, you ride the wave right after its crest breaks into consciousness. Answers may come cloaked in metaphor, in words, as visceral sensations, or as a knowing that has no form. The answers are never complex — however they reveal themselves the Witness will recognize them and know their meaning.

Once you have addressed the reasons why you couldn't imagine change, an internal shift will have taken place, and you will then be in a position to engage the Active Imagination and move from wishful thinking into expectation. Or you may find that you no longer need to work with your Active Imagination because you are at peace with your situation. In either case the blockage is gone — all because you "made it up" and witnessed the meaning of your own story.

The capabilities of consciousness are truly awesome. I do not pretend to fully understand all that goes on in these dimensions, but that is no reason to dismiss them. To think that our rational abilities are the only aspect of awareness worthy of attention is the equivalent of assuming the iceberg is only as big as what is above the surface. When we become adept at inviting, recognizing, and responding to the information our Receptive Imagination brings us, we will be better able to avoid wrong turns.

THE PERPETUAL DANCE OF CONSCIOUSNESS
The Boundaries Between the Subjective and the Objective Dissolve
When you start directing the imagination synchronous events become commonplace. Symmetry runs not only through the physical world of snowflakes and dandelions but through time, too. That is why I say that the imagination is the stuff of which probabilities are made. I used to take my imagination for granted, only taking its contents seriously when I was doing an art project. After the training in which I did my first psychic case reading, however, I began to direct my imagination more consciously. I imagined avoiding my usual reaction to poison oak, getting parking places right in front of my destination, and finding my dream apartment — all of it worked! My life lit up with magic! I kept finding myself in

the right place at the right time — on every level of my life from the mundane to the profound. It was as though synchronicity became a way of life. Now if synchronicity disappears from my daily experience I know that I have fallen out of harmony — my life becomes discordant.

Our imagination is always creating a story to make sense of the world and to anticipate what will unfold. The fabric of these stories is woven from our beliefs (what we have concluded from our experience) and from intuitive information that reveals, through psychic awareness, the current state of reality.

The world inside is as vast as the world outside. Each mirrors the other. View every thought as though it were a living, conscious, independent entity that is both affecting and affected by everything. Inner consciousness is suspended in universal consciousness. Think of it as a river of the collective unconscious. The Witness sits on the bank, viewing the flow of energy. The river brings information in (receptive) and carries your projections out (active). The picture that sticks is what is currently true; the ways in which you can shift the picture constitutes what is possible. Witness; dance with your imagination, and energy flows.

Letting Go into the Wholeness of Being

Wholeness is the natural state. Nature continually moves into ever-greater states of equilibrium and dynamic expression. This is the self-regulating capacity characteristic of ecosystems — to maintain balance and evolve. To reject a part is to reject wholeness; everything we experience needs to be integrated into the whole, not rejected.

Our rational minds tell us that the best way to deal with life is to keep everything under control. Behind the need to control is the assumption that somehow life, itself, is antagonistic and certain aspects of it must be rejected. We tense up and hold on in order to keep out unwanted experience. The problem is that when we do, we block life force energy. We cannot harmonize with our environment without perceiving what is true about it. The more energy we spend in the perpetual holding of control, the less energy there is left to perceive what is so.

Creative and healing energy can only be tapped when we let go, relax, and trust the process. Constriction restrains psychic circulation, blocking life force energy and the healing process. It is not a natural state. When constricted aspects of ourselves are in control we have tunnel vision, and our experience is correspondingly narrowed. For instance, when Pollyanna is in charge blind spots keep vital information from view. Remember the blinders of denial in the ESP experiments?

Life is fluid. It is in a continual state of movement. That is why breathing is at the center of this work. Whenever constriction occurs, breathe, and ask yourself how you can connect. With full breath comes openness, without which there is no learning. With full breath there is space for the harmonizing energy intrinsic to life to emerge. You find yourself simply knowing what is needed. In wholeness there is no dissociation. In wholeness there are no secrets. Without the toxic energy of repression or obsession, without the toxic energy of blame or shame, there is room for change.

What is true for individuals is also true for groups. Meditative awareness resides in the realms of universality. Groups that meditate together call out a collective knowing; people come into accord in a mysterious way and collectively move into symmetry. Teamwork takes on an aura of grace, and synchronous events spontaneously occur. (Indeed, people often feel that they are reading each other's minds.) Everyone works and plays as though connected by an invisible energy field of shared resonance. Whether you work on your own or in a group, when you let go into wholeness you witness healing.

In Spacious Awareness the Active and the Receptive Dance Together

When you reside in wholeness, your awareness is spacious and encompasses all of you. The Witness has moved into the forefront — it has full peripheral vision and catches the instantaneous impressions that break into the light of awareness. These impressions are the keys to understanding what is presently true, both subjectively and objectively. In wholeness we experience the "Aha!" of sudden insight and creativity.

With spacious consciousness, instead of getting caught in judgment or denial there is room to acknowledge all of what is happening. In your knowing there is no pushing, no pulling, and no cowering. Humor, grace, and compassion replace blame and shame. All that is, simply is. When you are in your wholeness you perceive clearly, for you've created space for witnessing what is so. Not invested, you can acknowledge whatever is currently true, both within and around you. You have space to choose direction.

When the Witness is present all aspects of the self work in concert with each other rather than at cross-purposes. It is not that you stop thinking or feeling — these aspects of experience just occupy a different position in the schema. When you are projecting what you want with your Active Imagination the Witness listens, senses, and recognizes the stuck spots. Then when you engage your Receptive Imagination to play with the stuck energy, the Witness recognizes the places where opening can occur and where new experience can be had. When you choose to move into the opening a shift takes place both internally and externally — everything moves into a different alignment. You feel differently about what is happening and what happens is different. No one aspect takes over.

In spacious awareness there is room for you to perceive your entire process and to ferret out the inner assumptions that are congruent with external limitations. You discover the ways you collude with the problem. When the Witness is present you are gentle. There is no need to be defensive or aggressive — the internal energy that corresponds to the problem can be acknowledged and nudged out of its holding pattern. Openness is created so that a new way of being can be experienced. In spacious awareness there is room for shifts to take place. Healing happens.

With Applied Meditation you will come to know life in the most intimate way and will be empowered to align your life with the healing forces that move deep within All That Is. Knowing is both simple and elegant — there is nothing complex about it. When we join with one another in wholeness we return our world to its natural order; we remake our culture to one that is sustained by the natural order. We move into balance and rejoin the elegant symmetry of the universe. Together we heal the future.

PART II

Applied Meditation

Applied Meditation in Practice

IT IS IMPORTANT TO UNDERSTAND the nature of inner awareness. If you apply the usual criteria for determining if you are on course, chances are you will conclude that you are not. When you come to appreciate the contours of the subjective realms, you will find it easier to navigate in them. Applied Meditation in Practice provides you with some guides so that you will be better equipped to move through your inner dimensions and work with whatever you come across.

Although you can use the meditations on your own, whenever possible it is best to use them in your circle of family, friends, and coworkers. The meditations provide an easy way for people to tap into their own creative and intuitive resources, making any effort more meaningful and more successful. Your meditations increase in power if you work in a group because the inner experience is synergistically more potent when you meditate with others. If you verbalize your meditative experience it helps to make it tangible and begins to move the insights gained in meditation into daily life. And when you share a practice with others it becomes easier to incorporate meditating into your routine.

CREATING A CONTAINER FOR MEDITATION:
WHEN, WHERE, AND WITH WHOM?

I highly recommend that you establish a regular Applied Meditation practice; life takes on a hue of joy when you do. Consciousness is energy. The specific concerns you focus on during your regular meditation carry much more potency than anything else that may occupy your imagination during the rest of the day. When you practice meditation you will develop a deeply intimate relationship with your inner world and greatly improve the overall quality of your life.

There is no one way to establish a meditation practice. The issue is your relationship with your inner life. The meditations are effective whether or not you have any meditation or visualization experience. The language they use speaks directly to the imaginative and intuitive consciousness. When you are engaged in any kind of rhythmic activity your state of consciousness is relaxed and receptive, so your imagination is fluid. Some people find that they have a better time using recorded meditations when they go on their daily walk.[1] Some people like to play soothing music. Just make sure you keep your spine straight. Whether you are lying down, sitting, or walking, energy flows more easily if your spine is straight.

Try to make the space you use comfortable and beautiful; it will set a tone that is conducive to your meditation work. You might want to make an altar. Some people use their altars for items that represent what they cherish in life or to remind themselves of what they want to cultivate. An altar can be a good place to put a statement of a personal commitment, the picture of a loved one in need of healing, or a drawing of a symbol that represents something to which you are aspiring. If you meditate with a group you may want to have a table on which people may put items of significance. Then when you meditate, your altar becomes a place of refuge — you are surrounded inside and out with what is sacred to you. If, on the other hand, you find an altar too cumbersome or senti-mental for your needs, don't worry. Paying attention to what feels right to you and following your inclinations are fundamental to this work: you are developing an intimate relationship with your inner life.

I recommend that you keep a journal. It is especially important that you write down any insights you gain and agreements you make with yourself. What comes forth in meditation can be like dreams, which are as clear as day upon wak-ing but fade in the bustle of activity. When you write down or draw your experience after a meditation, however briefly, you provide a clear record of your experience and assure memory. You also initiate the movement of energy from your inner world out into your life.

A journal tracks your progress and helps you give credit where credit is due. If you forget that you have focused on a particular issue, when change occurs, you may neglect to appreciate the contribution your deeper self has made. That decreases the effectiveness of your inner work. Acknowledgment develops your faith in your own inner powers. The more it works the more you expect it to work the next time; and the more you expect it to work the more it does. Keeping a journal demonstrates to your inner self that you take it seriously.

A meditation session can last anywhere from fifteen minutes to a few hours to a whole weekend retreat. You can work with one person or with many. Whether you meditate with a group or by yourself, it is best to have a regular (preferably daily) practice. You need to take time to get to know your inner landscape and to discover how working with it best fits into your life.

As with anything new that you want to incorporate into your life, meditation benefits from repetition. I suggest that you meditate for five to fifteen minutes once or twice a day to begin with. Although it requires an act of will to develop new habits, once they are established you will easily be able to keep up your practice. In time you will find that you can spontaneously access inner resources whenever you need them — anywhere, anytime. Since inner consciousness revels in repetition, it is good to use the same process to enter the meditative state every time you practice — that way you create a well-worn path into your inner dimensions and will find yourself better able to receive the insights and energy you need.

The meditations can be used to help in specific situations that arise in daily life. For instance it would likely be helpful to read *Getting Ready for Surgery or Other Treatments (68)* to a family member in the hospital or to share *Team Spirit (146)* with coworkers when you are about to embark on a new project. When a friend is in crisis you don't have to avoid them because you feel inept at helping: instead offer to read a meditation. However you choose to use Applied Meditation you will find that it has a significant influence on your life and on the lives of those with whom you share it.

Signposts to Guide Your Inner Travel

Many people think that meditation is something exotic and outside of our usual experience, and that it has to be quiet and peaceful in order to do it. But they are mistaken. Applied Meditation pays attention to and works with a part of you that is always present; it is nice to have quiet but it isn't necessary.

Meditation is the art of focused attention; you choose what to focus on. You learn that awareness and attention are not the same thing — just because a clock is ticking doesn't mean you have to listen to it. The meditations carve out new paths for your thoughts to travel. Once the paths are laid down you can use them to access resources in you inner realms whenever you like.

When you meditate your horizons broaden. You become more aware of what is taking place both inside and around you. The more relaxed you are, the more you notice. As you develop a relationship with your inner self, you will be able meditate anywhere — even on a rush-hour bus or standing in line with people talking right next to you.

Working with Breath

Breath holds the key to the inner dimensions. Full breath brings about a relaxed state, releases your imagination, makes your creative/intuitive powers accessible, and draws out the inner Witness. Your breath is your anchor. When you meditate endeavor to breathe with full, relaxed breaths — as relaxed as those of a sleeping baby. Full breath evokes your fullness, wholeness, and holistic consciousness. Whenever you find yourself tensing up, your inner consciousness gets pushed out of the light of awareness. Just take a deep breath, and you'll find your deeper consciousness surfacing again.

While meditating you can use your breath to deepen awareness and to heighten alertness. When you get distracted breath can bring your attention back to the issue on which you are focusing. You can use it to release tension, to intensify and direct specific energy, or to open space for problem-solving. Breath is the vehicle of the life force; working with it opens you to healing.

Although all the meditations use breath, three are especially intended to focus on breath work. *The Transformative Power of Breath (45)* is especially helpful. Use *Breath is Home; Breath Heals (1G)* at the beginning of a meditation or whenever tension arises. To end your meditation you might use *Energize Transformation with Breath (13G)*.

Rational Consciousness Dismisses While Inner Consciousness Evades

Your rational mind is afraid of losing control. Most people notice it injecting a string of thoughts, discounting anything that is taking place in their meditation. "You are not relaxed enough." "You just made that up." "That's stupid!" As with the ticking clock, you need not listen to it. The rational mind is doing what it is supposed to do — judging.

People usually think that the presence of the discounting voice is a sign that they cannot meditate. It is important to understand that your rational mind does not disappear when you are meditating. If you try to banish it, it will just dig in its heels. Do not take its bait and argue with it about your inner work. When you do, you are no longer doing the work. The question is where you focus your attention. Give your critic a box seat from which it can run its critique while you get on with your inner work. Let it sit back and be entertained by the theater of your imagination.

In contrast to the rational mind, the inner consciousness would rather play than work. It has a much easier time doing what it pleases when you are not paying any attention to it and is used to being ignored. Its most common tactic is to evade the issue at hand by drifting off and leaving you in a snooze. Or it may bring in distractions — making you itchy or confronting you with grotesque imagery— anything to avoid work and divert your attention.

Both your rational mind and your inner awareness feel threatened by the possibility of success. Take the presence of conflict as a good sign. In my experience it is often when you are doing the most effective inner work that dismissal and evasion become the most pronounced. In the spacious awareness of the meditative state there is ample room for all aspects of consciousness. Eventually your inner consciousness and your rational mind will make peace and welcome each other's contributions. In the meantime, the tension between them need not hinder the work at all. It is simply a bit of a nuisance.

Don't expect the meditative state to feel different than your usual state of awareness. You are paying attention to and working with a part of you that has always been present. The important thing is doing it, not how it feels when you do. The effectiveness of your inner work will reveal itself by how your life experience changes.

As a beginning meditator you are likely to want to know if you are doing it right. Rationally assessing your inner process is like asking your eyes what something smells like. You can have a sense that it feels right, and at the same time you might think you are doing it wrong. The problem is that the question itself is either/or, a judgment call, and therefore a question for your rational mind to answer. But your rational mind is not objective on the subject and is ill equipped to address it.

Strive to assume that you are doing fine. Even if you are convinced you are doing it wrong, go through the process anyway. A word of caution though — because we are always trying to validate our perspectives, do not look for proof that you can't meditate or that it makes no difference in your life. That is not suspending judgment and watching with open curiosity for what might transpire; it is proving a point. If you take a skeptical approach you will sabotage yourself. You needn't be a believer, but you do have to be open.

CHARACTER OF INNER CONSCIOUSNESS
Fluid, Fickle, and Fancy-Free

Inner consciousness is fluid, fickle, and fancy-free — full of humor, puns, and metaphor. Trying to focus it is a bit like attempting to control the movement of a leaf fluttering in the breeze — before you know it, it flits off. Take joy in it. Don't assume that everything of import is solemn. In fact it is usually in lightness that insight and creativity come through.

You want to fly — even soar — with your inner consciousness, not catch, control, or stop it. This is easier said than done, so be patient with yourself. When you find that your attention has been carried off somewhere else, just bring it back to your breath and recreate what you had been working on. To re-focus, you need not start back at the beginning — inner dimensions are not linear. Just go back to where you were. Before you do, though, note where your awareness got carried off to — often you'll find that what is taking place metaphorically provides insight into the issue on which you were working. You may discover that, rather than being carried away, you were transported into a dimension better suited to supply insight. Inner consciousness tends to be quite playful, so never dismiss out of hand what takes place in deeper awareness.

Modes of Inner Perception

For each exterior way of perceiving the world, there is a corresponding interior sense. Just as we often favor one mode of perception, so we often favor a particular way of experiencing our imaginations. For some the visual may predominate; for others the visceral or auditory. I've worked with people whose imagination works mainly through smell. However your imagination works is fine.

Generally, what you imagine will not be nearly as vivid as what you experience in the objective world or in your dream world. However, the more you work with your imagination — fleshing out your first impressions — the more vivid your inner experience becomes. (If you want to further develop any one sense, simply pay attention to it or make up what it would perceive.) Keep in mind that although it is captivating to have vivid sensations and images, this is not the goal. It isn't as important to be able to smell the imaginary rose as it is to understand the meaning the rose has for you.

Suggestible and Literal

Inner consciousness is not the aspect of our consciousness that judges. It is not critical; it simply experiences. That is why it is suggestible. When you hear or read the phrases "lemon" or "don't imagine a lemon," the same thing occurs: you imagine a lemon. Inner consciousness is literal. You want to be sure you keep it occupied with positive suggestions (not worst-case scenarios). Without resorting to denial and repression always strive to move the focus of your attention away from negativity and toward what would be better. (For example, when your throat feels scratchy, vividly imagine drinking soothing syrup.)

WORKING WITH INNER CONSCIOUSNESS

Sharp demarcations or linear order do not exist in the world of inner dimensions. When I strive to write my understanding of the nature of inner consciousness, I often feel that I'm searching for the beginning of a circle. I have described the different aspects of inner work as the knowing of the Witness, the projection of the Active Imagination, and the insight of the Receptive Imagination. In fact you will not experience them as distinctly separate processes, and you work with them simultaneously. Your thorough understanding of each aspect and how they work together will ensure a skillful use of Applied Meditation. The principles that follow are crucial for you to understand if you are working with your inner dimensions independently; they can also equip you to optimize the effectiveness of the meditations in this book.

Engaging the Witness for Mindfulness

We all have a Witness, but we must pay attention to it if we are to hear what it perceives. When it is present life is graceful. It is as though the Witness sits on the ground of being, itself. Through its observations, what will increase harmony becomes evident. Awareness takes on a soft and spacious quality.

The Witness holds the key to freedom. Real choice resides in the space between what takes place and your response to it — by expanding the space between, you claim your optimal well-being and effectiveness. The Witness both opens up and resides in this space. It is here that you recognize the answers that are right for you.

Full breath draws out the knowing of the Witness. To evoke its presence just stop, relax, and breathe; the Witness will always surface when you relax and focus on your breath. In the space created by full breath, constriction evaporates and horizons widen. Here awareness is spacious; choices are made out of a sense of wholeness. You respond instead of react. You are mindful.

Life is a perpetual dance of energies that resonate with each other. In the presence of the Witness that which is providing coherence in each particular situation and that which is incongruent is revealed. It shows where the concentrations of energies are — energies that determine what will come to pass. You are able to witness underlying assumptions, intentions, and expectations and to discover the beliefs that shape the past, the present, and the possible — not only yours but also the beliefs of others.

The Witness is mindful of both what is coming in and what is going out. For some it sits in the back of awareness, watching what emerges; for others it resides "in the gut" and feels out situations. In the presence of the Witness you can detect when new impulses arise and can catch a sudden leap of thought — the insight that illuminates the way out of a bind. You can notice when the currents in a situation shift or when transformation is needed to make room for positive energy. It knows what you should embrace and what you should avoid. Everything that you learn in the presence of the Witness is vital for making fully informed choices.

The Witness does not reason; it simply knows. It exists in the perpetual present. Not living in time, it does not experience cause and effect in the usual sense, so it can't explain why it knows what it knows — it just knows. Don't expect explanations from it. It reveals energy resonance: what congeals, what repels, what's harmonious and what's discordant in any given situation. The Witness is not emotionally attached to its perspectives. Its knowledge is simply there, and you can take it or leave it — there is no drive behind the information itself.

The Witness will not chase after you with information; in fact you only find out what it knows when you pay attention. Some other aspect of you may have a strong reaction to the information it offers, but the Witness itself resides in a perpetual state of non-judgment. It has a keen sense of what is best; it knows how you could move into greater states of well-being or what you need to avoid to protect yourself. Its knowledge is nonattached and neutral in tone, and its message never comes with a command. If you find that any information you are getting includes either an explanation or a mandate, then the messenger is not the Witness.

When you are familiar with the Witness it is easy to pay attention to it when you need to survey a situation. When you move into the space between stimulus and response, you have room to see a range of options. The Witness doesn't get caught up in fighting what is; instead, it is as though it breathes space into tension areas. This widens the context and changes your vantage point — you move from being inside the problem to seeing it from the outside. A change in your point of view reveals new possibilities; you can shine the light of awareness in a different direction.

So bring forth the Witness. Remember, all you need to do is breathe fully. Breath provides the space needed for you to perceive all that is taking place. You will find yourself residing in spacious awareness — this awareness is the Witness. To work with the Witness always use the section of the opening meditation *Inner Witness (1H)*.

In the Presence of the Witness Limitations Are Revealed and New Beginnings Are Found

The Witness has a knack for revealing where positive energy may be found so that you can initiate change. In spacious awareness you may:

- **catch first impressions.** Our first impressions are carriers of intuitive information. They are the ones that haven't yet had time to be contaminated by bias.

- **recognize realizations.** Realizations are like shooting stars: if you are not watching at the right moment you miss them. Catching the flare, you have a full view of the realization being illuminated.

- **become aware of new impulses.** When change is your intent, impulses may arise that invite you to do something differently. When acted on they are often the first steps on a new road.

- **detect correspondences between internal and external limitations.** You may not have power over what takes place externally, but you do have it over what takes place inside. By altering your side of the dynamic, you opt out of the rules of the game. Your energy shift causes different circumstances to be drawn to you. In the presence of the Witness you can see the internal belief/energy patterns you hold that resonate with external limitations.

- **reveal outdated beliefs.** When an old belief remains in place new information has nowhere to settle and form a base for new behavior. In the presence of the Witness you can detect contradictions between what you have learned would be better and what you continue to do.

- **enter old memories of pain.** In the presence of the Witness you can re-visit difficult times of the past and breathe space into them. This enables you to shift the energy so that you carry the memory differently. As a consequence you free yourself from repeating history.

Intention Is the Determiner of Result

You can change the path your thoughts move along with an act of will. All inner work is determined by underlying beliefs and intentions: these form the roads along which your projections move and your insights come; they dictate which direction your consciousness moves, and therefore what comes into view and how you interpret it.

It is human nature to try to prove that your perspectives are accurate; anticipation, therefore, angles the light of awareness. If your basic attitude is that any particular projection (or projection in general) will not work, then it won't. If you think it might and are curious to see if it does, then you will be on the lookout for signs of success. If your perspective is one of curiosity and delight with new information, then you will find that your beam of light is significantly wider and your range of options correspondingly greater than if you dogmatically hold to a single idea. The Witness is always aware of underlying attitudes; your job is to pay attention to what it reveals and to make adjustments where necessary. See Mental Housecleaning (Part II, Page 43) and the meditation *Clearing Space Inside with Mental Housecleaning (11)*.

The Active Imagination: Conjuring Up Probabilities with Projection

The premise that imagination is the substance of which probabilities are made implies that every idea/sensation/feeling/vision that crosses your awareness is energy — both affecting and affected by what is taking place in the world. The most important tenet of this work, then, is to keep your consciousness positive and open. Consciousness is magnetic. Like energies are drawn together: you are attracted to what is congruent and resonant with the contents of your subjective experience, and what is congruent and resonant with your experience is attracted to you. Affinity is the way of the universe. Whatever you do, you have imagined it first, and your expectations fuel probabilities. Always witness what you are expecting and notice if it is desirable.

We Are All Connected: The Ethics of This Work

Cultivate the attitude that your work with the Active Imagination is to benefit all beings. The power of the Active Imagination is awesome and, like any power, is to be used responsibly. Reality co-arises in the interaction between spirit and matter: we neither solely create our own reality nor do external forces solely determine our fate. The possible is in a continual state of flux; the Active Imagination influences but does not direct probabilities, and the Receptive Imagination discovers what is probable at any given moment in time. The Active Imagination, then, provides each of us with the opportunity to co-create reality and contribute to the cosmic co-arising. This work is sacred. It is unethical to use these energies to get what you want at the expense of others.

Never put forward a positive projection with the investment that it is the only way the issue should unfold. For any projection you work with it is vital that you extend your awareness beyond yourself and witness what its impact would be on others if it were to manifest — not just for the people with whom you come in contact, but for whole groups of people and the planet itself. (The Witness will safeguard you from imposing your will on others if you keep it present.) Each one of us is part of the larger whole. Each projection has an impact on the whole.

In the U.S. we have been so socialized to a "me-first" way of being that we don't know how to think in terms of "we." We are seeing what happens when greed drives history, and it is essential that we train ourselves to broaden our view.[2] When the future of life is at stake everyone has to take responsibility for widening horizons and refraining from being single-minded. Think in terms of community, of the planet. Think wide. Think of the ancestors and of the generations to come. Think far.

Good intentions are not enough to ensure that no harm is done. It is much more difficult to maintain humility the more power we have, yet it is increasingly critical to remember that we don't necessarily know what is best. In hierarchy the more privilege we have, the more cut off we are from the impact of our actions. When we have power over others it is that much more difficult to see the underbelly of our projection. When arrogance and ignorance combine with power the effect can be devastating: what is construed as progress from one standpoint can be experienced as genocide from another.

Be humble. If you are projecting a new work project, for instance, put yourself in the shoes of someone on the bottom rung — how does it affect this person? If you don't ask, then the impact of your plans is unlikely to come into the light of awareness. If the Witness is present, you can catch yourself when a projection is rooted in selfish motives. *Ripple Effect: Check Out the Consequences (101)* and *Ensure Your Vision Benefits Everyone (13J)* will help with relevant questions. Listen deeply, and never assume you know what is best. How could your ideas of how things ought to go be better than the natural symmetry of the universe?

I cannot emphasize enough: never put forward a positive projection with the investment that it is the only way the issue should unfold. Think of your projection as an offering not as a command, and maintain the attitude that it will only come to pass if it is in everyone's interest. Intention is the determiner of results: assume your projection will only take hold if it is of benefit to all beings.

Creating a Positive Projection

Pay attention to what occupies your imagination when you focus on an issue: in the spacious awareness of the Witness notice anything stuck or constricted, and ask yourself how you would like it to be instead. Always ask yourself what you want, what would feel better. Many of us never have been given permission to dream, much less to take our dreams seriously. Stretch your imagination; dream.

Find a vision that inspires you! Your use of the Active Imagination increases the probability that what you want will happen. It will help you to believe that what you want is plausible and creates a context for new expectations to settle in, making it easier for you to expect what you want.

The way to cultivate new and open energy is to imagine that what you want is already true. Unlike rational problem-solving — which is concerned with why conditions come about and what steps are needed to bring about change — when you work with the Active Imagination you do not need to know why, how, when, or where. (In fact explanations and justifications are counterproductive — they evoke rational processing and distract you from experiencing what the condition you're striving for would actually be like.) Instead assume with as much conviction as you can muster that your projection is actually so. What would life be like if you could take it for granted that what you want were an ongoing part of your experience?

When you explore how it would feel to actually have what you want, it both generates energy for your intuition to realign itself and attracts resonant circumstances into your life. Although all of the meditations engage the Active Imagination, *Making Magic (43)* and *Manifest Your Ideal (52)* are especially good to use in this context. To reinforce your process, use *Active Imagination (1J)* every time you meditate.

If you have trouble finding a positive perspective refer to Methods to Find a Positive Point of Reference for ideas that might help you locate one. If you still cannot find a vision toward which to strive, then use your Receptive Imagination to discover what is needed. You may also want to do Mental Housecleaning (Part II, Page 43).

Methods to Find a Positive Point of Reference

- Ask yourself what the opposite state of affairs would be. Pretend that is the case, and adjust your perspective until you find something you would like.

- Find an area that is free of the constriction. For instance, if you are working on healing a sprained ankle, remember how your other ankle feels; project that experience into the injured one.

- Think of someone who excels in the particular area you are concerned about. Imagine what that would be like.

- Bring to mind an arena in which you are talented. Superimpose your feelings of competence onto the problem area.

- Ask yourself what would it be like if you were at peace with the current state of affairs.

- See Positive Subjective Resources (Appendix).

Getting to Know and Adjusting Your Projection

Strive to imagine vividly. The more three-dimensional your visualizations, the more energy they contain. Choose a context where the desired reality might plausibly take place. Don't worry if that is really the context — the purpose here is to give yourself a way to imagine the details. It is not the object of your desire that is at issue. (The results of visualizations are never exactly as projected anyway.) Free your imagination to create, then elaborate, embellish, and exaggerate. Imagine the look, feel, sound, smell, and mood of the scene. See the colors. Feel the textures and hear the sounds.

Imagine as though what you want has already taken place. Transport yourself into the future and imagine what it would feel like. (If you only imagine what you desire as occurring sometime in the future, that is where it will stay — beyond your grasp. Remember the difference between wishful thinking and expectation?) Don't concern yourself with how or when you get to this future time. Simply use your imagination to experience what it would actually be like. How does it feel? How does it shift your sense of self? How does your day-to-day experience change? How does it affect others?

Imagine stepping into the body of yourself in your positive projection. What would your hands be doing? What would be below your feet? By embodying the experience you avoid wishful thinking. Get to know the experience intimately. Breathe it. Notice what happens in your relationships. Let your imagination explore the multiple aspects of it. When you feel the experience from the inside — discovering what life is like from that vantage point — you will be able to witness if your projection is as desirable as you had thought. Now is the time to be sure, not later when it has already manifested.

Always keep the Witness present so that you can sense how the energy moves, where it gets stuck, what opposing messages get provoked, and how it affects others. If something doesn't feel quite right, make the appropriate adjustments. When the Witness is present you can see what in your subjective landscape needs attention to make room for new experience. You will discover if you have any outdated beliefs that are obstructing your vision. It is important to understand that investment in a particular projection signals the absence of the Witness, which means that what you are projecting is more likely to cause problems than to solve them. If you keep the Witness present, your reactive aspects will not be able to conjure up projections that will cause trouble.

Your Receptive Imagination is also operative when the Witness is present. As you explore projections your Receptive Imagination reveals what is objectively possible at that moment. (Remember the imagination is the medium of psychic awareness.) If you have difficulty imagining something it doesn't mean your imagination is limited: you may simply be tuning in to the fact that circumstances are not conducive to the fulfillment of your desire — information worth having so that you can make choices before becoming frustrated. Witness if your projections develop or not, noting what is pervasive and what persists. Then, as needed, you can further engage your Receptive Imagination to discover how you can adjust your projection or find places more open to it.

Empowering Your Projection

When you have established a projection for an issue you would like to transform, you will want to work with it to further increase its power. Use your breath. As you inhale imagine that you are concentrating the new energy; then as you exhale aim it to the area that needs it. Use several breaths to concentrate and direct the energy. It is also good to create an affirmation, symbol, or gesture that represents your positive projection. (See Creating a Symbol for Calling Up Energy; and Affirmations Part II, Pages 39 and 41 respectively.)

Once you have chosen something that represents your projection, bring it to awareness every time the issue comes up. Have it be your last thought before you move your awareness on. Last thoughts are important because they are like the flashlight beam in a dark room. It is as though when you leave the room the light of your intention continues to shine in the positive direction.

After you have worked with a positive projection, forget about it. Let it go, and assume that change is taking place in its own time under the surface. If you keep comparing your current experience with your projection, you will only highlight and reinforce your dissatisfaction. Instead suspend judgment and watch for incremental changes, subtle inklings, or novel impulses to appear. If you keep the Witness present you will notice these impulses, at which point it is up to you to act on them and bring your behavior into alignment with your projection. Your actions will put you on a new path.

The result of projecting with the Active Imagination is magical, although your rational mind is likely to reject any possibility of causality and will invariably judge your projections as unrealistic. Its messages have no impact on whether or not they will work. When you work with projection subjective and objective reality shifts — your subjective energy both draws you into and attracts different circumstances. It is a given that you won't find your projections as plausible as the familiar state of affairs — if you did then you wouldn't have to work with that particular concern in the first place. However the very act of focusing your attention on what you want breathes life into your projection and awakens your intuition. Your horizon expands; thoughts move along new routes, and you find that you notice things you have previously overlooked. You will also find yourself inclined to act in new ways. Coincidence frequently occurs. What takes place won't be exactly how you imagined it, but it will be congruent with it. It is unpredictable and mysterious but it works.

It is good to make a gesture of faith to reinforce the change that is taking root in your life. I suggest that you do something you would not ordinarily do — something that feels congruent with your positive projection. You may want to express your gratitude in some way. Or you may want to refrain from doing something you usually feel obliged to do. Your gesture could be small, and it is likely to feel awkward, but it initiates change on the material plane. An act of faith demonstrates that you are serious about change, that in fact you expect it. When you act as if it were so, you become more open to new patterns establishing themselves in your life.

As your life changes be aware of what energy is now freed up within you. Make an offering to show your appreciation and to acknowledge the interconnectedness of All That Is. *Act of Faith (13F)* is intended to help you honor the mysterious and give thanks.

Creating a Symbol for Calling Up Energy

Symbols are the language of inner consciousness. A symbol is something that carries a significance that goes beyond its literal meaning. Consider, for instance, the meaning we associate with such symbols as a white dove, a red heart, or a burning torch. Every religious tradition uses symbols to speak to the spirit; in ritual they are used to focus intent and to evoke specific powers. When you create a symbol to represent the energy evoked in meditation work, you develop a personal language that speaks to your own deepest processes. (Remember your whole self moves into alignment with whatever is in your imagination at any given moment. When you bring a symbol to mind it enables you to embody the power of any positive projection.) The symbol ought to be vivid and meaningful to you. Keep it simple and easy to bring to mind — anything complex takes too much time to recall.

Once you have created a symbol it is good to bring it to awareness for a moment each time you meditate — every time you work with it, you energize it. It is also a good idea to draw your symbol and put it on your altar (if you have one), on your bathroom mirror, or on the dashboard of your car. Then, each time you look at your drawing you will reinforce transformation. When you create a symbol in advance you will be able to access its energy in the midst of any stressful situation — from job interviews to street protests. See *Create a Symbol to Tap Energy In Daily Life (13A)*.

Affirmations

Affirmations are positive statements describing a state to which you aspire and are a powerful way to engage your Active Imagination. They are also an effective means by which you can further strengthen specific work you have done in meditation. You can work with them by repeating them to yourself in the beginning or ending of any meditation sitting.

Affirmations will work regardless of what you rationally think. Inner consciousness is suggestible. To work with an affirmation effectively it is important that you assume it is true (as much as you can muster) at the moment you focus on one. Imagine what life would feel like if what you are affirming were an accurate description of your experience. When you use affirmations you realign yourself to be in accord with them and will find yourself intuitively acting in ways that invite them to manifest.

If an affirmation feels completely unattainable yet represents an experience you desire there is likely an underlying belief that needs to be transformed. When this is the case notice what messages get provoked; then you can do Mental Housecleaning to transform the belief. It is also good to create an affirmation that makes a statement that is the opposite of your negative belief — it will shift the energy and make room for change.

Affirmations should be simple, positive, and in the present tense. Straightforward sentences are good; use whatever adjectives help you imagine exactly the quality of experience for which you are striving. Since inner consciousness is not critical and will not understand a negative injunction, it is important to frame your affirmation as a positive statement: "I eat only those foods that nourish my body in healthy ways." Also, inner consciousness lives in the perpetual present and does not comprehend time, so keep your affirmation in the present tense: use phrases like "I take good care of my body."

Affirmation work is easy to incorporate into your life. Some people work with affirmations every time they meditate; others repeat them whenever they are doing anything rhythmic — when they are cleaning, walking, or swimming laps, for instance. Some people write them over and over. Others find it helpful to post them on the wall or bathroom mirror. Work with them when you are doing activities that require no thinking, such as when you are waiting in line, riding the bus, or washing the dishes. During these times your inner consciousness will be predominant. *Affirmation of Transformation (130)* can be used to create affirmations specific to the work you do in a meditation session; use it when you finish your inner work and before you return to an outer focus of attention.

The Appendix has affirmations from which you may pick and choose. Work with the ones that speak to you. It is best to work with no more than a dozen or so at a time because you do not want to overload your inner consciousness. Feel free to refine them; just don't keep switching around. Make your own series and then use the same wording in the same order every time you focus on your affirmations. The more regularly you use affirmations, the more you increase their power.

Affirmations in Groups

Getting ourselves to think in terms of "we" rather than "I" is at the heart of community-building and helps transform the isolation caused by our acculturated patterns of individualism. Nearly all of the affirmations listed in the Appendix can be adapted to family or group use — simply change the pronoun from "I" to "we." Thus, instead of saying, "I cultivate a joyous heart" say, "We cultivate a joyous heart." Notice how this feels different. Does it feel good to be part of "we?" If it doesn't, then that may point to a pattern in your belief structures that would be good to shift. If you like you can further stretch your sense of connectedness by creating affirmations that are about everyone — not just "we" but "all." Say, "All people cultivate a joyous heart."

Building Faith

The success of any particular positive projection that you are working with is proportional to your expectation. Your expectations are loyal to your beliefs, which are the conclusions that you have drawn about your past experiences. Having faith means expecting your projections will come to pass. The more you expect them to work the more they do. The things that you are likely to be focusing on are the very things you don't expect to unfold as you want them to. If you did you wouldn't be working on those particular issues. You need to trick yourself into expecting what you don't expect. The operative principle is that you are able to believe in your projection at the same time as you are contending with the problem. In other words when the problem is present, it is not interpreted as a sign of failure.

There are two ways to address this. One is to assume that your positive projection is already true far enough in the future that it is plausible. For instance if you want to be in a loving partnership, then assume that three years hence you will already be in one. That way your current state of loneliness is not a symptom of the projection not working, yet you could start a relationship tomorrow. Another tactic is to assume that the issue is incrementally improving. If you are contending with chronic pain, then project that each moment, gradually and imperceptibly, you are feeling more comfortable and will eventually feel fine.

Another way to increase your faith in the power of the Active Imagination is to work on issues that you don't have any reason to assume will not work — issues you can have an experimental attitude toward. (For instance, the bus arriving as soon as you get to the stop, a mosquito bite not itching, or a parking place being available in front of your destination.) Work on issues that you can suspend judgment about. They will demonstrate the power of consciousness. Small successes enable you to expect it to work in the areas that are more important to you. You shouldn't go through your day focusing on whether or not your projections are working, but you do want to note when progress has been made and your experience is different. This is one of the reasons why I have recommended that you keep a journal.

Building faith is an important component of group work, too. When you are working with a group find small things to imagine together. For instance if you have begun to open meetings with a meditation, then make a suggestion that you will finish at exactly fifty-seven minutes past the hour — it is best to name an unusual time — or suggest that the phone will not ring until all work is done. Such strategies will help the meeting. Furthermore, when something that has been suggested does occur, people will notice and be more willing to take time in their over-packed schedules to meditate. We all do things when we expect them to work. Whether you are working alone or with a group, when you've seen something work once you expect it to work again. You build faith.

Channeling Positive Energy to Those in Need

The world of probabilities is not a private one — we share it. The energy that is available to us as we direct our inner resources can be channeled wherever there is need. If a friend is having an operation, for example, take a moment when you are meditating to envision her as fully recuperated and in greater health than before.[3] If you become aware of anything that feels out of balance, try to move it back into equilibrium — doing so shifts the energy and often metaphorically reveals what your friend might do to increase well-being. When you channel energy to someone, do so with humility. Don't be attached to how or if the energy is received; just make it available.

An Energy Circle is a powerful way to channel healing — see *Grounded and Open: Working with Earth and Sky Energy for Centering and Circles (39)*.[4] *Making Magic (43)* and *Easing Another's Pain (130)* are designed to be used to support someone else in their healing process, and all the meditations in the section Healing Happens Naturally can be adapted to support others if you change the pronouns.

It is also important that we think well of one another and not pollute the subjective landscape with constricting energy such as greed, vengeance, envy, resentment, etc. *Emotional Metamorphosis (84)* will help you keep your subjective climate clear.

Mental Housecleaning:
Transform Negativity to Make Room for New Experience

You do not want to repress negativity; this only increases its power and drains energy. Avoidance causes a portion of your consciousness to be perpetually occupied with the task of keeping negativity out of awareness. The self-regulating, self-healing processes intrinsic to life itself can only take place when energy is moving. Both life and consciousness are fluid — stuck energy becomes toxic. Mental Housecleaning is a technique that you can use to clear out self-defeating thoughts, beliefs, and attitudes. It takes advantage of the suggestible and literal nature of inner consciousness. All you need to do is symbolically imagine a transformation process and clearly tell your deeper self that this is what is needed to transform whatever attitude you name.

Create an imaginary ritual of metamorphosis. Symbolize the stuck energy and imagine putting it into the transformation process: you can imagine burning it — fire transforms, breathing through it — breath transforms, or composting or grounding it. (When you imagine the stuck energy going into the ground as waste, it becomes rich soil for new life. Inner consciousness is literal so you don't want to throw the energy away — that just stores it out of view. You want to transmute the stuck energy.)

However you imagine your Mental Housecleaning process, use it consistently — that way your inner consciousness will come to recognize that you want transformation each time you imagine your ritual, and it will do your bidding. You don't need to know how change will occur or what form it will take. Clear intent, positive expectation, and imagining the ritual is all you need. Assume that transformation is taking place under the surface, then forget about it (as you do when you work with a positive projection). If the limiting idea comes to mind again, then momentarily envision your Mental Housecleaning ritual to reinforce the transformation process. Your rational mind will scoff — the technique works anyway. Sometimes it feels like magic. You will find that your subjective climate is much more amenable to positive experience and is open to any learning that will help you to move forward.

When You Can't Focus on a Positive Projection

Sometimes our experiences have been so contrary to what we want that it is extremely difficult to make a positive projection plausible. If you find something in your subjective landscape that tenaciously holds the center and blocks your ability to focus on a positive projection, then other work is needed before your Active Imagination can be effective. I am not referring here to the rational dismissals that are usually present: those thoughts do not keep you from focusing in a positive direction — they only judge you for doing so. Rather I am referring to those deeper messages that are provoked in reaction to the presence of a positive projection.

Deeper messages feel as if they emerge from inside the meditative experience itself. If, for example, an internal message broadcasts, "It will always be this way; you are just too _____," it has emerged from a deeper source. Messages like this arise because your positive projection contradicts limiting conclusions you have drawn about the nature of yourself and/or the world. They need to be transformed to make space for your new projection to take root.

Do not take these deeper messages as a sign of failure. Working with the Active Imagination does not mean that you have to fully expect your projection to unfold — that takes time — but you do need enough space to focus and explore. It is good to draw limiting beliefs into the light of awareness, since they are likely to be holding you back in more ways than what is apparent from the immediate issue you are working on. You now have the opportunity to do significant transformation work.

Self-Defeating Beliefs

A belief is self-defeating if it is no longer accurate. In many ways we are creatures of habit. It is not as though we think about and then choose which response to have for each moment we are awake — generally we respond automatically, though the more we engage the Witness the more mindful we become. Our responses are determined by our belief systems, which are the ways we have made sense out of our past experience. Beliefs determine how wide or how narrow our horizons are; they also determine interpretations, which in turn determine expectations. Our expectations form the basis of all decisions. It is as though each belief routes our thinking: the routes become so well worn that they seem to make grooves, and cognition automatically takes the familiar path. Beliefs become the maps that tell us what to expect — we use them to navigate through life.

It is not that beliefs are bad; the question is whether or not they are taking you where you want to go. Some beliefs may be empowering: these you can use to augment your meditative work because they will expand your positive frame of reference. Some beliefs may be limiting: these you can transform with appropriate meditations. Sometimes a belief is simply habituated: it is familiar, though the actual reason for it is long past. If you do not update your map as actual conditions change, you will recreate old dramas with a new cast of characters. And if the route to a particular destination is not on the map at all, the chances of getting there are not great.

It is easy to change your subjective landscape with meditation practice. If the conditions that caused you to draw certain conclusions are no longer operative, *Clearing Space Inside with Mental Housecleaning (11)* will help. For ferreting out beliefs that it would be good to transform, see Beliefs: Surveying Your Subjective Landscape (Appendix).

The Receptive Imagination

The Receptive Imagination is the sense organ of the psyche; through it we psychically access information at will. You engage the Receptive Imagination when you feel stuck, have no vision to strive for, and therefore need insight to illuminate a new approach. To be receptive means to be open. (*Clearing Space Inside with Mental Housecleaning (11)* will help you attain an open state.)

The mysterious and the ordinary combine and create a peculiar mix when you work with the Receptive Imagination. Questions angle the light of awareness: if you do not question, then the answer does not come into view. When you use your imagination to make up stories you create a context to intuit what is going on. Keep in mind that rational critiques often get louder when you are onto something: don't give them center stage; rather, take them as a signal and pay special attention to what you are imagining at the moment your rational mind chimes in.

Work with the Receptive Imagination calls for a combination of humility, trust, and playfulness. Story-making provides the context for your intuition and creative resources to come forth and address the issue at hand. Give yourself permission to play — the more you let go, open to, and work with your spontaneous responses, the more successful you will be. As I describe in Part I, everyone has these abilities, though we have been systematically taught to discount them. We have been taught that "making it up" is exactly the wrong thing to do. But this is the way that we intuit information.

A feeling of vulnerability usually accompanies work with the Receptive Imagination. Don't let this deter you. It is strange to work with a dimension of consciousness we have never deliberately used, and we have all been taught to base our sense of security on knowing why. In these dimensions we never know why. Though it is not easy, try to put your faith in your imagination. With time and practice you will get to know how powerful the receptive aspect of your imagination is, and your capacity to work with it will increase.

To work with your Receptive Imagination, bring an issue into the light of awareness. Create a focal point by personifying the problem so that you can easily interact with the issue in which you feel stuck (or in which you become stuck during a meditation). What would characterize it? Is it hot or cold, dense and heavy, or fuzzy and amorphous? Is it hyperactive or lethargic? What is its tone of voice? What color is it? Give the energy form: maybe it is a wall or a cloud or a cartoon character. Don't worry about whether or not the way you have personified the problem is "correct" — this process is your own, so whatever you come up with is, by definition, correct.

Don't wait for the experience to happen to you — that would be like getting into a car and, without turning on the ignition, expecting it to transport you. It is up to you to activate your imagination. You will be most effective if you keep your attention on the instantaneous responses that break into the light of your awareness. Catch your first impressions, and then play with them. Fill in the details. Don't worry about what anything means or how valid it is. Just flesh out your sensations and color in your visions. If you enter this work with a spirit of play you will have many spontaneous responses.

Pretend that the personification has an intelligence of its own. Animate it. Make up a story about it. Create an imaginary scene. Play with your imagining. Talk to the personification. Be inquisitive. Find out what its worldview is. What is it striving for? What motivates it? Who is it loyal to? What agitates it? Talk over the immediate situation with it. What is it protecting you from? Find out what it believes is at stake. What insights does it offer? What is it invested in? How might it use its sensibilities in a constructive way? Ask it. You might want to imagine being the personification: look through its eyes; move with its body. To do so will bring further insight.

Once you have become acquainted with the character, negotiate with it. Find a way to address its concerns and meet your needs at the same time. How might it be helpful? Ask it for what you want. Imagine how you can apply the understanding that you have gained. Decide if you are willing to act, and tell the character what you are willing to do. Imagine doing it. Tell yourself what your commitment is. In the presence of the Witness examine your commitments; if it is unlikely that you will abide by them, then make needed adjustments. At this point you will be able to use your Active Imagination to empower a different and desirable experience, or your attitude toward the issue will have made a qualitative shift. Either way, you will no longer be stuck.

Inner consciousness is not constrained by the same limitations of space and time that you have to contend with: it sees the picture whole, and when you are meditating so do you. You envision everything that would need to be different for a desired state of being to manifest. If, over time, you find that you have not kept all of your agreements (having bitten off more than you can chew) that's all right. You cannot expect to eat a full banquet in one bite. Have patience with yourself. You may have committed yourself to more than you can handle in the short run but not in the long run. The fact that you can imagine something makes it possible. You do not have to do everything that occurs to you all at once, but you do need to keep in good communication with your inner self.

If you do break a commitment, go back and talk it over. Come up with a manageable course of action, or your inner self will feel betrayed and won't provide the insights you need the next time. Your rational mind can augment your meditation at this time because it thinks logically and will likely be helpful in coming up with a way for you to attain your goal.

You always work with the Receptive Imagination in every meditation; use it whenever you come across anything that feels out of balance. It will always offer insight when you need it. Four meditations have been designed to work specifically with the Receptive Imagination: *Send an Invitation to the Solution (99),*

Invite Insight (100), Blocks to Creativity Become Stepping Stones (103), and *Visiting with the Future to Address a Matter of Import or to Prepare for a Momentous Occasion (104).*

The Receptive Imagination Lives on Sacred Ground: Recognizing Insight

Inner consciousness lives in the perpetual here and now. Therefore when you ask a question with the Receptive Imagination, the answer does not enter your awareness from somewhere else; it is already there. The act of bringing the question into focus is the same act that makes the answer apparent. You focus on a question and simultaneously find yourself sensing the answer. The answer does not feel as though it originates from somewhere else; on the contrary you might feel that you knew it all along.

When you work with the Receptive Imagination never wait for an answer to enter from somewhere else; instead, notice what is already there. Since inner consciousness is simultaneous, if it were just to "come" it would be there already. If it seems that nothing is there, then make it up. When you make it up you discover the same information that "comes to" you. The experience feels different but the content is the same. (Remember, when people do psychic readings those who feel that the information just "comes to" them are as accurate as those who just "make it up.") Avoid the mistake of dismissing an answer because it didn't "come to" you — this is one of the prime ways that we abdicate personal power.

The answers that emerge as you ask questions can take various forms. Many answers will seem trite, even corny — that is because inner consciousness resides in the realms of universality. It doesn't matter if an answer is cliched or not; what matters is whether or not it is helpful. The idea that nothing is valid unless it is new and unique is part of the modern existential angst, and we end up cutting ourselves off from the wisdom of the ages because of it. Sometimes answers will surprise you, and sometimes they are full of humor. Often it feels like they came out of nowhere — they have a way of just popping to mind. For some people, conversations with aspects of their inner world do happen the way we are used to: one comment follows another. For others the communication feels telepathic because knowing happens with no words attached.

Dialogue is not the only source of insight offered by the Receptive Imagination.

How your imagination depicts an issue is just as important as what it depicts, pay keen attention and keep the Witness present so that you can note subtle nuances. (This is equally true when you work with the Active Imagination.) The Receptive Imagination reveals truth metaphorically. For instance if it characterizes a problem as cold rather than warm, that provides you with valuable information that reveals what would bring balance. Remember, you may feel that you are just "making it up," but your imagination is what connects subjective experience to objective reality — its offerings are always accurate.

Nothing that your imagination offers is insignificant. Wherever you have ease in imagining and wherever you have difficulty mirrors what is true for you. Always notice what comes easily and what is not so easy, what is open to a different way and what quickly reverts back to the status quo. Whenever you find yourself imagining anything that is constricted in some way, bring in the Witness and breathe space into the situation. Then, however it occurs to you, strive to imagine the scene opening up. As you work you will discover the places of flexibility that point to where change can happen. The specific way you create balance in your subjective landscape will metaphorically represent a viable strategy that you can implement to make change in your life.

The childlike imagining of your Receptive Imagination is the bearer of the wisdom asked for in Reinhold Neibuhr's Serenity Prayer: "Grant me the serenity to accept the things I cannot change, courage to change the things I can, and the wisdom to know the difference." As your imagination engages with your dissatisfactions and endeavors to shift energy into a more open state, it reveals when you can and when you cannot make change. The gift of the Receptive Imagination is that it reveals what is currently possible and what is not. The terrain of the Receptive Imagination is truly sacred ground. When you discover that change cannot happen, then you turn to the Witness because it knows how you can come to terms with the situation.

Augmenting Receptivity

When you work with the Receptive Imagination you work with your spontaneous responses — a difficult thing to do if you are guiding yourself through meditations at the same time. (Having to think about what to do next takes you away from the very state of awareness in which spontaneous responses arise.) So how can you augment the receptivity of your Receptive Imagination?

- You may find that if you read the meditations while in a meditative state, it works just fine.

- You can record the meditations to listen to at a later time.[5]

- You can work with a friend and have them read appropriate meditations.

- You can engage your Receptive Imagination for another. When you direct your imagination to work with your friends' issues, insights are often more forthcoming — spontaneity is easier to unleash when you have no personal stake in outcomes.

- Most effectively, you can join or create an Applied Meditation group in which you use Energy Circles.[6] Your regular practice with others will increase your capacity to tap the powers of the Receptive Imagination. See *Grounded and Open: Working with the Energy of the Earth and Sky (39).*

Embarking on Your Journey

When you tap into greater intelligence and approach problem-solving with Applied Meditation you will transform your life. As with any new endeavor, you will need practice and support. It is a good idea to periodically review The Principles of Applied Meditation (Appendix) — they will help you to focus on the keys to transformation. (If you forget the principles, chances are that you will dismiss the most important aspects of your meditative experience.)

Group meditation will exponentially increase the potency of meditation practice. Do this work with family, friends, and colleagues and you will deepen your relationship with your inner dimensions and your relationships with others. Ironically it is in the presence of others that you will be able to contact the deepest and most intimate aspects of your own psyche. When you work with inner consciousness you embark on a journey that holds great promise.

Making the Meditations Fit Your Needs: How to Use This Book

The meditations are designed for regular use to help you deal with the myriad of issues that arise in daily life. You can use them on your own, with friends, or in groups. You may want to use them before you go to sleep to help digest the day or when you waken to ready yourself for what is in store. You may want to read one while you are riding the bus to work or listen to a tape recording when you go on your daily run.

The meditative journey itself is a highly private experience, but your experience will be more powerful when there are others with you who are also meditating — like watching full color instead of black and white. The power of meditation increases synergistically in group settings. Even if you meditate with just one other person, it will qualitatively deepen your experience. To receive the full benefits of Applied Meditation practice do both — use the book on your own and, whenever possible, meditate with others.[7]

USING THE MEDITATIONS

Each section in Part III: Meditations for All Occasions contains meditations that you can easily mix and match for specific purposes. Section One: Creating the Container, however, deserves a special mention since you will be using some meditations from it in every meditation session. Designed to open, set the context for, and close a meditation session, the meditations in this section provide a container for your inner work.

- **Induction: Relaxing into the Reverent and Awakening Your Imagination.**
  Breathing into Wholeness (1) is the opening meditation and acts as an induction — it will carry you into a meditative state. The rest of the meditations assume

that you are already there, so use this one to begin every meditation session before proceeding on. In the last sections you will be invited to work with breath, the Witness, and both the Active and Receptive Imaginations. I recommend that you use these sections repeatedly. *Breathing into Wholeness (1)* can be used in a short or an extended form.

• **Deepening: Constructing Meditation Context and Enhancing Inner Awareness.**
The meditations found here set the context for your meditative work, enabling you to enter a more enhanced state of awareness so that your imagination becomes more fluid and your inner knowing more accessible. If you choose to use a deepening, it should be inserted after an induction and before any topical meditation/s. Any meditation in this group can be used in whole or in part; some can also be used on their own as a full meditative journey.

• **Endings: Completing Work and Returning to Outer Focus**
Endings provide a process for you to complete your inner work by reviewing, reinforcing, and projecting your meditation experience into your life. They establish an intuitive alignment with your goals, making the inner resources you discovered in your session accessible in daily activities.

Section Two: Gathering the Forces contains summoning meditations that draw out the qualities, sensibilities, and energies that you would like to have accompany you in your inner work. In this section you will find meditations such as *Courage (20)*, *Calling the Ancestors (29)*, and *Pacing: Making Friends with Time (36)*. Unless otherwise noted, summoning meditations come after a deepening (if you use one) and before any topical meditation/s. These meditations, too, can be used on their own.

The meditations in the remaining four sections are designed to address specific topics. Section Three: Maintaining Well-Being contains meditations that help keep you well-balanced and strong. In this section you will find meditations such as *In the Quiet, Greet Yourself (41)* for centering, *Manifest Your Ideal (52)* for empowerment, and *Claim Your Space (60)* for holding your own.

Section Four: Healing Happens Naturally contains meditations relating to physical and emotional wellness. Meditations such as *Harnessing Healing (66)*, *Food: A Blessing (82)*, *Cut Loose the "Shoulds" (85)*, and *Disrobing Outdated Beliefs with Attitudinal Redress (93)* can help transform self-limiting patterns.

Section Five: Life's Activities offers meditations that can help you keep your life together while meeting life's many challenges. Here you'll find meditations such as *Juggling Hats: The Balancing Act (96)*, *Invite Insight (100)*, and *From Procrastination to Productivity (109)*.

Section Six: Creating Wellness Together offers meditations that can help you address issues related to intimacy, getting along with others, and building and maintaining just and harmonious communities. Meditations in this section include *Parenting (118)*, *Just Relations: A Balance of Exchange*

(136), *Enriched by Diversity (139)*, and *Claiming Integrity: Living True to Your Values (151)*.

The meditations can be used in multiple ways. Some you may use many times; others seldom or not at all. They have been designed so that you can use them in any order. Mix and match them to fit your own sensibilities and situation. The meditations can also be broken apart and arranged in different combinations. If you just lost a job, for example, you might want to use parts of *Illuminating Your Path (53)* and *Grief Heals (132)*. You will find that individual meditations can often address a variety of circumstances. *Rite of Passage: Transitions (106)*, for example, is good if you are getting married, retiring, or moving across the country. When you are deciding how you will use the meditations, always pay attention to your own inclinations and let them guide your choices.

Some meditations need to be used together; when this is the case the introductory note will say "designed to...." Others can naturally enhance or augment another meditation; you'll find recommended combinations in the introductory notes to the individual meditations. Meditations that are intended to enhance or augment others are optional — if you were to use each listed meditation in its entirety your session would probably take hours! Remember to use what speaks to you; often less is more. When you are fully engaged in doing the work you need to, the rest of the meditation may just be a distraction. Always feel free to skip over sections of any meditation with which you work. If a particular passage deeply resonates with you, it may be most effective to repeat it many times without using the rest of that meditation or any others.

You may want to use ribbons or sticky notes as bookmarks to help you move from one meditation to another so that you can avoid fumbling for the right page when you are in the midst of reading.

Finding the Meditation Best Suited to Your Needs

The Table of Contents and the Meditation Use Index will help you to locate the meditations that are most applicable to your situation: use them pragmatically or intuitively. When you know what issue you want to address, look in the Table of Contents and scan for specific meditations. If you have to meet a deadline, for example, you could look under the heading Aligning Your Energies for the Challenges Ahead. You would find a listing *On Time: Meeting a Deadline (110)*. You can also look up the word "deadline" in the Meditation Use Index.

If you don't know which specific issue you want to address — you want to feel better but aren't exactly sure what would help, for instance — use your intuition as a guide. Read the Table of Contents or Meditation Use Index with soft awareness and pay careful attention to your spontaneous responses — notice what seems to jump out.

There is no need to worry about which meditation is the right one. Since each meditation is simply a container to facilitate your process, spending a lot of time trying to figure out which to use is like getting stuck deciding if you want to drink from a glass or a mug. If you are not drawn to one particular meditation, any that you are considering will do. If several meditations call out to you when you read the Table of Contents, arbitrarily pick one with which to work. Usually the issues you need to work on will surface regardless of which meditation you use.

Meditations That You Use Repeatedly

You may find some meditations so helpful that you will use them time and again. When you use a meditation repeatedly it creates a well-worn path in the psyche, and eventually you will no longer need to use it in its entirety. With a meditation such as *Inner Refuge: Your Sacred Space (9)*, for example, you will not need to repeat the sections that have you create your refuge — you will be able to call it up simply by reading one or two paragraphs or ad-libbing a sentence to remind yourself of it.

Over time you will also be able to invoke the benefits of one meditation at will and use them to enhance the work you do with another meditation. For example you may regularly use *Making Magic: Conjuring Energy to Spread Well-Being (43)* as part of your practice. If you work with *Claiming Integrity: Living True to Your Values (151)* and get to the section that has you review your earlier life, you will be able to enhance your process by bringing forth the energy-body you created in *Making Magic (43)*.

How to Listen to the Meditations

The meditations provide a container for inner consciousness so that you can tap the universal healing energies flowing through inner dimensions; they are written in a style that speaks directly to deeper awareness. Rhythm, repetition, rhyme, metaphor, and memory — the language of inner consciousness — rouse the imaginative and intuitive powers of the psyche. It doesn't take work, in the usual sense of the word, to use the meditations effectively. Just read or, better yet, listen to the meditations being read, and they will transport you into your inner world. Consciousness, like all life, naturally moves toward a state of greater equilibrium when given the chance. All you need to do is relax, trust yourself, and open to the discovery of your own inner dimensions.

The purpose of the meditations is to draw out your inner consciousness and to create an atmosphere conducive to your inner work. The lines in the meditations direct the angle of the light of awareness, bringing into view what had previously been in the dark. Your task is to pay careful attention to what the meditations inspire in your imagination and to work with whatever feels out of balance.

It is unnecessary for you to work with every single line — in fact you will be overwhelmed if you try. Do not get caught up in trying to figure out exactly what any particular sentence means — they are often intentionally vague to make room for the varied experiences of readers. Just work with what the sentences mean to you. Similarly your attention should always be focused on your responses to the words and not to the words themselves. If your main focus is on the words rather than what is taking place in your own inner dimensions, you will miss the boat. When you are in the midst of meaningful work, guidance is no longer needed; at that point let the words become background ambiance and expect that you will notice what matters.

It is also unnecessary for you to work with everything that you come across as you journey through your inner world. Follow your own inclinations. It is your process that you are working with. Remember that awareness and attention are not the same — you choose where to focus. The essential thing is to notice what is meaningful to you. Use the lines in the meditation to find what you are looking for and then work with it.

How to Read the Meditations:
Pacing with Rhythm, Reinforcement, and Repetition

While you meditate you want to be in a receptive state of mind so that you can spontaneously respond to cues as you work. The operative principle is that you do not want to have to decide on what to do next when you are in the midst of meditating. The process of figuring out What next? will cause you to leave the meditative state because your rational processing will have taken over. Numerous approaches will inspire and enhance a receptive state. Some people work with the meditations while reading them to themselves; if you use this method the effect of the meditations will be optimized if you sub-vocalize. Furthermore if you close your eyes and take a few breaths as you move through the meditations, it will give your inner consciousness time to absorb and respond. Another approach is to gather ideas ahead of time for what you want to reflect on in your meditation session. I recommend that you highlight particularly meaningful phrases or that you make a crib-sheet so you can briefly open your eyes and find cues to guide your next step. In general, though, it is best to listen to the meditations — use a recording or have someone read them to you.

The meditation experience will be greatly enhanced when you pay attention to pacing, rhythm, repetition, and reinforcement. Pacing is integral to meditation work. Inner consciousness is simultaneous, and though it does not take a long time to do inner work, it does take some time. Each meditation contains a series of questions for reflection or tasks to carry out. You want instantaneous responses, but they cannot come into full view if you ask and immediately read the next question or task. (If you don't pause, it is as if you are continually being handed things when your hands are already full.) The meditations are punctuated by ellipses to help with pacing. A three-dot ellipsis signifies a pause corresponding to the length of time it would take you to take one full breath (5 – 10 seconds); it allows you enough time to reflect but is short enough that your attention is unlikely to wander off. A six-dot ellipsis signifies a pause corresponding to the length of time it would take you to take three or four full breaths (15 – 30 seconds); it is used when work of substance needs to be done before the meditation can proceed to the next step.

Rhythm is another important part of your meditation experience. If you read rhythmically and melodically and your breath is slow, deep, and relaxed it will call inner consciousness to the forefront of awareness. Some people find it helpful to gently rock while they read.

Reinforcement is also important. In addition to validating experience, reinforcing statements allow for work to be completed before you move on to the next stage of a meditation. I recommend that you include them regularly as you read, especially during the longer pauses indicated by a six-dot ellipsis. Inner consciousness is fluid, and long silences create an opening through which attention can easily slip and wander off. For work of substance, insert one or two reinforcing statements at ten-second intervals — they will help maintain focus and allow time for inner consciousness to work through and digest what is taking place. You can also repeat statements in the meditations to reinforce the work. It is good to insert statements as a reminder of the context. In health meditations, for example, insert lines about the resilience of life. The sound of reinforcing statements in the background creates an atmosphere that is conducive to focusing.

Repetition also enhances the meditation experience. For the rational mind repetition dissipates meaning and is boring. For inner consciousness repetition deepens meaning. To tune to one's own truth often requires that one go into deeper and deeper layers; repetition aids this process, which is why many of the meditations instruct you to repeat certain sections. If you come across a particular section that is especially meaningful, it will enhance your meditation experience to repeat it. In meditations that ask one question after another, repeat the list once or twice and periodically insert reinforcing statements. Lists of questions can tend to call rational consciousness out of the background — a reinforcing statement such as, "Sense what is so," keeps inner awareness primary.

You will optimize the impact of the meditations if you take advantage of the suggestibility of inner consciousness and insert positive suggestions. When you make suggestions to inner consciousness, keep them in present tense. You will find a wealth of such suggestions in *Endings (A – W)*; also see Positive Reinforcing Statements. If you are listening to the meditations, in those places where they invite you to "Tell yourself...," it is important that you sub-vocally give yourself suggestions. When you talk to yourself in a deliberate manner it paves new roads for your thoughts to travel on.

Positive Reinforcing Statements

The sentences that follow make effective reinforcing statements.

- In this level of awareness you always know what is best.

- The very fact that you can imagine it makes it possible. The energy exists.

- Feel change happening. Feel what it is like to live in this new and empowered way.

- Expect the best to take place....

- Know that you are fully capable. You are now able to....

- Know that you will now act in accord with this new way of being, as naturally as breathing.

- Breathe; know what is true for you.

- Trust your knowing; you do know.

- Breathe through this.

- Feel the energy shift.

- Sense what is so.

- Note the truth of the matter.

- Share presence with the truth of the matter.

- Breathe fully. Let your breath settle on what is true.

- Notice your first impression. Follow it.... What is it telling you?

- Let yourself be with your own knowing.

- Trust what occurs to you.

- Let your imagination depict what is taking place.

- With the exhalations of breath, aim the healing wherever it's needed.

- As you breathe, draw into your whole being the wellness you are experiencing.

Personalize the Meditations to Fit Your Circumstances and Sensibilities

Personalize the meditation wherever you can; their effectiveness will increase many-fold if you name the particular conditions, relations, or endeavors with which you are working. Naming brings the issues into focus. If you are making a speech, for example, name its subject matter; and if it has a title, use it. When you refer to other people in any of the meditations, use their names. When you are leading someone else through a meditation, it is good to elaborate by naming what you know is the case for your listener. (Always refrain from explanations — they call out the rational mind.)

Use description to flesh out the meditations and activate the imagination. Name any symbols that you use, and if you have an inner refuge, describe it. Many of the meditations work with memory to establish positive points of reference or to reveal where inner work is needed. Insert *Recollection (16)* and you will greatly enhance the effect of such meditations.

Stay positive — you are working with a suggestible state. For instance, if you are healing an abscess, be sure to say, "My leg is healing" and not "My abscess is healing."

Adjust the language of the meditations to match your internal dialogue. In several places I have used feminine pronouns; male readers may want to change these. Since you are working with your subjectivity, it is best to use words or terms that are meaningful to you — this is especially important in regard to religious perspectives. You may want to replace the phrase "All That Is" with the word "God," "The Great Spirit," "Quan Yin," "the Goddess," or "Allah" — call upon your experience of the sacred often.

I recommend that you adapt the meditation scripts to fit your predominant imaginative mode. Usually I have used the generic term "Imagine...." If you are a visually oriented person, you may want to replace "imagine" with "envision"; if you are more kinesthetic use "feel" or "sense." Always strive to speak to your experience.

Skip over lines or sections that don't fit. The whole point of Applied Meditation practice is to enable you to form an intimate relationship with your inner dimensions. There is no point in moving yourself through material that is not applicable to your situation.

You will find that the meditations are very versatile and can be easily modified to speak to a variety of circumstances. *Spirit of Place (38),* for example, is designed to help you appreciate the area in which you live. If you are about to lead an event somewhere or are moving, you can easily adapt the script by replacing all references to home with "conference site" or "new home." Again, insert the name of the place you are referring to and describe some of its characteristics to bring them fully into your imagination's view.

Supporting Each Other

The meditations can be used as a great resource for providing or receiving support. Ironically we are least likely to want to meditate when we most need to. It is at these very times that we should offer to lead or should ask for a meditation. Keep in mind that the meditations are most effective when they are read to you. Anyone — even someone who has not read the instructions and knows nothing about meditation — can read one to you and you will still derive its benefits.

The meditations are ideal to use with family and friends. The decision-making and healing meditations will prove to be especially valuable tools for support. If a friend is having trouble in a relationship, for instance, offer to read *Assessing a Painful Relationship (126)* so that she can get below her emotional turmoil to discover her own answers. If someone has recently lost a loved one, you could offer to read *Grief Heals (132)*. If you have to decide between two job offers, you might ask a friend to read you *Crossroads: Detecting the Right Course of Action (102)*.

Emotionally Charged Issues

When you are meditating on especially difficult issues it is best to have someone with you. Another person can lead you through, support you, and combat isolation; by their very presence, they convey the conviction that you are fully capable of addressing the challenge you face.

When you bring a problem to mind you naturally tense up, making it next to impossible to maintain spacious awareness — tension crowds out the Witness. Your guide will be able to notice when tension arises and can direct you to breathe and release it, enabling you to move through difficult feelings rather than getting caught in them.

When You Lead Another

Before you lead a meditation for anyone else it is best, though not required, to ask them to describe the experience they are striving to understand, overcome, and/or attain. Ask how the issue feels to them and what their vision is. You don't need any history or explanation, only a description. Listen carefully so that you will be able to use their language and to insert specifics into the meditations that will make them speak directly to their experience. If they meditate regularly, find out how they enter the meditative state and if there is anything they always do before they begin their inner work.

It is important that you be sensitive to and honor the other person. Applied Meditation can transport people into a highly private and personal experience. When you support another you need to honor that they may not want to share all that has transpired for them. (This applies equally to groups.)

A word of caution: meditation work is very powerful and addresses deep-seated issues. It is critical that you believe in the other person's ability to claim power and address their situation. If you are intimidated or in any way doubtful of their process (and doubt is different than feeling awkward about leading a meditation), then you are not the one to lead them. Refrain from agreeing to lead if you are fearful that something may come up and make things worse or if you feel they are not really willing or able to make change. It does not matter if your perceptions are correct or not: the person will sense your doubts and, since the meditative state is suggestible, your doubt will undermine their process.

If you know that the issue the person will be working on is highly charged emotionally, use *Protected View (12)*; it will help them to do the work without getting caught in emotional reaction. Always watch their breathing and body language. If tension arises, then momentarily stop reading the topical meditation and direct the person to work with their breath until relaxation returns — use *Breath Is Home; Breath Heals (1G)* — then go back to the topical meditation where you left off. Return to working with breath whenever needed. If you are not certain that the person you are leading is ready to go back to the topic, ask. Be patient; they may need to enter the work gradually, taking a few steps the first session before going further in the next. It is critical that you honor their process.

After you have read a series of questions and before you continue you might ask, "Are you ready to move on?" If the person needs more time they will tell you. Take your cues from them, while paying very careful attention to your own intuitive hunches. Intuition, more than anything else, will help you to guide in a manner that best fits the other person's needs. If you take your cues from the other person and remember to guide them to their breath, they will improve their ability to deal with whatever issues and feelings that come up.

Passages from *The Transformative Power of Breath (45), Pain: Reframe It (70), Emotional Metamorphosis (84), or Avoid Breaking Point (133)* are especially useful for this kind of work. You can also search in the Meditation Use Index for additional approaches that might be of help.

Creating an Applied Meditation Group

I highly recommend that you form or join an Applied Meditation group that meets regularly.[8] Individual meditations become exponentially more powerful and a group, itself, becomes stronger when people meditate together. A group of six to ten people is optimal. (You can, of course, also meditate regularly with your partner, members of your family, a friend, or housemates.) As with individual practice, it is good to create a beautiful environment in which to meditate — use flowers, candles, music, an altar, etc. to create an atmosphere encouraging to heart and spirit.

There are a variety of ways in which to work with the meditations themselves. You can obtain pre-recordings of the meditations, record them yourself, or rotate the reading among members of the group. You can also read the meditations using a round format.

If your group chooses to read using a round, sit close to each other so that the book can easily be passed from hand to hand as you take turns. When it is your turn to read simply open your eyes, read your section, and then pass the book along, showing the next person where to start. When you have finished reading, close your eyes and follow the meditation as before. (The energy created in groups is so potent that you will be able to sink right back into your meditation.) As the book passes from hand to hand, you might want to leave longer silences than usual in order to allow the most recent reader to bring their process up to where the group is. Experiment and see what works best.

It is also possible and beneficial to focus in on each other's issues as you meditate. Each person will derive more energy and greater insights from other members of the group when you do, and you will receive the psychic benefits of the Receptive Imagination, making it much easier for everyone to appreciate the power of that part of our consciousness we usually dismiss. Remember, it is much easier to free our imaginations if we do not have any emotional investment in the outcomes of what we are exploring. See *Grounded and Open: Working with Earth and Sky Energy for Centering and Circles (39)*.

The Receptive Imagination relies on spontaneity and can be tapped more easily in groups. In my weekly meditation group we focus in on each other's issues, give each other feedback, and generate energy to channel toward our goals. Once when I was getting ready to visit my partner at a conference (we were living in different cities), one member said that she saw us having a wonderful time in a room full of soft, downy feathers. I didn't take her literally, thinking she had just used that image as a way to imagine a positive scene. In fact I forgot all about it, until the quilt that we were sleeping under sprang a leak and there were feathers everywhere! Knowing transcends the limits of time and space, and when you work together regularly in the meditative state you invite magic.

The world inside is as vast as the world outside. When people meditate regularly together and share their experiences it provides a window through which to view the incredible richness of the inner realms. In today's frenetic culture of crass consumerism, it makes the heart smile when you come together to focus on what is important. Your meditation group becomes an oasis where you can gather the forces to spread well-being into all of life.

Empowering Groups: Meditating Together Creates New Culture

When used by a group Applied Meditation provides a way for people to experience their intrinsic connectedness. We have been taught to believe that groups somehow obstruct individual expression, so when people come together for a shared purpose they do not necessarily know how to act in the collective spirit rather than out of solely individual agendas. Group meditation brings out shared resonance and creates cohesion — people move into alignment and naturally act in ways that are in accord with the whole. Each individual member is not only able to feel themselves part of the whole; they are also able to feel themselves taken care of and supported by it.

The meditations can be used in group settings to foster the creation of a life-affirming culture. *Disrobing Outdated Beliefs with Attitudinal Redress (93)* or *Breaking Down the Barriers: The World Opening to You and You Opening to the World (149)* can help the members of a group to transform isolating patterns. As people share their experience they will be able to deepen their understanding of what is holding them back and to develop a sense of what is possible. Section Six: Creating Wellness Together provides numerous meditations that will enhance collective sharing and vision. With vision comes the power to change.

MEETINGS, CLASSROOMS, AND LARGE GATHERINGS

Unless people have come together explicitly to meditate, it always feels as if you are going against the grain when you lead a meditation. Especially in our fast-paced society where no one ever has enough time, meditation feels out of context. In our culture it is out of context. We need to remind ourselves that, for millennia, people have taken time to reflect together — it is we who are out of whack for not doing so.

We always have deeper intelligence to tap into. I have led meditations in all kinds of settings from Bell Labs to food co-ops and from the League of Women Voters to a gathering of activists getting ready to protest the activities of the World Trade Organization. If one can use a bullhorn to lead an effective meditation with 500 activists in a warehouse while being interrupted every few minutes by reports that tear-gas-wielding police are getting closer, then one can lead a meditation in any setting.

When a group uses meditation as a tool for collective reflection, it breaks the Western cultural norms that make it extremely difficult for us to access our creative and intuitive resources. According to Western culture, before we speak up we are supposed to have it all figured out and be able to justify our point by explaining why. We are required to always be objective, making it nearly impossible for us to use our inner resources to contribute to problem-solving. When innovation does happen it is despite, not because of, the context.

Group meditation slows us down, cutting the urgency mentality that grips most of us and giving us enough time to reflect together. Organizations are under the same pressures of modern life as individuals. There never seems to be enough time to reflect on practice, so mistakes go unexamined and decision-making is based on immediate survival or expediency — people don't look at the big picture. Meditation gives us a moment to collectively take a breath and minimizes the likelihood that we will make unwise choices. Ultimately, we'll save enormous amounts of energy not having to clean up messes. The meditations themselves create a climate that is conducive to cooperation and creativity and are especially suited to augmenting any planning or decision-making process. A meditation can transform a deadly meeting into an enjoyable and productive experience. They are ideal team builders for teachers, facilitators, and leaders. Their use substantially contributes to the building of shared commitment and community.

The act of meditating together invites authenticity, heart, and spirit to inform group process. It establishes a respectful atmosphere in which genuine listening can occur. As a result care, patience, innovation, vision, and intuition all become part of group culture. People find it easier to be honest with each other and to learn from mistakes. Conflicts become opportunities for learning and not for scapegoating. In the natural cohesiveness fostered by meditation, competition melts into cooperation and decision-making becomes easy. Consensus arises almost effortlessly.

The benefits of meditating together apply equally to leaders and participants. At *Tools For Change* my associates and I do a great deal of training, mediation, and facilitation work around contentious issues such as diversity and oppression. We believe in collective leadership and often work in teams. We find that when we meditate together before we begin, it equips us to work well with each other and to be fully attuned to the groups with which we are working. (When we neglect to meditate because of time pressure, we pay, having to work twice as hard to stay in synch with each other.)

Similarly, when you start any meeting or gathering with a meditation, it sets a common intention and helps prevent the manipulative and controlling behaviors that obstruct group work. I always begin mediations by inviting all parties to find that place in themselves where they can be simultaneously open and true to their convictions. Setting this intention at the start inspires people to put their best foot forward. The meditations set a tone that invites people to be both playful and to act in heartfelt ways. People's anticipation moves into alignment and the path of collaborative endeavor is illuminated — even in highly conflicted circumstances such as during the mediation of a dispute. Just as your steps fall naturally into a matching gait when you go for a walk with someone, so people come naturally into accord when they spend time together in a relaxed state of awareness. Rather than feeling separate from the whole, people experience themselves and others as part of the whole. You don't need to think about it, it just happens. You can't point out who changed or how it came about; it just does.

Collective suggestion is powerful. I was once called in to mediate for a university department. There were 50 people present, much tension in the air, and each person wanted what they personally thought was critical to be dealt with by the department. The meeting was scheduled to last two hours. Having a productive two-hour session with 50 people is a challenge in the best of circumstances but even more so when conflict is the reason for the meeting. I led a short meditation at the beginning; in it I set the expectation that we would finish exactly at ten o'clock. It became evident that everyone needed to have the opportunity to express their views. The last thing we did was go around the circle, with each person taking a turn to speak. Usually when I facilitate rounds of this sort, I time people to be sure that we end punctually. There was something sacred in the air that evening; I knew I couldn't time them even though my experience told me a circle of 50 extremely tense people could easily require three hours to say everything that needed to be said. It was magic: we finished exactly to the minute at ten o'clock — not a minute before; not a minute after. This kind of thing becomes a common occurrence when everyone sets the intent in meditation. Remember, it is from the inner consciousness that our behavior springs. When we invite its presence we drop into the implicate order.

Many of the meditations in Part III lend themselves to group work, especially those that appear in the second half: *Visiting the Future to Address a Matter of Import or to Prepare for a Momentous Occasion (104), Optimizing a Meeting*

(143), *Inspiration is Infectious: Collaborative Creativity (145)*, or *Team Spirit (146)* are just a few that are ideal for groups. If you are assisting people to work though conflict, *Communication Makes Conflict Healthy (135)* will help. If people in your neighborhood are meeting about a controversial issue, for example, you could start the meeting with a passage from *Listening with the Heart: Create Listening Space (140)*. The meditations also lend themselves to special occasions such as family gatherings, reunions, or ceremonies. To use any of the meditations in a group setting, simply change pronouns from singular to plural: use "we" and "our" instead of "you" and "your."

When you don't have the time to do a full relaxation induction or you would encounter resistance if you tried, you can lead a reflection that only takes three minutes or so. See *Group: Coming into Accord (2)*. If it would be inappropriate to ask people to close their eyes, you may want to just use the questions that are embedded in the meditations to frame a discussion — many meditations contain questions that are invaluable for exploring issues in a collaborative manner. They are written in a way that bypasses the rational mind and awakens the imagination. Used at the beginning of a discussion they will inspire people to be more creative and comprehensive in their approach. For example, see the questions in *Ripple Effect: Check Out the Consequences (101)* or *The Dance of Leadership (144)*.

If it is possible, allow a few minutes after the meditation for people to share their experience if they so choose. Invite people to take turns and ask that no one respond or refer to what others have said until everyone who wants to has spoken. This time is for story-telling and calls for descriptions not explanations. A different kind of listening happens: people tend to listen from their hearts, with no need to decide what they think about what is being said. When people reflect on the same issue, patterns emerge that are always enlightening. They make it clear what a good approach would be. As a result decisions don't need to be negotiated because it becomes evident to everyone what the wisest and or most inspired course of action would be.

Tips for Leading Groups in Meditation

- Prepare yourself in advance for any upcoming meditation session that you are going to lead: see *Grounded and Open: Working with Earth and Sky Energy for Centering and Circles (39)*.

- If it is possible, arrange the room to be inviting of the spirit and to reflect the tone you wish to set. Display your organizational logo, mission statement, pictures of role models, flowers, or anything else you think will act as a reminder of shared commitment. If you think an altar would not be scoffed at, set one up and invite people to put objects of meaning on it.

- Imagine that you are fully tuned to the energy in the room; this step sets the intention that you will stay aware of the needs of each person. It will help considerably if you literally imagine bands of energy that move from the members' minds and hearts to your inner consciousness.

- Trust the process. Remember that you are not carrying the group but are providing an invitation to heart and spirit, both of which will emerge when people simply slow down and breathe.

- Use *Group: Coming into Accord (2)* as an induction and *Group Closing (13U)*.

- Remind people that the group supports each of them and that its capacities surpass those of any one individual. Suggest that everyone tune to the power of the whole group, and ask participants to remember that others in the room share their cares.

- Always elaborate with specifics: name the shared purposes and goals of the group.

- Make some suggestions that will help build faith in the process of inner dimension work. Be sure that the suggestion does not carry any emotional charge: you could set the intention of finishing at an exact time — 11:15, for example. Or suggest that the group will easily fix a date for its next meeting. You could even suggest that everyone imagine something happening that ordinarily wouldn't happen — no interruptions until the session is over, for instance.

- Remember that repetition and universal imagery bores the rational mind, but that inner consciousness revels in this kind of language.

- Speak clearly and rhythmically.

- Leave ten-second silences periodically.

- Remember your breath. Breathe from your belly, and if you are ever unsure about how to proceed, return to your breath and suggest that the group do the same. Then pay attention to your own inclinations — they will let you know what to do next.

- It is important that you pay the finest of attention to what your inclinations tell you. Read only those parts of a meditation that you feel will be helpful and cut the rest. (See "tone setting" in the Meditation Use Index for meditations that you might want to use. *Visiting with the Future (104)* may also contain passages that you will find helpful.)

- If the group is working with positive projection, describe any relevant imaginary scenes and include specific details, remembering to use the present tense. For example if you are describing an upcoming event, name the intended venue, time, and any attendees; then invite the group to project themselves into the event as though it were taking place right then. Participants can then imagine the future more plausibly.

- Assume that all participants will come along in their own way. Most people are open to or willing to try an Applied Meditation approach to shared endeavors. Occasionally some people will be really resistant, but you need not fall into the trap of trying to convert the resistor to your point of view. Simply affirm that everyone who wants to will be given the opportunity to try this approach — a statement that other members of the group are likely to support — and then when you lead focus on those participants who are most receptive. Remember that when the tide rises every boat is lifted.

- Recognize that some people who keep their eyes open are still participating.

- Afterward you may want to invite people to draw a picture of what they experienced in the meditation and have them describe its meaning — a strategy that helps everyone to keep their imaginations open.

- When people share at the end of the session, be sure to let them know they need not say anything. You might ask that no one speak until everyone who wants to has taken a turn, and that people not refer to others' stories. Establish that this is a time to listen with heart, not to assess people's remarks. This sharing is nonlinear, and there is no need for remarks to have any direct relation to what others have said. Emergent patterns become evident.

Points to Set the Tone for Groups That Don't Usually Meditate

The points that follow can help you to set the tone of a meditation session if you are going to be leading a group that doesn't usually meditate. People want to know what to expect, so before you start, tell everyone how long the reflection will take and how you will proceed afterward. Make statements like: "We will share what we are inclined to with the person next to us and then bring what we want to the whole group"; "Afterward we will start work on the first agenda item"; or "We'll take time to do a round and hear from everyone who would like to share. You are welcome to pass if you wish."

Do not use all of the points that appear here — people will only get impatient. Instead choose those points that fit the tenor of your group and use them in whatever order seems best.

- It is nice to have peace and quiet for concentration, but it isn't necessary. If you get distracted just bring your attention back to your breath, and then proceed with what you are reflecting on.

- It is best to close your eyes when you reflect, but do whatever is comfortable. If you prefer to keep your eyes open, then you might try maintaining a soft focus at a point on the floor that is about five feet in front of you.

- If your belt is tight it is a good idea to loosen it so that you can breathe more easily — it is impossible to put our full minds to anything when our breath is constricted.

- Think of this exercise as a tuning fork for group cohesion and creativity. Here we have a moment to let go of our individual concerns and to put our hearts and minds together.

- When we share a moment of silence together it invites us to move out of separateness and into accord — just as your pace naturally moves into accord with a person you are walking with.

- Imagine that as we meditate together it invites spirit and sets the stage for synchronicity, opening us to our greater purpose.

- Call upon your own sense of the sacred, whatever it may be. The issue at hand is important, and we want to be informed by all the wisdom we can muster.

- A moment of reflection gives us the opportunity to gather our thoughts and concerns so that nothing gets lost in the shuffle.

- Take a moment for deep listening. Listen to your own deeper thoughts and to one another.

- This opens us to our collective genius.

- When we approach problems the same way as we always have, we end up with more of the same. Questions carry us to new thinking. There will be a series of questions. Pay special attention to your first responses, and follow what you find interesting.

- This exercise gives us an opportunity to employ our imaginations and intuition to the challenges at hand.

- This is a time to unleash the imagination for visioning. Don't get caught up in the "how's" or "why's; we will talk about those later. This is a time to open our imagination to change.

- This approach works best if you give your imagination the freedom to make up stories.

- When we are in a reflective state of mind, it is beneficial to get ourselves "on the same page," so we will be setting a collective intent. If you have a phobia of dogs, you don't need to have a dog in the room to get your adrenaline pumping — all you have to do is imagine one. We will use the same principle to our advantage by imagining how it feels when we are working well together. You will be invited to create a symbol that represents that experience for you. Then later, if you are ever feeling out of sync with the group process, all you have to do is bring your symbol to mind, and it will cause you to know what is needed.

- It is always helpful to simply breathe and silently share presence with any concern that you are focusing on. Just be in a receptive state; there is no need to do anything except be open to what arises in your awareness.

- The words are only creating a way for you to explore your perspectives — ignore them if they are distracting. The reflection uses rhythm, repetition, rhyme, and some universal imagery that you may find corny. Respond to what works for you. Generally the imagination finds this language stimulating.

When we tap into deeper intelligence we feel our connectedness. We gain the courage and wisdom to face great challenges. Spirituality has been the ground on which many have stood as they moved for justice. Every spiritual tradition has provided both a refuge for people to better survive oppression and the vision and courage for them to struggle for justice. One of the advantages of Applied Meditation is that it invites people from different spiritual and religious traditions to share time together in a way that enables them to come into accord without having to leave behind their religious convictions. The meditations make it possible for everyone to tap the powers of inner consciousness without giving primacy to any particular religious tradition.

The answer to the global crisis is not a technical one. We need to re-map the ways in which we think and act together. When we open to spirit, recreate the architecture of our minds, and envision together we can discover and bring about more sustainable ways of living on this planet we call home. When we tap our deeper intelligence and apply it to our lives and organizations, heart rather than greed becomes the driving force of history. By envisioning and acting together we both heal ourselves and secure the future.

PART III

Meditations for All Occasions

SECTION ONE:

Creating the Container

RELAXING INTO THE REVERENT AND AWAKENING YOUR IMAGINATION

When you are going to meditate, give yourself space; let people know you are unavailable for a while. Turn off beepers and telephones. It is a good idea to dress warmly: in meditation it is likely your metabolism will slow down and you can chill easily. Also be sure there is nothing tight around your waist so that you can breathe freely. Find yourself a comfortable position is which your spine is straight.

The following meditation — which you will use time and again — is designed to carry you into meditative awareness: from it you can proceed into any other meditation that you want to work with. You can deepen the effect of every meditation by repeating the parts that speak to you and skipping the sections that don't. **Three dots mean a short pause of five to ten seconds; six dots mean a longer pause of thirty seconds or more.** Trust your own rhythm.

To complete your meditation session use the sections you would like under Endings (13A – V), and then return to outer focus with Count Out (13W).

Please also see Grounded and Open (39) as an alternate method for entering into a meditative state — recommended if you tend to fall asleep easily.

Breathing into Wholeness (1)

You will want to use the subsections of this meditation over and over again to set the stage for your meditation work. **The first time you use it, skip the paragraphs with single brackets. Instead insert the paragraphs with double brackets that invite you to create a symbol for each relaxation section (body, mind, emotions, and spirit). Once you have created your symbols, use the paragraphs with the single brackets to bring each of your symbols to your awareness.** Henceforth you can use your symbols to quickly enter your inner dimensions. With a little practice you can dispense with an induction and bring your symbols to awareness independently. If you do not want to use symbols, then skip the bracketed paragraphs altogether.

This meditation works with the power of suggestion. When it invites you to tell yourself something you will get the best results if you actually do so sub-vocally; repetition will even further reinforce your intention. Please see instructions for *Creating a Symbol for Calling Up Energy* (Part II, Page 39) for more information on how symbols work.

Relaxing in Body (1A)

B ring your attention into your body.... Be aware of the position you are in.... Focus on your breathing.... Let your breath find its own most comfortable rhythm....

[Bring to awareness your symbol for physical relaxation.... Feel your whole body relax...more and more relaxed with each breath.......]

Imagine that your breath is as easy and relaxed as the breath of a sleeping baby...full and easy.... Feel your body breathe...the rise and fall of your belly as breath moves in and out of your body...the sensation and sound of air moving through...breath rolling through your whole body... renewing every cell of which you are composed.... Breathing...soft breath.... Feel your breath caress you.... Imagine your breaths are like waves that roll up onto the beach and caress every granule of sand, then roll back to sea again....... Breathe...waves of breath...in and out.... Each breath caresses every cell of which you are composed. Every cell in your body breathes....... Breath washes through; imagine each exhalation carries away tensions.... Breathing....

As you relax, feel your body let go.... Feel your weight sink into the support of whatever you are sitting or lying on.... Relax into this support.... Appreciate that the Earth always supports your weight...always sustains your life.... Relax into this support.... Trust it. Let go into it...relaxing.... Feel the Earth supporting your body....

You may want to imagine your body being supported in a warm pool of water...gently moving up and down as breath moves in and out....... Tell your body it can relax...fully relax now....

Feel all the parts of your body relax...your face relaxes...your jaw relaxes...breathing...your neck relaxes...your shoulders...your belly relaxes...breathing...your whole body relaxes.... Feel your whole body relaxing.... Notice if any areas need extra attention.... If there is any holding anywhere, send your breath there.... Breathe.... Feel the area breathe....... Relax.... Feel yourself relax more and more.......

[[Create a symbol that represents this physical relaxation. Imagine something that symbolizes this relaxed state — however you wish to represent it. Make it up; create it. It could be a picture, a tone, a gesture — be specific....... Tell your body that the next time you bring this symbol to awareness it will relax as deeply as it is now relaxed in a matter of moments.... Tell your body this.... *Expect* it to be the case.... Know that every time you bring your physical relaxation symbol to awareness, it will cause your body to enter deeper states of relaxation more quickly and more easily....]]

Expect that your body will continue to relax even more as you move through this meditation....

Relaxing in Mind (1B)

[Bring to awareness your symbol for mental relaxation.... Feel your whole mind relax into spacious awareness...more and more open with each breath...lots of room for whatever thoughts move across the sky of your mind.......]

Bring your attention to your mind. Be aware of the various thoughts running through your mind.... Appreciate the expanse of awareness.... Imagine giving your mind permission to relax into its natural state of spaciousness.... Breathe....

To help your mind relax, you may want to imagine yourself in a very peaceful place; imagining all the details of the scene.... You may want to imagine soothing music.... You can simply listen to and feel your breathing; whenever you rest your attention on breath your mind relaxes.... Breathe.... Draw in calm.......

Feel your mind relax into its natural state of expansiveness…. As though your breath were like a breeze that clears the air, imagine sending your breath right through your mind. Breathe…and your mind opens. Feel your spacious awareness…. Breathe…. Sense lots of space for whatever thoughts cross the sky of your mind…. So much space you can begin to detect space in between your thoughts……. Imagine that your thoughts are as free as the birds that soar through the air…. Feel your mind relax into its natural state of spaciousness — however you experience this….

Imagine your mind opening as though it were to extend as far as the horizons…. Imagine your mind relaxing into the vast intelligence of the universe. As your body relaxes into the support of the Earth, your mind relaxes into universal intelligence — however you experience this…. Breathe…. Each time you exhale your mind relaxes even more…spacious…open…ample room for whatever thoughts cross the sky of your mind…. Your mind is as open as the skies….

[[Create a symbol that represents this mental relaxation. Imagine something that symbolizes this relaxed state of mind — however you wish to represent it. Make it up; create it. It could be a picture, a tone, a gesture — be specific……. Tell your mind that the next time you bring this symbol to awareness it will relax as deeply as it is now relaxed in a matter of moments…. *Expect* this to be the case…. Know that every time you bring your mental relaxation symbol to awareness, it will cause your mind to relax and open, entering deeper states of mental relaxation with greater ease each time you practice. Relaxed and alert.]]

As your mind continues relaxing tell yourself that you will remain relaxed and alert throughout this meditation….

Relaxing Emotionally (1C)

[Bring to awareness your symbol for emotional relaxation…. Feel your whole emotional self relax…more and more relaxed with each breath…. Your heart opens…. The heart's natural state is compassion….]

Become aware of your emotional self...aware of all that you have been feeling lately.... Pay attention to your heart.... Notice the emotional climate in which you reside...notice the feelings present now — especially all the difficulties that you've been having lately...all the "shoulds" — feelings that judge how the world should be...how you should be...how your life ought to be — all the pushing and pulling energy...all the dense energy, all the edges, frustration, anger, anxiety, disappointment, judgment...all that makes you tense up and withdraw from life.... Just notice.... Put attention to your heart.......

Now give yourself permission to relax emotionally.... Tell yourself that as you meditate you can let go and emotionally relax.... Imagine that you can send your breath right into any constriction, breathe space in....... Sense your breath dislodging all the difficulties, all the stuck energies.... Like a lightning rod, imagine grounding out all this energy...as though all the negativity drops down into the ground by the sheer weight if itself...fertilizing the earth.... Let the "shoulds" go.... Breathe them out....... Each time you exhale let go.... However you imagine it. Breathe and release the "shoulds"....... Feel your heart lighten.... Breathe and let constriction go.... Breathe it out...breathe it all out.......

Now take time to comfort yourself — you deserve it. Appreciate your goodness.... Acknowledge all the efforts that you've made lately.... Tell yourself just what you need to hear.... Listen.... Be kind to yourself; you deserve it.... Be loving.... Breathe it in.... Be gentle with yourself.... Have compassion for yourself.... Feel yourself soften inside.... Feel your heart open...be warm.... Appreciate yourself for all you have been through...for all that you have given.... Appreciate your goodness.... However you experience it, let your heart relax into loving-kindness....... Feel your heart open — smile....

[[Create a symbol that represents this emotional relaxation. Imagine something that represents this relaxed state. Symbolize it however you like; make it up....... It could be a picture, a gesture, a tone — be specific....... Tell your emotional self that the next time you bring this symbol to awareness your feelings will relax as they are now relaxed in a matter of moments…. *Expect* this to be the case…. Know that every time you bring your emotional relaxation symbol to awareness, it will cause you to enter deeper states of emotional relaxation with greater ease. Your heart opens….]]

Let yourself relax into the goodness of life itself….

Relaxing into the Reverent (1D)

[Bring to awareness your symbol for your creative self-restoring center…. Feel your gratitude to be alive…. Feel your connection to all life…. Glad to be alive. Sense your whole being open…. You are in healing space, sacred space…. Receptive…. Creative…. Mindful…. Alert…. Relaxed…. Ready to do your inner work.]

Take time to bring to awareness what you are grateful for…to appreciate the goodness of life itself…. Remember what you hold in your heart…. Remember your connectedness……. Feel your gratitude…. Remember the sacred…. Let all of this have a quiet presence in the light of awareness…. Take time to appreciate what you love and cherish…. Acknowledge the blessings…. Feel reverence…. Life is sacred….

When you reside in the awareness of the sacred you are in your creative self-restoring center from which you can do your inner work. This is your creative self-restoring center. This is the place where you commune with the creative and healing energies intrinsic to life itself….

[[Create a symbol that represents this reverent state of awareness. Whatever represents this for you, create it…. It could be a picture, a gesture, a tone — be specific……. Tell yourself that the next time you bring this symbol to awareness you'll enter your creative self-restoring center in a matter of moments…. *Expect* this to be the case…. Tell yourself this…. You will enter this state of awareness more and more easily every time you meditate using all of your relaxation symbols. Each time you do they will carry you into exactly the state of consciousness needed for your inner work. Know that this is so….]]

Feel yourself connected to All That Is; you are held by the universe.... Feel the presence of your receptive/creative awareness.... Here you can tap healing energy. Here creativity is released; probabilities are formed, and intuition comes forth. This is where insight is found. Here you can be in the presence of the Witness. In spacious awareness the ring of truth is always revealed. You can always discover what is needed to regain balance. Trust spacious awareness....

Deepen Awareness (1E)

As you hear the sounds of these words move through your awareness feel yourself going down, deeper and deeper with each exhalation of breath...below the chatter of the day...deeper.... All the frenzied energy simply evaporates away as you go down into your deeper self.... All the sounds around you cause you to be even more deeply aware.... Breathing...relaxing into the depths of being itself....

Alert and Agile in Inner Realms (1F)

You will remain *alert, focused,* and relaxed in this meditation. Tell yourself that you will remain alert, focused, and relaxed through this whole meditation.... Know that you will maintain exactly the level of awareness needed and you will remember all that you experience....

Know that as you work in these dimensions you are increasingly able maintain whatever level of awareness you choose for as long as you choose. Your power of concentration increases, and your imagination becomes more and more fluid. Your intuition sharpens, and your creativity blossoms. Here you always witness what is true. Know that all of this is so....

Breath is Home; Breath Heals (1G)

Breathe.... Arrive here in this meditation. Breathe.... Rest your attention on your breath.... In meditation your breath is your home. You can always return to your breath...take refuge in your breath.... Your breath centers you. Breathe.... Your breath clears you.... You can breathe in calm and breathe out any energy you wish to release.... Your breath renews you.... Your breath heals you.... Your breath returns you to the embrace of life itself.... Your breath is your home.... Breathe.... Let your attention rest on your breath. Breathe.......

Let the rhythm of your breath gently rock you...soothe you...calm and quiet you....Breathe...breathe out tension.... Breathe.... Healing happens.......

Breathe in calm.... Breathe space in.... Breathe in kindness.... Breathe space in, space to discover what is...accept what is.... Breathe...let the past go...arrive in the present.... In full breath there is openness, even with the greatest difficulty.... Breathe.... Healing happens.... Breath heals....... **(Repeat as much of the meditation as you like.)**

Inner Witness (1H)

Breathe...be with quiet awareness.... Breathe...be aware. Listen to the quiet of awareness....... Experience awareness.... Breathe...be in awareness...held by awareness.... Breathe. You needn't do anything; just be in awareness....

There is a quality of awareness that is all-encompassing. It sits in wholeness, as though it is the center of being. This awareness resides inside everyone. This awareness just is.... A quality of patient knowing that is as vast as time itself.... It is always to be found right here in present time...completely present. Here is where one can glimpse the divine. Breathe.... Rest attention on breath and you open to spacious awareness....

Whatever you bring into the light of this spacious awareness becomes clear. In the light of awareness what is true is apparent. In spacious awareness there is no attachment, no investment, simply acceptance of what is so...no definitions, no decisions, no words, just knowing.... Rest attention on breath and you open to spacious awareness.... Here you witness what is so. Breathe....... **(Repeat as much of the meditation as you like.)**

Active Imagination (1I)

Here your inner visionary is alive and thriving. In open awareness it has ample room to play.... It scouts out the best route and cuts a path for you.... Cast into the future it provides a guiding light. You find that your heart and mind generate feelings and thoughts in accord with the vision.... Your intuition chimes in with impulses and insights. All of this begins in meditation and moves out into life's activities. You walk the path naturally.

Here your inner visionary gets you oriented to what lies ahead. As it moves forward it awakens all resonant energies. It is charismatic; it draws to experience all resonant energy. It has far-reaching vision and is drawn to resonant energies.... Possibilities discovered, probabilities energized.... Magic happens...usually surprising you and sometimes surpassing your dreams — mysterious!

Receptive Imagination (1J)

Here intuition is awakened. Here consciousness is clear; there is room for insight to appear.... In spacious awareness creativity is released. In story, truth is revealed.... Sometimes it's quirky, sometimes obvious, sometimes simple, sometimes subtle.... Truth is always revealed in whatever form; it's waiting.... All you need do is turn your attention to the matter; create story and it delivers the truth...sometimes cloaked in metaphor, sometimes delivered in telepathic knowing; sometimes it comes through the gut, or just pops up as an insight. Occasionally it's vague — abiding with it invites clarity. Intuition points the way with no rhyme or reason why. It's eccentric — ask it to explain itself and it goes into hiding; invite it to tell you a story and it blossoms into its own reality, gifting you with a view of actuality. Remember to watch closely, because your imagination often reveals reality by how it carries your projections. Welcome your intuition in all its quirkiness....

Group: Coming Into Accord (2)

Use only as much of the following meditation as you like; take just one minute or as long as ten to complete it. Combining it with lines from any part of *Breathing into Wholeness (1)* will augment it. See *Optimizing a Meeting (143)* for a more elaborate exploration. Name the particular purpose that has brought people together, and suggest that they imagine success. You might want to add a suggestion about the group coming to agreements easily. Please see Tips for Leading Groups in Meditation, (Part II, Page 64). Also note the ending *Group Closing (13U)*.

Take a breath and allow yourself to settle in; be present with each other and the purpose at hand.... Take a moment and focus on your breath.... Imagine as you inhale, you gather yourself and become more present.... Imagine as you exhale you let go of the clamor of the day, of distractions, and settle into this meeting.... Let your breath relax...breathe with your belly.... Extend you awareness to include everyone in the room, everyone breathing....

Imagine as though we literally begin to breathe together. Imagine that we move into accord with one another, however you imagine this. Sense this happening, as though we are one breathing.......

Take a moment and sense each person here. Feel all of us coming together for a common purpose....

Imagine that we listen deeply...our differences inspire collective brilliance.... Inspire a generosity of spirit.... We celebrate each other; we celebrate together....

Imagine that we bring our hearts and minds together. (Name the purpose of the meeting and suggest success.)

Find that place inside where you stand in your truth, where you stand in your integrity, in your openness....... Now feel yourself open and connected with each person here....... In our openness we are powerful.

If there is anything that you need to do to maintain an openness...imagine what that is.... Imagine doing it....

CONSTRUCTING MEDITATION CONTEXT AND ENHANCING INNER AWARENESS

Although most of these meditations can be used on their own, they are designed to enhance the others; used repeatedly they will achieve their effect if you read only a couple of the paragraphs. Use a small section when the other meditation you are working on is long. Once you complete the enhancement meditation go directly to the one you have chosen to work with.

Reside in the Quiet (3)

Recommended for days that are filled with demands that seem to come from every-direction. Leave long pauses between lines. If you want to use your inner quiet to become more conscious of your current state being or of any other concern, then continue on to *In the Quiet, Greet Yourself (41)*. Any or all of the paragraphs in this meditation can be repeated to enhance their effect.

L et the sounds invite you to be present. All sounds you hear invite you into this moment. Present…. As you hear the sounds of my words…as you hear all the sounds around you, become acutely aware of your own being…. Breathing. Focus on your breathing…. Each time you inhale, feel your energy…. Each time you exhale, settle into yourself…. Each time you inhale, feel your energy…. Each time you exhale settle into yourself…breathing…. Witness yourself…. Fully present with yourself…observing yourself breathing…inhaling, exhaling…inhaling, exhaling…. Watch yourself breathe…. Listen to the sound of your breath….

Let yourself reside in the quiet of your own being……. Feel your energy…simply reside in the presence of yourself, quietly…. Reside in the presence of yourself…with yourself, breathing…. Witness yourself…. Be with yourself…fully present with who you are…your whole self softly settling down, residing with yourself…. Experience your presence in the present…wholly present…. Feel peace as you settle into being present…breathing…being….

As you breathe, the clutter and clamor of the day dissipate…. Breathe in calm…. Breathe out calm. Peaceful. Let this peaceful energy wash through you as you breathe.... As it washes through you, it replenishes you...it renews you...it returns you to yourself.... Let yourself simply reside in this peaceful energy.... It washes through you...cleanses you, clears you... returns you to yourself... to the ground of being itself.... Breathing...in and out.... Breathing.

In quiet, in stillness, room is made for healing body and soul.... Breathing, quiet, healing, quiet.... Breathing...just breathing.... Peaceful energy washes through you like waves...breathing calm...absorbing it...bathing yourself in it...peaceful energy.... Breathing peace. Cleansing and clearing you.... Just as water brings out the true colors of the stones in the streambed, breath reveals truth. Be with your breath, and the clamor and clutter dissipate, revealing what is true. Be with your breath, and what is true becomes apparent.... Breathe.... Here awareness is spacious and knowing is deep....

Open to your experience.... Give yourself permission to really believe in your experience.... Breathe.... Be with your breath and what is true becomes apparent.... Breathe.......

Integrity of Your Being: Unique and Belonging (4)

This meditation transforms deep alienation — the feeling that you never are quite good enough and don't really belong.

As you hear the sounds of these words you can feel yourself moving into your deepest knowing. Notice how the sounds of these words carry you down into the very bedrock of your being, of being itself — however you experience this.... Here you experience your connectedness to All That Is. You are made of the same stuff that All That Is is made of. Every molecule that composes you moves in concert with the solar system itself.... Feel yourself as part of All That Is.... Experience your connectedness to the universe —yourself a part of it all.... All life breathes; you breathe.... What you breathe out, plants breathe in; what plants breathe out, you breathe in.... Breath weaves all of life together. You are part of the fabric of the universe. Rest in this knowledge.......

The great unifying forces of the universe move through you.... Feel yourself in communion with All That Is.... Feel the spaciousness...the serene security...however you experience this. Feel yourself exquisitely attuned with the great unifying energies of the universe — a universe in a perpetual state of becoming....

Every being has an integrity unto itself.... Every creature lives in a time and space particular to itself; yet it is part of All That Is —supported by All That Is.... The creative force of life is always expressing itself in new ways.... Acknowledge how you express life like no one ever has — a combination of qualities that only you possess — particular to you.... You express universal energies like no one ever has or ever will.... Only you express life as you do.... Rest in the knowledge that you belong.... The universe holds you.......

As you hear the sounds of these words you can feel yourself moving even deeper into your own essence. From this deep level of awareness you become acutely attuned to the unique quality of who it is that you are, the distinct way you give shape to the life force. Experience the very tone of your being...the particular combination of energies present only in you...the tone of your being...without words, without description, simply experience the deepest tones of your being. Experience the distinctive ways you give form to life...the bedrock of your being — however you experience it.... Know it.... Feel the deepest core of who you are...the quality of energy you express in the world is like none other — no one ever has expressed or shall express life as you do....

Appreciate and honor the integrity of your being...of who you are.... Feel spirit flowing through you...the expression of who you are...your character...the ways you give expression to life.... The distinctive way you express your humanity is like no one else. Feel your integrity; appreciate who you are.... Know that as you appreciate who you are, you open to your true self.... You give yourself space to be true to your own self.

Imagine as though the particular qualities that make up your being come together and form waves — waves of light or music, color, vibrations, or simply pure energy. Imagine that as you breathe, these waves roll through the whole of your body and mind.... Sense energy invigorating, revitalizing, rejuvenating who it is that you are. Imagine it.... Breathe...waves roll through. Waves of energy returning you to your own truth — like returning home. You are distinct, yet part of and supported by All That Is.... Acknowledge that you have a place in the universe... Breathe....

Smoothing the Edges: Soothing Irritation (5)

This meditation is for dissolving feelings of aggravation.

Imagine all that you find soothing...soothing...maybe music...maybe the soft fur of an animal friend, maybe smooth cloth...soothing qualities...comfort...soothing qualities.... The touch of a loved one...the warmth of the sun...soothing qualities...softness...flower petals...a warm drink...a hot bath...soothing qualities...pastel colors...the scent of flowers...gentle rocking...soft humming...fire in the hearth...being held, hearing a beating heart.... The smell of food cooking.... Imagine feeling soothed....... What makes you feel comforted, quieted, reassured? What makes you feel like you can let go and receive?... Remember moments you've felt this way before.... Evoke these qualities now. Let yourself be comforted. Feel these qualities, these soothing qualities.... Conjure them up now.... Imagine them vividly. Breathe.... Open to them.... **(Repeat the first paragraph here.)**

Now imagine that they merge together and become a warm stream.... You can float on it. Imagine that this calming, comforting stream is below you. It is carrying you.... Imagine that it carries you down deeper and deeper...deeper into yourself, and you relax even more as you go down...down...floating on this warm stream...gently carrying you...a current of tranquil energy.... You might hear music now...soothing music.... Feel yourself bathed in the harmonizing energies of the universe...like you are suspended in this energy — warm, supportive, buoyant, beautiful.

Imagine the caress of this energy; let the energy, this soothing energy, roll through your whole being.... Breathe and feel it roll through.... Feel your spirit being soothed.... Breathe, and your mind is quieted.... Breathe, comfort your heart; feel your body being soothed, comforted, quieted.... Feel a shift taking place deep inside you as you are soothed by the harmonizing forces of the universe.

Imagine these harmonizing energies spread.... Let the energy, this soothing energy, roll through all of the things that you've found irritating lately...all the rough edges...all the dense energy...the part of you that has been over-worked....... Imagine all the edges, confusions, anxieties, tensions, as they all simply dissolve into this soothing harmonizing energy. Feel your whole self and your whole life relaxing into this harmonizing energy.......

Lake of Reflection (6)

This meditation may be used on its own, in conjunction with *Countdown into Deep Awareness (7)*, or with *Clarity (46)*.

Imagine yourself in a mountainous place in the springtime. There is a meadow with a lake in it and falls that feed the lake.... The sun shines down through the falls, creating rainbows.... Trees reach to the blue sky.... Birds sing.... Imagine it...the sounds...the smells...the dance of light here...the beauty — an exquisite place. It is breathtaking.... This place is sacred.... Notice how grasses dance with the breezes. Wild flowers burst in a celebration of color and scent.... The majesty of the mountains surrounds you. Feel yourself becoming so in tune with this place that every cell in your body sings.... Notice how the lake is so still and quiet that you can see the mountains reflected in it as clear as day.... The whole world is reflected in it. This is a magical lake of reflection....

Countdown into Deep Awareness (7)

Recommended for use in conjunction with meditations in which the Receptive Imagination is the main focus. This meditation will help you to enter a deeper level of awareness below the usual mind chatter. It is designed to be used with *Lake of Reflection (6)*, but it can also be used independently, in which case skip the first paragraph. Read with an emphasis on the numbers.

Here you can safely journey into the world of reflection... down into the depths of reflection.... In this world of reflection you'll experience everything in its true light — just as water brings out the true color of stones. In this world of reflection you'll come to know what is at the bottom of whatever you choose to focus on. Expect this to be so. This is a magical place.

In a moment I'm going to count on a descending scale from *Ten to One*, and on each descending count you'll feel yourself going deeper and deeper into the world of reflection. At the count of *One* your consciousness will have adjusted to *exactly* that level where you can do your most creative, receptive inner work, where you are fully insightful about yourself and others. Your consciousness knows itself intimately; your consciousness knows just where it needs to be to do the reflective work at hand. You'll be centered at that level at the count of *One*.

Ten, moving down, deeper and deeper into the world of reflection, deeper and deeper into yourself. Each exhalation gently carries you down.... *Nine*, it feels good to relax into yourself, to simply return to yourself, to be present with yourself, moving down deeper and deeper into your world of reflection. Breathing.... *Eight*, softly, gently returning to yourself, deeper and deeper down, deeper and deeper down into the depths of being itself. *Seven*, softly and gently moving down, feeling the essence of yourself, feeling the essence of being itself, deeper and deeper; it feels good to return to yourself. *Six*, relaxing, returning to being itself.... *Five*, your inner world expanding out in all directions around you. *Four*, deeper and deeper; at the count of *One* your consciousness will have adjusted to just that level where you can do your pure reflective work. *Three*, deeper and deeper. *Two*, moving down now.... *One!* Your consciousness has now adjusted to a very stable level of awareness where you are acutely attuned.... Your consciousness is exactly where it needs to be to do the work at hand. Here you are attuned to the underlying rhythms that permeate everything.... You are aware of subtle energies. Here your reflections are pure and clear....

Soaring High in the Skies (8)

This meditation is helpful to use if you are prone to depression; feel oppressed, trapped, or overwhelmed; or need to cultivate an open mind.

Here your consciousness expands. In this spacious awareness you can soar through your world inside like a bird that soars in the sky. Imagine being carried by the breezes...relaxing into the breezes...high in the sky...floating through the air...supported by the air.... Sense how your own consciousness moves like the bird that glides through the air...relaxed, carried by the breezes.... You can see your whole life clearly as you look down over the landscape of your inner dimensions.... Feel yourself able to fly high through the great expanse of awareness itself. However you imagine it, feel it.... Envision the contours of the land below....

You can see all the contours of the land below...just as the eagle sees the slightest movement way down below — the subtlest movement in the grasses.... Imagine that your awareness is as keen as the awareness of the eagle soaring through the skies....... Open, free, alert, and relaxed. (Repeat any of the above.)

Imagine that from this view, you can look down on the contours of your own life....

Inner Refuge: Your Sacred Space (9)

This meditation creates a place of power that you might want to use regularly in your inner work. It creates a deep sense of safety and is especially good if your life is usually filled with meeting the demands of others. The paragraph that invites you to welcome helpful spirits is optional. If you do use it, you may want to augment it by inserting *The Spirits (32)*. If you have already worked with Inner Refuge, skip the first paragraph and use as much of the rest as you like. You may want to move directly from this meditation to *Magic Is the Power of Transformation (10)*.

Imagine a special place, a sacred space for you to be...a peaceful, serene place.... It could be a place you know or a place that exists only in imagination. Create an imaginary place of power....... This place causes a deep calm.... This is your place of power — your sanctuary — a sacred space. You can come here to be calm, to heal, to transform energy.... It is a magical place.

This is your refuge, your sanctuary, which you can always come to. Make yourself comfortable. Sense all that is around you...above you...beneath you.... Listen to the sounds.... Notice the scents in the air, the colors.... Sense the quality of energy here.... Breathe in the beauty and peace of this place...the magic.... Feel yourself bathed in calm.

This is your place of power for your inner work. Feel the sense of well-being in this place. Despite life's trials and tribulations, here in your place of receptive power there is peace. You are entirely safe and secure here. You can always take refuge here.

Take a few moments to absorb the tranquillity of this sacred space.... Breathe...with each inhalation feel yourself becoming as much a part of this place as all that's here. Commune with the spirit of this place.... Feel it.... Feel the calm begin to spread through your whole being.... Breathe it in. Bath yourself in it.... Feel it spread through your body...through your mind...your feelings...your spirit...through all the energy centers of your being....... Breathe and commune with the magic of this place....

If you like, you can invite in spirits who will guard your space and protect you.... Invite spirits who will guide you in your healing and transformation work.... Sense their presence.... They reveal themselves through your imagination....... Welcome them one at a time.......

This is your place of power where you come to do the work of transformation. However you're inclined, imagine doing a ceremony to sanctify your place of power.... Do a ritual now.... Sanctify your sacred space with song or dance or simply with focus of intent — however you imagine it....

Magic Is the Power of Transformation (10)

This meditation is greatly enhanced when opened with all or parts of *Inner Refuge (9)*.

Magic is the power to manifest transformation. Magic is the way of life in sacred space.... Here impediments transform into strengths — assume this is the case; here consciousness is fluid.... You shape it....

Acknowledge the regenerative powers of life itself. Life naturally heals itself, balances itself, reproduces itself, recreates itself.... Life is intrinsically creative...resilient. The creative power that transforms constriction resides here in sacred space.... Here wisdom is born. You receive exactly what you need to transmute energies — for the power of receptivity resides here.... Lessons are offered and energy is released here.... Life naturally moves into balance here....

In the depths of the Earth, all that enters is transformed into power.... Here in the depths of inner consciousness, transformation is always taking place. Here all difficulties ferment and become invitations to embrace life fully.... As in the bowels of the Earth, where all that is no longer needed is converted into nourishment for new life, the Earth creates out of darkness.... This is the place in the depths of consciousness where all that is in need of transformation is converted into a new form that life embraces.... Acknowledge the magic of transformation.

Here you can draw up energy from the deepest levels of being.... Know that this is so. There are no limitations of space and time here.... Trust it.... Here you can delve into truth.... This is where transformation takes place. With faith and clear intent anything is possible....

Clearing Space Inside with Mental Housecleaning (11)

Use this meditation anytime you want to transform defeating beliefs, attitudes, or feelings or when you are working on an issue you are unhappy about (see Mental Housecleaning, Part II, Page 43). It is designed to follow all but the last paragraph of *Magic is the Power of Transformation (10)*. If this is the first time you are using Clearing Space Inside with Mental Housecleaning, skip the third paragraph. Once you have created your mental housecleaning process, skip the second paragraph and use only as much of the rest of the meditation as you wish. Use the same imagery whenever you work with the meditation again.

Know that your deepest consciousness is very loyal to you. It is receptive to your messages. It *will* respond to your suggestions and do your biding. You are now going to communicate with the part of you that stores your beliefs and offers up habituated reactions. Know that when you provide it with offerings, it comes alive — happy to have the opportunity to make revisions. These revisions create openings for new experience.

Imagine how you would like to communicate your intent. Imagine a process of transformation. It could be using fire, or it might be using breath; maybe composting is what's best.... Or maybe there is another process you'd choose; be sure it is one in which a transformation takes place. Create a process that you will use for your mental housecleaning now....... Know that every time you work with it your deepest self becomes even more responsive to your intentions.

Bring to awareness your mental housecleaning process.... Know that you can use it whenever you come across anything that is in need of transformation.

To work with it now, bring the concern you would like to transform to awareness. Remember the details.... Feel the energy that it carries.... Notice the thoughts that belong to it. Notice its limitations.... Breathe.... As you inhale, gather up the energy and make a symbol with it....... Now as you exhale, put the symbol with all its energy into your mental housecleaning process.... Release it. Breathe.... With deliberate and clear intention, tell your deepest self to transform it. Tell your deepest self that you fully expect it to convert the energy.... Tell it that you welcome new approaches and look forward to new experience.... Now thank your deepest self for doing the work of transformation.

Expect that every time you use your mental housecleaning process for transformation your deepest self will respond by creating space for fresh approaches and new insights. Tell yourself this now. Appreciate the power of transformation. Let yourself feel relief that change is taking place.... Now you can free your attention to move on to other concerns knowing that your deepest self is taking care of the matter. If by chance you run across residues of the old ways just put them in your transformation process and expect change....

Protected View (12)

Use this meditation to work with issues that are emotionally charged. It is designed to work with *Inner Refuge (9)*. Pay attention to your breath as a signal of rising tension. If tension rises, let go of what you are doing and return to the protection of your inner refuge and work with your breath. When you have re-established your well-being continue where you left off. You may also want to use *Breath Is Home; Breath Heals (1G)* or *Inner Witness (1H)*. Parts of *The Transformative Power of Breath (45)* will prove helpful if tension arises. *Magic Is the Power of Transformation (10)* will further reinforce this meditation.

Protected View combines well with any problem-solving meditations; simply adapt the scripts by replacing the words, "bring to awareness" with "project into your viewing area." Feel free to skip the last two paragraphs and go directly to the other meditation you are working with.

In this sacred place you can work with energy; you can transform energy.... Here it's as though you are the alchemist of all your own feelings...especially the feelings that undermine you.... Here it's as though you can look at a film of patterns that undermines you...your emotional patterns — when you get tangled in your own feelings...when you get upset.... You can sense how the energy moves you...how you get pulled off center.... You can witness the unfolding of events past, present, and future.

From inside your sacred space, you can see outside.... Now, create a viewing area just *outside* of your sacred space...maybe a screen or stage...some place where you can view situations, circumstances, feelings.... Imagine a viewing area where you can explore and get to know the true nature of the issues that concern you...where you can perceive energy patterns. Create a viewing area — however you imagine it.

Whatever you observe outside in your viewing area, whatever you project there, you come to know its true nature. You come to know just what you need to do to maintain your integrity, safety.... Whatever you view from your place of power, from your sacred space, you discover exactly what's needed to bring balance about.... You can transform energies from the inside of your sanctuary. You can dull the picture by simply turning down the light, or you can reframe it altogether; you can even turn it upside down, shake it up, and see what falls out. You can change your view, and you can change what you are viewing.... Either way you change your relationship to the issue.... Know that this is so, for you are now in the realm of magic where problems transform into gifts

Whenever you are in your sacred space and perceive anything outside it, you always remain safe and secure — your integrity intact. Know that this is so.... If you ever feel that you've lost your sense of well-being, it's only because you left your sanctuary; all you need to do is to return to your sacred space and you'll regain your well-being. To return, just focus on your breath; imagine being inside your sanctuary; make yourself comfortable, and then go back to watching your viewing area *outside* your sanctuary in the safety of your magical space. Know that this is the case. Tell yourself that whenever you find yourself off center you'll notice, breathe, and remember to return to your secure refuge.

Now project images that represent the concern you have chosen to work with into your viewing area.... Watch it outside your sacred space.... Observe.... Witness.... Keep them *outside* your sacred space and witness them.... Perceive them however your imagination conjures them up — notice their energy; they may not take a visual form. Breathe and witness....

If you like, change them...or change your perspective.... Smoothe out the feelings with breath.... Turn the picture all around — maybe even upside down...turn up or down the light and sound.... Shift the scene however you like.... Know that in doing so you shift your relation to the issue. Expect this to be the case.... Breathe.... Imagine change.... Experience transformation taking place...subtle; notice the shift.... What is the message?....

COMPLETING WORK AND RETURNING TO OUTER FOCUS

Coming Out of Meditation (13V) and Count Out (13W) should be used to complete every meditation; they will help you to integrate the insights and move the energy you have discovered while meditating into daily life. *Endings (13A – W)* focus on what is needed to integrate new approaches into your life and take advantage of the fact that you are in a suggestible state of awareness. Utilizing the power of suggestion, they effectively reinforce transformation and increase both memory and resolve. When they invite you to tell yourself something, it is best to sub-vocally do just that. Always refer to transformation in the past tense — as if it has already taken place. It is important to name the specific meditative work you have done, especially if you have made any agreements with yourself. *Endings* may be used in any combination.

Endings (13)

Create a Symbol to Tap Energy in Daily Life (13A)

Use this ending to create a symbol if you want to easily and quickly access the positive energies you experienced in your meditation work. Or, use it to further empower a symbol you have already created — just name your symbol in place of the section that tells you to create it. Whenever you bring your symbol to awareness in the midst of your day that energy will become accessible, and the more you use a symbol the more powerful it becomes. Don't worry if the symbol you create is the "right" one. Whatever you create is right for you. You are working with your own associative process and the power of suggestion. Keep it simple; your symbol has to be specific and easy to call to awareness. You can use a gesture, a sound, or a visual image. It is important that you stick to whatever you create; if you keep changing symbols they become meaningless.

This method is simple and profoundly effective because your whole self responds to whatever is in your imagination at any given moment. For more information on how symbols work see Creating a Symbol for Calling Up Energy (Part II, Page 39).

Create a symbol that represents this experience. Imagine something that symbolizes this way of being. However you would like to symbolize this experience, make it up, create it.... It could be a picture, a gesture, a tone, an affirmation, a rhyme — be specific....... Whatever your imagination conjures up is what is right for you.... This symbol encapsulates the fullness of your experience. Imagine that this symbol has a magnetic core, and it draws into itself all the power of this meditation...all the energy.... As you inhale, concentrate the energies.... This symbol embodies the energies you have evoked. The energy is so vibrant that it lights up the symbol. It hums with energy.

Know that whenever you bring this symbol to the forefront of your awareness it causes your entire being to move into alignment with it, enabling you to tap these powers on the spot.... You will find that you naturally act in accord with this power. Expect this to be true. Tell yourself this is true.... Know that your symbol aligns your energy and empowers you to draw from your deepest knowing. You intuit exactly what is needed....

Tell yourself that you'll remember to bring your symbol to awareness whenever the need arises in the midst of activity.... Imagine that when you do, it evokes these energies and empowers you to act on them.

If ever you are in a quandary about how to move forward, all you need do is imagine asking your symbol. As you do, you'll sense what's needed.... There may be a concern you would like to ask it now; imagine doing so....... Trust the knowing that comes.

Know that as the energy is present in you, others are inspired by these powers, too.... It's magnetic.... This symbol causes all that resonates with it to come forth. *Expect* this to be true.... (Optional: continue with the following ending, naming the use of your symbol.)

Energize Transformation with Breath (13B)

You can energize your whole being with this potent energy. Use your breath to direct it wherever you choose. Inhale; gather the energy....... Breathe;

concentrate the energy.... Exhale; channel it.... You can energize any dimension of yourself and your life.... Channel it into your body now, bathing every cell of which you are composed with this energized breath....... Breathe it into your mind; experience all your thoughts infused with this energy.... Breathe it into your feelings.... Feel your heart open to it....... Fill your spirit with it....... Breathe...and send it into your future......your past......your whole self, your whole life infused with this empowering energy.... Imagine it. This way of being becomes so familiar it is like the air you breathe. Breathe its power.......

Keeping the Energies Moving Through the Day (13C)

Tell yourself that these energies will continue to move through you in this way throughout this day.... Imagine this is the case.... You have now established the energy pattern — the passageway is in place. These energies will continue to move through you and aid you. *Expect* it.... When you move your attention on to other concerns, this energy continues to move through you in this manner. Tell yourself this.... Tell yourself that occasionally as the day unfolds, you will turn your attention to the energy moving through. Know that doing so further empowers you and the energy too.... This energy keeps you centered, clear, open, and contributing your best. It gives you all the energy you need to be fully tuned, to learn, and to meet the challenge.... *Assume* it is true....

Spirit of Change (13D)

Imagine all this energy coalescing into an animated spirit who will guide you in this new way of being....... Talk to the spirit of change.... Get to know its temperament.... It has offerings...lessons, insights.... Commune with this new experience....... Breathe.... Draw this fresh approach into yourself. Feel it.... Embody it.... Welcome it into your thoughts.... Invite the spirit of change in....

Feel change taking place inside.... Open to it; believe in it.... Breathe it.... Feel a shift of consciousness.... Welcome the spirit of change; ask it to make itself at home....

Imagine what you might do day-to-day to make it feel at home....

Let Go and Welcome Change (13E)

When you release the old ways of being you make room for the new ways to move in and take root. Witness if there is anything that you might need to let go of to make room for this new way of being to take root in your life.... Do you have any habits, self-images, or beliefs about the world that stand in the way of change?...... Anything that might sabotage this new energy?... Notice what is invested in the old way, what is more comfortable with everything remaining the same.... Talk this over with yourself. Have patience and generosity toward yourself.... Decide what you want to do.... Imagine doing it.... Breathe.... Release....

Be patient with the change process. Change takes time.... Feel yourself letting go of the old patterns.... Breathe them out.... Release them.... Feel a shift inside. Know that you are making change. Feel it.... It might feel awkward and unfamiliar at first. In time this new experience will have grown into your life and become completely ordinary — what has been will live only in memory. Know that this is so. Welcome change....

Act of Faith (13F)

Imagine what is needed to honor the energy, to invite it to flourish in your life.... Notice what in particular would be good to do to cultivate this energy in your life this coming week...act as if it were already manifest.... How can you prepare the soil of your life for this experience to grow?... What is an offering you might make?... How might you express your gratitude?... Imagine doing what you're willing to do....... Have faith.... Trust the energy; open to what it might offer you in your life....

Putting Your Will to Work (13G)

Acknowledge that this vision feels right....... Know that when you choose to act in accord with it you make it manifest.... Sometimes other things will cross your path and beckon you — but you choose where to focus your attention and what to do. Imagine doing what is right for you....... In every single situation in your life you have choice. Know this is true.... Invite your Witness to be with you; make space for clear choice....... Make a commitment to yourself that you will act in accord with this vision....... Tell yourself you will do what is best.... Feel your whole self tuned to your sense of purpose. As though it softly vibrates inside....

Reside in your resolve. Only you choose what to do. You determine how you move forward. Make a commitment to choose what is right and healthy for you whenever distraction appears.... Invite your will power; invite your determination to accompany you as you move forward.... Have clear intent.... In doing so, know that you make this vision your reality. Be deliberate; the choice is always yours.... Imagine that you always focus on what is most important. Be mindful....... Have clear intent. Imagine always choosing to act in accord with your vision.... It has become your compass.... Imagine how this is day-to-day.... The choice is always yours. When you choose in accord with your vision, you bring it about. *Expect* it....

Support (13H)

Others want the best for you. Notice what support there is for you.... Is there anyone you would like to confer with?... Take a moment and open to the support that is there for you....... Is there anything that it would be good to ask for?...... Or anything that it would be good to communicate?... With this new way of being notice how you are better able to connect with others...better able to support others....

Communicate Insight and Change (13I)

Now notice if there is anything that would be good to communicate to others in your life about the insights you have gained or the changes that you have embarked on....... Imagine doing so...what you'll say, to whom...when, where....

Ensure Your Vision Benefits Everyone (13J)

Everything is connected in the wholeness of life. Everyone is part of the great web of life. Honor the wholeness of life; extend your awareness to include others...your family...your community...your coworkers...even people you do not know....... Experience how this vision affects the well-being of others.... One at a time, focus in on particular people and witness....

What impact will this have on others?... How will different individuals experience these changes?...... Look into the future; notice the consequences.......

How do these visions resonate with your principles?... with your values?... Make any adjustments you need to so everyone benefits.......

Sense how these changes will affect the natural fluidity of life itself.... You may want to tune to a particular place and the life that lives there.... Listen deeply.... Make any adjustments that are needed so that the sanctity of life is fully honored....

Hold the intention that your meditation brings wellness to all....

Embody the New You (13K)

Let yourself be who you truly can be.... Embody this energy.... Feel the energy informing your whole being.... Envision it moving out into your life...creating your life anew...becoming who you truly can be....... Step inside of your vision.... Feel it in your body.... Imagine how your body moves when it is informed by this energy....... Embody the change you want to make....... Open to its offerings.... Open to its lessons....

Vision Becomes Experience (13L)

Acknowledge that everything begins with a vision. Vision, choice, and action combine and change manifests. Expect that more and more of your vision moves into reality.... Imagine specifically how your life begins to shift.... Change happens.... Eventually you will find that your vision and your experience are one and the same.... *Expect* it.... Bring the future into the present; imagine your vision has already come about.... Feel what this is like.... Now your vision is your guiding light. Walk the path it illuminates; learn the lessons if offers and it becomes your experience......

Intuitive Alignment: Visions Guide; Impulses Call (13M)

Know that every time you bring these energies to awareness you empower yourself to act in accord with them. Every time you focus on your vision you give it more power.... Believe in your ability to manifest your dreams.

You have moved into alignment with your vision, and you'll find that you intuitively act in accord with it. You'll find your inclinations are congruent with your vision. You'll find impulses and insights arise in daily life that guide you into this way of being...as though this way calls you into this experience.... *Expect* change. Trust yourself. Trust life....

The Imagination Builds Probabilities (13N)

Your Active Imagination has conjured up new patterns of energy. The imagination builds probabilities. Know that the very fact you can imagine it makes it plausible, makes it possible; that in fact, it makes it probable — the energy exists.... Appreciate the fact that you can feel, sense, imagine new ways of being — this means they are real. The energy exists. Your vision is magnetic, drawing into experience resonant circumstances. All you need do is act on the energy and you'll find it manifests in experience.... *Expect* this.... Trust the future.... Know the future welcomes you....

Affirmation of Transformation (13O)

Experience how this way of being is.... Create a sentence in present tense that describes this way of being...simple, positive, describing the change as though it has already taken place. You needn't explain it or say what it is not — just a sentence that describes exactly what it *is*....... Tell yourself you'll remember your affirmation....... Know that every time you repeat it to yourself you bring the reality it describes closer to actuality. You align yourself intuitively to it. You discover new ways of being. You draw resonant circumstances into experience. Eventually the affirmation and reality are one and the same. Meanwhile every time you focus on your affirmation, pretend it is already true — open to it....

Well-Being Spreads into Life (13P)

Feel the knowing you have come to.... Imagine that each time you exhale this energy extends out.... It dissolves all that is worrisome, like the sun melting ice.... As you breathe out, this well-being extends further and further and further out...spreading over more and more of your life.... Secure always...throughout your day...throughout your life...as secure as knowing the sun rises tomorrow.

If you like you can channel some of this energy wherever it is needed.......

Calming Influence (13Q)

A sense of well-being surrounds you and touches the heart of others.... Imagine that everywhere you go you have a calming effect on others. Wellness spreads out.... Feel how this is increasingly so as time passes....

Spreading Through the World (13R)

After using this ending in a group setting, you can encourage people to share their new visions with each other.

Imagine this new way of being extends out and encompasses everyone...as though a whole cultural awakening happens.... How is daily life transformed?...... How does it feel for everyone to embody these new ways of being?...... Experience life this way.... Imagine the culture shifting.... Learning new ways, creating new ways.... Imagine the world embraces this way of being.... Envision it.... Breathe it.... Believe in it....

Bidding Farewell to the Spirits (13S)

Use this ending with *Clearing the Self (13T)*, which follows.

Thank the spirits for accompanying you in your meditative work. Note if there is anything you would like to do to honor them, to pay your respects.... Imagine doing it.... Tell them what you will do.... If you wish, invite them to be with you at particular times that are upcoming....

Clearing the Self (13T)

Use this ending for any meditation work that has involved others in order that you fully clear yourself from any of their residual energies — especially important if you have been doing healing work on behalf of another. If you have had a particularly dramatic experience, it is critical that you return to your usual sense of self: use *Cleansing After Violation (59)*, and shake out your hands and feet.

Now, say goodbye.... Imagine them departing.... Now that they are gone, feel your own energy clear.... Breathe.... Return to the quiet of your own presence. Listen to your breath.... Breathe.... Be in the quiet of your own self.... Clear. *Only* your own energies present....

Group Closing (13U)

Use any of the other endings and substitute "you" with "we" where appropriate.

Begin to finish what you are doing. Be aware that you are sitting here with others.... Sense everyone being attuned with one another.... Imagine all of us working well together.... Know that our visions and sensibilities weave together, supporting each of us. Empowering us all to do exactly what we set out to do…learning together, creating together…. None of us can do it alone; together, we can. We are.

As we breathe together imagine that each time you inhale you set the intention…. With each exhalation send this energy into the group, into the scene, into our common endeavors……. The stage is set…. Trust it….

Coming Out of Meditation (13V)

Use any or all of what follows to come out of your meditation.

Imagine yourself moving through the coming days in such a way that this energy surfaces whenever it's needed…. Imagine going through the routine of your life fully attuned…….

Now go over the details of your meditation experience…. Acknowledge the healing and creative energy that availed itself…. Review any insights you have gained…any choices you may have made…. Acknowledge any agreements that you may have made with yourself…. Imagine further opening to and acting on this energy…. Embody it…. Breathe it…. Project it into the future….

If you like, before returning to an outer focus of attention you can channel energy to anyone that could use a little additional support. Imagine bathing them in healing energy, however you imagine this……. If there is another that you would like to channel energy to, do so now…….

Know that this energy is like an underground spring. You can always tap it. It is always there. It always supports you. Know that this energy transcends space and time; it simply is. All you need do is remember it, and in so doing you invoke it…. It is always a source of power…empowering you to act in the way that is best for you, for everyone, for the future….

Take a moment to fully inhabit your intent to cultivate this harmonizing energy throughout life…. Hold the intention that your meditation practice brings balance and harmony into the world…. Hold the intention to be open to what life offers — all the gifts, all the challenges, and all the lessons — each day a new experience. Welcome life....

Finish what you're doing.... Note anything that you may want to return to the next time you meditate.... Tell yourself that you will remember to focus on this next time you meditate.... You may want to choose when you will meditate again....

Take a moment to acknowledge and appreciate the gifts and challenges of your life, to feel your gratitude....... Be thankful. Take a moment to express your thanks to any energies, spirits, or aspects of yourself that have been with you in this meditation.......

Know that every time you meditate you tap the harmonizing energies of the universe; you become more and more acutely attuned to your intuitive knowing throughout your daily life.

Know that every time you meditate you heal yourself and come to know what's needed to bring about healing around you. True empowerment emerges out of receptivity. The more you meditate, the more harmonizing energies flow through you. Know that this is so.... The more you meditate, the more you open to the healing and creative forces intrinsic to life itself.

Know that each time you meditate you develop more and more agility to navigate through the inner dimensions; you become increasingly able to maintain whatever level of awareness you choose, for as long as you choose. Your imagination becomes increasingly fluid. You are increasingly able to keep your inner Witness present in all your meditation work....

Know that this is so. Tell yourself that this is so.

Tell yourself that you will remember everything that you experienced in this meditation. Every time you meditate you are increasingly able to enter deeper and deeper states of awareness with greater and greater ease....

Count Out (13W)

Use this ending to close your meditation session. Read the numbers with emphasis, and change your tone of voice to one that sounds definite. A bell or handclap can be substituted for the snapping of fingers.

Now, make yourself ready to return to an outer focus of attention.... Know that you can again return to deeper dimensions of awareness whenever you wish.... Bring your attention to what is around you now.

At the count of *Five*, you'll open your eyes — alert and remembering all that you have experienced...feeling refreshed, revitalized, and relaxed.... Bringing with you all the energies you have tapped...ready and able to act on this energy in your life.

One, coming up slowly now....

Two, becoming more aware of the room around you....

Three, at the count of *Five* you'll open your eyes feeling relaxed, revitalized, and refreshed, and remembering all that you've experienced....

Four, coming up now, bringing with you all the energies you have tapped in this meditation.... Feeling yourself alert.

Five! (***SNAP*** *your fingers*), eyes open, feeling refreshed, revitalized, and relaxed; remembering all that you've experienced; ready and able to act on the energies you have tapped.... Alert and feeling a sense of well-being.

SECTION TWO:

Gathering the Forces

SUMMONING THE POWERS

The meditations in this section are designed to augment the rest. They call to awareness specific energies, perspectives, and sensitivities that will enhance your meditation experience. Feel free to repeat the passages that speak to you — it will deepen their effect. Insert meditations from this section after you have used an induction (including a deepening from Constructing Meditation Context and Enhancing Inner Awareness, if you use one) and before using the meditation you have chosen to work with. You may find that you want to use only a portion of one, or to insert a paragraph in the middle of a meditation: use your own inclinations to create the meditation experience that best applies to your situation.

Nearly all of these meditations can also be used on their own; in fact you will find many to be exactly what you need. Several are well suited for getting yourself into the right frame of mind when you are faced with a challenge. If you simply want to work with a particular quality in this section, *Making Magic (43)* will help you to do so more deeply.

Highest, Wisest, Deepest Self Has the Patience of an Ancient Tree (14)
Please change the personal pronouns as needed.

I magine that there is an aspect of you that has the patience of an old and ancient tree, a tree that has witnessed whole centuries go by.... Pretend that you have an aspect of consciousness that has the patience of a very old tree.......
This aspect resides quietly inside all the time. Quiet, yet when you notice, she has an immense presence.... In the quiet of breath you invite her presence....

Sense this part of yourself. She may be your higher self or may be your wisest self. Or she might reside in the deepest core of your being. She may quietly make her home in your heart or speak through your soul. She may have no form; she may simply have a presence.... However she manifests, she is part of you, yet she is more than you.... She is fully present, always present — feel her presence now....... It is as though she is awareness itself. Acknowledge and appreciate her. She resides quietly inside all of the time. It is as though omnipresent intelligence speaks through her.

Listen to her; in her silence is her knowing. She is patient and kind. Loving. Experience how she embodies all these qualities. She has profound patience; she knows what is so. She resides on the fulcrum of balance, always recognizing what rings true. There are no sides to her views — she sees all sides in wholeness...no attachment...no investment; she simply accepts what is so.... She is your conscience.... She recognizes the answers that resonate with the highest reaches of spirit and the depths of soul. She always knows.... She is.... She is powerful in her receptivity.

Sense her spacious awareness.... Feel her openness, her kindness.... She is fully present. Wherever her attention turns, understanding arises as naturally as leaves turn to the sun. She holds total respect for what is so — an appreciation that all things take their own course, that there is purpose to all that comes into being and all that passes away. That all that is has its own place and its own time.

Welcome her into your inner work. Invite her to call your attention to intuitive insights and impulses. Invite her to remind you to let go and open to new perspectives. Invite her to share her wisdom with you all the time. Know that when you share presence with her you receive the gift of life's lessons. She believes in you completely. Invite her to join you in meditation.......

Resilience (15)

This meditation is good for awakening or regaining vitality. Use it as a prelude to any healing meditation.

Every being has the drive to survive and thrive.... Every living cell composing all beings has the drive to thrive. Inborn in every being is the drive to reach to the sun...to drink the waters...to ride energy through time...to be alive! Feel the pulse of life. Feel it.... Resilient, driven to prosper, to discover life, to express life, to be alive!... This drive resides in all that is alive...powerful life force energy...resilient...vital. Life recreates itself, replenishes itself, heals itself. Innate to cellular life is the intelligence to self-regulate, to heal, to regenerate, to perpetuate life. Feel the vitality of life moving through you.... Witness the presence of intelligence intrinsic to life.... Mysterious. Miraculous.......

Feel the blessing of being alive. Feel your own drive to thrive.... Feel the healing powers that reside inside you. Your body is a self-cleansing, self-regenerating, life-perpetuating organism. Sometimes its energies move in subtle and steady ways, sometimes in dramatic and spontaneous ways. Appreciate the mystery.... Appreciate the blessing of being alive!... Remember times you have witnessed the miraculous regenerative powers of life itself: from new life emerging every spring to the cells on torn skin knitting back together again.... Life provides for life. Life gives life. Life protects life. Life sustains life. Life is sacred.... Feel the life force pulsating through your body.... Trust it....

Recollection (16)

Insert any of these paragraphs when meditations call for you to pull up memories. Fill in the blanks with the particular times or quality of experience that you want to bring forth. Repeat any of this meditation to deepen the effect.

In this state of awareness the limits of time evaporate. All of the future and all of the past live in this present moment. From this moment you can journey into your past. You can pull powers right out of your past.

You can shift the energies of the past and carry the gifts of times gone by the way you choose to carry them...for now is your point of power. You carry the past into the future the way you choose to.

Remember times that (____). Recall; vividly recall (____). Revisit one scene at a time. Choose one. Recreate it.... Imagine the details. Let yourself feel it all over again.... Imagine yourself in the middle of the situation as though you are there this very moment.... Was there anyone else there?... Feel (___) all over again.... What are your hands doing? What is below your feet? Recall the mood in the air...the smells, the colors...sounds.... Remember what you may have been wearing.... Recall the details of the scene.... Remember; vividly remember....... Let yourself appreciate the gift of the time even more....

Compassion (17)

Acknowledge how gravity holds all close to the bosom of the Earth...and the sun holds the solar system in light and warmth. Contemplate this.... Imagine that compassion is the glue of the universe. Compassion holds All That Is in the light of care, in the warmth of care.... Compassion.... Hearts touch....

All That Is is interconnected. All that is under the sun, all that lives upon the Earth, matters.... Imagine that compassion is the glue of the universe. Everything is connected to everything else. An effect here is felt everywhere.... Anything that happens elsewhere is felt here....

All is connected. It is as if compassion is the gravity that holds the universe together. Breathe it in.... Your heart breathes compassion. Breathe it out.... Suffering inspires care; we touch in our vulnerabilities.... This is the lifeblood of the heart. The heart holds all; for everything is of everything else.... Compassion is the center of the universe.... Contemplate compassion.... Your heart breathes it....

Intelligence (18)

Intelligence is intrinsic to life.... Acknowledge the existence of intelligence...admire the miracle of intelligence. Awesome. Appreciate the gift of learning — the gifts of lessons you have gained — they are always helpful. Like the water that washes over stones bringing out true colors, there is something magical about learning...delightful.... Acknowledge that you are perpetually learning. Appreciate your own intelligence.... Let your awareness relax into a state of open appreciation...as though your awareness smiles. Just as your body can relax into the support of the Earth, imagine your mind relaxing into the support of universal intelligence.... Open...interested...curious...creative...brilliant.... Alert to the flash of insight....

Personal Power (19)

Let the sounds of these words tune you to your own sense of self...your full self, your whole self.... Remember times in your life when you felt the most alive...times when you felt creative and powerful...when you felt dynamic and whole...times you felt connected...appreciated for who you are and what you offer.... Remember those times now, times when you experienced your own personal power.... You totally came into your own.... You stretched the limits, broke the limits, discovered yourself, discovered life.... If no times come to mind, imagine what it would have been like.... What it could have been like if you were loved and respected for who you are and what you offer.......

Conjure up your magnetism....... Feel your dynamism.... Feel personal power.... Feel the energy.... However you experience it, this energy is always with you; bring it forward now....

Courage (20)

Feel the substance of your body...your bones giving you a frame to stand on...your muscles giving you form, strength, flexibility....... Feel your heart; in receptivity great power emerges.... Now focus on the strength of your character....

Your character gives your spirit ground to stand on. Sense how this is so.... Appreciate your integrity.... Feel the power of your convictions.... Know that as you acknowledge your character you awaken your courage. As you breathe, feel courage stirring inside you now.... You are rooted in your convictions. The trees draw nutrients from the ground; as you inhale, imagine drawing strength from your convictions....... Feel courage stirring inside you now....... Courage; breathe it.... Stand in your character; feel yourself courageous.... You are completely equal to the challenge....

Love (21)

Invite into the light of awareness all the different faces of love. Remember the moments of love in your life...moments when your heart opened.... Love.... Love of another.... Love of life.... Love of nature.... Love.... Invite love in all of its faces to be with you now.... Feel its many faces: warm, radiant, gentle, glowing, passionate, powerful, vulnerable, tender, touching, laughing...all the different qualities of love.... It makes your heart smile. Breathe it in.... Feel how it softens and strengthens you at the same time.......

Love is to truly recognize another, to look deep. Love is to be recognized deeply...to hold...to be held. As you receive and offer love, as you offer and receive love, the separation between you and everything else becomes blurred.... Loving energy almost makes you feel like you can let go and melt into All That Is.... The energy is very warm, fluid, and buoyant.... Feel this energy fluid inside you...and all around you. Like the fish that swim in water, imagine as though your whole being is immersed in this loving energy.... It supports you...like the ocean waters supporting all fish that live in it. Loving energy supports All That Is....

Faith: The Beneficent Dance of Matter and Spirit (22)

It is as though there is an underlying intelligence that moves through All That Is and connects everything into a grand cosmic matrix in which every little part from the minuscule to the magnificent has its own particular place and its own particular time. It is as though there is an energy that moves through everything, connecting All That Is through the infinity of time and space, as though an energy is perpetually creating connective tissue through All That Is. And everything moves in synchrony — from the solar system to the electron. As though everything is infused with spirit — matter and spirit dancing together....

Remember coincidences in your life: times when events just seemed to fit together like matching gloves.... To this day, part of you may be dismissing it all; yet you know that what you witnessed was profound. Remember times when seemingly unrelated events transpired together as though there were some invisible hand orchestrating it all in a marvelous dance of energy resonance.... Maybe you met the right person at the right time...or exactly the book you needed was given to you...or you got a call from a long lost friend you were just thinking of.... Everything fell into place so well it seemed supernatural — almost fated. Mysterious.

From the mundane to the profound, from the commonplace to the momentous occasion, matter and spirit dance together. Maybe there have been times that you had the honor to witness healing — profound healing...or times that a sudden shift in a dangerous moment brought about safety — as though heaven and earth touched in that moment....

These times caused an uncanny sensation: it's as though the divine was reading your mind and you were being addressed personally, as though the universe were speaking to you directly — auspicious.... Somehow you felt connected and cared for. In times like these, you may have felt yourself held by All That Is, somehow belonging to the mysterious. As though the whole universe were completely coherent.... The divine appeared. As though you belong to life — that you must be on the right path. Feeling reassured that you are given exactly what you need when you need it. Feeling that you move in harmony with the way of the universe...that life is enchanted.

Appreciate how your heart and spirit already know this to be true. Elegant.... Mysterious.... Awesome.... Blessed.... Experience faith. Imagine that you can let go and be held by the universe itself. Supported. Experience faith.... Humbled by it all....

Dynamic Center (23)

This meditation is helpful for combating depression and for focusing when one's energies are scattered. It works with the interdependence of what seem to be opposites: calmness and vitality, discipline and spontaneous creativity. Whenever you use this meditation as a prelude to another, skip the last paragraph.

Imagine that you have a magnetic core of energy in the very center of your being.... However you imagine this, sense a core of concentrated energy within you.... It is very quiet and powerful at the same time.... It may be tingling with energy.... It may be pulsating with energy or vibrating. Imagine it full of color, sound...energy, pure energy.... Imagine it at the core of your being...pure energy, vibrant, radiant, sparkling, pulsating, vital energy.... Experience it at the very core of being...energy, powerful energy.... Breathe....

This great concentration of magnetic energy emanates out from your center. Imagine the magnetic center rooting you to life itself.... Energetically it is connected to life force energies the way the trees are rooted in the Earth.... This inner core of energy always draws in strength from the universal spirit of life.... Feel it breathing....

Imagine this magnet in the center of your being pulling in universal energy — as indeed it does — drawing in universal life force.... Your dynamic center roots you in the ground of being, itself.... To empower yourself, you can work with universal breath. Your center is renewed by breath; your life is renewed by breath. Experience how your breath revitalizes this energy in the core of your being.... Notice how each time you inhale, it gets a little stronger...and each time you exhale, it expands...inhaling, your center becomes more vibrant...exhaling, the energy spreads.... Inhaling, vitalizing it.... Exhaling, spreading it.... Inhaling, it becomes more powerful, glowing.... Exhaling, it expands out.... As you breathe, this energy extends through your whole being.... Inhaling, energizing.... Exhaling, expanding.... The energy spreads...vibrant, magnetic, tingling...radiant energy.... Breathe and feel it spread through you.... Experience it.

When you relax and feel the energy move out from your core, feel how it centers you, clears you, returns you to your power. This center keeps you balanced through all the ups and downs of your life — the fulcrum of your life.... Your center enables you to maintain balance amidst change.... Feel yourself fully present with yourself, self-contained and yet connected...fully grounded and yet open.... Notices how this is — powerful and receptive, grounded and open...self-contained and connected...substantial and fluid...autonomous and a part of All That Is. Dynamic. Through the quiet calm, deep within, power emerges.... Your mind is full of content; yet it is receptive, ready to receive and respond.... Discipline and order create channels through which artistic creativity spontaneously erupts.... Rest provides energy.... Feel the dynamism within you.... This magnetic center of receptive power enables you to maintain balance amidst continual change. Experience how this is so....

Sense how energy from the center of your being shines out to the periphery of your life.... Your center glows.... It receives the vitalizing life forces and expresses your truth in a continual exchange of renewing energy as natural as breath itself....

Call Upon Your Life-Affirming Values (24)

Use all or parts of this meditation. You may want to follow it with *Courage (20)*.

There are some truths in life. There are the ethics you live by, the principles you aspire to. Take time to bring to the forefront of awareness all that you believe in.... What is basic in life, to be honored...revered?... What do you care deeply about?...... Acknowledge it.... What do you hold sacred?... Bring forth your convictions.... How do you honor the heart?...each other?...the Earth?... What is truly important?... Bring forth your principles.... What are you committed to?

Who do you love?... How is it they should be treated — honored for who they are?... What does it mean to live honorably?...... to be respectful?...to be fair and just in all your relations?... How should we all treat one another...in health?...in conflict?...in hard times? Everyone belongs.... Everyone deserves to be treated with dignity. What does it mean to live with integrity?...

How to be honorable, ethical...how to work...how to be family...how to be community....... How to care.... How to share.... How to be trustworthy.... How not to be.... How to honor the ancestors.... How to honor future generations.

How to be in place. Are there places, sacred places, that you especially care about?... How should these places be appreciated — cared for?... How to honor nature...and all its creation.... What is important?...

Let yourself be humbled.... All of this is what matters. These are truths that cannot be argued with.... Bring all of this to the fore. Take a moment and align your whole self with your values.... Feel yourself embody your heartfelt values.......

Acknowledge your convictions. Breathe energy into your convictions.... They are the lifeblood of your integrity. They are important...most important.... Believe in their importance **(Repeat beginning of paragraph.)** Honor them; take them seriously. Take yourself seriously — life demands it. You do care.

Imagine that as you embody your values you inspire others to do the same. Your very presence calls forth ethical ways of being.... Know that this is true.

As you stand rooted in your convictions you are strong, equal to whatever challenges you meet.... You are courageous — empowered by what is important. Believe it....

Inspiring Your Very Best (25)

You might want to use *Create a Symbol to Tap Energy in Daily Life (13A)* with this meditation.

Tune into yourself. You know yourself. You know where you shine out.... Remember the inner satisfaction of having done really well.... You know when you shine. You know when you have contributed your best.... Call forth those aspects of yourself now.... Ask them to join you in the challenge ahead.... Welcome them....

Your capacities are stronger than ever.... Every time you exercise them, they develop even more, and you discover new ones that you hadn't even known before. You surpass your own expectations; you amaze yourself....

Imagine going forward with all of your capabilities ready to be called upon.... Imagine contributing your best. Breathe.... Feel each and all of your capacities on the alert. Ready to contribute.... Each is coordinated with the rest. Each aspect in the driver's seat when needed.... Your sensitivities are so sharp that you have a way of learning just what is needed when and for moving through with such grace that it is amazing! A dance. Imagine it....

Support Sustains You (26)

Bring to awareness those who support you.... Remember the moments in life that you received a smile in support.... Remember those who encouraged you...maybe family...maybe friends...remember people who stood by you.... You knew you were supported...cared for.... People believed in you.... A teacher, a friend, a neighbor, a colleague...remember the support.... Let the times parade through your mind....

Maybe times when there was a great challenge ahead, or a time you finally graduated, or maybe a time of crisis.... People came forth and offered support.... They believed in you. They applauded your efforts. They still care.... They take pleasure in your success.

Breathe it in.... You are not alone; their spirits are with you now. Let it in. You are supported.... People believe in you. People are rooting for you. It is true. What would they say?... Listen to their voices.... Feel this support make your courage grow.... Open to it.... Believe in yourself as they do.... They're with you in spirit; they are behind you. Feel their support. It empowers you to move forward...to do well....

Calling Upon Your Allies (27)

If you want to explore these issues more deeply use *Conversing with the Spirits (29A)*. At the end of your meditative work use *Bidding Farewell to the Spirits (13S)*.

There are others who share your care. There are others who share your convictions.... Widen your awareness to include these people who share your concerns.... There are people you know.... There are people you haven't even met who share your concerns — whole groups of people who share cares. Extend your awareness to include others who understand and share your convictions.... Appreciate that all of these people are with you in spirit. Breathe...feel yourself empowered by your allies.... They stand with you. They are rooting for you....

Imagine joining forces in life and letting your spirits glow in the care and support you share.... They'll stick with you. They are behind you. If there is some way or other that you would like them to watch your back, imagine asking for that.... Notice if there is anyone in particular that you may want to ask into your life....... With your allies you'll do great!

The Elders (28)

If you want to explore more deeply use *Conversing with the Spirits (29A)*, and at the end of your meditative work use *Bidding Farewell to the Spirits (13S)*.

The elders. Appreciate what those of the older generations have offered, have learned, what they know now. Bring to awareness those who have graced your life.... Appreciate the great wisdom of those who have lived through so much, witnessed the decades gone by.... Invite their spirits to be with you for the challenge before you.... Open to their presence.... Open to their wisdom....... Give thanks for their gifts....

Calling the Ancestors (29)

To complete your meditation session make sure to use *Bidding Farewell to the Spirits (13S)*.

Acknowledge those who have gone before who have made your life possible.... Acknowledge your ancestors.... Acknowledge the ancestors....

Remember the great people who have passed before — some without recognition, some with it.... Those who have gone before dedicated their lives to the generations to come. They worked hard for their children, for their children's children.... Appreciate the gifts they passed on.... Give thanks to the ancestors. They made your life possible.... What can you do to honor them?...

There may be particular ancestors who could be of great help in the challenges ahead. Invite these ancestors to be with you now.......

Conversing with the Spirits (29A)

Imagine them. Let them come to you, through your imagination.... Welcome them.... Feel a sense of safety in their presence.... Commune with them. Your imagination is the medium through which they talk with you. Bring your concerns to awareness and notice how they respond to them.... Listen deeply; pay attention to what occurs to you — they may not use words when they offer their knowledge.......

Open your awareness to the knowing that is received from the spirit of their lives.... Converse with them.... Commune with them.... Draw upon their powers.... Gain courage from them; feel yourself become equal to the challenges that lie ahead.... Imagine what you should do to honor them....

Invite them to join you through the rest of your meditation....

The Future Ones (30)

Summon the powers of the ones who live in the future. Travel into the future, the distant future, generations from now or maybe decades from now. Travel into the future and let the future generations tell you how this is important to them.... Listen to what they say about all this....... Sense what is so for them.......

They are rooting for you. What you do matters to them, too. It makes a difference. As you breathe, draw in the spirit of their lives. They want you to succeed. Breathe in the spirit of their lives. What you do counts. They stand with you....... Let yourself embody their concerns; let yourself be empowered by it. Their spirits are with you. Move forward on their behalf....

The Spirit of the Children (31)

Remember the children. Remember all that they love...and all the children you love. Remember the children.... Bring in the spirit of the young. For them it matters. Breathe in their joyous spirit.... Fill yourself with love of the children.... Fill yourself with the spirit of the young.... Let it sing to your heart.... Let it lift your spirits.... Let it give you the courage to meet the challenge ahead....

The Spirits (32)

There are spirits who would stand by you — offer moral support, loan you their sensibilities, guide you in your meditative work.... Spirits embedded in nature, or maybe they come from other dimensions.... Invite any spirits who would like to join you in your meditation to come forth now.... They will offer guidance. Maybe one, maybe more; you may know them well; then again they may be entirely new.... Whoever is ready to be with you, invite them into your meditation now. Sense their energy.... Imagine the spirits that are here for you.... Welcome them.

Imagine their presence.... Do they have form?... What do they look like? What quality of energy surrounds them?.... Is there anything they have to say? They may communicate telepathically — spirits often find language too clumsy to bother with. You might find yourself knowing what they know directly.

Appreciate their presence. Commune with them.... Tell them what you are working on and ask if they will join you....

Fun (33)

This meditation is good to use if you want to enhance the lucidity of the Receptive Imagination.

Some days you may feel happy — maybe lucky. The air seems to glitter; joy is inside and all around. You're happy. The heart sings. Life has a sparkle to it. Imagine these times. If none come to mind, imagine what it would have been like.... Life sparkling!

Remember times when you were a kid and play was the point of it all — just having a good time. Playful. Laughing. Remember good times.... You may have had particular friends that you always kidded around with — had a good time with.... There may have been places that were especially fun to be. Remember the fun times you've had.... Spontaneity. Laughter.... Feel the light-hearted energy all over again.... Recreate it.... Embellish on it....

As you inhale draw in the lighthearted energy.... It sparkles and tickles inside.... As you exhale imagine making magic; spray this sparkling fun-loving energy into any scene you wish. Choose a scene you'd like to enchant with this energy.... Bring it to mind.... Magic dust rains down and everyone is gifted with a playful fun-loving energy. Imagine it....

There is delight in the air. Color...song...laughter is there.... It is a joy to be alive! The situation begins to glow from all the sparkle in the air.... Smile at the very idea of it.......

Sometimes pranksters have been with you. If you like, invite the prankster spirit to come and have fun with you now....... In the fun, this trickster is a great teacher.... Delightful!

Well of Nourishment (34)

If you have suffered abuse this meditation will help you to establish a point of reference that encourages self-expression and to supplant the default position, which is often defensive (withdrawing from experience).

Imagine immersing yourself in a pool of pure nourishment, whatever that means to you...as though you were to lie in a warm spring.... Like a baby, you're supported in a well of nourishment...warmth...warmth that gives life...warmth that gives comfort.... Imagine it...warmth that supports you...warmth that provides all you need to grow into the fullness of your being.... Create this quality — whatever nourishment means to you — music, color, texture...song...scent...touch of love.... Conjure up warm, nourishing energies.... Vividly imagine it; feel it.......
Imagine as though you could suspend yourself in it; almost like you could return to the womb.... Here you can hear the heartbeat of all life. The pulse of life quietly caresses you.... Breathe.... Receive nourishment...enveloped by nourishment.... Breathe.... Let it soak in.... Let it roll through....

Let yourself be received into it.... This energy welcomes you.... Imagine being fully cared for.... The energy supports you.... Feel this in the deepest portions of your being...your body...your heart all nourished, cared for.... Nourishment makes you strong, empowers you.... Breathe...you receive all the energy you need to be equal to whatever challenge you face.... This energy gives you the strength to express the fullness of your being.... Know that this nourishing energy is always here — just like the underground springs which perpetually flow. All you need do to awaken the energy is bring it to awareness....

Moving Moments (35)

This meditation will lift the spirit! It is particularly good for someone who is suffering with pain or depression or is in the last days of their life. If you are working with someone who is dying, then leave out the last paragraph. Read this meditation slowly.

Bring to awareness those moments in your past when you felt deeply blessed.... Blessed with the gift of being alive and able to experience the magnificence and the magic of life.... Bring to mind those times when you have been especially moved by the beauty of it all — those moments when you have been so moved, your whole being seemed to quiver to make room for the experience.......

Remember them, times of deep beauty...times you were deeply touched by a loving moment...aroused by music...exhilarated by nature's splendor...warmed by new life coming into being...moved by another's story...transfixed by a work of art...transported by the exquisite scent of a flower...awed by a spectacular sunset or a magnificent panorama.... Remember the moments.......

There is a multiplicity that moves you.... That is part of the miracle of it all. Remember particular moments; remember them in detail.... Just let these times parade through your mind now.... Awesome moments.... Recreate them now — times when the air glowed with a silent grace...or sparkled with joyous excitement.... Let yourself be moved again, blessed again, as though you glimpse divinity....

Breathe...feel your spirits lift...your heart open.... Feel reverence.... Remember those moving moments. Blessed.... Humbled....

Happy to be alive! The world is sacred. Open to the sacred in life — your regular life is sacred, too — feel the blessings.... Give thanks....

Pacing: Making Friends with Time (36)

If you are using this meditation with another one, move to the next one any time after completing the first three paragraphs. Name the activities you are tuning to.

Feel your breath. Feel the rhythm of your breath...in and out...in and out...the rise and fall of your belly...breath moving in; breath moving out.... Feel the rhythm of your breath.... Just as breath brings life into your body, enlivening your body, rhythm brings life into time, enlivening time. It is as though rhythm carries time.... Rhythm gives shape to time.

Everything in its own time, carried by rhythm.... Everything is part of the whole concert. The sun rises in its own time. The sun sets in its own time. The seasons come and go in their own time. Everything that exists has its own place; everything that exists has its own time. Acknowledge this.... Everything comes and goes in its own time. Let yourself trust this as deeply as you trust that the sun rises on every new day.... Just as you trust that after each exhalation, an inhalation will follow.... Everything has its own time; everything alive has its own breath, its own rhythm.... Some as slow as the centuries-old trees, some as fast as the humming-birds.... Trust that everything has its own place, its own time, its own rhythm....

Tune to the timing of the particular activities in your life now. Tune to them one at a time....... Each has its own tempo.... Bring one to mind; witness it....

Feel the rhythm.... As you listen deeply, you find yourself harmonizing with it.... When you are in harmony with each activity, you find yourself in the right place at the right time. It all comes together like music.... If you like, bring another activity to awareness and tune to its rhythm....... (Repeat paragraph as many times as you like.)

Imagine how all your activities form a great concert.... Experience the pacing and the transitions...always in the right place at the right time.... You have a knack for knowing when to move forward, when to lie back...when to slow down, when to speed up.... Naturally pacing yourself. Graceful.... Elegant.... Like the bird that catches the breeze and is carried by it, imagine catching the rhythms as they carry you through.......

Imagine moving through specific activities with time as your friend.... Feel the pacing in your body....... Imagine the transitions between activities....... Graceful. Time is your friend. Time supports you.... It is always there for you....

In the Seasons' Embrace (37)

Following the opening there is a paragraph for each season; read the applicable season last. For instance if you are about to enter the spring, start with the paragraph for summer, then go on to fall and winter and end with spring. Then go on to the last segment of the meditation and fill in the blank with "spring." You may want to use *Spirit of Place (38)* to augment this meditation.

The Earth carries us. It is as though time carries the Earth. Time cycles. Life cycles. The Earth cycles round and round the sun.... Moving through warm and light times, then cycling through cold and dark times. Each cycle completes a year and another year begins.

Winter. In the dead of winter the air has a bite. We go inside. Wintertime is a time of inward focus. Quiet, reflective, like sleep; deep in the winter, we gather our strengths. Winter is a time of reflection and replenishment...a time to take stock of what has gone on before and what is to come. Winter is a time to appreciate the comforts of home life...a time to show love of family. Winter is a time to make home and to be cozy with the comfort of loved ones near by. The short days gradually grow longer...all is getting ready for the spring. Replenished, time delivers us strong and ready for the spring.

Spring. Life bursts forth...fresh green...blossoms...colors...scents in the air. A time to care for the soil, a time to plant. Life is excited; it moves, quickened by sunshine. Spring is the season of enthusiasm.... Spring is the season of new birth, birth of new life...of new ideas, new projects.... Spring is the season of creativity....

The light returns; the sun returns. Then all the enthusiasm of spring slows into the meander of summer.

Summer. In the summer, time stretches; the plants take their time to bear their fruit; life luxuriates in the sun, drinks in the warmth.... The air is heavy; it embraces you, even holds you. In summer it is as though time itself yawns and stretches out...as though the Earth slows down in her cycling round and round the sun. In the warmth everything has the time to appreciate the fullness of life.... Celebrate the splendor of the sun...of long days...lots of time...lots of warmth.... Summer, a time to have fun and enjoy life.... As water evaporates in the heat of the sun, the summer itself evaporates.... Days begin to shorten and the fall arrives.

Fall is harvest time. All the fruits are ripe, the food abundant.... Fall is a time of gratitude.... Fall is the time to reap the fruits of the year.... The sun recedes...the days shorten; the air gets cooler. Life draws back into itself — withdraws from the surface. Leaves shrivel and dry. They carry the colors of the sun. They flutter in the winds and land, making a blanket to protect the ground. Life draws back into the core of itself.... Making ready for the winter to come.

All in flux, carried by time...through the seasons. Here we are in (____) again. Cycling through.... Notice the changes all around.... Tune to the plants and animals.... Look closely; notice how they change with the time....... Feel the shift in your own being, as (____) moves through your body and spirit....... Welcome this time. Notice what is needed to honor this time in your life.... Review the season past and notice what needs to be released or completed to free you to be fully present in this season...to let go into its embrace....

Feel yourself move in harmony with the great cycles of time.... Appreciate the gift of being part of the great motion of the universe.... Carried by time. Nourished by the Earth. Embraced by the seasons as they unfold around and within you.... Imagine what you might do as an offering of thanks....

Spirit of Place (38)

When you use this meditation replace the word "place" with the name of the place you are exploring. If you are exploring a place other than where you live, simply delete the words "that you live" and any other references to home.

Tune to the place that you live...the nature of the place, the character of the place.... Tune to the place that you live. Listen to the voice of the place...the spirit of this place. Imagine that this place has a personality, as in fact it does.... Sense the knowing of this place...its history...all the stories of this place...all the stories that took place here...all that this place has witnessed...all that has transpired over the years here.... What has built the character of this place?...... Tune to the reality of this place. Witness.... Listen to the spirit of this place. Let this place speak to you.... Listen.......

Remember the vistas of land and sky here.... How water moves through this place.... How weather dances here...how the seasons travel through.... Extend your awareness to appreciate all the life that this place gives home to.... The Earth and sky are generous; they make home for all life. This place is generous; it makes home for a multitude of creatures. Appreciate how this place makes space for you, how this place makes home for you....

Open your heart to the care you feel for this place.... Breathe with this place.... Feel the life here — as though the place breathes...the patterns of weather here...the dance of light, the shape of the land here...what people have built here...the nature all around.... All that has been created here. Be in this place. Relax into this place.... Feel yourself held by it.... Belonging.... Breathe.... (Optional: repeat as much of the preceding as you would like.)

If you would like, let yourself go back to the times when people lived in total harmony with this place.... Imagine how it was in those times; let yourself visit those times now.... Imagine....... There may be ancestors of this place that you would like to visit; imagine them.... Imagine how they lived here......what they knew to be true to this place....... When you are ready, bring yourself back to current time.

There may be some life that is calling your attention...a particular tree...a creature who makes a home here. Focus in now.... Imagine simply sharing presence with this being.... Listen deeply.... Sense what this being knows, how this place is home for it.... If you like you can tune even deeper; imagine as though you are this being....... Imagine your experience as this being. How does it feel to move in this body?... Imagine living through the changes here...in season......in the changes that people have brought.... Imagine.......

Is there anything that you want to do that honors this place?...... Offer this place a thank you for all that it has given you.... Imagine what you might give this place as an offering of gratitude....

SECTION THREE:

Maintaining Well-Being

CENTERING

Grounded and Open:
Working with Earth and Sky Energy for Centering and Circles (39)[1]

This meditation is an alternative method for inducing a meditative state of consciousness and is especially useful if you are having trouble maintaining an alert state while meditating. If you are using it with other meditations, you may prefer to use only a couple of the paragraphs in each section and to skip those beginning with the word "intend."

Grounded and Open is a versatile and extremely powerful meditation in its own right. It can be used to reduce stress, steer clear of burnout, avoid codependency, claim control in the presence of an obsessive habit, diminish depression, get focused, or strengthen visioning abilities. If you are scattered, disorganized, or unable to focus, then working with Earth energy will prove especially helpful. If, on the other hand, you feel stuck, lack vision, need more creative energy, or want to overcome depression, then work with the energy of the Sky. This meditation will also enable you to maintain your own center when you are in the midst of demanding situations — particularly if you are leading, working with the public, or caring for others. When you imagine energy moving through in the way it suggests, you will avoid absorbing other people's energy and getting invested in how they receive what you offer — habits that cause exhaustion and burnout. It is best to use it immediately before beginning your challenging activity. Grounded and Open is designed to be used with the ending *Keeping the Energies Moving Through the Day (13C)*. Then, whenever you have a free moment in the midst of your activity, pause for fifteen seconds or so and imagine the energy is still moving through you the way you imagined it in the meditation itself. With regular use you will soon be able to work with this technique with a simple, momentary focus of intent.

You can also use this meditation in group settings to create what I call an Energy Circle. For more than 20 years these circles have been the center of the weekly meditation groups I lead. Energy Circles have proven to be the most effective form for sharing support or collectivizing meditative work. An Energy Circle can be used to pull a group together before it embarks on any shared endeavor.

It is also a very effective practice for gaining insight, increasing probabilities, and channeling healing. Have people hold hands — this magnifies the energy. After people have imagined the energy of the Earth and Sky moving through, suggest that they imagine it moving around the circle and building momentum. At this point people can take turns, inviting the rest of the group to focus on their issues. One at a time people name their issues slowly, refraining from explanation and trying to frame issues in positive, or at least neutral, terms. (For instance they do not send healing to "cancer" but to the affected body part.) It usually takes about three breaths to focus on each issue. After you focus on each, take a moment to refocus on the Earth and Sky energy before going to the next issue. If your use the meditation in this way, please see the section Affirmations (Part II, Page 40) for instructions that will help you frame issues. Also see We Are All Connected: The Ethics of This Work (Part II, Page 34) and Channeling Positive Energy to Those in Need (Part II, Page 42). After a group has used an Energy Circle I recommend that people share what they imagined — this sharing promises to be rich with helpful insights.

Earth (39A)

Imagine a very old, maybe a favorite tree....... Imagine that like a tree, you have roots that stretch deep down into the ground.... Feel as though you have roots that extend deep into the Earth, weaving around and among the rocks...touching underground springs.... Your roots pull the sustenance of the Earth right up into you, making you strong.... Feel the Earth giving you strength and nourishment.... The Earth always sustains your life.... The Earth always supports your weight.... The Earth is your home.... Feel it.... Just as you are fully rooted in your body, your body is rooted to the Earth.... Feel yourself supported, sustained, nourished by the Earth.... (Optional: repeat this paragraph.)

Imagine that the roots stretch deep into the core of the Earth...that there is a magnetic connection moving between the magnetic core of the Earth and your own center.... Magnetic energy moving between you and the Earth.... Imagine that as you breathe, it is as though you are breathing with the earth. As you inhale you draw up sustenance....... As you exhale you release energy no longer needed, which the Earth transforms into nutrients.... The Earth breathes; you breathe. You breathe with the Earth...a continual exchange of replenishing energy.... Feel your magnetic connection breathing.......

Draw up Earth energy.... It tunes you to the substance of which you are made...made of the Earth...every molecule that comprises your physical being has been in other bodies — in rocks, in plants, in animals.... Every molecule of which you're composed is of the Earth and has been of the Earth from the beginning of time. Every molecule composing your body has witnessed all of history. You are of the Earth.... Feel the power of Earth energy inside you....

All that has ever happened before has been witnessed by the Earth.... The Earth has witnessed all of history...lived through all of history. The knowledge that is carried by the Earth is awesome! All that lives returns to her.

Let yourself relax into the support of the Earth — the Earth always supports your weight, sustains your life...feel it.... As your body provides your spirit with a home, the Earth provides your body with a home.... Feel yourself at home wherever you are.... You are of the Earth. Breathing with the Earth, continually.... Earth energy continues to move through you in this manner.

Intend for this to be the case. Tell yourself this. When you have Earth energy moving through you this way, you always remain centered, focused, and relaxed. Present. Know that this is so....

Sky (39B)

Like the trees, feel how it is to reach up into the sky...to turn to the sun, as all the plants turn to the sun.... Imagine stretching up into the vast expanse of the skies....... Extend awareness to include the vast expanse of sky...patterns of weather...clouds, rains, winds...the sun...the moon...the planets...the whole solar system...the stars, a multitude of solar systems.... Breathtaking!... Breathe....

Imagine sky energy drops down through the top of your head and moves though your whole body, just as your breath moves though...in and out...back out through the top of your head, or maybe down the roots into the ground; imagine the energy moves in and out, in and out continually.... As easily as breath.... Imagine sky energy moving through you as the Earth energy moves through. Carried by breath. Moving in and out, in and out as you breathe; sky energy moves in and out.... Feel yourself as open on the inside as the skies on the outside. Imagine the skies move through you as you breathe.... As the sky moves through you it opens you to new experience. Exhilarating.... Spacious. When sky energy moves through your vision opens. Know that this is the case. (Optional: repeat this paragraph.)

Intend that the sky energy continue to move through you in this manner.... Tell yourself this.... Sense the Earth and sky energies mix inside as they do all around you.... As the Earth and sky energies move through you, all the elements move through you, continually replenishing you. Fire...Earth...Air...Water. Giving you vitality...stability...openness...fluidity. Energized, stable, open, and fluid all at the same time....... Life rides these energies. Awesome. Feel it. Breathe.... Draw strength from it. Expect these energies to move through you just as they are now moving through you throughout this day, keeping you energized, grounded, open, and centered all day long....

Being Present (40)

This meditation can be augmented with *Highest, Wisest, Deepest Self (14)* or *Reside in the Quiet (3)*.

Be aware of the climate of your consciousness as you move through your life.... What textures your thoughts.... What do you find occupies your mind most of the time?...... How often do you keep going over the same thing time and again?... How much of the time do you reside in the future — caught in anticipation?...or reside in the past — rerunning events gone by....... How much consciousness is confined to worrying about what will unfold or in rehashing how things could have?...... How often do you think the same thing over and over again — occupying the space of your mind with repetition, obstructing discovery of anything new?...... Is there any attention left to experience the present moment?

Witness what your awareness tends to focus on.... Simply witness your propensities....... Like weeding a garden, imagine moving through your consciousness and uprooting all that gets you stuck in reruns...all that obstructs the light of awareness...all the reruns, all the debris that keeps you from experiencing the moment.... Weed it all out.... Breathe it all out....... Clear it out. Imagine it becomes compost, nourishing the ground of being for new growth.... Detach from the past; detach from the future....... Witness the light of awareness spread out into the moment as you clear the space.... No obstacles casting shadows and blocking the light. Breathe.... Settle into the ever-changing present.... Breathe...let go of preoccupation....... All the shadows disappear as the light of your awareness expands....

Breathe.... Settle into the present, for this is where all life really takes place....... Each moment carries you into the next.... Each moment different from the one before — alive anew, fresh experience....

Feel yourself settling down and relaxing into the present — welcoming the moment — completely present, letting go of what was or what might be...being in the moment....

You may want to heal those spots where you have uprooted the thoughts....... Send compassion and healing breath to those spots where you have uprooted the thoughts.... Shine gentle, compassionate energy there....... Be kind to yourself.... Witness the light of awareness expand and you can see very clearly....

You have released all that pulls your awareness out of the present.... Tell yourself you can't control it all anyhow.... Notice how when you let go, you get to live in present time. You get to respond to whatever unfolds in wholeness. Let yourself be....... Let your life be.... As you reside in present time your life opens up like a flower. As you settle into present time your horizons expand. Sense opening.... Breathe.

As at noontime there are no shadows. When you reside in present time, what is true is fully apparent.... The light of awareness reveals what is so.... When you reside in the present, old habits die, and all actions spring out of knowing what is true in present time.... The present is your point of power.... Feel this....

Breathe...your breath can always keep you present.... Just as gravity holds all in Earth's embrace. The present is the gravity that holds us in time's embrace.... When you breathe, relax. Time carries you....

Imagine moving through your life fully present in each moment; as you open to each moment, each moment expands and opens to you — welcomes you. Each moment carrying you to the next — welcoming life.... Only in present time can life be appreciated.... Let go into the embrace of present time. Breathe....

In the Quiet, Greet Yourself (41)

This meditation is good to use on stressful days, for general malaise, or for confusion. You can use the last section to witness whatever is true for you on any particular issue, whether it is focusing on your health, reviewing the day, making a decision, being mindful about something that is upcoming in your life, or contemplating what justice means in a particular context. If you want to focus on an external concern, you may want skip everything up to the optional section.

This meditation is designed to follow *Inner Witness (1H)* and/or *Reside in the Quiet (3)*. Leave very long pauses between sentences. Deepen its effect by reading any part twice.

As you share presence with your being, widen your quiet awareness to include recent times — maybe the last few days.... Widen your awareness now.... Witness how you have been doing lately.... In this quiet, notice your moods.... Witness your experience.... How it has been for you....... How your body has been......your spirit.... What's taken up space in your mind.... Witness your heart.... How is your heart?......

In the quiet be present with your experience.... Let it be there.... You need not do anything with it; just be with your experience.... In the quiet, acknowledge yourself as you are.... Be with yourself.... Share presence with your experience.... Offer yourself open attention.......

As you do, you'll find yourself knowing if there are areas that need special attention to bring about balance and well-being. Note this awareness as it occurs to you. Just note it....

(Optional. This section can be used for different concerns. Just repeat and fill in the blank with the new issue: heart or justice, for example. Give long pauses between each sentence and an even longer pause — three minutes — between each use of this section.)

Breathing.... Being with your breath.... Listening to it.... Breathing....

In this quiet extend your awareness to include your (____).

Share presence with this. Let it be in awareness. You needn't do anything with it; just be together — you and awareness of (____).... As you breathe just let it be in awareness.... Breathe.... Be aware of (____).... If you find that you get caught up by it, just let it go; breathe and you'll again find space to be with it, to witness it....

In the quiet of breath you naturally become attuned to what is so.... Even though you don't feel like you did anything — it happens in the quiet of being present; what is true becomes apparent.

Notice as you focus on (____) if you find yourself opening into connection or withdrawing and closing down.... Witness what happens as you hold this in awareness.... Breathe....... Open to it.... You needn't do anything; just breathe and let it be.... Notice if anything arises in awareness. Listen deeply to what arises.... Notice.......

This arising makes it evident what is so, what is needed for increased well-being — or maybe you find a patience, an openness to uncertainty. Pay attention to any inclinations.......

Choose what you'll do.... Imagine yourself doing it.... Notice how that feels....

(Always end with the following section.)

Be with yourself in silence as long as you wish. You need your own company. You deserve it.... You may choose to simply bathe in the quiet with your breathing. Quietly breathing.... Take refuge in the silence, in the breath....

(Remain in silence as long as you like. If you are leading this meditation for someone else, allow about four minutes, or ask them to signal their readiness to finish.)

Whenever you wish you can return to outer consciousness. When you do, take a moment to appreciate yourself, to appreciate the spirit, and choose what you might do with the awareness that arose....

Open Heart, Sharp Mind (42)

As you breathe, you draw in replenishing energy, inspiring energy.... Imagine drawing in energy that sparkles and tingles throughout your body...throughout your whole being...breathing vibrant energy....... Your whole self glows and sparkles as you breathe in life force.... Imagine yourself sparkling, glowing, bubbly, vibrant as you replenish yourself with life force.... Breathe out all the stale energies no longer needed.... Breathing in renewing energy.... Replenish yourself. *(Repeat paragraph.)*

Now become aware of your heart.... Notice whatever may weigh on your heart...whatever may be shielding your heart...anything that may be making your heart stiff and disjointed, cold, and disconnected....... Breathe out and release these energies...with each exhalation let go.... Feel your heart soften.... To comfort yourself, tell yourself about your goodness.... Appreciate yourself for all the efforts you make.... Listen!... Let your heart receive love and appreciation. You deserve it.... Breathe in love.... Feel your heart softening...opening.... Feel it warming....

Remember times in your life when you felt joyous...times you felt love...the good times...the times you cherish.... Recollect them and let your

heart be nourished by these times all over again....... Remember how you felt....
Draw on these memories now. Breathe in.... Let your heart bask in the
energy...joy for life...in communion with others...alive, together...the joy of sharing...caring...living...laughing...crying...all that warms your heart...all that gives
life meaning.... Bask in it....

Imagine creating an atmosphere around your heart that protects its sanctity so it remains open.... However you imagine it, place an aura of protection
around your heart.... When your heart is protected its sensitivities are acute —
your heart knows what is so. As you open your heart, your mind opens and your
thoughts shine....

Be aware of your intelligence, the part of you that processes information....
Imagine that your mind is as clear as the blue desert sky...clear.... You can see all
the patterns of weather.... Your mind is that vast.... You can see millions of stars
at night...and all the dances of light infusing the dawn and dusk with a symphony
of color.... Your mind is as miraculous as the desert skies.... Your mind is as vast
as the desert skies...open...yet piercingly sharp with each thought.... So open
that each thought has its own distinct place, space, movement, just like the stars
in the desert night.... Your thoughts sparkle and shine.... Feel the precision of
your mind.

Each thought can be clearly seen for what it is, telling you just what you
need to know to be clear about what is so.... Your mind works well — integrating all that you know...bringing you intuitive information, bringing you logical
information, pulling in what you already know.... Your mind receives it all clear,
distinct...enabling your whole self to make good choices.... Experience this.
Trust your intelligence.... Imagine moving through life with a sharp mind and
an open heart....

Making Magic: Conjuring Energy to Spread Well-Being (43)

You can use this meditation to evoke any positive quality you like. For example if you want to work with resilience, replace the word "generosity" with "resilience." If you want to go through it again, use a related word like "vitality." If you are working with the past, then you may want to use "forgiveness." If you are working with the future, then "patience" is likely to be helpful. Some meditations in Summoning the Powers may be useful, depending on what quality you evoke: you might want to insert *Recollection (16)* after the first paragraph. *Inner Refuge (9)* will augment this meditation. You may want to use this as a group meditation to send support to someone in need. Switch pronouns as called for.

Magic is the ability to transform energy. In these states of inner awareness you have magical powers. You can evoke energies and come to a deep appreciation of them. You can shape, transform, and channel energies. In this state you have magical powers. With these powers you are about to create a body of energy, which will be of great service in spreading well-being. This body gets brought to life by calling up and concentrating specific beneficent qualities.

Bring forth the quality of (generosity). (Generosity).... Feel it in your heart. Recall times when you have witnessed it...times you have felt it...times it has been in the air.... Let these times parade though your mind, leaving the warm glow of (generosity) as you go from one memory to the next. Sense the energy of (generosity) building in awareness.... Recall (generosity).

Sense its presence. (Generosity). Feel it.... Be intimate with it.... Recall what it is; what it feels like...it may even have taste or smell to it. Recall (generosity).... It is not complex, but it is profound in its simplicity.... (Generosity); feel its energy.... How does your body feel when your are in its presence?... (Generosity) makes the heart smile.... Sometimes it can even make the spirit swoon.... (Generosity). Remember times you have been graced by its appearance.... It touches the heart.... It has an openness about it.... There is a spacious quality about it.... It has a light aura about it. Remember times you have been graced by its appearance.... Draw on these memories now. (Generosity). Invite it to be with you now.

Breathe with it.... Feel your heart warming as you open to the energy of it.... (<u>Generosity</u>). Breathe with it. Bathe your being in it.... Let your spirit be lifted by it...your heart be warmed by it. (<u>Generosity</u>).As you inhale gather it.... As you breathe in you can feel yourself concentrate it.... Imagine that there is an energy-body in front of you. As you exhale direct (<u>generosity</u>) into this energy-body. As you exhale send it. Charge the energy-body with (<u>generosity</u>). Imagine it.... Feel it.... Breathe it.... The energy-body fills with color, vibrations, music, knowing, even poetry.... It becomes animated with (<u>generosity</u>)...vibrates with (<u>generosity</u>). Hums.

(Optional. Repeat the preceding three paragraphs, replacing the word "generosity" with "compassion." To augment the meditation use Compassion (17) *before you repeat the preceding paragraphs. If you like, go through the process again, using "patience" or any other positive quality you choose.)*

Imagine the energy-body animated with all this marvelous energy — lots of energy. Feel its vibrational level. Whoever and whatever comes in contact with it begins to vibrate at the same level. It evokes these qualities wherever it goes. This energy-body is very versatile. It transcends the limitations of time and space. It resides in the world of intention. The clearer the intention the more powerful this energy-body is.

Take time now to work with this energy-body. Feel the power of the energies: generosity...compassion...(____).... Feel it. Breathe with it....

(Use any of the following sections you like; then go to the ending of 43D. Or invite the energy-body to accompany you into another meditation.)

Healing Mission to a Discordant Situation (43A)

You can send the energy-body on healing missions. It is especially helpful for agitated and discordant situations. Imagine the particular situation that you would like to send it to.... Bring to awareness the people and activities involved.... Vividly imagine the details of the scene....

Imagine the energy-body going there and entering the scene. The energy-body works magic and the climate gradually shifts. Quietly, subtly, its presence awakens resonant energy in the people there.... It touches the innate goodness that lives inside everybody's heart. Imagine how that might be.... Generosity.... compassion, (____)...aroused. Energy that may have been dormant in people's hearts and spirits awakens — it's possible.... The whole mood shifts.... Magic is possible. Imagine it.......

Notice how the interactions take on a different tone.... People become kinder, more open, honest, caring.... Generosity...compassion, (____)...fill the scene. Trust begins to emerge. Everyone knows people are doing their best...that they'll get through it together...and maybe even celebrate one another while they're at it.... People begin to trust that one way or another everything will work out in the end.... When generosity...compassion, (____)...are present everything works well. Everyone wishes everyone well. Imagine how this happens. Imagine it in detail.......

Healing Mission to a Friend or Loved One (43B)
Use the ending from *(43D)* and *Clearing the Self (13T)* for this meditation.

Bring to mind the person you would like to make this energy available to. Imagine her or him clearly. Ask the energy-body to be with her or him. Expect that all this healing energy becomes available....... Sometimes as you do this, you may find a knowing arises that points to what might help your friend increase well-being in her or his life. Listen and awareness arises. Note it, and keep yourself focused on the healing that is present for your friend. Let your awareness be soft and hold clear intent.... Imagine that the energy-body provides healing in whatever ways the person needs it.... Honor whatever process may unfold.... Hold good intent.... Healing happens....

Embody the Powers (43C)

To empower yourself with the energy, to embody the energy, breathe with the body.... As you do invite it to come inside you. Breathe...inhale.... Welcome the energy. Sense it coming inside.... Feel it settling in.... Breathe. Commune with all the energies.... Your own energy vibrates with them.... Your energy field shifts. Notice this.... Feel the tone of your being shift some....... Your body, your heart, your spirit have all subtly shifted as this energy spreads through you. Sense the change.... A subtle glow has begun to emanate from your center. Become familiar with it....

Wherever you go you inspire generosity of spirit. You inspire compassion; (you inspire_____). Discover how this happens in particular situations. Pick one to explore.... Bring to awareness the people, the place, the details.... As you bring the situation to awareness, notice how it looks a little different in the glow of the energy you now embody.... Note the difference.......

Imagine how you are.... Imagine how the energy of generosity and compassion awakens in others.... The energy field of the whole scene opens up.... Imagine the interactions.... Feel what it is like.... People become kinder, open, honest, caring, light-hearted.... It's almost magical.... Hearts and spirits dance....

Note what would be good to remember for when you are in this situation again.... Tell yourself about it.... Ask the energy to accompany you....

Healing Yourself (Past, Present, or Future) (43D)

Use whichever section that is most appropriate; change the personal pronouns as needed.

You can heal your own self with the energy-body. You can bring to mind hard times that took place in the past, or even those that may unfold in the future. Healing happens when the hard time and the energy-body share presence in awareness. You can also send the energy-body to anything that ails you in present time. Healing happens when you hold whatever concern you have in spacious and soft awareness along with the energy-body....

Past

You may want to invite a past self in. One who got hurt, abused — harmed in some way. Maybe this part of you was assaulted; maybe she was abandoned. There may be a part of you who has been shamed or blamed, a part of you that has been caused to suffer in some way.... She may have been judged harshly...or may have sustained an injury. This part of you still has a difficult time of it.... Invite her in to be with the energy-body....

Focus on the particular part that you would like to give attention to.... She may be cold. She may have gotten stiff. She may be hot. She may be numb. She may be scared. She carries some sort of charge or stuck energy.... She is reactive; be gentle with her.... Tune to her.... Invite her to be with you and the energy-body now.

Welcome her. She brings back memories. Let the memories parade through your spacious awareness. Breathe.... As memories move through the aura of the beneficent energy-body they receive some healing.... Witness it.... Breathe....... As you remember, be careful not to let the memories carry you off. Breathe...stay present. Be with that part of you that has had a difficult time of it.... Invite her to relax in the presence of the energy-body....... Give her space to share presence with the energy-body.... Tell her times are different now.... Tell her how courageous she was....... That she didn't deserve to be treated as she was.... Tell her about her goodness.... Sense her energy shift.... Be gentle with her.... Breathe together. She had a hard time of it; now she can be treated with generosity, compassion, and (____). She deserves it.... Give her time to experience the fact that she is not alone.... Sense her soften and receive the energy.... Kindness.... Witness healing.... Sense her breathing it in....

As she discovers present time she may want to reclaim her dreams.... The stars in her eyes reappear.... Life energies flow again.... Breathing brings new life.... As the healing happens you can feel your own heart open (and/or feel your body heal)....

Present

Bring to awareness whatever is troubling you in your life now. There may be a part of your body that is ailing you. Or maybe a relationship or some other situation is difficult for you.... Bring to awareness the specific concern you would like to work on.... Imagine the details.... Recollect your feelings as you dealt with this....

Invite into spacious awareness the part of you that has been having a hard time of it.... Feel the difficulty become present...and share presence with the energy-body. Use your breath to keep your awareness both spacious and soft. Breathe.... Imagine that this part of you communes with the energy-body.... As though this part of you is bathed in generosity, compassion, and (____). Feel it open to healing.... Imagine it loosens up and breathes.... Breathe a sigh of relief....

As they commune together — the part of you that is receiving healing and the energy-body — pay close attention, for you may find that you become aware of what this aspect needs to better handle the circumstances....... Note what arises in awareness....... Tell that part of yourself what you will do, that you appreciate her struggles and will support her.......

Future

There is a challenging time that you are facing in your life now. Bring it to awareness....... Acknowledge the enormity of the situation.... Invite the energy-body to journey with you into the future and pay this upcoming time a visit. Ask the energy-body to grace the time with its beneficent energy.... Project yourself into this time. Imagine it.... Imagine the energy-body infusing the whole scene — all who come in contact with it harmonize with the generosity, compassion, and (____).... Magic; the climate gradually shifts. Quietly, subtly, its presence awakens resonant energy inside everybody and draws out the innate goodness.... Imagine it....

End

You may want to converse with the energy-body about any further concerns.... You'll find yourself knowing how well-being could be increased.... Choose what you will do with this knowledge.... Thank the energy-body for all its blessings....

Home (44)

Good for when you find yourself getting ragged from being in a competitive and/ or oppressive environment, this meditation creates a place of refuge where you can safely let down your guard.

Imagine evoking the quality of comfort...completely comfortable...warm, secure, satisfied, cozy....Bring to mind particular times and places where you felt this way — however momentary they may have been.... Imagine feeling comfortable... cozy...content...secure...satisfied...relaxed.... Experience it.... Comfort; breathe it....

Imagine the feeling of a very comfortable home...a nest, a space that's yours, that you belong in, just as a tree belongs to the place in which it roots.... There may be loved ones who share this space with you...making home together.... If you've never quite felt this way, imagine what it could have been like.... Imagine a place where you completely relax.... All your guards melt away, for you are truly safe and comfortable here.... Imagine it; feel it.... There is beauty here...maybe smells of food cooking.... It's warm, cozy, beautiful.... Home. Whether this place exists in the world or in your mind's eye, vividly create/imagine it...so comfortable and secure you can relax entirely.... In this place every cell in your body hums, purrs...basking in comfort....

Home is full of gentle energy....energy is so smooth, so good, so warm that only that which resonates with this good energy can transpire here...for anything else would simply not occur here..... Like roots that draw nourishment from the soil...breathe in this tranquillity; feel it spread through your whole being —

bathing every cell in your body...every feeling in your heart...every thought in your mind.... Breathe it....

Breathe through the shield, the shell, the rigidified energy that you've protected yourself with.... Breathe through.... Feel a softening...a melting away of any hardened energy.... As you relax in this place you replenish yourself; you heal yourself.... Your whole being hums, smiles as you replenish yourself in your home space, your comfortable space.... Breathe in these energies....

Home is your place to be safe...secure.... Where you completely relax. Feel it.... Smile as you savor your home inside....

The Transformative Power of Breath (45)

This meditation will help you develop your skill for working with your breath. After repeated use you may want to work with only the last two or three paragraphs of this meditation.

Life is miraculous. It is in the regular processes of life that transformation takes place. Nutrients turn into energy; energy turns into waste; waste turns into nutrients for the life of another — transformation is always taking place. Follow breath: oxygen is inhaled, moves through the entire body; every cell in the body inhales and is renewed. Then each cell is cleansed. Then the body exhales. Breath released becomes fresh air for plants to inhale.... Transformation is always taking place. Life is miraculous. Life processes are always in a perpetual state of transformation.

Breath encompasses us all. Breathe and heal yourself. Breathe and renew yourself.... Breathe and cleanse yourself.... Breathe.... All that is necessary to heal is to breathe.... Let go and breathe. As the body breathes imagine that consciousness breathes too.... Consciousness is also perpetually transforming energy. Feel how deep breathing opens awareness...and holding breath shuts awareness down. Breathing opens it. Breathe deeply...notice awareness opening into its natural state of spaciousness.

Intrinsic to life is the movement toward equilibrium and creative expression. Breathe and it just happens.... Anything shut down, controlled, made cold, outside the flux of energy becomes toxic. Thoughts that move round and round or the feelings that freeze.... All these stuck energies block the life flow process and take you out of the present moment. They come between you and being fully alive. All you need do is breathe into them.... Breathe through them.... Let go...breathe, and transformation happens. Nutrients turn into energy and waste is released. Emotionally, mentally, breathe.... Keep the energy moving, flowing, alive.... Breath opens space and insight appears; learning happens and difficulty transforms. When you breathe you ride time and nothing stays the same. When you breathe everything is fluid...free. Let go. Breathe. Just breathe and transformation happens. Breathe and hard feelings loosen...open, become fluid and transform as naturally as breath moving in and out of all the cells in your body. Know you can transform whatever stands between you and present time....

Witness in your subjective landscape what causes a dam-up of energy flow...stuck energies, stuck feelings, stuck ideas...things you tell yourself over and over again, making yourself withdraw and shut down.... Maybe you tell yourself that you are not okay in some way — plague yourself with put-downs...or maybe you judge others.... Maybe you distrust and feel like you have to take control...or give up, expecting that it won't work anyhow.... Maybe you're jealous or envious...or maybe your energy caves in on you in shame or guilt.... There are many ways that you could be harboring stuck energy. Worry, control, cynicism, anger, anxiety, dogmatism, denial, blame — all these stuck energies stand between you and open experience. They narrow your experience. Witness in your subjective landscape what causes a dam-up of energy flow.......

Choose one particular issue that you would like to transform; you can work on others another time. Choose one now.... Focus on it now.... What do you tell yourself about it?... Picture the issue...feel it...sense it...create it in your mind's eye; characterize it.... Notice where its corresponding energy resides in your body…. Imagine breathing into it — however you imagine it, breathe into it…. Imagine breathing through it. Breathe through it however you imagine it. Feel it loosen…open……. As though it begins to breathe…. Energy begins to flow again. Breathe into it. Breathe through it…breath rolling right through…. Imagine it transforming, releasing….

Don't worry about how this happens; just assume it does. Don't worry about what it is like after transformation is completed; just trust that positive change has begun and will continue. Your experience changes, sometimes gradually…sometimes suddenly an insight appears and shifts your experience. Trust transformation, however it happens. Trust it…. As you breathe through, assume transformation is taking place. Tell your deepest self about it……. Know that in transformation you develop new habits of the heart, new routes for your thoughts to travel upon…. Transformations open life for you. *Expect* it. Expect transformation…. Breathe and energy flows again…. If ever this issue arises in awareness again, just breathe. Knowing breath transforms, opens, heals consciousness. Consciousness breathes too….

Whenever you want to transform and release stuck energies bring to mind the thoughts, feelings, body sensations surrounding the issue; hold all of it in awareness and witness it as you breathe…open to it and breathe…breathe through it. *Expect* transformation. Expect the deepest dimensions of consciousness to transform difficulty into wisdom, transmuting experience — like your body which converts food into energy and nutrients — your deepest consciousness transforms stuck thoughts and feelings and provides space for new perspectives to emerge, bringing with them different experience. Breathe and expect transformation. Tell your deepest awareness that you would like it to transform and release this energy…. Have clear intent. Expect change. Breathe and release. With breath and time healing happens. Trust it.

Work with the power of transformation intrinsic to consciousness now. Bring to awareness one issue at a time. Breathe with it. Breathe through it.

Open...let it go...and expect transformation to take place.... All you need do is breathe with clear intent.... Work with the power of breath now...one issue at a time.... Breathe...open.... Breathe...release....... Whenever difficulty comes, breathe. Breath opens. Transformation happens. Transformation is intrinsic to life. Breathe.......

Clarity (46)

This is a good meditation for cutting through confusion or for clearing yourself of other people's energies. It is designed to follow *Lake of Reflection (6)*.

Feel the magic. This lake offers you cleansing and healing. Take time to do a ritual of purification — however you imagine that — you may want to swim or take a shower in the falls, drink the water or drop all the burdens you carry, letting them dissolve in the lake.... Do an imaginary ritual, however you are inclined....... Feel...sense yourself becoming as clear on the inside as the water in the lake....... The water cleanses...purifies...tingles inside.... Feel yourself becoming as clear as the water....

The water brings out your true colors.... Imagine it washes away all the debris that stands between you and clarity.... Feel it wash away.... Now you reflect all that you come across as perfectly as the peaceful surface of the lake. The truth sparkles here....

Choose a concern you would like to bring clarity to.... Imagine taking the water from this lake or falls and splashing its magic on your concern. Imagine it becoming purified and sparkling clear....... The way the water sparkles when the sun shines upon it. Truth is revealed.......

Imagine taking this water and cleansing your whole life and washing away the debris...the truth is revealed.... The spray and the light make rainbows...everything shiny bright...clear...defined...self-evident.... Trust it....

Unwinding (47)

This meditation helps you leave your work life at work. It is designed to have *Inner Refuge (9)* inserted after the first paragraph. Where the meditation invites you to shake out tension, you may want to shake out your whole body. Change personal pronouns if appropriate.

Survey your own inner landscape and notice which aspects of yourself are still out and about — running, spinning, buzzing, busy, busy…. For the moment just witness them. Notice how your mind is still working away…. Notice the places in your body that are taut…. Note any feelings that keep pulling at you…. Witness all of this. Breathe….

Now let all this activity be for the moment, and refocus your attention. Let your imagination transport you into your inner refuge……. Return to the quiet. Make yourself comfortable here…. Soak up the peace and calm that's here….

Now go to the entrance and call in whatever aspects of yourself are still out there running about. Invite them to come in and relax. Imagine them. Find them. There may be one who is still running after all the details or another who is anticipating what's needed next. Or one who is still striving. And don't forget the one who is immersed in concentration…or the one who is still caught in conversation…. Find them. Invite them all back in…. Now listen; is there anyone else out there bustling about?… Call everyone into your sanctuary….

Welcome all aspects of yourself. Welcome them into your peaceful inner refuge. Imagine each of them coming in…. Greet them…. Invite them to hang up their hats and make themselves comfortable…. Give them a moment to make themselves at home…. Let them get settled; some may have to take off constricting clothing or put equipment away. Some may need to shake out the tension, ground the excess energy into the Earth, or make a note so thoughts don't get lost…. Imagine each doing whatever she needs to do so she can finally settle down and relax……. Feel how your body, your mind, and your feelings relax as all settles down……. Breathe a sigh of relief….

Tell them they can relax and replenish themselves now. They deserve it. Assure them that everything can wait. They can let go of obligation for the moment.... They, too, can absorb the peace of this inner refuge. Take time to acknowledge the efforts of each of them.... They have had a hard day. Let them debrief and appreciate each other....... Listen; maybe one has a request that would make her job a little easier when she goes back out again....

Now give each of them special gifts. Bring in tender, loving energy and bathe them in it...music, massage, flowers, a warm drink. Imagine whatever is called for.... Sense each receives exactly what she needs.... Give them special gifts. Sense each being comforted.... Feel your whole self quieted...comforted... calm...relaxing into well-being....

Harmonizing with Nature (48)

This meditation will help you become completely comfortable in your body — as comfortable as animals are in theirs. It also provides for an appreciation of the elements upon which all life depends. It is designed to start with *Inner Refuge (9)*; it can be augmented with *Body Care (80)*.

In this place you can fully settle into your own nature.... Here the beauty of nature is especially exquisite.... Imagine the colors, the sounds, the scents.... Here you feel at one with yourself and all of nature.... Give yourself permission to settle into your own naturalness.... Reside in your body as easily and comfortably as the animals do.... Relax into your own naturalness.... Feel it....

Reclaim your naturalness.... Love your naturalness.... Love nature...like the rivers that flow, the sun that shines, the air you breathe, all the life that springs from the Earth.... Breathe.... Feel yourself part of all of it...your own naturalness.... As you relax into your own nature, into nature itself, it is as though you have returned home.......

Let yourself commune with the Earth — feel the substance of which you are made — made of the same substance as the Earth.... Remember that the

Earth always supports your body and provides the sustenance your body needs....

Let yourself commune with the air — the air gives you breath — breath that continually renews your life. The air opens you...clears you...refreshes you with each breath....

Let yourself commune with the fire of the sun — the gift of warmth; your body is always warm — warmed by the sun. Appreciate the sun's penetrating heat, which warms the whole of the Earth and sky....

Let yourself commune with the water...water that cleanses all that it touches and brings out the true color of everything — water, fluid; it dances everywhere it moves....

Feel yourself solid, warm, open, and moving all at the same time.... Feel the spirit of life vibrate, glow, sing and dance inside you.... Feel the spirit of life within you and all around you.

As you relax into your naturalness, you can feel the intelligence intrinsic to life itself...the harmonizing qualities of life itself.... Life regenerates itself.... Life cleanses and clears itself. As you relax into your own naturalness, you can actually feel yourself regenerating, revitalizing.... As you relax energy flows.... Witness every cell of which you are composed teeming with resilience.... Feel yourself becoming increasingly comfortable in your body as you relax into your own nature...fully relaxed in your body....... Experiencing the natural intelligence of your body.... Your body heals itself, cleanses itself, revitalizes itself of its own accord...all you need to do is relax and your body takes care of itself naturally.... Feel that....

As you relax well-being happens as naturally as water flowing down to the ocean.... As you relax well-being happens as naturally as the leaves turning toward the sun...as naturally as birds soaring through the sky.... Relax into your naturalness.... Be comforted by your own nature, a part of all of nature.... The harmonizing forces of life itself flow through you as you breathe.... Feel them caress you.... Feel them heal you.... Trust nature; trust your nature.... Feel your whole self harmonizing with nature....

EMPOWERMENT

Heal Alienation: Relax into the Web of Life (49)

In our competitive culture our preoccupation with individual identity alienates us from mutuality. We find ourselves plagued with a deep psychic malaise, perpetually feeling we are never good enough. Individualism has created tremendous negative effects — ranging from the stress that underlies the most prevalent diseases to an economic system that ignores social costs and rewards greed. When we remember that we are supported by the interdependence of life, we don't feel isolated — and we act in ways that take one another into account.

Focus on the miracle of the natural world. Bring to awareness the great landscapes...the infinite variety of flowers...of animals...of trees...the worlds under the sea...the microscopic worlds you can't even see.... Appreciate the miracle of the natural world. Stretch your spacious awareness to ponder nature.... Witness the awesome....... Life is expressive. It is in a state of perpetual becoming. Life is resilient. It recreates itself.... It is as though an underlying intelligence maintains balance and invites all beings to express their life and leave behind a new generation to do the same.......

As awesome as the variety of life forms and places is the relatedness of all that lives in any particular place — a web of interdependent relationships in each habitat. Move your attention from focusing on particular beings to what is taking place between beings.... The web is spun in the exchange between life forms...relatedness forming patterns of energy exchange, weaving the web of life.... Sharing of the elements — energy moves. What we breathe out the plants breathe in — complex patterns of energy exchange — intricate patterns of mutuality.... Water flows through bodies, through earth, through air. The web is spun in the exchanges. Imagine the movement of energy...luminous.... This is the web that supports life. Consider the continual exchange of energy between life forms — a continual flow and flux of energy supporting life.... What is waste for one provides nutrients for another. The life of one provides life for another — even death supports life. Life recreates itself. Life brings death; death brings new life, bringing death, bringing life in a great wheel. Life is in a constant state of becoming. Interdependent, all supporting, all supported.... All life weaves the web.

This web is strong. You are of it — you cannot fall through it.... You comprise part of the fabric of the web of life.... This is true by the very fact that you exist. This is true for each of us. This is true for all of us. You are of it. The web of life supports you. Rest in the knowledge that you are of it. Let yourself inhabit your larger identity.... Let yourself relax into the web....

Life lives in community. Intricate patterns of exchange meeting basic needs. Constant exchange of giving and receiving — of taking care of needs.... Take a moment and focus on what you are wearing. All the different relations and materials that made it come into being....... All life on the globe forms great patterns of mutuality. Acknowledge the interdependence in your life.... Take time to appreciate all that supports your life: what you receive to sustain your body.... Give thanks.... What you receive to sustain your spirit...your heart...your mind.... What you receive to sustain you....... Give thanks....

Now remember what you give. You, too, give offerings. You make the web of life stronger.... Remember what you give....... Feel yourself as part of this great flow of energy supporting life. Remember what you do.... Appreciate yourself for your offerings. Imagine that the universe thanks you....

Imagine the myriad of supportive relations weaving community, everyone contributing.... Witness the exchange of energies...at work...in family...in community...in private, in public, all weaving a great web of kinship.... Life resides in community.... The needs of our lives are taken care of in community.... Feel the give and take, the exchange of energy with others, with other life forms...continual exchanging of energy supporting life, your life, other's lives, other forms of life...weaving a luminous web....

Feel yourself as part of this flow that supports life — your life, others' lives, other forms of life.... Let your awareness encompass how you are part of the great interdependent relatedness of All That Is...how you are inside the connectedness of it all. The web of life is strong. You are of it. Trust that you are being supported...that everyone is being supported.

Relax into the support.... Let go into mutuality. As you open the flow of life, energy moves with ease. You are supported. Trust it.... As you relax, you open and the energy moves more easily. It opens up the circulation of community.... Relaxing contributes to the well-being of all life. Relaxation brings strength in flexibility; tension causes brittleness, weakening the web. Relax into the pulse of community, and know that it supports you. Feel it.... As you are connected you experience and act out of the collective power. We need each other. We have each other. Trust community.... Relax...open, and the energy easily moves, vitalizing the circulation of community. Relaxing contributes to the well-being of all life. Let go...let the energy flow.... Relatedness is the natural state of being....

Witness your life. Notice the ways in which you isolate, withdraw, tighten up.... Imagine how it is you can turn it around: relax, trust, and be connected...to be a part of the connectedness that exists.... Remember everyone belongs.... Diversity makes the web strong....... Celebrate collective strength. Let your individual consciousness expand out to include the community of life in which you are embedded. Celebrate it.... Take time now to tell yourself whatever you need to hear, so you remember you are of the web...of the community...supported by life. Trust it....

Character Building (50)

This meditation is useful for getting to know one another, particularly in support groups. Lead the meditation before people share their stories with one another. The meditation can also be useful in the beginning of a therapeutic relationship. You may want to use different sections in different sittings. *Soaring High in the Skies (8), Lake of Reflection (6), Recollection (16),* and *Highest, Wisest, Deepest Self (14)* will augment this meditation. Character Building does not include the best times; for these, use *Personal Power (19), Moving Moments (35), Fun (33),* or *Support Sustains You (26).*

In addition to reclaiming times that have been empowering, this meditation directs you to acknowledge unfinished experiences. To work with unresolved issues, at some later time use meditations such as *From Reaction to Response (86), Forgive Yourself (89), Declaring Boundary Lines and Healing Past Violations (62),* or *Making Magic (43D, Past).*

In this state of awareness there are no limits of space and time. Here you can look through time the way you can look through space. Here the past opens up before you and you can witness the whole of your experience, appreciating the influences that have shaped you.... Here you can note where there may be psychic congestion in need of healing.... Here you can acknowledge all the building blocks of your character. You can give thinks for the gifts, let your heart smile again...take pride in the becoming....

Heritage: Those Who Went Before (50A)

Now look back into your past, way back, maybe even before you were born. What is your heritage?... Who are your people?... Some may be related by blood.... Some may be related by spirit...or by place.... Who are the people who went before you?... What are the gifts they gave you?...... What is the legacy that you carry today?... What do you take pride in?...... What ways of being were you given?...... If you come across anything that you would prefer to leave behind, breathe through it, thank the past, and tell yourself that the times are different now.......

Give thanks to all those who went before you.... Appreciate all that they gave to make what's present today possible.......

Your Own Callings (50B)

Notice what you have a propensity for.... What are you particularly good at?... What do you love?... What do you thrive on?...... At what times in your life have you come closest to feeling completely in your own element?... comfortable ...welcome...supported...creative...spontaneous?... Times you may have marveled at learning.... Times your heart may have sung with joy....

Has there been a yearning to do something that you have never done?......

Life's Turning Points (50C)

From this place of feeling the wholeness of who you are...witness the turning points of your life — pivotal times in your life.... Recall them; let them run through your mind like a film....... Turning points in your life...pivotal choices you made......crucial lessons you learned....... Times you've been touched deeply...good times...hard times...pivotal times in your life...opportunities that opened up for you......or doors that closed in front of you.... Then again there may be doors that you closed....... Losses you've endured....... Let these times run through your mind.... Recollect turning points in your life.......

How were you transformed by these experiences?... Focus on those particular times and appreciate how each one has shaped who you are.... Notice them — the turning points in your life...where you changed...transformed...grew into yourself...times when the fiber of your character was strengthened.... Remember turning points in your life.... And remember life choices you made....... What are the moments?...and the ways you met those moments that have made you who you are?...

Life's Challenges: Lessons Learned and Some to Be Completed (50D)

How have you responded to what life brought your way?... difficulties you never asked for, hard times you were dealt.... How have you responded when the going got tough for you?... When have you been able to influence or shape the scene?...... When have you had to fully adapt, having no power to influence it at all?...... When have you had to withdraw and protect yourself? Or maneuver around so as not to get trapped? How have you responded to what life brought your way?... Has any negativity soaked in?...

At what times in your life have you felt different?... How has this built your character?... What do you take pride in?... Are there ways you have been treated that just aren't right?...

Look back to life's rough spots.... Did you exit from any scene before you could learn the lesson it offered?...... Make note of the spots that could use some attention.......

If any old wounds were uncovered in this meditation, decide how you will take care of yourself.... Comfort yourself.... Imagine sending healing energy to yourself inside the memories of those times.... Give your past self the compassion you deserve.... Note if there are any areas you want to do healing meditations with....

Lessons Learned (50E)

Appreciate the times in your life that you have received the gift of wisdom.... Recall the important lessons you learned.... Recall these now....... Feel how all of this gives you great strength of character....

Now you can go back over any times that you didn't fully allow yourself to learn from at the time.... You can go back and claim the full offering of the situation.... You may want to do that now.... Reclaim your wholeness. Feel your wisdom deepen....

End (50F)

You have been shaped by life...and you shape the life that is yours.... Feel appreciation for what life has given you...and for what you bring to life....

Acknowledge all the building blocks of your being.... Feel the strength of your character.... Feel the strength of your character...equal to whatever challenges the future holds....

Life Is Magnetic: Cultivating Faith (51)

This meditation is helpful for creating an open subjective climate, cultivating faith, and/or combating cynicism. It is designed to follow *Dynamic Center (23)*. *Active Imagination (11)* will augment it. If you have a particular issue you want to work on you may want to continue into the next meditation, *Manifest Your Ideal (52)*.

You now reside in this very quiet, yet potent state of consciousness...still, quiet, yet vibrating with energy.... Like the center of a whirlwind, it's completely quiet, yet enormous power is propelled out from its center.... You are now settled into your own center — completely still, yet full of potent, powerful energy. The core of your being is magnetic. Know that corresponding energies magnetically attract each other. Know that by expecting the future to be good, you make it so. Know that this is, in fact, true — everything is attracted to what it has affinity with. Affinity is the way of the universe....

Take time to remember moments in your past when you felt completely secure, completely trusting, when you knew that your needs were covered.... However momentary these times may have been, however true your expectations turned out to be. Remember those moments in your past when you felt completely secure, when you knew all was well.... If no times come to mind, endeavor to imagine what it would have been like to be fully secure.... Imagine what it feels like to know all is well...to trust the future.... Just as you know that after each breath another will follow.... Imagine feeling just as secure that all is well in the future.... For the moment pretend that this is completely true.... Breathe in security.... Fill up your magnetic core with this quality of knowing all is well.... Exhale and relax into knowing all is well.... Breathe.... Experience this at the very core of your being.

Trust the future just as you assume that the Earth always supports your weight — it's a given.... Feel yourself relax into that, knowing that your needs are fully supported. Take it for granted that the future is secure.... For now, endeavor to completely fully believe everything is okay.... There's enough.... All is safe....

All is well.... Your needs are supported in the future as your weight is supported in the present.... Life provides.... Trust it.... Experience this at the very core of your being. Breathe it in.... Give yourself permission to believe that this is true....

Know that as you relax into trust, energy blockage dissolves, and your core draws into your experience exactly what you need.... A magnetic energy that pulls into your experience just what you need...and those whom you need...just what you offer.... There's an exchange of giving and receiving between yourself and others. Everyone's needs are met.... Just as what you breathe out the plants breathe in, and what the plants breathe out you breathe in. All is supported by life.... Feel yourself secure, knowing there's enough.... Take it for granted that all is well.... Feel this knowing soak into the very center of your being. As trust soaks in, witness residual anxieties dissolving.... Feel it.... Know it in your bones....

This energy acts like a compass inside you, guiding you in the direction that is right for you.... Have faith — know you are drawn right into the situations that are right for you. Trust your core energies — they are magnetic.... Imagine that you draw into your life and are drawn into the lives of others, that you give what you offer and receive what you need.... Giving and receiving...a balance as natural as breathing in and out. Feel it.... Trust it.... All fits together as naturally as your breath flows. As you relax and trust, you harmonize with the movement of the universe.... As you align yourself with universal energies your life moves smoothly — for the forces are with you. Energy is congruent.

From this center, this magnetic core, you can mix energies.... You can generate energies.... You can create new probabilities.... Take time to work with energy....... Drawing in exactly what you need and offering up what is needed....... As you welcome the future, the future welcomes you....

Manifest Your Ideal (52)

This meditation is one of the best for using the Active Imagination. See The Active Imagination: Conjuring Up Probabilities with Projection (Part II, Page 34). You might want to precede this meditation with *Active Imagination (11)*, *Life Is Magnetic (51)*, and *Inspiring Your Very Best (25)*. It is designed to be used with *Endings (13A – W)*; use the three or four that speak most deeply to you.

Bring to mind a particular area in your life you would like to improve.... How would you like it to be instead?... If you could create it however you wanted, what would you like this area of life to be like?...... Create an ideal vision.... How would it be?... How are you doing in this vision? Get to know it.... It is conceivable...the more plausible, the more possible. Give yourself permission to believe in your vision.......

Project yourself right into the vision.... Try it on for size.... Feel what it's like to be inside this reality.... Imagine it is already true....... Focus on a specific scene. Don't worry about when or how it happens; just experience it as though you are in the midst of it. Imagine how it plays out.... Become very familiar with it....... Make any adjustments you need to, so you are fully comfortable with it and it fits just right.... Notice how it impacts others....... Make needed adjustments.

You can manifest the changes you choose.... Trust change.... Imagine moving forward, being very gentle and patient with yourself, yet steady and strong.... Each day welcoming and manifesting more of your ideal.... Change happens.... One day you find that you and your ideal are one and the same.... *Expect* it....

Illuminating Your Path (53)

This meditation helps you to set your priorities and regain a sense that your life is on course. It is designed to be used with *Dynamic Center (23)*. Preceding it with *Active Imagination (11)* will augment it. Use the first two paragraphs of *Coming Out of Meditation (13V)* as an ending.

Your magnetic center projects light.... It illuminates the path that's right for you.... In the quiet, you can feel and see the path that is right for you in your life now. Assume this is so.... Sense the light and magnetism.... Your center is a compass guiding you.... You are always drawn in the right direction.... The light in your center illuminates your path as you go…. You always know what is right for you when you reside in your center. Experience how this is true…. Trust it…….

As you breathe, the light shines brighter on what is before you…. As you look down your path, you'll find yourself drawn into the areas of your life that deserve attention. Breathe…. Listen deeply…notice what draws you…. Give it the attention it deserves……. Anything else need attending to?……

Your center has great magnetic resonance…. Notice how your energy matches the energy that's needed for each area as you come across it. The inside is congruent with the outside…. Feel the subtle shifts in your energies as you move through the different contexts along your path……. Listen deeply…as the energy shifts you may find yourself with particular inclinations…….

As you're centered, you focus on the places that are right in the middle of your path, illuminated by your light…. All the rest fades into the distance, becomes peripheral…. Feel yourself focused — the light on your path is very focused…. Notice what is in the middle and what has faded……. If there is anything obstructing your path, take time to clear it…….

As you're centered, your inner compass guides you in the direction that is right for you…. Your life rolls forward smoothly, going just where you need to. Feel yourself harmonizing your energy with the energy that is calling you……. Your life has a natural order. You always find yourself in the right place, at the right time, with the right energy — as though your life is a choreographed dance…. You do what needs to be done, and you receive what you need to do it…. Feel yourself a part of the natural order of All That Is….

Serenity Washes Away Inhibitions (54)

This meditation helps to transform awkwardness into spontaneity and encourages authenticity.

Imagine yourself in a very serene place with a stream running through it…….
Imagine the beauty of this place…the sounds and scents in the air…the colors….

It is beautiful here, peaceful here.... Imagine it in detail....... Breathe...feel the beauty of this place come into you. Breathe.... Feel peace spreading through you.

Notice how this place elicits serenity.... The magical qualities of this place act like stream water washing over stones and bringing out their true color.... In this place, serenity washes over you and brings out your true character.... Enabling you to be who you truly can be...washing away all the crud that obscures your true self.... Breathe...draw in this serenity...waves of it washing away your inhibitions and self-doubts.... Breathe them out.... Feel peaceful energy wash through you...washing away all the debris that demeans you, that diminishes you — the doubts...the anxieties...the ways you always check yourself...the awkwardness — all that makes your emotions feel jerky or heavy...drags you down or stops you altogether sometimes.... Feel this peaceful energy wash through...cleansing out all that obscures your lively self. Clearing out all that stifles your zest for life.... Breathe and release....

Your true self shines.... Feel your zest for life stirring...spontaneity...your own particular way of expressing your joy to be alive.... Feel it.... Appreciate it.... Imagine expressing your true self.... Let your truth shine out.... Imagine shining in all sorts of different settings....... Feel yourself as relaxed as you are in this place wherever you are...your true self shines.... You are welcomed for who you are...as you are.... Imagine it in detail.... Feel it...the energy flows between you and others...expressing yourself...being appreciated for who you are.... As you experience yourself welcomed, notice how you can fully delight in others just as they are....

Know that whenever you come back to this relaxing, serene place all the inhibitions that may have accumulated — the edges, the anxieties are washed away and your true self emerges.... By simply imagining this place, serenity moves through and clears out all that causes you to shrink from life.... Tell yourself this.... You needn't withdraw; instead you will express your truth and celebrate life.... Glad to be alive!

Mustering Courage and Confidence to Express Your Truth (55)

This meditation is good to use if you are overly self-critical. It is designed to follow the first paragraph of each section of *Grounded and Open (39)*.

Imagine in the same way that you stretch into your life with the fullest expression of your truth, rooted in your own particular expression of life, like none other.... You are who you are — only you are who you are.... Feel yourself expressing life, as though you gain energy when you turn to the sun.... The sun warms you, encourages you. You're cleared and opened as the breezes blow.... You stretch to the sky in your expression, the fullest expression of who you are....

The plants turn to the sun; all the planets revolve around the sun. Imagine that you turn to the sun.. Imagine that the radiance of the sun is the warmth of love.... Imagine that the light of the sun is love — however you imagine that.... Pretend it's true.... You gain strength from being loved for who you are.... Simply being who you are is enough.... Feel warmth spread over you...soak it in.... Love makes you bloom.... Encouragement draws out the fruits of your expression.... Warmth inspires you to create.... Let yourself receive love for simply being who you are.... Love welcomes you, makes room for you to be who you are. Lots of space to be you.... Surround yourself with love.... Turn to it.... Bask in it.... Feel love soak into your whole being; breathe it in....

Feel it making you strong...inspiring you to express your true nature — what comes naturally.... All that you offer flows through you as easily, as naturally as sap flows through trees, as underground springs flow through the Earth and come up to bask in the light of the sun.... Imagine expressing your own nature...what you truly feel...trusting your nature...trusting your expression...being received, as all that lives in the light of the sun is received. Standing in your own true nature makes you fully open to the blessings life offers.... You receive; you offer.... Imagine dancing with all that inspires you.... What is calling you to dance?......

Anything inside you that craves to see the light of day?... that longs to dance, to play?... Listen deeply.... There may be something that wants to be created; there may be something that needs to be communicated, or something that longs to commune with life in the light of day....... Let it bubble up to the surface of consciousness....... Watch it emerge.... Feel the energy.... Be with your truth....

The flowers bloom in greeting the sun — life is about expression. The world welcomes your expression as the sun welcomes the flowers. Feel this; assume this is true.... Feel how easy it is, how natural it feels to express the full-ness of your being....... Imagine expressing your truth....... Notice the love and support there is for you to express yourself.... Absorb this encouragement.... Breathe it in.....

The sun sheds light onto all life — whatever its form.... Affirm the expression of your nature.... The sun shines upon it.... Love shines upon it.... All life yearns to be expressed, to offer itself to the great verity of life expressions that this Earth provides home for, that the sun provides light and warmth for. Life is about expression. Your expression is a gift to the world....

Go For It! (56)

This meditation helps overcome self-sabotage and gets you in touch with what you have always wanted to do, replacing self-doubt with the enthusiasm and curiosity needed to do it. Use *Support Sustains You (26), Reside in the Quiet (3),* and *Clearing Space Inside with Mental Housecleaning (11)* to augment this meditation.

As you settle down, everything quiets down and smoothes out. Horizons become visible. You can sense the vast expanse of All That Is...vast expanses, conscious-ness, life, the planet.... Let yourself be opened by the expanses of life itself. Breathe. Listen. Open...opening more, opening to the vast expanse.... Breathe in.... Draw in openness.... Let it exhilarate you.... Imagine yourself as open on the inside as the vast universe around you.... Breathe openness.... Sense the expansiveness of being.... Like the sun that moves out from behind the cloud — suddenly everything gets bright and warm. Feel expansiveness.

Evoke the quality of curiosity — experience curiosity — your curiosity...desire for discovery.... Pull into awareness the urge to explore.... Feel anticipation.... Feel inspiration.... Excitement.... Feel the desire to discover, to learn, to play in the vast reaches of experience...and infinite potentiality. Remember what interests you.... *(Repeat this paragraph.)*

With discovery comes the urge to express.... With coming to understand comes the urge to express.... To create is to discover.... They feed each other.... In the creation comes the understanding...each carrying the other forward...each feeding the other...expression and discovery, like inhaling and exhaling....... This dance has many others who are contributing to it. You dance together; notice how this is.......

Become aware of your own creative energies.... Sense your connection to the universal creativity that permeates everything...the creativity that brings forth change itself.... Imagine the essence of creativity within you....... Now bring to awareness your sense of where you are poised in your life. The chapter of life you occupy.......

The future is as expansive. Inhale and feel that the future is as open as the skies themselves....... Pay careful attention; what calls you in the future?... Listen deeply....... What in the future draws you?... What interests you?... Sense where the pull is.... There may be something inside that the future calls out.... Let it awaken.... What is brewing inside?... Anything needing expression?... What do you yearn to create, to explore, to discover...maybe creative expression, maybe particular ways of being with others?...... Give yourself permission to give it life, to bring it to the light of day...to discover it.... Give yourself permission to create, to go for what you want...to explore, to learn, to express, to commune...to give those feelings inside form, to bring them to life....

Release yourself into the expansive future.... Notice if there are any reins pulling you back, any voices telling you, "Don't even try." Any voices that tell you, "You better not." "You can't." "Nobody will like you if...." Invite these voices to take a back row seat and just be entertained for a change; they need not do anything.... Or you may prefer to simply invite them to leave.... If so breathe them out....

Notice what in particular you want to do this week to honor the expansiveness of life, to celebrate life, to appreciate your freedom to discover, to create.......

HOLDING YOUR OWN

In a culture driven by the profit motive the perpetual striving for more makes it very difficult for us to love and honor the blessings of our lives. From the daily barrage of media images in public life to the violence in private lives, coercion and manipulation are the norm. The very structures of our psyches have been invaded, and despite ourselves we often find that we act in accord with those forces. We need to reclaim and protect our respect for ourselves and for life itself. The meditations in this section are designed to address the effects of unhealthy societal forces so that we can fully appreciate our lives and become more effective contributors as we work to bring about a life-affirming culture. *Clearing Space Inside with Mental Housecleaning (11)* will augment any of the meditations in this section.

Self-Esteem (57)

Designed to follow the first four paragraphs of *Claim Your Space (60)*, this meditation counteracts those images from the media, our families, or peers that undermine our sense of self. If you are a man or are using this meditation in a mixed group, you may want to skip the word "beauty."

You're bombarded with images of what to strive for — of what it looks like to be okay. Feeling that if you just lose weight, get this, accomplish that, then finally you'll be okay. To make things worse, maybe you were mistreated in some way, and you concluded that you were not okay.... Now the judges reside inside and taunt you....

Remember when you have felt this way.... Remember when you felt you had to hide yourself, or maybe you had to display yourself.... Breathe out all the false images; breathe out all of those feelings that tell you that you are not good enough....... Remember what they tell you.... Remember how they make you feel.... How do they torment you?... Are you always checking yourself?... Gather any feelings of disdain you have for yourself and let them go.... Breathe them out.... Let them all go.... Breathe all of them out.... Feel your breath cleanse you. Release all the judgments that tell you that you are no good in some way.... Breathe out your frenzy toward perfection.... You are who you are; accept yourself.... Claim your body.... Claim your beauty.... Claim your life. Breathe....

Feel your breath return you to your authentic self.... You are already who you are supposed to be.... This is true. Reclaim your dignity.... Breathe. Relax into the idea that you are already okay just as you are. You are already worthy. Breathe.... Relax into the knowledge that you are worthy whatever your size, whatever your looks; whatever you have or don't have, you are already okay.... More than okay. You don't need to prove anything. You are already more than okay. Reclaim your dignity....

Imagine looking in a mirror and telling yourself that you are glad to be you.... Breathe out any residual judgments and welcome yourself to be who you truly are....... As you exhale relax into your true self.... Open your heart to yourself — to your whole self.... Welcome your whole self.... Let your sense of well-being emerge from inside yourself.......

Feel yourself welcome in the world. The world welcomes you; feel it.... Believe it. In your wholeness, even the parts you don't like so much are welcomed by life. This is true.

Be at ease with your true self. Pretend that you are totally contented with who you are. Imagine how that would feel.... What would that be like? Imagine feeling good about yourself in the different settings in your life.... Offer yourself this contentment as a gift. Imagine it makes you want to sing...dance — it is true that you are good just as you are!... You are you; feel good about your own self.... As you breathe fully, open to yourself. You are sacred, as all life is sacred. Reside in the dignity of who you are now. Love yourself; you deserve love.... Let your heart smile in appreciation for the life that you have been given.

As you breathe, sense how it is that you are completely lovable...lovable just as you are. Imagine that this is the case.... Reside in the knowledge that you are lovable....... Let yourself smile inside; like the sun that emerges from behind the clouds and warms the Earth, let your whole being be warmed by the knowledge that you are loved.... Take some time now to tell yourself all about some of the things you especially appreciate about yourself.... Love yourself....... Trust yourself.... Trust your own intelligence....

Tell the voices that have judged you that if they ever show up they have to change their attitude...loosen up...drop their perfectionism and be forgiving...even be friendly...be loving. Or you will pay them no attention. Feel them transform....... Breathe. Talk to them and decide how you'll develop new habits of the heart.... Invite the presence of new voices.... Listen.... Imagine what will remind you and the voices of your dignity...of your worth. Feel yourself welcome in the world....

Sacred Sexuality: Claim Yours (58)

If you are working with a loved one you might want to combine this meditation with *Making the Sacred Container of Love (123)*. If you are not working on sharing your sexuality with another, skip the last paragraph. (You may want to skip the second-to-last one as well.) If you are not working on reclaiming your sexuality, you may want to skip the second and third paragraphs.

Sexuality. Experience how life force energy celebrates itself in sexuality. Sacred life in celebration of the pure joy of life. Sacred. Sexual energy is the vitalizing energy of the universe. Feel your sexuality — sometimes dormant, sometimes vibrant.... Witness your sexuality...when it is aroused and you move with this energy. You feel the spirit of life sing in every cell of which you are composed. Your whole being comes alive and communes with life.... It is sacred; it opens and brings joy. Your sexuality is yours.... Celebrate it; honor it....

If you have any feelings of shame or obligation find them now.... Gather these feelings up as you inhale.... Find all those ideas that tell you how you are supposed to be.... However you imagine doing so, gather them up, any and all messages that cloud and obstruct your ability to experience the beauty of your own sexuality.... As though your breath scours through your entire inner landscape and dislodges any directives obligating you to anyone else.... These feelings do not belong to you.... As you breathe, dislodge these energies.... As you inhale, gather them.... As you exhale, discharge them; cleanse yourself.... Breathe....... Release.... As you scan your inner landscape you may find that someone else's energy has attached itself to your sexuality.... Banish it — only you have claim on your sexuality. Expel anyone else's energy. Take command; be definite.... Exhale and release all that clouds and obstructs the integrity of your sexuality.... Breathe it all out.... Feel your breath purify you.... Breathe.... Negativity is transformed.... Tell yourself that if ever these energies reappear you'll clear them out...breathe them out.... Celebrate who you truly are....... Welcome yourself.... Open; be fully alive!

Feel your own sensuality....... Remember the ways you thoroughly enjoy your body, yourself as a sensual creature.... Remember how you relish being alive — the sheer joy of it. Breathe love of life.... Breathe in love for yourself.... Claim your whole self.... Claim your sexuality.... You get to express your sexuality when and how you choose to. It is yours.... Reside in this knowledge now.... Your sexuality is sacred.... You, only you, choose who to share it with and how. Sexuality is sacred...beautiful.... As you breathe, channel this loving energy into all those spots where you have dislodged the negative energy. Let love be there.... Love belongs there.

Breathe it in. Sexuality is the embodiment of love. Pleasure spreads through one's whole being.... Every cell in the body dances, sings, melts in communion with vital life force energy. Sensuality…. Sexuality…. Sacred. Imagine how you can create safety for the sanctity of your sexuality…. How do you give it the place of honor it deserves?… What kind of boundaries are needed to be safe?…… Imagine honoring your sexuality with the protection it needs…. Respected. Safe to express and discover itself…. Give yourself sacred space. Imagine setting the boundaries you need to create so you provide a sacred and safe container in which your sexuality flourishes….

Imagine expressing what you need to provide for the sexual experience that is right for you. That is safe for you…. Imagine what you need to say. What to tell…. What to ask…. Your sexuality is sacred energy…. When to say "no"… when to say "yes"…. You, only you, decide what to do or not do with your sexual energy…. It is yours to celebrate life, to celebrate love…. Honor your sexuality in whatever way is right for you. It is sacred. It is yours……responsive, expressive, alive!

Welcome your sexuality to come alive, fully alive in sacred space. Sexuality transports you into the center of the essence of life force energy: Awesome…. Joyous…. Spontaneous…. Love of life embodied…. Sensuous…. Rhythmic…. Playful…. Sacred…. Alive…. Aroused…. Life discovering itself. Awesome…. Aroused…. Erotic…. Creative — feel it. Give yourself permission to open to all its gifts, to discover its offerings…. Open to them; let them carry you into experiencing of the primal source of life itself….

When you share your sexuality you experience deep connection, primal connection with life…. You experience the sacred life of another…. Another experiences the sanctity of your life. You move in deep resonance with one another…together in sacred embrace…to give life, love, deep pleasure…to receive life, love, and deep pleasure…. The energy of the communion of life celebrating itself. Breath brings it…. Riding breath. Riding life rhythms together. Sensuous…. Sensuous touch…flesh…desire…touch…delicious. Moving together…riding waves of energy…following the energy…discovering love….

Moving, breathing; sometimes long journeys of discovery, sometimes quaking spasms of ecstasy.... Touch. Love. Energy of love. Love thriving in the body. Energy building.... Bonding.... Intimacy.... Melting into union...a communion of loving — a blessing....

Cleansing After Violation (59)

In U.S. culture, where systemic oppression and aggressive behavior are so prevalent, our boundaries are violated all the time. Whether minor or life-threatening, assaults leave negative energy in their wake. This energy hurts, sometimes causes shame, and always undermines the claiming of one's personal power. This meditation will help you to clear yourself, reclaim your integrity, and heal from abusive treatment — the more traumatizing the experience, the more times you may want to use it, and the more important it is to have support as you work through your experience. (See Supporting Each Other, Part II, Page 57.) You may want to open this meditation with *Breath Is Home; Breath Heals (1G)* and to follow it with *Claim Your Space (60), Protected (61),* or *Declaring Boundary Lines and Healing Past Violations (62).*

Use Cleansing After Violation to clear yourself of anyone else's energy after you have engaged in healing work, if you have provided support to someone in distress, or have been in any situation that was fraught with negative energy. If you are using the meditation in this way, omit the references to shame and contamination.

This meditation is designed to follow the first three paragraphs of *River of Life Dissolves Blockages (83).*

This is the energy of purification.... It may be bubbly like soap, or maybe it has a magnetic consistency to it, or it might be purest water to be found anywhere.... Feel this energy going into your whole being.... It rides on your breath. Feel it.... It sparkles and bubbles and picks up all that needs to be removed, returning you to your own self, cleansed. Breathe with it.... Send it where it is needed.... Breathe in and energy comes through, cleansing you.... Imagine it flowing through...picking up and clearing out anything that doesn't belong.... In whatever ways you have been contaminated it absorbs all the foreign energy and clears it out of you.... If there is any shame anywhere it takes that, too....... It scours through your entire insides, leaving you purified.... Feel it....... It picks up and takes out anybody else's energy...cleansing you, healing you. Breathe.... Send it

wherever it is needed.... *(Insert specific guidance, naming where to send energy —
body parts, heart, etc.)* Experience your body being cleansed. Feel energy move
through, purifying you.... Breathe out.... It cleanses and washes away anybody
else's energy. Breathe out.... Feel yourself returned to your own
self...cleansed...purified. Your whole being. Sparkling, tingling clean. *(Optional:
repeat.)*

You may want to return to the river bank now and bask in the sun.... Relax
into the support of the Earth below you....... Healed...

Claim Your Space (60)

You may want to augment this meditation with *Integrity of Your Being (4)*. The first
paragraph of *Protected (61)* will enhance its effect. This meditation should be read
using a definite tone of voice.

As you breathe feel the rise and fall of your belly. Feel the substance of your
body.... Feel your weight supported by the Earth.... Feel your breath come in and
move through your entire body. Every cell of which you are composed is breathing. Feel your heart beat inside your chest; you are alive! Feel your bones; feel
your flesh. You are endowed with life. You are supported by the Earth....

Acknowledge the substance of your being. You take up space; you exist.
Claim your space on the Earth. As you breathe in, feel the substance of your
being.... Claim authority over your own being.... Honor yourself. Only you have
dominion over your being. *(Repeat paragraph.)*

Grant yourself your entitlement; the fact that you exist is the reason you are
entitled. Only you can be you.... You are endowed with life. Claim authority over
your own being.... Honor yourself. It is not only your right, it is your obligation.... Honor the life that that is yours. Feel the substance of your being. Know
that you are worthy. Treat yourself with dignity....

Take some time to settle into yourself; experience the dignity of your being.
As you exhale let yourself relax into yourself and take up your space. Take up the

space that is yours. You are entitled: entitled to your own thoughts...entitled to your own feelings...entitled to the entirety of your experience. It's true.... You are entitled. As you inhale fill yourself with your sense of entitlement. You exist. You are worthy. You are unique, special; only you are you. Give yourself permission to be your own self....

In whatever ways you may have been overpowered before and you had to disappear, give up, dissociate, or recede into the background — you had good reason at the time — but now you need your whole self. Call yourself back.... You deserve your whole self; the world needs you whole.... However you may have relinquished your wholeness, call yourself back now.... Welcome yourself.... However you have been diminished, reclaim the fullness of your being. Expand.... Inhale...bring yourself back now. Exhale...open to yourself. Breathe.... Inhale.... Reclaim your whole self.... Exhale...expand. Take your space back.

Welcome your whole experience to be present. Take up your space. Be whole again. Be all here...all of you present. Reside in the wholeness of your being. Claim your power. Expand into all of the space that is yours. However you imagine this. Psychically...emotionally; take your space.... Physically take up the space that your body occupies.... It is yours. Feel yourself expand.... Be expansive. The world needs you whole. The world invites your particular contribution. Trust yourself. *(Optional: repeat this and the preceding paragraph.)*

Claim your experience. Claim your voice. Express yourself. Step forward.... Engage. Encourage yourself. Remember those who have passed before — they care for you.... Remember there are those who stand with you now.... You are cared about.... You count. You matter. Claim your life. Claim your right to be you. Have the courage to be you...fully you. Take yourself seriously...you deserve it. The world needs you whole. In wholeness you fully receive the blessings of life....

Protected (61)

This meditation is designed to follow the first three paragraphs of *Claim Your Space (60).*

As you exhale imagine energy moving out of your body, creating a force field around you that announces you.... Breathe.... Sense how each breath makes this field become more vibrant.... This field of energy announces your integrity.... You are to be counted. You count; you exist! You inspire respect.... You are taken into account. Breathe.... You are part of All That Is. The space you take up is yours.... No one else has the right to determine what is so for you. You determine for yourself.

Breathe.... Experience the force field of energy around you. This field arouses respect wherever you go, with whomever you encounter; this force field inspires respect. Sense that your spirit is grand.... Imagine it.... Know that this is true. You are protected. You are respected.... Feel the energy glow...vibrate. You may want to give this energy field color. You may want to invite sprits to accompany you.... Know that you are always protected...always respected.... Feel it....

(Optional: continue with the next meditation.)

Energetic Field of Protection (61A)
This meditation is designed to follow the preceding meditation, *Protected (61).*

This energy field is versatile. You can use it to protect yourself. You can also send this energy to surround someone who needs protection. Whatever this energy surrounds it announces its integrity — it protects its integrity. Send this energy wherever you like.... Channel it with breath....... Imagine it surrounding. Sense the energy protecting.... Know that integrity is protected — honored...respect is inspired. When this energy surrounds, it protects. *Expect* this to be the case.... Breathe power into the energy field now.... Protected.... Safe.... Respected.... *Expect* it.......

Declaring Boundary Lines and Healing Past Violations (62)

This meditation is designed to follow *Claim Your Space (60)* and *Protected (61)*. If you are using it to heal past abuse, rape, or hate crimes I recommend that you use it in its entirety and work with it when you have support around you. (See instructions for Supporting Each Other, Part II, Page 57.) You may want to use *Cleansing After Violation (59)* and *Making Magic: Healing Yourself (43D, Past)*. You may also want to use *Protected View (12)* as a substitute for the beginning. Use parts of *Breath Is Home; Breath Heals (1G)* if tension arises.

If you only want to establish your boundaries rather than to heal past violations, skip the section Repairing the Ruptures and go directly to the section Securing Yours. This part of the meditation is recommended if you are under major stress — for instance if you are dealing with a life-threatening disease and need to conserve your energy.

As you breathe feel this field of energy around you. An aura of your energy surrounds you. This aura establishes a boundary between you and the world. You choose what you want to let in. What feels good can be let in. What feels bad can be kept out. You control this boundary line. Feel it.... Trust yourself: you know what feels right....

Like the cells that compose your body, each cell has an extremely sensitive and alert membrane around it. These membranes know what is to be let in for nourishment and what is to be kept out. These membranes know. Feel the energy field surrounding you. Feel your boundary now.... You decide what is good for you. You decide what is not. You control your boundary lines.... Fortify your boundaries now. Imagine that they announce to the world that they are to be honored. Your boundaries are to be respected. You control your boundaries. Feel how this is the case.... Only you control your boundary lines.

Repairing the Ruptures (62A)

In the past your boundaries may have been violated, betrayed, or torn in some way. Now you can repair the tears.... Imagine doing so now; send your breath to the tears and repair the damage done.... Breathe.... Make your boundaries strong again.... They are your boundaries. You decide what to let in. Make them strong again. Imagine it — however you imagine it.......

For some of us, our boundaries have become fuzzy, confused. We may have combined and conflated love and abuse.... Take time to move through your subjective landscape.... Keep the love; reject the abuse.... They are not the same — they do not have to accompany each other — you know that now. Love honors that you control your own self — only you determine what you do, how you feel, and what is true for you.... Abuse takes that control away from you. Comb through your subjective landscape; retake control.... Reject abuse; invite only love, for love will always honor your choices.... Breathe out the energies that don't belong....... Retake control of your subjective landscape.... Cleanse yourself of anyone else's controlling energy that you might run into. Breathe out.... Clear it out.... These times past may have left behind residual shame, blame, maybe some sort of disdain; cleanse yourself....... Breathe it all out....... Reclaim yourself.... Forgive yourself.... Trust yourself....

There maybe fear lurking somewhere. Just because it happened before doesn't mean it has to happen again. You are in charge now. Tell yourself that.... Tell all aspects of yourself that. Shout it out!... This is your terrain! Reclaim it.... As you inhale feel your own integrity.... Occupy your own self.... Feel the life energies returning throughout your whole being....

Clear out all those leftover energies now. Let your breath dislodge them and wash them away.... As you breathe in feel your entitlement. Feel the integrity of your being....... As you exhale clear out all that doesn't belong. Let it go; breathe it out.... Only you have dominion here. Trust yourself.... Occupy your whole self....

If you come across any places that are still in pain, breathe.... Breath is healing. Breathe in healing.... As you reclaim yourself, as you clear yourself, you make space for healing.... There may be tears there — it's okay.... Breathe.... Breath into those places inside.... Healing happens. Comfort your past self....... Be with your whole self — yourself whole…your boundaries healed…. Reclaim your life; it is yours, only yours….

Securing Yours (62B)

Your body's immune system is always on the lookout for what is disruptive to its health; your energy field is keenly aware of what feels right and what doesn't…. It repels what doesn't feel right and welcomes what does…. Imagine setting up sentry posts that protect you. Give them radar or antennae in which your intuition can be on full alert. Tell the sentries to distinguish between what is good and what it is not. Tell them to be very discerning…. Give them clear instructions…. Be specific…. Sometimes negativity comes in seductive disguises. Tell them what to watch for so they are not fooled….

Your boundaries have a great capacity to welcome what is healthy and resist what is not. Feel that. Imagine what in life you want to invite in…what nourishes you…. You decide what to welcome and what to reject….You decide what feels right and what doesn't…. You protect yourself…. You protect your boundary lines. Notice if there are any particular individuals who are invasive…. Imagine what you need to do about it……. Imagine saying "no" when you need to…. Imagine expressing what you do and don't want. You maintain your boundaries….

Make your boundaries strong. This is your life. You need to pull in what nourishes you…and keep out what weakens you…. Imagine moving through the different situations in your life with family, with coworkers, with the different people in your life, and notice what you'll invite and what you'll keep out……. Sense what is best in the different settings in your life……. Imagine communicating what is true for you…what you need and what you don't. Imagine saying "no" when you need to…. Imagine what you need to do or say to declare your boundary lines. Witness how it feels to do so…. Imagine doing so…. Imagine that the integrity of your being is honored. You deserve it. It is necessary for maintaining well-being….

Protecting Yourself From Being Devalued (63)

Competition and prejudice are so prevalent that most of us find ourselves in circumstances in which we often have to protect our integrity. This meditation is
particularly useful if, at work, those who have more rank than you are ignorant
and/or disrespectful and your speaking up would put your position at risk. It is
designed to follow *Dynamic Center (23)*.

Know that this magnetic core of your being is where your deepest character is
rooted.... Your integrity, your talents, your sensibilities are all rooted here.... The
full power of your persona shines out from here.... Feel your magnetism, your
charisma.... Acknowledge all that you offer — your talents, your intelligence, your
sensitivities, your humor...your creativity, your spontaneity......your generosity.
Feel all of this — the particular ways you manifest these qualities — they emerge
from the core of your being....

Breath energizes the power of your persona. Breathe.... Feel your
power....... When you breathe from your magnetic core, you neutralize all
that keeps you from expressing your truth.... When you fully occupy your
center your magnetism draws in only that which has affinity for your truth —
all else loses its hold.... Anything that could have undermined you, all the
messages that discount or trivialize you, all these lose their charge. They
have no resonance with your center; there is nowhere for them to hook in.
They can no longer undermine you. All negativity loses its influence; there
is nowhere to connect. Negativity gets no standing from which to
influence you.... Experience how this is true.... Breathe from your center of
power....

When you occupy your truth, undermining messages lose their meaning....
They simply dissipate.... When you reside in your center all that devalues you loses
its power.... Sense how this is the case.... Let out the pulsation of the deepest core
of your being.... Let the glow in the deepest center of your being shine out into
your life...powerful energy, magnetic energy...vibrant.... Breathe.... Vitalize your
center.......

Sense that it shines right through and dissolves all the ways you get discounted or trivialized.... When your magnetism is clear you draw in only the positive; the rest dissipates.... Feel this....

Reclaim Your Power (64)

Designed to follow *Personal Power (19)*, this meditation will help you deal with internalized or current oppressive circumstances. As long as another has power over you, you are not free to fully express a different perspective because doing so may put you in jeopardy. Sometimes your inhibitions may not be rooted in the present but are a result of past conditioning. It is crucial that you be able to discern which is the case in order to determine the best course of action. This meditation helps you assess what you need to maintain your power and to express yourself without getting in trouble. If tension arises, use parts of *Breath Is Home; Breath Heals (1G)*.

Now scan your life and witness when you let your power recede.... Review the different contexts in your life and observe when you leave your power behind.... When you withdraw from your own experience....... Notice under what circumstances you shrink from the fullness of your own experience....... When do you suppress your expression?... Are there times when you take someone else more seriously than your own self?...... Notice under what circumstances you diminish yourself. Witness.......

When do you find yourself with one experience inside and another that you express to the world?...... Notice what part of your experience gets relegated to silence....... Notice how come you do that. What's at stake?... Would you be rejected?... Would you provoke trouble?... Are there areas in your life where people assume something about you that isn't true and you let it go?...... Bring to mind the times in your life when you give away or simply concede your power....... Notice the times when you don't or can't express your truth.......

Imagine what you might need in these situations to be able to be your full self, to express the dynamism of your being, to express the creativity of your being, to reside in your power...to offer your gifts to the world...to tell people what you truly think...to reveal what you really feel.... What do you need to be your full self?...... Maybe there are allies who can accompany you in body or spirit...or maybe there is something you need to remember.... Is there anything you may need to protect yourself from?.... What do you need to be your full self in the different settings where you tend to relinquish your power and become compliant?... You may need different things at different times.... Explore how it is you can keep your power.......

If there are any arenas in your life where you simply can't express the fullness of your being, notice what price you pay....... Acknowledge the pain it causes you to have to hide some aspects of who you are.... Acknowledge your dignity — the integrity of your experience.... Affirm your truth.... Be sure that despite having to keep part of your truth inside, you still reside in your own power, maintaining your integrity.... Tell yourself that the problem is not of your own making.... Comfort yourself with this knowledge.......

Notice how you can care for yourself.... What is needed so no aspect of your being atrophies?... What can you do to honor the aspects that have been relegated to silence?... How can you bring them to the light of day?...... What can you do to take care of yourself and make it safe to be your full self?...... What's needed to maintain self-respect?... What can you do so you continue to grow into the fullness of your being...to express your authentic self...be who you truly are?......

Is there anything that you need to do in those situations where you keep silent?... What can you do to express your truth and be safe at the same time?... Imagine creating a psychic protection so you don't internalize any other people's false projections.... You might want to imagine an invisible shield or mirror surrounding you so their energy bounces back....... Summon the courage you need to live by your truth.... Remember those who believe in you.... Give yourself permission to reside in what is true for you.... Believe in yourself....

Imagine yourself moving through the world effectively, fully residing in your personal power.... Envision yourself contributing what you have to offer to the world.... Know that as you claim your power, you have more to contribute and people welcome your contributions.... Notice what arenas in the world are hungry for what you have to offer.... Where can you be your full self?... Imagine it — people welcome your full humanity, your creativity, your thinking, your sensibilities, your care and concern.... People welcome your authentic self.

Give yourself the gift of expressing the fullness of your being...coming into your power as you claim yourself...grounded and open. You are a gift and you have gifts for the world....

When you claim your power you empower others to do the same.... Experience this.... When we claim power we create power together...in connection, in communion, with one another, with life itself.... With the power of this connection we protect ourselves in those places where integrity is not honored and respect is not present.... Imagine successfully protecting ourselves where respect is not present...in our power, wherever we are, whatever we do...inspiring respect in life itself.... Truth is honored....

Healing Happens Naturally

COMMUNING WITH YOUR BODY

All of the meditations in this section will help you become more intimate with what is taking place inside your body. They will help you to discover what you need to increase your well-being and empower your healing process.

You can also use these meditations to support others: read them to the person whose healing process you wish to support. Or, if you want to help move energy and gain insight, imagine the other person's body instead of yours when you meditate; have someone read the meditation to you, and ask them to adjust pronouns as necessary and to name the person you wish to support. If you use any in this way, it is important that you review Channeling Positive Energy to Those in Need (Part II, Page 42). Be sure to use the ending *Clearing the Self (13T)* before you complete your meditation session.

Inside the Body (65)

This meditation is designed to follow *Resilience (15)*. If you want to continue with specific healing work, repeat some of *Resilience (15)* and then go directly into *Harnessing Healing (66)*.

The miracle of life reveals itself in the living processes continually percolating inside your body. Your awareness is about to embark on a journey to explore the world inside your body. As you travel your intuition will offer insights, revealing what is taking place. Your intuition works in partnership with your imagination. As you focus on the different areas inside, invite your imagination to create the area's story. Create story and discover truth — however you imagine it is what is true for you…. The very act of directing attention illuminates what is so inside. Just as if you were wearing a miner's light, wherever you turn your attention what is taking place is illuminated — sometimes symbolically, sometimes literally, sometimes with feeling, sometimes with knowing — wherever you turn your attention inside your body, what is happening is apparent. Expect this to be the case.... Awareness is very versatile. It can widen focus to view the whole or narrow it to view minute detail. Your awareness can sense what is true on the cellular and the whole system level.

Breathe.... Follow your breath. Your breath rolls through your whole body...waves of breath rolling through.... Every single cell of which you are composed breathes.... Now imagine that your awareness is a point of light riding a wave of breath down into your body. Ride a wave of breath; travel down into your lungs.... Imagine being inside your lungs.... Imagine what it looks like in there.... Imagine hearing the air swishing as breath moves in and out of your lungs. Notice the moisture in the air. Imagine how it feels inside your lungs.... Imagine what the lung tissue looks like....

If, as you explore inside your body, you run across any areas that have suffered injury or illness, stop and witness the awesome capacity of the body to heal itself...all the complexes of systems cooperate in healing. You may choose to channel some vital energy to the area while you are focused there. In your journey, if you come across any imbalance imagine it returning to a state of well-being — however it occurs to you to do so. You may want to stop and converse with the area; you may want to channel positive energy there, or you may decide to return later.... Do what feels right....

While you're inside the lungs, turn awareness to the beating of the heart — listen. Travel over to your heart. Imagine what it looks like as it pumps. Your heart is always pumping, keeping the currents flowing, keeping the rivers of blood moving though out the landscape of your body. Rivers of blood carrying breath, carrying nutrients to every single cell composing your body. Blood flows through your whole body, carrying oxygen.... Feel this.... See this.... Imagine the rivers of blood traveling though your whole body.... Take a journey through your circulatory system.... Imagine being carried through the land-scape of your body.

Pay attention to the muscle tissue.... Your muscles give the body form and movement. They are flexible, supple, and strong. Feel their strength and flexibil-ity.... Notice how they change from one area to another. Go to somewhere that you know you tend to store tension.... Sense the muscles there. Draw in some extra breath here so that they may loosen some.... Be aware of the ligaments at your joints...connective tissue. Be aware of how this tissue is different than the muscle tissue....

Now, focus on the frame your body stands on — your bones.... They are firm and durable.... Move your awareness deeper inside one of the bigger bones.... Witness the factories making healthy blood, continually replenishing the rivers of blood flowing through the entire landscape of your body — through every nook and cranny of your entire body.... Blood carries breath, oxygen, nutri-ents...and then carries away the wastes — what is no longer needed and is ready for discharge.

Your digestion, all the organs are working together, transforming food into nutrients, into energy.... Your mouth then your stomach break down the food.... Your intestines accurately discriminate between what is needed and what is not...absorbing all the nutrients for your blood to supply your whole body with nourishment and passing the rest out. Sense it. Imagine it. Your digestive and excretory systems keep your body nourished and cleansed. Sense your liver.... Your liver detoxifies your blood.... Be aware of your kidneys filtering fluids and cleansing your body of all the dead cells and toxins.... Your bladder flushes it all out of your body. Watch it.... Sense it.... Imagine all the organs of your digestive and excretory system in good working order. Imagine how well they work with each other....

Tune to your reproductive organs. Imagine them in good health.... Your reproductive system celebrates life and can reproduce it. Your reproductive system moves through time in harmony with the grand cycles of nature. Imagine all the organs in good working order....

Tune to your nervous system — an elaborate system of communication. Be aware of complexes of nerves sending signals back and forth from your brain — alert, efficient, passing on all information. Alive. Alert. Electric.... Be aware of your brain...processing and storing massive quantities of information. Keeping everything in order. Imagine it.... Notice how your networks of nerves move from one side of your brain then cross over to the other side of your body....

Tune to your lymphatic and immune systems as they move fluids through your body, keeping your body protected.... Your lymph nodes watch for anything that doesn't belong. If anything is detected, the immune system is notified and it moves into action...maintaining the integrity of your body. Your immune system is adept at correctly discerning what is okay and what is not.... .

Imagine your endocrine system of glands sending out chemical messages that maintain the body's energy balance — tracking what's needed and sending out hormones to carry messages throughout the landscape of your body. All systems harmonized. Always keeping your metabolism working optimally.

Your skin contains you. You skin breathes and releases. Your skin is supple.... Tune to each of your senses and to their related organs that transmit what is happening in the outer world. Feel how keen they are....

An elegant system of communication among all functions, among all parts...not a single cell is left out.... Witness each of the systems cooperating with the others...each dependent on the others...each contributing its part. Feel it...the miracle of the interdependence of life.... Each part has its own place in the whole scheme of things — from the whole system level to the cellular level.... Tune a little deeper; sense the cellular structure.... Sense it in different areas of the landscape of your body. Notice how the cells communicate and cooperate with each other...each doing its part in providing and maintaining your body's wellness....

There may be areas you would like to explore in more detail.... Do so now....... Talk to your body.... What does it have to say to you?....

Harnessing Healing (66)

This meditation is designed to be used after *Resilience (15)* and can be adapted to channel healing to another. If you are using it for healing another, use the first four paragraphs and replace any reference to your body with the name of the person to whom you want to channel healing.

Let all this energy concentrate itself. Every time you inhale feel it concentrating. Breathe life force energy.... Let this energy concentrate. However you imagine it: it may have sound, music, vibrations, color, light.... It may not have a form; it may consist of clear intent. However you imagine it, concentrate life force energy as you inhale.... Feel it build. Concentrate it. Healing energy. Powerful energy.... Vital energy. Breathe it....

Using your breath you can channel healing energy wherever it is needed. Bring to awareness the area in your body that is in need of healing. Focus on what needs healing.... Sense how it is doing. Rest your attention right on the area. Feel it.... Imagine it....

As you exhale imagine sending healing there.... Surround the area with healing.... Every time you exhale send even more of this powerful healing energy to the area.... Imagine the area opening...becoming receptive to this energy. Imagine the area inhales this healing energy.... Take your awareness down to the cellular level. Cells breathing healing.... Sense healing happening there.......

Breathing.... Healing.... Breathing healing. Healing happens...sometimes slowly, sometimes quickly...sometimes subtly, sometimes miraculously. Healing happens. Breathe healing. Trust healing.... Sense healing.... Vital healing energy, trust it.......

(Optional: repeat paragraph.)

Rest your attention on the area.... Notice if there is anything it needs.......
Any changes in your life...or your activities.... Pay attention to what arises in
awareness....... You may want to bring specific concerns into awareness and witness what it wants.... Notice if there are particular foods...exercises...or ways of
resting that would be appreciated....... Imagine communicating with the area....
What does it have to say?...... Imagine doing what is needed to honor the area
with good care...to help healing happen......tell it what you'll do for it....
Experience healing happening.......

Treatment Choice (67)

You can use this meditation to help determine which medical and/or alternate
health treatments are best when you are trying to decide among different options.
It is designed to follow *Resilience (15)* and the first three paragraphs of *Harnessing
Healing (66)*. Repeatedly name the treatment and graphically describe the process
it is meant to catalyze.

Extend your attention to include your whole body along with the particular area
that is in distress. Feel the intelligence of your body. There are ways that the healing process can be supported. Your body knows what it needs. Feel the
intelligence of your body.... Tune to this intelligence. Breathe in its presence....

Imagine each possible supportive treatment. Bring them to awareness one
at a time. Bring the first treatment that you would like to explore to awareness
now.... Talk to your body about *(name treatment)*....... Pay attention to whatever appears in awareness.... Imagine using this treatment.... (If you can,
describe what it is supposed to catalyze.) Witness if your body responds as
hoped....... Envision; feel specifically what happens.... Rest your attention inside
your body and sense its experience....... Is *(name treatment)* helpful?...... Are
there ways you can augment its strength?... Are there ways you can minimize
side effects?... Are there any conflicts?... Talk it over with your body.... Imagine
what it tells you....... Listen deeply; notice what arises in awareness....... Are
there issues or questions you need to take up with your health provider?....

(Repeat paragraph, replacing "first" with "another." Continue until you have finished exploring treatments.)

Now imagine how the treatments may work in concert with one another.... Sense what is optimal.... Notice what opens to life.... Decide what is best to do.......

Feel how providing your body with this care brings well-being.... Appreciate the blessing. Appreciate how hard your body is working to be well.... If you have any feelings of distress, breathe them out.... Breath transforms them into pure energy, which can be utilized to make the treatment even more effective.... Imagine getting better.... Be patient with your body; feel yourself getting better.... Envision it in detail....

Getting Ready: Surgery or Other Treatments (68)

This meditation is designed to follow *Resilience (15)* and the first three paragraphs of *Harnessing Healing (66)*. If appropriate you can replace the word "surgery" with the name of the treatment you are about to begin. When you are anesthetized you continue to hear; therefore it would be advisable to play a pre-recorded meditation during your surgery — check with your surgeon for permission beforehand.

Take a moment to gather up any anxieties you may have. As you inhale gather them together.... Remember the scary thoughts.... Remember the distress.... As you inhale draw them together.... Gather them up.... Now as you exhale breathe them out.... Let them go.... Know that as you breathe them out they transform.... They are a reflection of tenacious life force energy that moves through you. Breathe....... Trust the life force energy that is pulsating through you. *(Repeat second half of paragraph as needed.)*

Focus awareness on the area that is going to have surgery. Tell it what is going to happen. Imagine holding council with the all the parts of the affected area.... Brief them....... Take your awareness all the way down to the cellular level. Brief all affected areas....... Tell them how this will help your whole body to regain well-being.... Be specific.... Imagine showing pictures or evoking sensations of how much better you'll feel afterward.......

Talk over how all affected parts can avoid adverse reactions and cultivate a swift and easy recovery. Talk about what is needed for recovery.... Say what you will do.... Imagine success.... Feel it.... Breathe; draw in life force energy.... Imagine your body basking in healing energy...especially all the affected parts....... Know that this energy will be with you through this difficult time.... Know that this energy will carry you through.... *Expect* it....

Taking a Vacation from Pain (69)

This meditation is designed to follow *Smoothing the Edges (5)* and to precede *Fun (33)*, *Love (21)*, and/or *Moving Moments (35)*. Name specific times, interests, or relationships that have been especially gratifying — particular art works, landscapes, or moments with a loved one, etc.

Those places in your body that have been calling your attention...tell them you are leaving for the time being. Tell them you are taking some time off because you need to simply have a good time for a change.... Tell them they should make themselves as comfortable as they are able. You may want to give them a special place to be...their own room maybe — whatever seems right. Tell them you'll be back later to check in on them. Tell them they can always reach you if need be, but that it is best for them to rest. Life has been difficult all the way around lately. You may want to leave them with something to entertain themselves with.... Turn down the volume of the room monitor. Bid them farewell and close the door behind you....

Pain: Reframe It (70)

This meditation is designed to follow *Inner Witness (1H)*. Repeat any parts to deepen its effect.

There is a place in you that is screaming for attention or is maybe just gnawing at you. Focus your awareness into this place now. Quietly rest your attention there now.... Just be with this place. Just be there. You need not do anything; just be there and breathe.... Breathe.... Breathe full breaths.... You may want to breathe through the area. It may be thirsty for breath.... Feel it breathing.... Bring in the quality of kindness.... Breathe kindness.....

Breathe through the area — however you imagine that.... Sense the area breathing.... Breathe....... If you find yourself pulling back, withdrawing, or tensing up, breathe; relax and just be with this place.... Breathe with this energy.... Be there. Focus there.... Gently rest your attention there.... What exactly is the sensation?... What if you interpreted it differently?... What if you gave it another name?...

As you witness you may find that this place changes form and energy...gradually it shifts...maybe color, maybe mood.... It shifts somehow; some way it shifts.... Just focus there.... Focus with soft awareness.... Focus with clear awareness. Breathe.... Rest your attention there.... Feel yourself relate to the sensation differently....

Breathe. Witness. Be with this energy. Witness it.... Relax. Share presence with it.... Breathe there.... As you share presence with this place inside, with this energy inside, open to it.... Breathe with it.... Not only is it shifting in some way; notice how you shift in relation to it....... Change happens. You need not do anything; just witness.... Being present with pain is a way to reclaim power. Pain contains an offering of power.... You may even decide to go into the center of it.... Feel your relation to it change.... Breathe.... As you do open yourself, it may speak to you.... You may want to converse with it.... Converse in knowing — this may not be a time for words....

Make friends with it.... It may surprise you.... It may even have a gift for you.... It may even have a new name. Breathe with it.... Quietly rest attention there.... Focus there,.... Watch it.... Witness it.... Share presence with it.... Breathe.... Breathe....

Listen to its experience; it has a message for you....... Breathe.... Witness. Be kind.... Breathe kindness.......

Life Cycles, Body Cycles (71)

This meditation is designed to follow *Resilience (15)* and the first two paragraphs of *Pacing (36)*. You may want to augment it with *Body Care (81)*. If you are using it at the beginning or ending of menses, you may want to use it in combination with *Rite of Passage (106)*. If you are addressing menopause and/or aging, continue directly into the next meditation, *The Grace of Age (72)*.

Tune to the cycles of your body. They move carried by time.... They move with the moon.... They move through time. Life cycles carry you.... Feel yourself completely harmonized with the life cycles of your body. Feel these cycles harmonized with the great cycles of the Earth and sky.... Follow your cycle.... Different activities are needed to honor the different phases in your cycles. Notice what you need to do to honor your life cycles.......

Imagine moving through your whole cycle comfortably...in balance...harmonized with the cycles of the Earth and sky...supported by the cycles.... Feel it.... If there are rough spots, tune to your body and talk with it....... Ask it what it needs to come back into rhythm.... Tell it what you would like....... Imagine what would increase well-being....... Feel it.... Imagine taking care of yourself....

The Grace of Age (72)

This meditation is designed to follow the first paragraph of the previous meditation, *Life Cycles, Body Cycles (71)*, (along with the meditations it uses). If you are male, use only the first paragraph of The Grace of Age and any lines from the previous meditation that hold meaning for you.

Appreciate being carried by time. Time supports you. Make friends with time.... Time has always carried you. Make friends with aging.... Age contains the gift of experience.... Life gets deeper and deeper with each passing day..... Appreciate what time has given you...the time you have...the times you had.... Take the long view. Notice what gifts each life phase offers.... Notice the rhythm, the quality of life in each phase....... Acknowledge the gift of each.... They each have a different

offering. Appreciate this....... Love your body for the ways it carries time.......
Feel the dignity of your being.......

There are the short cycles of the moon...there are the long cycles of many,
many, many moons...delivering you to the other side of the moon cycles. Imagine
moving into menopause easily....... Imagine moving through menopause comfortably....... The hormones changing naturally.... You ride these changes in your
nature as easily as you move from one season into the next. Imagine it.... Life
force energy always supporting you...carrying you, carrying you through time....
Feel it. Your life is a gift...all phases of life a gift. Imagine what this phase offers....
Open to it.... Feel the blessing....

Inviting Conception (73)

This meditation is designed to be used after *Resilience (15)*. If you are partnered,
when the meditation refers to love, insert your partner's name and insert sentences
about your shared love wherever you are moved to do so.

Appreciate how life regenerates itself; life is the creative force, continually regenerating itself — creating itself. All forms of life naturally regenerate. Regeneration
is the miracle of life itself.... Sexuality, in a frenzy of celebration of life, creates
life.... Feel how your body naturally welcomes life. Fill your whole pelvis, your
womb with love of life.... Fill your pelvis with magnetic loving energy, energy
that draws new life in.... Expect new life to generate here. Invite a spirit in....
Welcome new life into your womb. Welcome conception.... Celebrate life creating life.... Invite the spirit in.... Trust your body, for your body naturally
conceives life. ˙

Breathe out all that may stand in the way of conception — any anxiety,
hopelessness, grief — breathe it out; let your breath wash it away....... Trust your
body to open and conceive. As you inhale welcome new life; welcome your
baby.... As you exhale let go of all that may get in the way of providing a nourishing place for this spirit to come into you.... Feel your body full of health,

vibrancy, fully embodying nature herself.... Nature replenishes, recreates herself. Nature creates through your body.... Welcome new life....

Talk to your body.... Sense if there is anything that will help.... Tune yourself to the timing, to the rhythm for conception....... This new life has its own timing; let it inform you....... Harmonize yourself with it....... Talk to the spirit.... Listen .... The spirit comes into your womb, into your lives — a baby is born through you into your life....

Imagine your body becoming pregnant.... Feel your body welcome conception.... Expect a healthy pregnancy and birthing.... Your baby joins your life.... You are a mother.... Expect it.... Breathe love into your womb....

Healthy Pregnancy (74)

This meditation is designed to follow *Resilience (15)*. It can be augmented with the first two paragraphs of *Birth (75)*. If you are partnered, when the meditation refers to love, insert your partner's name. If you are not partnered, appreciate the love between you and your baby.

Feel the love that has created the life in your body. Love; celebrate loving energy. Love creates a baby. Tune to what is taking place in your womb. Acknowledge the miracle of life.... Now your body is making life.... It is easy; it is natural.... Breathe with it.... Trust the life in your body, providing life. Let the love flow. Trust your body. Trust the life that grows inside you. Trust the life your body creates.... Nature is awesome....

Tune to what your body needs to optimize health and nourish the life developing inside you....... Channel loving energy into your womb. Feel your body smile.......

Greet your baby.... Sense how your baby is doing.... In the quiet of awareness open to the spirit of your baby. Commune with one another....... Imagine conversing.... Listen with soft awareness; the baby's spirit may have something to say....... Listen with deep awareness, for there may be no words

— only knowing.... Listen....... If you like, bring particular concerns to mind and witness what occurs to you.... Is there anything that would make your baby happier?...... Pay attention to what occurs to you.... Is there anything you would like to request?......

Welcome your child into life.... Imagine that together you have a healthy wonderful time through pregnancy...getting ready for each other...ready for your lives together.... Making family with love.... Offer a preview of the great wonders and pleasures life offers....

Birth: Getting Ready for Labor (75)

This meditation is designed to follow *Resilience (15)*. You may also want to use *Love (21)*. If you are partnered, when the meditation refers to love, insert your partner's name. If you do not have a partner, think of the love between you and your baby. For optimal effect repeat all the paragraphs as many times as you are inclined. It is good for your partner or other family members to also imagine all that the meditation suggests. Pay special attention to reading this meditation rhythmically.

Feel the love that created the life in your body.... Love. Celebrate loving energy. Love creates life. Feel the love you have for life, for the baby. Breathe it.... Let yourself relax into love.... Let it carry you, as you can relax on water and float.... Love supports you — just as your womb waters support your baby. Feel love support you.... Relax into it.... Let it carry you.... Flow with it.... Breathe with it.... Open to it....

Creating life, giving life, letting life flow through you. Life-breath flows through you.... Breathing.... Breathing life into your baby.... Life-breath moves through your baby. Breathe together.... Offer your baby images of the great pleasures in life that you'll share together. Welcome your baby.

Your baby is born with ease. Born into loving. Born out of loving.... Breathing in and out...breathing in love...breathing out, releasing, letting go.... Breathing.... The baby is born into loving.... Welcome the labor of giving birth. Labor brings life into the world. Welcome it. Trust it. Relax into it....

Feel the energy flow through you. Breathing...carried by breath...releasing, relaxing...a new life is born. Flow with it, as easily as the rhythm of breathing...the rhythm of contractions, the rhythm of life....

Fully tuned to the baby, the baby fully tuned to your body; together the birth is easy...all working in rhythm...with love...together...easy, flowing....each contraction, birth is closer, easier.... Talk to your baby....... With you and your baby working together the birth is easy, powerful, wonderful.... Welcome your baby into life.

Feel the power of new life moving through you; as you contract, life emerges.... Your baby is born.... Breathe...your cervix opens.... New life comes into the world — your baby, a new being, a gift to the world.... Moving with life. Giving life, giving birth — a baby is born. Moving with ease...trusting your body. Breathe....

Each contraction creates space and life emerges. Open to the contractions and your baby is born.... Let go; let your body do what comes naturally.... Releasing, relaxing, and your cervix opens. Each contraction and the baby moves closer into the world. Each contraction is easier.... Your cervix opens...opens...opens, and your baby is born. Breathe...open.... Love carries you, moves through you. Love creates life.... Life creates love....... Let it carry you.... Relax. Breathe.... Let go. Release. Let go; let the flow carry your baby into life.... Let the rhythm bring your baby into the world. Birth is joyous. Your whole being moves with the flow...knows just what is needed to make the birth easy for the baby, for you...together.... It all flows....

Pregnant but Cannot Have the Child (76)

You may want to use *Highest, Wisest, Deepest Self (14)*, *Love (21)*, and/or *Compassion (17)* to augment this meditation.

Tune into what is taking place in your body now. Tell your body what is true for you at this time in your life....... Tell your body that you are sorry....

Tune into the spirit who was getting ready to join you.... Tell the spirit what is true now....... Tell the spirit you are sorry....... Everything has its own time and its own place. Tell the spirit that this is not the right time or place — that this won't work.... Apologize for any confusing messages....... Wish the spirit a good home elsewhere.... You may want to do a ceremony together and release each other. Do what feels right.... Say goodbye....... Grieve....

Warn your body about the processes you are going to undertake.... Tell your body how you are going to take care of it....... Imagine that your body is receptive to resilient life force energies, which will assist it in making the internal adjustments it needs to.... Imagine this occurring....

Sleep (77)

If you are using this meditation to explore the gifts of sleep, use only the first two paragraphs. If you are using it to go to sleep easily, you may want to skip the second paragraph and augment it with *Smoothing the Edges (5)* and/or *Unwinding (47)*. Repeat the last paragraph as many times as needed. Dispense with using a count out; go directly to sleep instead.

Sleep, sound replenishing sleep — your body loves it. Your body melts into it.... Sleep is a gift. Remember the feeling of comforting, soothing, quiet, sound sleep.... Sleep. In sleep the magic of replenishment happens. In sleep dreams offer their gifts. Sleep is a gift.... Let your whole body smile as you remember how delicious sleep is — a gift...soothing sleep. Sleep brings the gift of being ready for a new day, refreshed...revitalized. Sleep is a gift. Sleep brings renewed life....

Imagine just how and when your body needs you to receive this wonderful gift.... Imagine sleeping. Imagine what you need to open, let go, to invite sleep in. What is the optimal rhythm for you?... How much sleep do you need?... Are naps a good idea?...

Imagine that all of yourself settles and opens to sleep's embrace. If any aspect of yourself is distracted, call it in.... Breathe and let it relax too.... Tell it there is always tomorrow, when you'll be replenished and ready to go forward with zest. Imagine letting go and sleep embraces you.... Breath shifts; sleep comes. Breathe.... Listen to your breath quietly move through. Breathe....... In the quiet your body drinks replenishment. In the quiet your whole being transforms all fatigue and you emerge fully renewed, revived. In sleep magic energy visits you. Tender.... Quiet.... Magic.... Tiredness is washed away and you are vitalized.

Let breath carry you into sleep, breathing in and out. Ride breath into sleep. Breathing. Sleep is nearer. Breathing. Breathing in, breathing out.... Listen to breath's soft sound.... Breathing.... Breathing in, breathing out.... Breath carries you to sleep's embrace.... Breathing. Focus on breath. Keep bringing your attention back to your breath.... Breathing.... Let your breath deliver you to sleep's embrace. Sleep is soft; breath is soft.... Breathing.... *(Repeat as many times as you like.)*

Dreams Are a Gift: Remembering Yours (78)

This meditation will help you to deepen or develop an active relationship with your dreams; it becomes increasingly effective with repeated use. Use it right before going to sleep and, if you wake up, before returning to sleep again. You will be more successful if you develop the habit of writing down your dreams upon waking — it gives your dream world the message that you take it seriously and increases recall as you write. Any paragraphs can be repeated to deepen their effect.

Sleep is a passageway into the dream world. Free of the limitations of space and time, dreams transport you into many dimensions. Dreams are a gift. They shift patterns of energy, bring healing, and offer insight. Dreams are a gift.... They digest what has gone by. They get you ready for what is to come.... Appreciate what they offer.... Dreams are amazing: they release and rebalance energy, awaken different perspectives, and reconfigure reality. They are filled with meaning. Dreams are a gift....

To bring your dreams back to your waking world, tell yourself that you will remember your dreams upon waking. Tell yourself this now.... *Expect* it to be true.... Know that with practice you will bring more and more back from the dream world. Your dreams offer gifts to waking life. Know this is true. Appreciate your dream world for helping maintain balance in your life.... Tell yourself that upon waking you'll remember your dreams.... Imagine it.... Expect it to be the case. Expect that every time you practice remembering your dreams you are better able to do so. Be deliberate; feel yourself welcome your dreams.... Be patient; know that they will come in their own time. Your dreams enrich your whole life. Sense how this is so.... Know that in time you are becoming increasingly able to receive and appreciate the gifts of dream life.... Tell yourself this now. Believe it....

Invite a Dream (79)

This meditation is designed to follow *Dreams Are a Gift (78)*; when you awaken after using it, pay careful attention to what lingers in awareness.

If you have a specific concern which you would like to dream about, focus on this issue now.... Bring the details to awareness....... Invite your dream world to dream about it.... Expect a dream that is helpful.... Dreams bring gifts from multiple dimensions. Dreams offer new perspectives. Dreams bring insight. Expect that upon awakening you will remember a dream that is helpful. You will awaken with a knowing about this issue. Your dream world will gift you tonight.... *Expect* it. Feel yourself welcoming whatever your dreams may offer up.... Thank your dream world for giving this concern some attention....

Revisit a Dream (80)

This meditation is designed to follow the first paragraph of *Dreams Are a Gift (78)*.

If there is a dream that is calling you back, you can revisit it now. Let your imagination recreate the dream now.... What was the mood?......the flavor?... Is anyone one else there? Recreate it now.... Assume that any fragments will soon coalesce. Sense what this dream is telling you.... Imagine bringing balance into the scene if it needs it....... If you like, you can project yourself into it.... Open to the meaning....... You may want to converse with a particular aspect of the dream.... Imagine what it has to say for itself....... What is the dream's story?... Imagine.......

Body Care (81)

This meditation is designed to follow *Resilience (15)*. You may want to augment it by using *Inside the Body (65)*. If you have emotional issues that you are acting out through your body, you may also want to use *Breath Is Home; Breath Heals (1G)* or *When You Are Really, Really Upset, Scared, or Obsessed (89)*. If your body is facing specific challenges, ask it what it needs. *Clearing Space Inside with Mental Housecleaning (11)* will augment this meditation.

Take a few moments to just be in your body. Feel it; feel it breathing. Be in your body.... Experience all of your senses.... Your body brings you the experience of the moment....... Be present.... Sense all that is taking place inside your body.... Be in your body.......

Your body is the sanctuary of your spirit. Appreciate your body for providing you with a home...whatever its limitations, it provides you with home.... Your body is sacred.... It depends on you to provide it with good care.... Only you can care for your body. You truly need each other.... Make friends with your own body.... Appreciate it for carrying you around all the time...appreciate it for the hard times it has been through.... Appreciate it for the pleasures it offers you.... Appreciate the joys you offer each other....... Be present in your body, with your body; make friends with your body.... Appreciate that the healing force that harmonizes life energies is always present in your body....

If you have bad feelings about your body or how you treat it, talk it over....... Breathe.... Be patient with your body, with your whole self.... Breathe.... Have good will.... Have generosity toward your body...toward your whole self....... Let yourself be one, be whole....... Your body offers you the gift of life...sensuous life; take joy in it....

Imagine going through the routine of your life and discovering just how your body feels about what you do.... Witness your life from your body's perspective....... Notice what it appreciates.... Notice where its aversions are.... As you bring your life activity to mind, be in your body; notice how it feels.......

Bring awareness to your routine, rhythms of activity and rest... lively and sedentary activities of your day.... How does your body feel about the rhythm?... Does it get the rest it needs?... Does it get the stimulation it needs?...... Be in your body; how does it experience the rhythm of your life?.......

Environment. Sense how your body feels inside the different environments that you spend time in.... At work, at home...notice how your body feels in each of these environments.......

Exercise. Tune to how you exercise...how your body feels.... Do you offer the right amount?...at the right time?... Tune to how your body experiences this....... Do you push too much, not enough?... Notice if any adjustments are needed.... Appreciate your body's strength, stamina, vitality.... Honor your body with the exercise it needs to maintain optimal health. Take joy in your body in motion.... Imagine how exercising fits in the routine of your life.... Exercise feeds your resilience.... Appreciate this.....

Food. Bring to awareness the ways you eat: what, when, where....... What quality of attention you bring to eating....... Review the foods you eat.... Witness how your body responds to the foods you eat....... Is it what your body needs?... Appreciate the satisfaction food brings.... If you eat for other reasons than what your body needs, what are you nourishing? What needs are you feeding?...... How can they be truly satisfied?... Imagine caring for all levels of need...care of your body and care for your feelings in healthful ways.... Imagine how this would be....... Cravings relax and the body smiles inside.... Imagine what a relaxed and healthy relationship with food would feel like....... How would it be as you move through the routine of your life?...... Your body needs food....

If there is anything you are not clear about, bring it to awareness. Imagine trying it out.... Imagine it in detail.... Listen deeply; notice how your body feels about it....... If there seem to be conflicting needs, negotiate.......Where is balance?...... Note any adjustments that would increase well-being.......

Tell your body what you are willing to do to provide it with care. Be specific.... Imagine doing it.......

Your body is sensuous.... Your body is healthy.... Reside in gratitude for your body. It offers the gift of life.... Imagine a healthful life....... Have joy.... Life is a sacred gift....

Food: A Blessing (82)

If you are working with some kind of compulsion related to food, follow this meditation with *Releasing Addiction: From Compulsion to Choice (91)*. It can be augmented with *Reside in the Quiet (3)*.

Food is life loving itself.... Food sustains life. Food provides us with life...with ways to celebrate life. Food is an invitation to commune with each other...with life itself...in celebration.

Food comes from nature. Food is our lifeline into our own nature. Nourishment. Food connects us to our bodies, to the Earth, to our natures, to nature itself.... Food brings us health. Food brings us pleasure. Food brings us life. Food. Contemplate it....... Give thanks to the Earth for providing food.... Give thanks to all who offered their lives and work to provide it....

Honor the sanctity of food in your life.... Relax into knowing what a healthy relationship to food is for you....... How and what may you eat in a manner that invites you to celebrate your own life?... How or what might you eat that invites you to honor your own body?... How or what might you eat that makes you healthy?...... What food does your body want for its strength, balance, and vitality?...... Breathe...be in your body.... Open to your experience.......

If you would like to know how your body responds to a specific food, bring it to awareness now and witness how your body responds to it.... In the quiet, experience your body and the food sharing presence.... Witness the resonance.... What do you sense?... Does it sing? Is it somehow off-key...or altogether jangled?... Witness the resonance.... If you would like to know how your body feels about any other foods, bring them to mind one at a time and experience your body response. Trust your body....... Trust your sense.

In whatever way you may have been compulsive about food, breathe through it....... Forgive yourself. Remember you are sacred as you are, and food is sacred.... Breathe through all the ways you have tension in relation to food. Give yourself permission to have a relaxed relationship with food. How would that look or feel for you?... How would your day-to-day life be if you were to have a fully relaxed and healthy relationship with food? Notice how that feels in your body.... How that affects the routines of your life....... Tell your body what you are willing to do to provide it with care, tenderness...to meet its true needs. Be specific....

Food is a gift to life, to your life....

River of Life Dissolves Blockage (83)

This meditation is for general maintenance of well-being. Use all or parts of it.

Imagine that it's summertime; you're sitting on a riverbank by a peaceful river which is gently flowing before you.... It is a warm sunny spot; there is lots of grass to sit in.... Imagine the ground below you...the river meandering down...the flow of the water...the sky above — puffy clouds float by overhead.... A gentle breeze makes the grasses dance gracefully...butterflies flutter among the flowers; birds sing. Create the details of this place...the quality of the air, any scents, the sounds.... Be in the beauty. Feel it.... Slowly absorb the serenity this place offers.... Breathe it in.......

Move your attention to the river in front of you. Watch the water flowing...flowing downstream...the constantly changing forms on the surface of the water...the movement of the water...the fluidity...watch the water move before you.... Listen to the sounds it makes.... Watch the water; watch the water so carefully, so intently, that you begin to detect the sensations of the water flowing in your own body...the currents that flow through you.... *(Optional: repeat paragraph.)*

Imagine the water transforms into pure life force energy that moves through you. Imagine placing your body in alignment with this river of life force energy. Imagine it comes in through the top of your head and flows down and out through the tips of your fingers and the tips of your toes.... Your breath, your heartbeat keeps it moving through...in through your head and out through your toes, continually flowing through.... Feel it flowing through, cleansing you....

Energy flowing through, just as blood flows through you, just as water flows over the riverbed, constantly moving downstream. Experience this life force energy flowing through you from head to toe, the river of life constantly flowing through.... It dissolves tension in your body...soothing you...smoothing the edges...creating openness, and the energy moves even more easily.... Feel it flow through every cell of which your body is composed.... Just as blood flows through you — feel life force energy flow through....

Dissolving Blockage (83A)

Sense how easily it flows. Sense where it doesn't flow through quite so easily...any blocks — anything that you're holding onto physically......or emotionally. What impedes the energy flow?... It may have to move around, like big rocks in the middle of the river. Notice where the energy has to flow around instead of through....

Focus on one blockage that seems unyielding.... Sense the mood of the blockage. Is it sluggish or brittle? Is it nervous?... What's its story?... Imagine it....... Ask the block what it is doing there. It may not answer you verbally, but you'll sense its experience.... Experience what's true for it....... Listen deeply...patiently.... Ask what it is protecting you from....... Ask it what it wants....... Ask what is needed in order to release...to trust and let go....... Sense what is so.......

Acknowledge what you need to do so it releases.... Decide if you are willing to.... If you are, imagine yourself doing so.... Feel the river of energy begin to dissolve the blockage.... Breathe...release.... If you're not willing to do what's needed, or the black won't dissolve, notice how you can live more comfortably with it for the time being. Breathe with it....

If there is any other blockage you would like to work through do this now....

(Optional: repeat the two preceding paragraphs.)

Breathe and release.... Notice how it is now easier to be supported by the river of life, to be carried by it.... Instead of expending your energy in holding patterns, you are carried by the energy.... Feel it support you.... Feel yourself flowing with it....

Flowing Through Life (83B)

Feel how it gives you vitality — the gift of life.... Just as the river goes through rapids...through falls...and meanders through twists and turns.... Imagine your body moving into activity, riding the energy through your days, as water travels through the land...through all the different landscapes of life.......

Sense the changing rhythms in your life as you move through the terrain of your days.... Witness activity and rest...active and then calm.... Let the life flowing through you give you all the energy you need for your activities.... Feel the currents of energy flowing through...sustaining you as you move through the different environs of life....

Feel the rhythms of your body — the rhythms that your health rides upon. Harmonize your activities with the rhythms of your body...with the currents of the life force........ Notice what changes you need to make in how you move through your days.... Harmonize your routine with the currents in the river of life.... You maintain good health when your daily activities and your body rhythms are in harmony with one another....

Make the shifts needed to move with the currents of life force energy.... When the energy flows you are fully healthy.... Trust the flow of life....

GETTING UNSTUCK: EMOTIONAL RESILIENCE

This section allows you to resolve unfinished experiences, face really hard times, and learn what you need in order to remain present. While you cannot change the past, you can claim power over your relationship to it. How you carry your past experiences immensely influences your current experience. It is when we let the past get stuck inside that we find ourselves cut off from the present and likely to recreate similar circumstances over again. All of the meditations in Getting Unstuck are designed to help you create emotional flexibility, empowering you to fully open to what life offers you in the present.

It is good to work with others when you are confronting areas that are particularly painful. See Supporting Each Other (Part II, Page 57). Tension is likely to come up during this work; you may want to use *Protected View (12)*. When tension comes up in the middle of your work, focus on your breath; use *Breath Is Home; Breath Heals (1G)* and *When You Are Really, Really Upset, Scared, or Obsessed (89)*. *Clearing Space Inside with Mental Housecleaning (11)* will augment any of the meditations in this section. Also see the Social Conditioning survey (Appendix). If you are addressing issues of abuse, see Emotionally Charged Issues (Part II, Page 58) and the meditations that appear under the heading Holding Your Own.

Emotional Metamorphosis (84)

This meditation addresses whatever weighs your heart down. It develops emotional resilience. *Inner Witness (1H)* or *Highest, Wisest, Deepest Self (14)*, *The Transformative Power of Breath (45)*, and/or parts of *Breath Is Home; Breath Heals (1G)* will augment it.

Your breath transforms your body with each breath you take. Your breath breathes in new energy, breathes out old energy.... Each breath renews you.

Your breath is magic. Your breath transforms you every moment of your life. You are now going to use your breath to transform your emotions — bring in new energy, release stale energy. Your breath renews your emotional body, too.

Bring to awareness whatever weighs on your spirit...feelings that drag you down...feelings you would prefer to avoid.... You may want to work with the recent past or a time long ago...feelings that weigh on your spirit...anxieties...hard times...disillusion...distress...aversion to yourself or another...humiliation... anger... feelings that come up again and again for you, for they seem to fester right below the surface.... Pull these feelings into the light of awareness.... Breathe. Invite the feelings you've put away into the closet of avoidance. They may appear to you in symbolic form...in colors, sounds, textures, snapshots of the past.... However you imagine it, welcome the feelings that have weighed you down.... Imagine that they appear in awareness symbolically.... Keep breathing; let your feelings breathe again.... Each breath transforms your body. Your breath draws in renewal; your breath releases and carries away stale energy.... Each breath rejuvenates you. Your breath transforms you every moment of your life.... Let your feelings breathe.... Bring in new energy; release stale energy — your breath renews your emotional body, too. Breathe....

Feelings you put away in the closet of avoidance develop a magnetic charge, drawing in dramas that will give them a role again.... The energy inside them is potent.... When you let them be...let them breathe, they transform of their own accord. Breathe....

Breath transforms them into power — your power. Feel it.... Feel yourself becoming fluid.... These are your feelings; you choose how to experience them.... They are your feelings; their energy moves.... You can choose the direction.... They are your feelings. They have great power.... Experience them build strength of character.... Breathe. Feel your emotions breathe.... Let them be.... Let them breathe.... Notice how their quality begins to shift as they are included in the great flow of life force energy.... Sense transformation.... Breathe....

Know that when your feelings breathe, they too naturally transform. Just as food becomes energy for your body, your difficulties become strength for your character.... Let your breath transform the feelings.... Feel a softening....

Sense the transformation.... Maybe humiliation becomes humility.... Witness; maybe frustration transforms into patience...pain into sensitivity...anxiety becomes discernment...hatred turns into forgiveness.... Maybe anger gives birth to courage.... Breathe. However your particular feelings transform themselves, feel a conversion taking place deep inside you.... Sense a shift in your emotional body.......

Feel your emotional body breathing.... Breathe new life into your emotional life.... Notice how the textures, rhythms, colors change.... Feel a different quality beginning to emerge within you.... Breath carries the resilience of life — the stiff and hardened energy yields, softens....

Just as your breath washes through every single cell of which you are composed, sense your whole emotional body taking deep breaths...transforming feelings lodged deep inside.... Imagine it.... As though your emotional self stands up and stretches like a cat...yawns.... Feel the atmosphere in which you reside softening, all the edges, all the hard spots cramped in your emotional body, softening. Feel your spirit lift.......

Sense your emotional body becoming agile and limber — responsive to new experience, fluid, free — for you have transmuted all the rigidified energy that caused you to restrain yourself.... Witness your emotional energy moving from constriction to openness...vitality flows through...emotional energy circulating again — carrying vital life force...fluid...feel it.... Breathe. Life is enriched with color, with depth.

In the presence of this conversion witness what gift these experiences have brought into your life.... What lessons are there for you?...... Sense how this metamorphosis will influence your day-to-day life.... Imagine how it changes the quality of your responsiveness....... Imagine yourself in a challenging situation, and notice how it unfolds this time....... Feel yourself opening to an entirely new experience.... Your life fills with color.... Feel a lightness opening in your spirit.... No longer weighed down; feel as though your spirit soars like the birds fly through the sky....... Imagine yourself moving through your life emotionally breathing — always....

Cut Loose the "Shoulds" (85)

This meditation enables you to discern what is motivating your actions. With it you can reclaim your ability to make choices that are rooted in your own values and priorities and avoid scrambling to meet other people's expectations. You develop emotional autonomy so you do not get caught in the trap of needing the approval of others. At the end it is good to specify family or peer pressure you do not want to succumb to. *Inner Witness (1H)* or *Highest, Wisest, Deepest Self (14)* and *Call Upon Your Life-Affirming Values (24)* will augment this meditation.

Make note: are there any voices that call you?... Any energy that tugs at you? Pulls at you?... Pulls you off balance, so rather than life proceeding gracefully, motion becomes strained, hard, difficult, jerky, or clumsy, confused, or disoriented.... Witness what pulls at you.... Witness what pushes at you.... What tugs at you?... Pronouncements on how it should be, how you ought to be, what should have been.... They may be feelings directed toward you from others — feelings you've let get under your skin and trip you up...obligations to prove yourself...voices that tell you, "You can't anyhow, so why bother trying?"... What nags you? Anything badgering you?... Judging you?... Energy that makes everything feel lopsided somehow.... Notice the quality of these energies...the textures of these energies.... They each want their way.... They each want to compel you.... They are all compulsive.... They are all controlling.... They are never satisfied. Witness them.... What do they tell you?......

Imagine as though each of the calls, the tugs, the pulls is an invisible cord crossing your path, tripping you up; or maybe it hooks right into you and yanks you off your path altogether — energy cords entangling you....... They each have a texture of their own.... They are all attached to this or that — how things should be, how you ought to be, what should have happened, wants, fears, regrets, expectations — yours or others... parental voices....They're always barking orders at you. They are never satisfied.... All these cords are attached to some idea of how things could have been, or should be otherwise, or how you should be. Energy cords sap your vitality. They jerk you out of balance. They pull you out of the present and drop you where you can't act anyway — for all action takes place in the present.... Witness what cords pull at you.......

Take time to cut or pull out the cords.... Unhook...detach...and let them go...one by one, or all at once, or a few at a time — whatever feels right. Breathe.... Detach.... Imagine disengaging.... As you exhale feel it all releasing.... Let go of self-recriminations.... Release anyone else's expectations of how you ought to be.... Breathe it all out.... Imagine the cords.... Cut them or pull them out.... Unhook.... Detach.... Bid them farewell.... Imagine disengaging.... Feel your energy untangling. Let them go.... Imagine that the cords snap back into the source of themselves, leaving you with what is so, fully present...in your truth.... They recede, leaving you in the expanse of present time.... Feel a sense of relief....

You may feel sad, relieved, vulnerable, a little disoriented — whatever your feelings — breathe.... Let them flow through you, healing you.... Breathe with the feelings, knowing that it is good to free yourself to be your true self.... Imagine that where the cords used to be attached a gentle energy comes in and soothes the exposed raw spots. Breathe.... Patience, compassion, love, forgiveness form a gentle caressing touch.... Sense it.... Draw it in with breath. Send it to the raw spots....

Know that the energy that held the cords in place is now available for you to live by your truth.... Imagine telling your past self how things are different now; you get to be your true self now.... You can relax, settle down in present time...experiencing what is so. Honoring who you are. Now you can move gracefully — no longer awkward.... Released, you are free to move forward on the path of your life easily, gracefully — unencumbered.... Imagine this in different settings in your life....... Notice if there is anything you need to say to anyone....... Trust that, in fact, you have let go and can take joy in life — dance.... Affirm yourself...and make choices out of your own truth. Free....

Love Yourself and the Future Welcomes You (86)

This meditation is good for reclaiming wholeness and for healing from the effects of being harsh on yourself. *Compassion (17)* will augment it.

Remember your own goodness.... Acknowledge yourself for all your efforts.... Appreciate yourself for all that you have been through.... Give yourself permission to relax into the source of your own good will.... However you experience that.... Appreciate all of the particular ways you have of being in the world that you enjoy, that enable you to enjoy the world.... Recognize those qualities in yourself that are capable of deep feelings of love.... Recognize those qualities you possess that are capable of deep feelings of excitement...aspects of yourself that respond with humor...passion...creativity...care.... The spark inside comes alive...sometimes it dances...sometimes it glows warmly....

Feel these qualities in yourself as though they were currents, like underground springs that feed the ground of your being.... Feel your goodness flowing.... It glows.... It sings and dances....

Now notice how you tend to judge yourself...all the doubts, the "shoulds," the ways you think you ought to be...the ways you think you are that you shouldn't be.... What arguments do you have with yourself?... Notice the areas where you constrict your energy, where energy is dense, hard or cold, brittle, constrained....... Give yourself permission to let go of constriction.... Breathe through it. Transform it. Breathe....... As you let go, notice that space is made for healing energy to come through.... Draw on the spring of all those marvelous qualities. Breathe.... Fill your whole being with these wonderful energies. Let the springs of goodness rise and fill your whole self with color, warmth, vibrancy.... Imagine it.... Breathe.... Open to goodness.

Bathe yourself in these wonderful energies...compassion...love...humor, kindness.... Accept yourself completely.... Listen to what you tell yourself when you are infused with these energies.... As you relax into acceptance, you no longer need to expend energy keeping parts of yourself pushed away; instead let yourself be bathed by the springs of goodness. Feel it; feel this in your body....

Notice where this energy is needed.... Let it flow into neglected aspects — rejected aspects of yourself...the tight places, the knots, the tensions, the empty spots, the sides of yourself you have ignored, the aspects you prefer to leave alone.... Let all the goodness of your being, of being itself flow into these parts of yourself.... Breathe.... Fill these places with the colors of life.... Breathe life into them.......

Welcome them.... Let those spaces that got tight and rigidified...that were neglected or rejected...let springs of goodness flow up into them.... Feel them soften...be made supple again.... Imagine it; all the self-doubt, all the self-hatred, all the confusion, dissolves with this good energy.... Breathe it.... Like ice that melts in the sun. Feel your whole self glow, dance, sing.... Breathe.

Tell yourself that who you are is all that you need to be. Know that as you fully accept yourself, you open to a fresh experience — in whatever way change is needed it happens easily, for your energy is no longer caught in constriction; instead it is free to rise to the occasion.... Feel yourself opening fully to life. As you welcome yourself, the future welcomes you.... Feel it...comfortable, appreciated, loved. Just as you're welcome in the home of a loved one.... Feel yourself fully welcomed into the future.... The future has a home for your life; it holds a place for you...to be fully who you are. Experience the future welcoming you....

From Reaction to Response: Turning Buttons into Pearls (87)

If you haven't fully healed from a painful experience, you will be hypersensitive when anything reminds you of it — a defensive mode automatically kicks in, and you will react rather than respond. This meditation creates a way for you to work through unresolved incidents, clearing the stuck energies so you are no longer locked into the past and doomed to repeat history. If you are working with especially difficult feelings, open your meditation with *Inner Witness (1H)* or *Highest, Wisest, Deepest Self (14)* and use *Protected View (12)* and/or parts of *Breath Is Home; Breath Heals (1G)*.

Now view how you've been lately.... Focus on whatever has been bothering you lately.... Witness what happens that makes you pull your energy back — withdraw...or maybe numbly barge ahead.... Notice how it is you shrink from life when you tighten up.... Recall what you say to yourself.... Witness what has been troublesome lately.... What has been bothersome lately.... What makes you tense up.... Bring it to awareness now.......

Notice the energy in others.... What incites you...a particular attitude...a tone of voice...an assumption?... What conditions make the sparks fly or freeze everything up?...... Where are your buttons?... What gets triggered in you?... What happens when you no longer respond openly?... Have you gone into automatic reaction? Do you feel like you've been here before?... What provokes you?... Find your buttons.......

What places get touched inside you?... Where are your sensitive spots inside?... Find them — there is a concentration of energy there.... This energy is the counterpart of the driving force outside — in fact this place inside you has such an intensity of magnetic energy that it pulls into your sphere of experience these particularly upsetting circumstances. What ingredients in the troubling situations ignite you?... It's like a chemical reaction — between the outside and the inside...and you're set off in reaction.... Notice the energy inside you.... It is as though you have a rough spot and certain kinds of things get hooked there....

Let go of the exterior stimulus for the moment; put away the reaction and focus on that place inside you that gets touched off, the sensitive spot that gets pushed on....... It might have a shell around it, protecting a tender spot.... Zero in on the place inside.... There is an intense concentration of energy there.... Imagine how you can care for that place inside you.... It may need some special attention.... It may have been neglected; it may have been hurt.... It may have become hard and cold; or maybe it has become hot and needs to be cooled.... Notice what qualities reside in this place inside.... What's needed so it doesn't numb out or get hypersensitive?...... Imagine talking to your sensitive spot.... Ask it what it thinks it's protecting you from.... Ask it what it's afraid of.... Ask it what it needs.... Sense what it wants.... What will give it more room inside so it's not so cramped?...

You have whole vignettes of the past trapped in this place inside.... Unresolved times, times that hurt in some way...as though these moments froze and got trapped inside you. It is time to liberate them.... This sensitive spot has a face from the past where some of its charge came from.... When did you feel similarly?... What happened at the time?... How did you protect yourself at the time?... What did you conclude at the time?... Did you surmise anything about life?... Or decide how you had to be?...... How were you hurt back then?...... Breathe. Revisit the past.... Witness it.

What choices did you make at the time?... Knowing what you know now, would you take care of yourself differently?... Did you have other options?... Was there any part of you that had to be ignored at the time?... Were there feelings that couldn't be expressed at the time?... Actions that couldn't be taken at the time?...

Now let your imagination roll with these past inclinations.... Imagine what you wished had happened at the time.... What did you wish you could have done?... Don't worry if you really could have or would have; simply give your feelings what they craved for at the time.... In the privacy of your mind, give life to the fantasies you had at the time.... Imagine it vividly, as though that's what did happen.... How would that have been?... Feel it.... Breathe...as you roll with the energy, it rolls right out of that place inside where it's been trapped all this time.... You no longer need to repress it. You no longer need to suppress it.... Let your imagination roll with what you wanted at the time. Imagine it vividly.... Set your fantasies free.... Breathe.... Release.... Watch them roll out of you.... Feel the energy go.... Feel relief....... Breathe it out.... Know that you have now changed how you carry the past inside you....

Imagine that your sensitive spot inside now treats these times past like an oyster transforming irritants into pearls.... Imagine it.... What pearls of wisdom have these experiences given you?... Let the irritants be transformed. What do you know now that you didn't know before?...... Is there anything you need to express to anyone about all this?...

If you have any other vignettes trapped inside that sensitive spot, work with them.... Let the energy be transformed; breathe out and release the energy.......

How can you protect yourself next time?... Notice what's needed to maintain your integrity.... Imagine how you would respond differently.... Tell that place inside how things are different now.... Be specific.... Tell that spot all about what you have learned and how it has empowered you and expanded your options.... Feel this new way of being soak into that vulnerable place.... Breathe.... Send breath there.... Feel it getting stronger.... Feel how the quality of magnetic energy has transformed; it is now entirely different in this place inside.... Feel the change.... Breathe.

Notice if there's anything you can give this part of you in the routine of your life...attention...care...so that this part heals, becomes flexible and strong.... Ask it what it wants.......

Now bring back to mind the circumstances you focused on earlier in the meditation — the ones that set off the chain reaction.... Transformation has taken place; witness how you respond this time.... Now you respond with clarity.... Your whole self responds, not just the automatic pilot.... Feel the difference.... Feel how your options have expanded.... Breathe.

Imagine it unfolding differently the next time the particular ingredients come together that in the past set you off. You've changed their chemistry, for you've changed your side of the scene.... Imagine it.... Imagine that the pearls of wisdom provide a presence of deep knowing that pervades the whole scene.

Now you experience your feelings clearly, knowing what you need to express or ask for from others.... Now you're able to let your experience flow, each moment being different than the moment before.... No more automatic pilot. Feel yourself able to be fully present with your feelings...no longer tense, withdrawn, or numbly barging ahead. Instead, fully present feelings flow through you, not getting stuck inside, not causing chain reactions later on.... Know that by giving your feelings life you give yourself the gift of being fully present....

Death: Coming to Terms with Yours (88)

Lake of Reflection (6), *Inner Witness (1H)*, or *Highest, Wisest, Deepest Self (14)* will enhance this meditation. If tension comes up use *Breath Is Home; Breath Heals (1G)*.

Life is never certain. The one thing that is certain is that one day death will come. It could be tomorrow; it could be decades away.... Reside in the knowledge that life is not permanent — that one day you will die. Breathe. Let yourself be with this knowledge.... Breathe. Aspire to be relaxed about it. Breathe.... Imagine your body no longer alive; you have already died. Imagine looking at your body dead.......

As if your death were imminent look back over your life and appreciate the gifts that it has brought you....... Acknowledge the gifts you have given — acknowledge your legacy....... Breathe and reflect.... Acknowledge what your life has been up till now.... Acknowledge the challenges...the joys...the lessons.... Review the chapters of your life....... Acknowledge the depth and breadth of your life.......

Be present with the idea that your death is just around the corner....... If feelings are screaming, take time to let your spiritual self care for your emotional self — whatever that means to you — let your spiritual self care for your emotional self....... Give your feelings the attention they deserve....... Breathe with them.......

If you knew you were to die in the next season, what would you want to be sure you said or did before your death?...... What is most important to you?...... How would you live this next season?...... Is there anything you have always wanted to do that you would make sure you really did?......

What is needed for you to truly rest in peace?...... Is there anything that you need to say to a loved one?...... Are there feelings that point to anything that needs attending to?...... Do you have feelings of being wronged somehow...or of having wronged another?... Is forgiveness needed anywhere?...... Are there feelings that point to anything that needs attending to?......anything that needs to be said...anything that needs to be done?...... Are there aspects of your life that need to be put in order so you may rest in peace?......any unfinished business that you never seem to get around to?...

What do you need for your spirit to be free?...... Reflect on all of this. Let yourself be with what is true for you. Breathe.... Reflect.......

Now take time to let these reflections illuminate what this means about how you are living now. Are you living in accordance with what is most important to you?... Are any changes in order?... Is there anything that you choose to do so that you could rest in peace if you did die tomorrow?......

What if you were to live each day as if it were your last?...... Review what is true for you. Acknowledge the gift of your life. Savor it....... Choose how you will honor it.......

When You Are Really, Really Upset, Scared, or Obsessed (89)

This meditation is designed to follow *Inner Witness (1H)* and *Inner Refuge (9)*; if you prefer you may use *Highest, Wisest, Deepest Self (14)* instead of *Inner Witness (1H)*. If you are using When You Are Really, Really Upset, Scared, or Obsessed to deal with a strong emotional reaction rather than a habituated pattern, skip the last two paragraphs. To help overcome compulsive behavior or a phobia, replace the word "upset" with "obsessed" or "afraid." Repeat the final paragraph as many times as you like. If tension comes up and really takes hold, direct yourself to leave the imaginary scene altogether, and use *Inner Refuge (9)* and/or *Breath Is Home; Breath Heals (1G)* until you are fully relaxed; then go back to the challenging scene in your mind's eye. Practice until you can maintain a relaxed state at the same time as you imagine the challenge. Have patience — it may take numerous meditation sittings before you are successful. *Making Magic (43)* will augment this meditation — insert it where indicated and invoke the quality of compassion. Use parts of *Breath Is Home; Breath Heals (1G)* and/or *Protected View (12)* if you are working with fear. Parts of *From Reaction to Response (87)* may also be useful, as will *Clearing Space Inside with Mental Housecleaning (11)*. Though you can work with this meditation on your own, it is best to have someone read it to you — see Supporting Each Other (Part II, Page 57).

Breathe. Witness.... Invite in the part of you that is really upset. Witness. Breathe.... Every time you find yourself in your feelings, breathe.... Breathe through them. Welcome the part of you that is upset and simply be with her.... Don't be in your feelings; be with your feelings........ Imagine seeing the part of you who is upset in front of you.... Breathe. Meet her with soft attention. Be with her.... Comfort her.... Let her have her feelings, all of her feelings. Breathe.... Let her scream; let her have a tantrum; let her wail; whatever she needs to do to express her feelings — let her do it. Offer her soft attention.... Be with her; breathe...witness.... Give her what she needs to discharge and balance her energy.... If she's hot bring in cool; maybe she could go for a refreshing swim.... If she's cold maybe she could soak up the hot sun.... Give her what she needs to discharge and balance her energy.... Shine compassion her way....... *(If appropriate, insert* Making Magic *here.)*

After she calms down, be with her and tune to the vulnerability.... What is the fear?... What does she want protection from?... Is there anything she feels she has to defend?...... How can she be cared for?... Reassured?... Be kind to her.... Imagine giving her what she needs....... Feel her energy shift....

Invite her to take up the challenge.... Tell her you will accompany her through what she finds most difficult.... Or maybe what is hardest is refraining from something and letting go....... Whatever the difficulty, imagine accompanying her through it....... Imagine that the Witness and the part of you who is challenged enter into the scene that has caused such distress in the past. Imagine it.... Imagine it in detail. Keep breathing.... Breathing through it.... Breathe together and do what is most difficult.... As soon as tension arises, stop and breathe...keep breathing.... Relax.... Clear your mind; if need be, shift your attention all together so you can completely relax. Breathe.... When you are relaxed again, then go back to the task. Notice that each time it gets a little easier....... Be patient; breathe, and know that as you breathe through, change happens. Breathe, and breath gets you through. Witness this is true....

Forgive Yourself (90)

This meditation addresses regrets. Begin it with *Inner Refuge (9)* and/or *Compassion (17)*. If tension comes up use parts of *Breath Is Home: Breath Heals (1G)*.

You occupy the space of transformation...the place of healing and empowerment. You choose how to carry yourself forward into the future.... Here you can use the past as a great source of strength. Your past is the ground in which your wisdom grows. Know that all that has transpired in your life is exactly what you need to be equal to what the future has in store....

Remember those times in your life that you did something, got involved in some way that you feel bad about now.... Remember your regrets...things you wish hadn't happened.... Maybe you wish you had been different...or made different judgments...or made different choices.... Somehow you feel you failed in some way.... Remember your regrets.... Recall them.... Focus your attention on the times where you shrink from your own experience...when you feel remorse.... You may shudder a little, recoil a little... it still feels bad.... Breathe.

Witness when you find yourself withdrawing from your experience...withdrawing from your own self...feeling aversion or anger...or maybe arguing with yourself. Maybe lying to yourself. Maybe part of you wants to get away from another part.... Breathe.... Witness your response to your own self.... Let yourself be with your whole experience.... Breathe....

What happened?...... Notice if you still harbor any feelings of blame or shame...any resentment...any humiliation.... Do you find yourself wishing, "If only...?" Breathe.... Let these times be.... Breathe through these feelings, for they get toxic if you hold onto them for long.... Breathe.... Accept what happened.... Forgive yourself; you did what you could.... We all make mistakes. Let yourself be humble.... Breathe kindness into the past.... Be gentle with yourself. Breathe....: Maybe invite some humor in...lighten up the scene....... Let yourself breathe; loosen it up.......

Whenever you recoil from yourself you give away your power. If ever you wall yourself off from your experience, you create psychic carcinogens.... Invite the transformative healing powers of breath to dissolve the walls inside.... Breathe through the walls now.... Welcome the feelings that arise as you breathe the walls away.... Breathe into them.... Breathe healing into these times.... Breathe healing into your feelings.... Breathe....

Assure yourself that you did as well as you could have....... Be kind toward yourself — you deserve it. Welcome those aspects of your being that have been walled away, pushed into the shadows.... Tell the part of you that was banished that you know it had a hard time of it.... Forgive it.... Welcome back all aspects of who you are. You deserve to be whole again.... Experience relief deep inside as you open....... Feel yourself healing.... Take a deep breath and relax into your wholeness....

Be compassionate with yourself. Express forgiveness to yourself.... Let yourself know the lessons learned.... Let yourself know and let go...move on.... Feel forgiveness in your heart....... Appreciate the wisdom you have gained...a gift for building character....

If you have trouble letting go, there is still learning to be gained.... Witness what is to be known here....... Listen deeply....... Is there anything that needs to be said and done to make amends?... What are the gifts of this experience?... As you acknowledge the lessons learned, tell your hurt self that you know better now and this won't happen again....... You have changed; times have changed. You know better now.... Reassure yourself.... Breathe and accept what is so.... The past is done; the future opens to fresh experience when you let go.......

Releasing Addiction: From Compulsion to Choice (91)

You may want to open this meditation with *Breath Is Home; Breath Heals (1G)*; then use *Resilience (15)*, *Personal Power (19)*, and the first four paragraphs of *Claim Your Space (60)*. If you are not dealing with a physical addiction, skip the paragraph that works with the cells in your body. The endings *Putting Your Will to Work (13G)* and *Support (13H)* will increase the effectiveness of this meditation.

Find that place inside you that values you.... Find that place inside you where the will to live is pulsating through you. Feel it....... There is a habit you have, a compulsion you have. Witness it.... There is a craving pushing at you, pulling at you.... Sometimes it seems to come from deep inside you.... It can be very demanding; sometimes it even feels bigger than you. Tune to this craving.... As you inhale gather up all of its energy.... Let it take form in your mind's eye. Invite this compulsion to reveal itself to you. Imagine it before you.... Witness it.... What kind of personality does it have? Is it dense?... restless?... Demanding? Agitated? Cynical? Manipulative? What kind of personality does this craving have?... Witness it. Breathe and simply notice the qualities it possesses....

Now, with breath, breathe space into the scene.... Imagine that with breath, with each exhalation of breath, you create a quality of openness all around this energy.... Breathe.... As you breathe, imagine the scene opens some.... Breathe. Breathe space all around the craving.... Breath carries the power of transformation. Breathe....

In the space you have created invite the craving to join you in ritual. Do a ritual of transformation.... With breath, draw in the resilient powers of life itself.... Draw in the benevolent forces of the universe.... Invite the powers you need to support you and you will succeed. Breathe.... Imagine that the craving itself breathes and relaxes some. Give it space to appreciate relaxing with breath.... Open to vulnerability; let it be okay.... Sense it loosening up some and gaining a wider view.... Invite this compulsion to talk to you. How is it doing?... Converse together. Imagine it....... Where is the charge?... What is the desire?... Is there avoidance? What's being avoided?...... What's true for you?...for it?... Let yourself know what's so....

Breathe together.... As you breathe, insert lots of space. Breathe together.... This is the space in which choice takes place.... Breath brings with it the gift of choice. Appreciate this.... The choice is always yours.... Breathe, and give yourself the space to make choice mindfully. Breathe.... First decide if you accept the gift of choice. There are two faces to the gift of choice: freedom and responsibility.... Decide if you want the gift.... If you do, then inform the craving that there is now going to be a transfer of power. Inform it that you are taking over now.......

Imagine a transfer of power.... Feel a shift of energy.... Tell the craving that the situation has changed. You are now in charge. It used to be that you would indulge and regret it. That is in the past. Now you might want to, but you won't. It is much better to want to and not, than to do it and want not to. You are in charge now.... Tell the craving it has a new role now. Tell it that its very presence reminds you of your resolve.... Life is sacred; your life is sacred. Only you can take care of you. Invite it to direct all of its energies into supporting you, so that together you both honor the life that you have been given.... You deserve it.

Do a ritual in honor of your being. Feel the craving transform into an ally who helps you look deep into the soul. Every time it appears you get another glimpse of your soul.... Ask your ally if it has a new name.... Ask your ally to join you on a journey to clean up your insides. Your ally knows you intimately, knows all your weaknesses, all the twists and turns of your thinking patterns.... Invite your ally to join you in cleaning up your inner world.... Tell your ally that you are now going to cleanse yourself of all that stands in the way of honoring your own self. Now find that part inside that has given in and decided you don't matter anyhow, or that says that nothing really matters anyway.... Breathe out all of that sentiment....... Breathe it all out....... As you inhale imagine that you and your ally project an aura that says, "I do matter!" Tell your whole self this is true! Shout it out, so your whole insides hear: "I do matter! I count!" Go through your inner landscape gathering up all of the thoughts that say otherwise.... Gather up all those thoughts and banish them.... Breathe them out. They are wrong; and they no longer belong.... You are alive; your body deserves to be honored. It is true. Apologize to your inner self for past abuse and neglect....... You deserve a good quality life. Reside in this knowledge. It is true....

With your ally, take time to care for yourself; be present with your inner experience.... There may be things you know that you wish you didn't and feelings you have that you'd just as soon you didn't have.... Now that you have taken charge, they surface — raw and exposed, no longer covered up by old ways.... With your ally, take time to take care of your feelings.... Be gentle with yourself.... Breathe.... Give yourself permission to have the feelings you have....... Breathe through your feelings. Trust breath to carry you through....... Remember you are not alone...there are those who support you.... Open to the support there is for you.... Remember life is resilient; it heals heart and spirit.......

Take time to converse with the cellular craving in your body.... Talk to the cells; tell them to relax and breathe.... Tell them that it might be hard for a while, but in the end everybody will be happier....... Tell them that if ever they feel that familiar sensation of craving, it has now taken on a new meaning. Tell them that a healthy response to these sensations is to breathe, to breathe in space...for in breath resilience is found; in breath courage is found; in breath choice is found. Give them a lesson in breathing.... Tell them that it is likely to be hard, but breath will carry them through....

Tell yourself that every time you feel the want, every time you feel the impulse, you'll remember breath and breathe through it.... The very presence of the want is a reminder of your strength of character, of your courage. It is an entry point for glimpsing your soul.... Tell yourself that all the craving is transformed into an invitation to look deeper into the soul...to be whole...to acknowledge your wounds...to heal.... Tell yourself this now. Feel this perspective sink into your body and mind.....

Stretch your imagination into the future and imagine how you'll respond if ever the old sensations appear again.... Imagine what support there is for you to hold on to your gift of choice, hold on to responsibility and freedom.... What changes do you need to make to hold your ground?... Imagine what you'll do differently. Imagine this in detail....... Notice how this feels.... Notice what you might do to make the going a little easier.... Remember your ally.... Build the boundaries you need to successfully take care of yourself. Who to see.... Who to stay separate from.... Insert new patterns of thought and action.... Imagine it specifically....... Embody the new you.......

If ever you relapse know that you can use it as an opportunity to hone your will even more skillfully and to come to know yourself even better.... You are fully capable of success. The choice is yours — always yours. Claim your life. It is yours....... Only you can care for yourself; you deserve good care. Tell yourself this.... It is true....

Premonition or Anxiety?: From Victim to Visionary (92)

This meditation is for exploring and transforming anxieties. You may want to lead into this one with *Protected View (12)*. Use parts of *Breath Is Home; Breath Heals (1G)* if tension arises.

Bring to awareness whatever has been worrying you lately.... What makes you anxious?... Bring it to mind. Now create a screen and project the very dramas you are worried may come to pass up onto the screen.... If you have a few that are unrelated, pick one and project it up onto the screen now.... Let your imagination play it out on the screen.... Watch, just as if you were watching a movie....... Get to know the dramas.... Become familiar with the different possibilities.... Breathe; relax, sit back, and watch.... Imagine the scenes unfold.... Let your imagination loose; paint the pictures of the possibilities.... Make it up...and watch.... Make it up and explore all the details.... Sense it.... Let your imagination loose.... Give the vague anxieties form; give them a role in the movie.... Get to know their character.... Breathe.... Watch.... What do they have to say?... What do they want anyway?... Sense what motivations are at play.... Imagine how the drama might unfold.... Familiarize yourself with the nuances.... Witness it all....

Now, defuse it, as though you are pulling the plug. Imagine draining out all the charge from the scenes.... However you imagine that, release the energy; pull the plug. Sense it.... Know that in so doing you've taken away its power.... As you exhale, feel energy begin to move, constriction dissolve; psychic circulation becomes fluid.... Breathe it out.... Ground it out.... Breath transforms. Breathe it out....

Now find your anxious self; assure this aspect of yourself that there is nothing to worry about since you are working with the energy that probabilities are made of.... Invite this part of yourself to transform from a victim into a visionary.... Invite this part to use its creative imagination to write new scenes — ones everyone is happy with.... Give it a constructive project for its creativity. Now repaint the pictures; rewrite the scripts so everyone is safe, secure, respected.... Paint over any troubled spots.... Imagine that you are the director — rework the scenes however it occurs to you....... What would be a happy ending? Imagine it.... Try it this way and that, till you discover how it works best. Experiment.... Create an open and secure ambiance.... Generate new energy.

Feel yourself as the shaper and shifter of the energy. If you can't imagine the energies shifting or the outcome changing, ask yourself, "What is the wise thing to do?"... What will shift the energies?......

If any vignette is still stubborn, somehow reticent to accept change, and keeps recoiling back into its constricted form, imagine how you might maneuver around the situation so all remains safe and secure....... Is there anything that would be good to avoid?... What could be done instead?... How can you protect yourselves?...... If the energy is tenacious and continues to be constricted, come to know the details so you can be very clear about exactly what to avoid. You choose where to engage, and you can avoid potentially hurtful situations and warn others to do the same, keeping the vision out of the material plane...keeping that particular combination of ingredients from ever coalescing.

In whatever way works, make the outcomes good for everyone involved...whether that is through engaging in entirely different scenes or through changing the ones you have been sensing.... Be a visionary.... It's all energy that is in a continual state of flux.... Participate; redirect the energies.... Rearrange the ingredients of the scene.... Use your imagination to rework the possibilities — make it all turn out okay....

Know that in so doing you have shifted the probabilities. You have redirected the movement of possibilities.... Know that this is so.... Expect that all will unfold in a harmonious way. Expect to intuit the choices that are safe for forward motion. Feel yourself relax about it all.

Note if there is anything that you need to let others know about so they support the positive possibilities and are able to recognize and avoid the negative.

Thank the part of yourself that used to be consumed with anxiety for helping to reshape the energy into positive forms.... Invite it to always work toward creating welcome experiences in its fantasies.... Tell it that this would be a much more enjoyable way to occupy itself and a more effective way to protect you. Trust your intuition.... Expect that all will unfold harmoniously.... Know that you can now truly relax and trust the future....

Disrobing Outdated Beliefs with Attitudinal Redress (93)

This meditation is particularly helpful for overcoming undermining self-images or detrimental social conditioning; use it to transform any limiting belief — for instance, to transform compliance into assertiveness or control patterns into trust. See Beliefs: Surveying Your Subjective Landscape (Appendix) for help with finding beliefs that it would be good to transform. Disrobing Outdated Beliefs is designed to be followed by the ending *Spirit of Change (13D)*. *Spreading Through the World (13R)* and *Communicate Change (13I)* are also good for closing this meditation.

In group settings this meditation will foster the creation of a life-affirming culture if you encourage people to share their insights once they have finished meditating. When people hear how others are releasing limiting beliefs and what they are replacing them with, everyone gains both a deeper understanding of what holds us back and what liberating ways of being might look like. What one person knows is a limiting belief, another may have assumed was an unchangeable reality. When we hear other people's visions of new ways of being it expands our imagination with positive possibilities and provides us with more options. When we have a vision to strive for change becomes possible. The Social Conditioning Survey in the Appendix would be good to use before using this meditation.

Bring to awareness a belief that you would like to change…an attitude that you know limits your life…an attitude that has become too narrow to comfortably fit your experience anymore…. Bring to awareness a particular belief that you have simply outgrown; it is out of date and no longer useful. It often gets you into trouble…. Bring it into the light of awareness….

Notice how this point of view makes you feel…. How does it make the world feel?… Just what does it assume is true?… What does it expect?… What does it presume is beyond possibility?… How does this notion narrow your perceptions?… How does it regulate your actions?… Sense all the ways it ties constraints around you, confining your experience…defining your experience…….

Assure yourself that this belief is not reality but only a way of looking at reality…. Remind yourself that the world is larger than this view allows for; so much is simply kept out of sight…out of touch…out of reach…. The expansiveness of the world is available to you; you do have more options…. Assure yourself that this belief was only an idea about reality, not reality itself….

Now just as if you are taking off a piece of clothing, shed the belief, for it no longer fits. You have grown out of it…. Now it ties you down, constrains your experience, restrains your progress…. Breathe and release. Feel yourself discard the antiquated image of yourself and the world.... Acknowledge change.... Breathe.... Imagine that the old beliefs coalesce into a form. Personify the outmoded belief.... Imagine it becoming animated.... It is extremely possessive, and it begins scurrying about gathering up all that belongs to it...claiming everything it created: all the presumptions, all the rules and regulations; everything.... You know what its holdings are; return them to it now.... Give it back all its effects.... Imagine it in detail. Notice what its belongings are.......

When it has gathered up all its stuff, tell it that it will actually be much more comfortable residing in the past. That's where its home is, and it is entirely too straining to try to keep up with the times. Tell it that it can go back where it belongs.... Tell it that it can go home now and that it can take all its stuff back with it.... Help it gather up all of its baggage so it can go back where it came from.... Help it pack so it can go back where it belongs.... Tell it that if it leaves any of its belongings behind, you will send them along as you run across them....

Acknowledge what it gave you in its day....... Thank it for the lessons you learned.... Bid it farewell.... Watch it leave and return to the past where it can live more comfortably....

Now that it is gone, feel how much more room there is. The clutter is gone.... There is room for the fullness of life's offerings. There is no longer the need to keep anything out of view or to remain out of touch.... Now you have space to cultivate an attitude that is expansive...empowering...open to the fullness of life. Experience the relief.......

Now create a new base for your experience. Name the new belief you wish to invite into your subjective opening.... Tell yourself about this new conviction you are cultivating....... Tell yourself about all the possibilities it offers.... Be specific. What is different?...... Imagine the atmosphere surrounding this belief.... Notice that the feelings and thoughts have a distinctive quality about them...and a new set assumptions.... Get to know them; they are different.... What realities does this point of view illuminate?... How do your horizons expand?... Let your imagination be carried along by this new belief.... Try it on for size....... What new experiences are now possible?...... How do they feel?... What is the world like?... How does this belief affect you?... How does it affect how others treat you?... Notice how much better it feels to have a belief in place that is in accord with your values.... Breathe a sigh of relief.... Energize the possibilities that can occur with this belief in place. Feel how expanded life becomes. Embody change.... *(Use* Spirit of Change *(*14D*)* *here.)*

Life's Activities

The meditations in this section are designed to help you meet the specific challenges of your life; to gain their full benefit it is crucial that you pay keen attention to what you cannot yet imagine as well as to what you can. Remember that the imagination is the purveyor of intuitive information, and it represents what is true metaphorically. You will find that insight blooms out of subtlety — the greatest meaning is found when you look closely. (See Working with Inner Consciousness, Part II, Page 32.)

You will increase the effectiveness of these meditations if you elaborate by painting the context of what you are grappling with: wherever you can, insert names of the people involved; the place, time, project, etc.; or a specific question you are facing. Be careful to use neutral terms.

Many of these meditations use metaphor to set the frame for exploring. The imagination is very versatile — feel free to switch back and forth from metaphoric language to the familiar images and language of your everyday life.

KEEPING IT TOGETHER: BALANCE AMIDST TOO MUCH

Meeting the Many Faces of Your Self (94)

This meditation addresses inner conflict. You can discover how different facets of your personality affect the others, which in turn invites integration. It is designed to open with *Dynamic Center (23)*.

Know that this wise, peaceful core creates an all-inclusive atmosphere in which every aspect of yourself resides. All the facets of your personality revolve around your center. Your center provides an expansive terrain for them.... Like gravity emanating from the center of the Earth — all that lives on this Earth is supported. So, too, all the aspects of yourself are connected and nourished by your center. All facets of your personality are supported by the core of your being.

Notice the different aspects of your personhood — all the different sides of your personality. Bring to awareness the various characters you give life to. Remember your different interests...your different talents, your distastes...bring to the light of awareness the different aspects of your personhood.... Remember the variety of your moods. Imagine whom your different moods belong to.... Imagine them — all the different personalities within you. Some come out when you are in one role; some come forth when you are in another role. Which situations bring out which aspects of your character?... Imagine that the different aspects of your being are distinctive personalities. These personalities each have different talents and foibles.... Maybe there is one who is especially curious...another who is very sensitive.... Is there a cautious one?...or a creative one?... Then there is the companionable one and the reclusive one...the responsible one and the lazy one...the nurturer.... Is there a clown around?... And the rebel; where is the rebel?... What happened to the awkward one? Is there a martyr anywhere? Some of these characters you may know well; some may never have emerged.... Who else is there? Who lives inside?... Which characters come alive in your home life?... Which in your work life?...

Notice all the different aspects of who you are....... Let your imagination invite them into your awareness as animated characters with unique personalities and very different temperaments. Personify them.... How do they appear?... Exaggerate them. They each have their own drama. They each have a personality of their own.... Which characters come into the forefront in the different settings of your life? Sometimes, one is needed more than the others.... Who is active in the different relationships in your life?... Has anyone been neglected?... Or has anyone been too demanding?... Is anyone discontent?... Now focus on them, one at a time.

Choose one.... Focus on her. What kinds of situations draw her out?... What inspires her?... What worries her?... What makes her thrive.... Talk to her. How is she doing? Is there anything she needs?... When you are ready take time to focus on another.... What's up with this one?... *(Repeat paragraph a few times saying, "Choose another....")*

Take time to check in with each of the rest....... Notice how they feel about one another...how well they get along.... Are there any conflicts between them?... Imagine what they have to say to each other?... Who cooperates? Who competes?...Is anyone antisocial?... Does anyone want a break?... Anyone need some special attention...or protection?...

Your core provides an expansive context for all of the different characters of your personality to thrive...to be embraced...loved for who they are — each and every one of them.... Each unique...each has her own contribution to make...and yet needs all of the others.... Experience this.... Welcome them into the wise and understanding atmosphere that emanates from the core of your being.... Like the mother who, in her loving protection, provides space for the discovery of self. Be maternal toward your whole self in all of your dimensions, in all of your moods.

If anyone is being rejected by another, or if there is any competition going on, you may want to take time to negotiate a way to cooperate....... How can each contribute her best?... Is each getting her fair share of attention? Is any taking too much air time?... What kind of room needs to be made for each to have full expression?... How can they each contribute and support each other?... Negotiate....... Make agreements.... Make commitments.... Talk it over with everybody.......

Imagine doing a ritual or dance with all the different characters.... Acknowledge the offerings of each.... Appreciate the complexity of your being.... Imagine all aspects making a team — each is needed; each has her place; each has her job to do.... Honor them all.... Together they empower you to be equal to all the challenges you meet and to appreciate the gifts life offers. Embrace your whole self....

Weaving Your Life Together (95)

It is best to use *Inner Witness (1H)* and either *Countdown into Deeper Awareness (7)* or *Soaring High in the Skies (8)* with this meditation. As you move through the meditation name the different activities and relationships that you want to focus on.

Relationships, activities, interests, commitments, talents...they all weave through your life, work life, home life, community life.... They all weave together and build the fabric of your life. Contemplate how this is the case.......

Notice the quality of exchange in the different relationships of your life.... This exchange of energy creates the fiber of your life.... Witness your relationships with loved ones....... Witness the nature of your relations at your workplace...the quality of exchange with people in your community...all these weave through your life...all these weave your life together. Where is the exchange soft and supple?... Where is it brittle or frayed? Are there any holes anywhere...or tangles some place?...

Feel how all the threads weave together...how they crisscross.... Do any get tangled? Which aspects of yourself do different threads feed into?... Acknowledge all the threads of your life...the interests, the activities, the relationships, the exchange of energy, the support, the sharing, the caring....

Witness if there are any frayed edges anywhere, or any places that are worn thin and need mending.... Notice if any energy gets lost or dissipated.... Are there any loose ends? Where is the weaving too loose.... Are there places that are woven too tight?... Notice if energy gets stuck, tangled, or knotted up.... Notice the exchange....

Witness if there are any areas that are soiled, in need of cleaning.... Notice if there's anything you need to let go of so all the threads weave together more easily.... Make whatever adjustments you need to.......

Imagine weaving all these threads together so your life is fully integrated...strong, vital, balanced.... Weave the threads together in such a way that all your relationships are cared for.... Imagine that each aspect of your life supports the other aspects of your life...all a part of the whole of the fabric of life.... Weave it together...let them feed off one another, support one another...all the threads of your life weaving a rich fabric....

Imagine you can wear the fabric of your life like a golden robe, or like a rainbow, an earthen or ethereal robe — however you create it.... Imagine wearing the fabric of your life like a majestic robe, all woven together.... It's beautiful; it's strong and durable...inside the fabric of your life you are protected, safe, and secure.... Empowered to receive the gifts of life and to offer your greatest gifts. Feel it.... Your life wraps around you — a perfect fit; let yourself feel comfortable in the fabric of your life. Each activity, each relationship supports the others.... Your life fits....

Juggling Hats: The Balancing Act (96)

Add and delete roles and change pronouns as needed. *Soaring High in the Skies (8)* and *Fun (33)* will augment this meditation.

Look down over your life and see yourself in all the different roles you juggle.... You do many things, play many roles — each role has a hat of its own.... In family life: as a mother, as a partner, as a daughter.... Then there are the hats you wear as a friend...all the hats you wear at work...and in community life.... Hats for making home, making family, making community...hats for work life, hats for creative life; many hats, different hats. Look down over your life and see yourself playing all the different roles life demands....... Look.... You're a good juggler; sometimes you wear more than one hat at a time.... Look over your life and see yourself in each, in every role you play.... Notice how well you are doing.... How do you feel in the different roles?... How well do you transition from one to another?

Each role entails different capacities, different responsibilities...different delights, different satisfactions, different challenges, different frustrations. Look at it all....... Take in the whole picture.... Is it an orderly picture...or a harried picture?... How does it all fit together? Does anything tend to get pushed out?... Something else tend to take over?... What are all the demands?... Which one seems to be always screaming the loudest?...

Is there energy scattered about?... Gather up the scattered energy with the particular hat in which it belongs.... As if you were catching butterflies with the hats. Gather it up.... Any hats that just don't fit anymore?... Imagine what you will do with them.... Give yourself permission to give away or put away any hats that you have outgrown or no longer have time for.... Feel the space created after you have dispensed with them.......

Now imagine that you can roll up each remaining hat...can roll each of them up into a ball.... Imagine that you can roll them all up.... Now like magic, juggle the balls.... Juggle till you get the rhythm right and it is easy to keep them all in the air. Is there any particular ball that keeps throwing you off?... Do you find that you drop others? Any ball that needs to be adjusted to fit into the swing of things?...... Any that simply should be put aside for the time being...or let go of all together?...

What would it be like in your life to juggle gracefully?... Imagine that you play each of the roles and easily make transitions from one to the next...or play a few at a time.... Imagine playing gracefully. As the very best jugglers do. Graceful. Amazing. Fun. It is all in the rhythm — a dance. Imagine it....

Widening Time: Creating As Much As You Need (97)

For this meditation it is best to start with all or parts of *Breath Is Home; Breath Heals (1G), Inner Witness (1H),* and/or *Reside in the Quiet (3),* and/or *Being Present (40).*

Each time you exhale you settle into the present — even more than before. Share in the presence of breath, of energy.... Simply be with your breath. With each breath you settle more and more into the present...more of you settles. All of you present. Whole. Be aware of your exhalations. Follow your exhalations. Imagine following your exhalations moving out from your body.... Breath moves out into the expanses of space. Breathe. Follow your breath. Imagine that your exhalations carry you into the expanses of space. Imagine it. Each time you exhale your horizons extend further and further. Breathe.

Follow your exhalations.... Horizons expand — lots of space, infinite space.... Breathe. Follow your breath.... Quiet.... Expansive. So expansive.... There is room for anything, room for everything. Follow your breath into the infinity of space. Quiet.... Expansive.... *(Repeat this paragraph.)*

Just as there is lots of space, experience how there is lots of time — all the time you need.... As you follow your breath, experience the broadening of time.... Sense how this is. You have all the time in the world — you always do.... As you rest in breath, feel time open up....... With each exhalation you settle into the present.... Openness happens.... Breath opens. Space opens.... Time opens.... With each exhalation time and space expand out as you settle in. Sense this.... Witness how as breath opens, space opens; time opens.... Relax into time.... Time carries you. Relax into it...lots and lots of time.... All the time you need. It is true. In the present, time is infinite. Inhabit time. Don't chase it. Relax into it....... It carries you. Time brings the gift of the future. Time holds the past. Time is a gift. Be friendly to it....... Time carries you; relax into it. You needn't chase after it or try to get ahead of it. Relax into it and it supports you, carries you....

Time is generous. You always have all the time you need. It is true. In the present, time is infinite.... In the present there is room for life. The present is where life lives.... As you exhale, send your breath to those places in your life that feel cramped....... Imagine that your breath opens space there...lots of space. Expansive. Breathe.... *(Optional: repeat any part of the preceding paragraphs.)*

Dealing With the Issue: Problem-Solving and Decision-Making

Witness the Issue (98)

This meditation is good for the cultivation of mindfulness and is useful for coming to terms with a major issue, a sudden loss or injury, world disaster, etc. It is useful for getting clear on any issue large or small. When you name the issue feel free to name it a little differently each time, but refrain from any explanation. Long silences as well as repetition of any of its parts will enhance this meditation. It is designed to be used with *Highest, Wisest, Deepest Self (14)* and/or *Inner Witness (1H)*. You *may* want to augment it with *Countdown into Deep Awareness (7)* and *Compassion (17)*. If tension comes up, use parts of *Breath Is Home; Breath Heals (1G)*.

B ring to awareness (_____), which you want to work on. Share presence with (_____). Let its presence be in your awareness.... Simply note the quality of energy that comes with it....... If you notice yourself tensing as you focus on the issue, breathe.... Be aware of the quality of energy you tend to bring to it — your aversion, your desire.... With your deepest, wisest, highest, most spacious awareness, witness all of this now.... Give it soft attention.... Just let (_____) be in awareness. Witness your various responses to it.... In your spacious awareness, witness.... Breathe through any contraction.... Breathe.... If you find yourself caught in reaction, let the issue go for a moment; breathe. Feel the soft attention of the Witness bring calm.... In the calm, space is provided to witness the issue. Breathe and put your attention back on the issue when you are ready...always, if tension arises — breathe. Witness what is so regarding (_____). As you simply let it be in awareness, understanding happens naturally — you need not do anything — just witness and notice what is so....... Understanding simply happens....... You find yourself knowing, as the Witness knows, how to best live in relation to (_____) .... Breathe; let yourself open to what is so....... Notice how you can be even more open....... Befriend uncertainty.... Have compassion for difficulty.... Breathe. Witness what arises in awareness. Trust it.......

Now you can know what you can change and what you cannot change.......
Here the Witness senses the contours of any limitations....... Here you can come
to accept things as they are....... Here you can see what your own contribution
can be....... Here you come to know what lessons await you, what challenges face
you....... Here you can let go, be whole again, be connected again.... Breathe....

Let yourself share presence with (_____). As you do, feel yourself, your
whole self, beginning to come to terms with (_____). As time unfolds you can
sense yourself truly coming to peace with all of this.......

Send an Invitation to the Solution (99)

Use this meditation for any problem to which you can't find a solution. Where the
text uses the term "the problem," give your problem a short name and refrain from
explanations and descriptions. This meditation is designed to follow *Receptive
Imagination (1)* and *Intelligence (18)*; *Open Heart, Sharp Mind (42)* will augment it.
You might also use the first two paragraphs of *Go For It! (56)*.

Bring to mind the problem you are grappling with — the conundrum you are
stuck in, the question you haven't yet figured out. Bring it to mind.... Open to
your own vulnerability; bring the issue to mind.... Don't do anything with it; just
let it be there. Let it be there in all of its quirkiness.... Breathe.... Share presence
with it....

The fact that there is a question means the answer exists. But the answer
has a life of its own. It picks its own time and its own place to appear. It will only
show up on time: not early, not late; just on time — its own time, on its own
terms.... Be patient. It is coming. Expect it.

Set your frustrations aside. Set your preconceptions aside.... Make room
for the unknown. Make friends with the unknown.... Let yourself be curious
without grasping.... Let yourself be inquiring, without an agenda that the
answer has to fit into — for the answer may not fit your idea of where it belongs.
If the opening you leave for it is too narrow, it will pass you right by. Just let
the problem be present in all of its quirkiness. Let the question be in your mind.

Don't do anything. Just breathe and let your mind be open. Just let the issue be there in all of its quirkiness. Breathe.... All you need do is reside in a state of open awareness.... You reside in open awareness by simply breathing.... Breathe.

Sit in quiet, patient expectation. Fully comfortable, sit in not knowing; for you know that things have a way of working themselves out when they're given the space to do so. Things always work out in time. Know this is true. Let go of preconceptions and settle into expectant listening.... Sit in trusting receptivity — open to whatever possibility arises. Patient. Breathing....

Know that when you align your energy with clear intent and trust the intelligence intrinsic to the universe, you do discover exactly what you need, when you need it. Trust the universe.... Put your consciousness on relaxed and ready alert — a bit like animals in the wild, relaxed and alert — always alert to change. Your awareness stands in attention, watching everything that appears in your mind, watching for everything coming in from every which direction. Mindful.

Feel yourself open without position, without contention, on the alert for the solution to leap out at any time, but in its own time. The larger pattern emerges. In the meantime purify your intent and wait patiently; wait.... Expect the solution to make itself known in its own way, in its own time. Honor that it does have a way of its own; it will come on its own terms. When it is ready, when you are ready. Be patient. Trust the process. A fresh perspective arises. Understanding happens.

You may decide to converse with the problem as though it has an intelligence of its own, as though it has a personality of its own. Characterize the problem.... Imagine that it represents itself to you as a character....... Imagine that it has a story to tell. Listen.... Let it talk to you.... Listen.......

Send an invitation to the answer. The answer often comes in a quirky way.... sneaks into your peripheral vision or slips in through the back door. When you notice, it seems to jump right out of the ordinary; yet it may feel like it was there all along.... The answer makes itself at home. It just feels right. A light dawns and illuminates the whole pattern. What is really taking place is evident. The best way to approach the whole issue is clear.

Expect to know.... Welcome a new way of seeing the world. Tell yourself to be mindful as you go about the activities of life.... Have faith in the intelligence intrinsic to the universe. Trust that the solution is on its way. It will arrive on time, on its own time. Expect to recognize it when it arrives. Welcome a fresh perspective....

Invite Insight (100)

This meditation is good for recurrent problems. It is best to read it with a quick, snappy, and definite tone of voice, which will inspire spontaneous response. You might want to use *Receptive Imagination (1J)*, *Countdown into Deep Awareness (7)*, *Fun (33)*, *Intelligence (18)*, and/or *Open Heart, Sharp Mind (42)* with it.

As you focus on the issues, mull over the circumstance, be mindful of your experience; you can invite insight. Given the opportunity your creative mind delights in making insight. All the various issues, the complications, the conflicting orientations are art supplies that your creative mind plays with. Imagine your creative mind is getting ready to present you with a gift of insight. It may come as a picture or in some other form.... It is about to offer you a metaphor revealing the patterns of energy at play. Your creative awareness is about to present you with a picture depicting what's so. It might give you a picture of a landscape or an abstract drawing.... Sometimes it offers up sound or a mythical creature.... Imagine that you are opening a present. Imagine opening a box.... Expect that inside is the gift of insight.... *(Snap your fingers.)*

Look and see what is there. Pay attention to what pops to mind. Make it up. What has your creative mind conjured up?... Fill in the color; give it sound. What's there?... Does it have a feel to it?... Imagine the detail...the energy patterns at play.......

Notice if anything would increase balance and well-being? Imagine changing the scene in whatever way occurs to you.... Play with the picture.... Know that
whatever you change on this plane affects the energy patterns in regular life.......
Notice how all this illuminates a good approach....... Imagine how it feels to act
on it....

Ripple Effect: Check Out the Consequences (101)

Use this meditation to explore the impact of anything that you are considering
doing. Groups may want to use it investigate the implications of decisions they are
about to make. The meditation is designed to follow *Lake of Reflection (6), Inner
Witness (1H),* or *Highest, Wisest, Deepest Self (14). Call Upon Your Life-Affirming Values
(24)* will augment it. You may want to use *History Empowers (143B)* to deepen
insight. If you are facing a number of options, then you may want to combine
Ripple Effect with *Crossroads: Detecting the Right Course of Action (102).* Name the
project and context (people, place, time, etc.) and refrain from any explanation or
justification. Ask specific but neutral questions, not leading ones. For instance, don't
ask, "Who feels bad about it?" Instead say, "Notice how different residents in the
neighborhood feel." Allow long pauses so that people have time to thoroughly
explore. It helps to keep people focused if you punctuate the silence by repeating
the question or making a suggestion such as, "Sense the truth of the matter."

The magic of this lake reflects potentialities. Whatever activity is of concern to you
bring it to mind now.... Reflect on all the complexities.... Bring it to mind.
Imagine that the clear reflective powers of the lake reveal what is true. The sun
creates a dance of glitter on the ripples that move over the lake. In the magic of
this lake you can discover what is so. Imagine that you take the issue that you want
to consider and drop it into the lake of reflection. Each ripple glitters. When you
look closely at each sparkle you'll discover a whole vignette — what would take
place, as if it were already the case. Your imagination fills in the details and reveals
the possibilities. Look in and see how it would be, how it could be; the ripple
effect becomes apparent.

Focus on the particular aspect of the activity you would like to explore....
Bring the details to mind.... Imagine the scenarios unfolding....... Let the details

float through awareness; witness the possibilities.... Notice the quality of energy present.... Is it open? Is it shut down? Is it light or heavy?... Is it trusting or controlling?... Is it driven or is it flexible? Is it expressive or secretive?... Who is being taken into account?......

Bring others to mind, one person or group at a time, and notice how they are affected...how they feel about all this....... Take everyone into account.... What vignettes play out? Imagine.......

You may want to put yourself in another's shoes. Choose another and imagine how it is from this person's experience.... Imagine being in their shoes, looking out their eyes, listening through their ears....... You may want to imagine consulting this person about it....... Now explore still another perspective....... *(Repeat paragraph).*

Notice the resources that it takes.... Track back; where do they come from?...... Notice how the Earth is affected.... Fast forward; imagine all the ripples that swirl out.... Where do they go?... What happens?... Imagine who benefits....... What's better for whom?... What's the cost?... Who pays?... Imagine all of this. Let the ripples reveal themselves..... Look closely. Who gains; who pays?......

Witness how it lines up with your values.... Imagine how it affects you....... Explore how adjustments could be made....... Are there people affected who could be brought into the process?...... Witness; is this activity a good idea?...... What is to be protected?... Where would change be welcome?...... What is the right thing to do?... What would be good for everyone...for the Earth? Notice this....

Now choose what you will do with your clarity. Is there more investigation needed?... Are there people who have been left out of the process who should be included?... Anyone impacted whose perspectives have been ignored?... Anyone's life experience that would enrich the understanding.... Anyone that needs to be communicated with? *(Explore possibilities as thoroughly as you like by repeating the preceding paragraphs a few time. If you want to explore different options, take them one*

at a time, and name them as you do.)

What is the right thing to do?......

Crossroads: Detecting the Right Course of Action (102)

This meditation is for decision-making. It explores all the options so that you can become clear about which feels the best and should be used in combination with *Clarity (46)* and *Call Upon Your Life-Affirming Values (24)*. Name the different options as you explore them. This meditation can be augmented with *Ripple Effect (101)*.

Focus on the decision you are facing. You have a couple of directions that you could go, or maybe a whole array of ways is possible.... Bring to awareness the options you're considering.... Imagine that you are standing at a crossroads, and the different options stretch out before you.... Give your imagination permission to fully explore the possibilities, the probabilities. Pretend that it can see into the future. It knows each route intimately. Invite your imagination to be your tour guide, telling you the stories that go with the sites...showing you what happens where. It will show you what each route entails.

Envision all the routes that branch out from this intersection. Imagine them.... What are all your options?... What are the names of the roads that branch out from here? Let your imagination illuminate where they each go.... How long is each route?... What are the road conditions on the different routes? What do you go through to get there?... Are any routes especially scenic or treacherous? Imagine it....... Now decide which routes you want to tour, for there may be some you have no interest in. Choose which route you want to explore first....

Imagine yourself embarking on this course of action...moving in this direction.... Make up what it is like to go this way.... Give it detail.... Let your imagination carry you along this road a bit and discover just exactly what's in store.... Imagine it is happening right now. Imagine what you would be doing....... Feel what it's like.... What conditions unfold around you?... Who else is around?... What are the interesting spots along this route like?... Imagine the details of the scenery....

You may see whole vignettes played out along the way.... Or you may find that your imagination transports you right into the middle of a scene. What happens?... How does it feel?... What's the mood?... Do you feel connected to the environs or is there something foreign about them?... Does it intimidate you or excite your curiosity?... Does this route lend itself to speed, or is it better to mosey along?... Or maybe it's full of potholes and requires careful navigation.... What difficulties present themselves along the way?... What demands does this direction place on you?... Imagine it....

How do the different aspects of yourself take to this course of action?... your body?... your heart?... your spirit?... How does it fit with your values?... How do those in your life feel about it?... What are the consequences of this course of action?... What are the risks?... How does it resonate with what you care about?... What do you learn from this way of going?... What do you bring to it?... Explore all of this.... Imagine it in detail. Make up a story about it.......

Now come on back to the intersection where the roads branch out. Clear yourself from the experience of that particular tour. Put it aside for the moment. Breathe.... Remember the other route/s you wanted to explore.... Choose another route to scout out.... *(Repeat the preceding three paragraphs until all directions have been explored).*

When you're ready come back to the intersection again and carefully sense if there are any pathways that were overlooked earlier...or if any of the routes can be combined using part of each to get you there.... If you want to explore any of the options more extensively, do so now.......

Bring to awareness others in your life; ask them their opinion.... Imagine how others feel if you go this way or that way.... Do any want to join you on one passage and not on another?... Have any of them been over any of these passages before?... Is there anyone you should talk to?...

The way water rolls over stones and reveals their subtle colors.... Notice the nuances of each possibility.... What will your day-to-day life be like if you go this way...or that way?... How does each option affect you?... How does each option affect others?... How does each alternative resonate with your values?... On which are you most relaxed?... On which are you most dynamic?... On which do you learn the most?... On which is your offering most welcomed?... Witness.......

Sense which road is best.... Or what information is still needed to make the right choice.... Or if a number of directions are really equally attractive.... How is it you can make a choice? Trust yourself, for you are the only one that knows what's right for you.... As clear as water, you know what is true for you, what is right for you.....

Imagine making your choice and moving forward.... Imagine the attitude that is best for what lies ahead.... Try it on.... Make any adjustments needed.... Open to possibility....

Blocks to Creativity Become Stepping Stones (103)

This meditation is for transforming barriers into the opportunities for insight that fuel forward motion. It is designed to follow *Integrity of Your Being (4)*. *Clearing Space Inside with Mental Housecleaning (11)* will augment this meditation.

When you open to your essence, your creativity releases and materializes in the world in a unique way. The energy flows through the essence of your being, out into the world.... Life is about expression.... Feel creativity flowing...flowing through you. Breathe.... Keep the channels open for your creativity to flow from the depths of being, itself.... Imagine that anything impeding the flow gets washed away by the waves, dissolved by breath....... Any self-doubt breathed out...whatever throws up resistance, dissolved by waves of breath. Breath washes it all away....... Break through.... Experience this....

Look closely for any remaining blocks, any limitations.... Understand this: they are only disguised as blocks; in fact they are really gifts...they are intelligent;

they have something to teach you. You need them to move forward on your path — in fact they compose part of your path....

Focus on one now. You can work with others later.... Remember the times when it is active....... Now it appears to make an offering. Sense the quality of its energy, the tone of its character.... Is it hot, cold; does it have texture, sound?... Feel its mood.... Imagine that all this energy comes together and forms a character.... Make it up.... Greet it.... Listen to what it has to communicate; it may not use words.... Sense what is so for it. What does it want?... What posture does it take?... What does it protect you from?...... What memories does it hold?...... What does it offer?... How can it support a fuller expression of your truth?... Breathe....... Feel the power released.... Acknowledge the lessons.... Feel yourself empowered.... Thank it for its offerings. Imagine what you will do.......

Now if you like you can choose another to communicate with.... *(Repeat paragraph if you like.)*

Blocks are steppingstones, offering exactly what you need to meet the future, to express your truth in the world.... Each step is a lesson along the path of your life; each step is a challenge...and you grow wiser.... Believe in yourself. Believe in your creativity.... Open to possibility; trust life....

ALIGNING YOUR ENERGIES FOR THE CHALLENGES AHEAD

Visiting with the Future to Address a Matter of Import or to Prepare for a Momentous Occasion (104)

This meditation activates the Receptive Imagination and invites insight. It can be used for any concern and in group settings when people want to explore a collaborative endeavor. Have people share their experience afterward — it will prove helpful for informing the group how to move forward. Replace terms such as "the matter" and "the issue" by naming what you are working on; if it is not major, then skip the first paragraph. You might want to open this meditation with both *Active Imagination (11)* and *Receptive Imagination (1J)*.

There is something important that is up for you. It may be an upcoming occasion or a special event; it may be something that has been calling your attention or something that is bothering you. There is something brewing. It is important.... This matter is the bearer of great gifts.... It is not quite clear just what these gifts are yet. They may be lessons offered, achievement honored, or doors opening to new opportunity...openings of heart, deep meanings for the soul...maybe all of these things or maybe something entirely different. This just might be the opening to a whole new chapter in life. This is a rite of passage. Open to it. Welcome it....

Take a moment and let all your associations with this matter parade through your mind now.... Remember particular times when it has made its presence known.... All the different things that come to mind — let them move through now.... Watch them.... Times that have led up to the situation.... What is the story?... Remember the details.... Witness; what is at the bottom of the matter?... What surrounds the matter?... Who else is around?... What is true for them?... What motives drive the matter?... What emotions give it fuel?... Any anticipation, any anxieties giving it direction?... What pleasures or pains are present? Is there pride?... Is there shame?... How does your body feel when you call this matter to awareness?... What are your expectations?...

There are your responses to the matter; then there is the matter itself. Breathe. Let the matter simply reside in awareness. Breathe.... Tune to it.... Witness it.... What quality of energy emanates out of the center of the matter? What aura surrounds it?... Does it have color, texture, tone? Imagine.... Are there any sounds or scents that accompany it? What is the mood?... What feelings does it have?... What quality of energy emanates out of the center of the matter? Or is there a whole collage of different energies?

As though this matter had an intelligence of its own, as though it had a personality of its own, let all that has been passing through awareness, let it all swirl together and form a character...as though a cartoon character were to form right there in your imagination now. Or maybe a future you, visits.... This character comes to you right out of the future where the matter has been resolved or when the event is unfolding. Conjure it up.... Create it. Make it up. Meet it.... Give it form. Give it personality — or maybe it has multiple personalities.... Welcome this character in all of its complexities.... However you feel about this character, welcome this being, for it is the bearer of great gifts. This being comes to you with offerings; it is visiting from the future. Welcome this being....

Talk over your concerns now.... Find out what's needed to prepare yourself properly to honor this rite of passage, to honor the offerings, to be equal to the challenge.... This being is acutely tuned to you and completely familiar with the situation. Talk over your concerns now. This being is telepathic. Sometimes its knowledge doesn't fit into words too well — language can be too confining. But it will convey its knowledge. Turn your attention to the back of awareness as you bring your questions to mind. You may find that the answers seem to have been there all along — as though they have just been waiting for you to get around to looking their way. The knowledge doesn't come; it is already there. Notice it. Form your question and find yourself knowing. Telepathy is simultaneous.......

Remember the issues that had been calling your attention before. Bring them to mind now.... Bring them to mind one at a time.... Choose a specific one.... Witness knowing.... If you have a particular anxiety, bring it to mind.... Discover what, if anything, is needed to protect yourself.... Know how you might cultivate positive results.... Imagine all of this. Your imagination is the window into the future...the medium this being communicates through. Imagine this character's story.... Make it up....... How does it take to different approaches? Display one at a time and discover how it resonates; after exploring one, clear from awareness and bring in another for display.......

Acknowledge what you know.... Breathe in your knowing. Draw in the future's gifts.... Fill yourself with this energy. As you exhale, settle into your own self.... As you inhale, embody your knowledge.... You are prepared, equal to the challenge, relaxed, and ready.

Together with this character set the stage for the act to go on.... What's the best approach?... What prep work is needed?... Are there friends and allies you want to be with you?... Who should be contacted? Anyone need forewarning?... Any closure needed anywhere in order to fully open to the gifts of the time? Set the stage. Imagine doing what is needed to ready yourself and the world for the gifts of this time.

Express your gratitude for the gifts visited on your life...the opportunities...the recognition...the lessons.... Express your gratitude to the future who welcomes you, who holds gifts for you.... You are ready to receive. You are ready to offer your contributions. The future welcomes you. Give thanks for its gifts....

The Work That Is Right for You (105)

This meditation can be used to explore a career or work that you may do outside of your job. It is designed to follow *Integrity of Your Being (4)* and/or *Mustering Courage and Confidence to Express Your Truth (55)*. It can be augmented with *Go For It! (56)*. If you are not sure what kind of work is right for you, pick something that might be. Pretend that it is precisely right, and this meditation will enable you to witness if in fact it does suit you. If you are considering different kinds of work, combine this meditation with *Crossroads (102)*.

Now take time to feel yourself doing the work that is right for you. Imagine it. If you are not exactly sure what or where this is to happen, let your imagination transport you into a context where it could happen.... Give your imagination permission to respond to your calling.... Imagine how you feel doing the work that is your calling.... It just feels right. It suits you.... It is exactly right for you. You are contributing your best. You are living in alignment with your values.... Doing what is meaningful.... Doing what interests you.... Imagine how this feels....

Feel yourself inside a life in which you are already doing the work in which you thrive; your talents come alive.... All your capacities come forth.... Imagine the context. What are you doing?... How are you feeling?... What kind of relations do you have with others?... Imagine it in detail.......

Feel yourself being appreciated.... You are truly welcomed. You offer what others need.... You receive the support you need.... Imagine what this support makes possible for you. Imagine it.... Imagine yourself in a daily routine as you do this work....How does it make the rest of your life feel?...

What are your challenges?... Where do they take you? What skill do you need to hone?... Imagine the projects that you do.... Imagine how they are received.... Imagine the nature of your relationships....

Take the long view — what happens down the road?... What have you learned?... What have you offered? What recognition have you received?...... Feel the gifts you offer being received.... Giving, receiving, as naturally as breathing in and out — a blessing.

As you experience all of this, focus on your life now, in present time. Notice what you need to do to make space for the work that is right for you.... You may need perseverance. You may need patience; you may need change. You may need to add to or maybe let go of what you are doing.... Are there connections with others that need to be made?...... Is there investigation that needs to be done?...... You know what is right for you.... What do you need to do in your life now to make room to answer your calling?....... Notice the support there is for you to do this....

Rite of Passage: Transitions (106)

This meditation is good for major life transitions such as graduation, moving, retirement, marriage, a career change, becoming a parent, etc. Name the particular situation from the past and the one you are about to embark on. It is good to use several of the meditations from Summoning the Powers (Section Two) to enhance this meditation; choose the ones that fit your circumstances.

Imagine yourself standing on top of a mountain. There are two great valleys that spread out from either side of you — great vistas are in view here.... Imagine it; this is a magic mountain.... Here you can see your life. On one side is all that you have been given and all you have done to get to this spot in your life. In the valley on the other side is where the future lives.

You stand in a momentous time of transition. You are about to descend into this valley where you have never been.... There is hardly anything familiar there. Now you stand between the worlds. Here you get to view both worlds. Take a deep breath, sit back, and take in the details of the vista that spreads out on either side of you....

This is a very powerful place. Here you can ready yourself for what comes next, and you can say farewell to the past.... You can invite friends from the past or the future to be with you here and join you in ceremony. Now is the time to perform your rite of passage. Invite your allies. Imagine them joining you — friends, family, spirits: whoever you would like to be with you at this time of great transition. Welcome them.... Greet each of them.......

This is the time to acknowledge the gifts you have been granted and the ones yet awaiting.... This is the time to make commitments and to show your gratitude. Imagine doing so.... It is time to gather up lessons learned and friends made and invite them to accompany you on your journey into the future....... You can ask the invited guests from the future to tell you about the journey ahead....... They can forecast the conditions you need to pack for so that you can gather the particular resources you may need....... In this ceremony you can come to know exactly what you need to leave behind to lighten your load....... When you make good closure with where you have been, you disencumber yourself and become more open to what the future offers.......

Take time to do the work needed to fully honor times past and coming times...to be ready for your journey. Confer with your guests. Do ceremony together....... You may want to recite the meaningful moments, what you've been given, what you've done, what you have learned....... You might want to name your commitments to the past...to the future.... You may want to say what you are looking forward to...what you'll be careful about.......

This is a time between the worlds of past and future. Now is the time to honor each. As you do you'll find that shifts begin to take place inside you. Your energy readies itself for your journey.... You can feel what it is going to take: what resources on your part...attitude... pacing.... You know what is needed to be equal to the times ahead.... Imagine it. Express your gratitude for the opportunities you've been given.... What offerings might you make?... Imagine what you want to do in your life to honor this time.... Who would you like to accompany you?...

Igniting Inspiration (107)

Read this meditation with an upbeat voice. *Dynamic Center (23)*, *Intelligence (18)*, and *Invite Insight (100)* will augment it and can be inserted toward the end. *Recollection (16)* can be inserted after the second paragraph. Use *Create a Symbol to Tap Energy in Daily Life (13A)* as an ending. If you are working with a group, use just the first two paragraphs of the symbol meditation and then continue on to *Inspiration Is Infectious (145)*.

Feel the charge of life force.... This energy is always pregnant with potential...always present and ready for the next moment, and the moment after that...each moment different than the moment before.... Feel the life force carried by breath...life force, radiant, electric, vibrant...life force. Feel it....

Extend awareness over your past, and notice the times when you were inspired...felt the electricity of life...creativity...intelligence...insight was pop-ping...energy moving, flying, flashes of electric energy.... Remember the times in your past when you were inspired, carried by the energy...as though it had a life of its own...and you discovered it, created it, immersed yourself in it...inspired in deep connection.... Times when you were highly inspired; brilliant, powerful energy that jumps and flies, that sparks and flashes, that sings, that dances.... Remember times in the past when you have been inspired.... Inspired with others, inspired on your own.... Inspired by others.... Times that the experience of life felt fresh — a new perspective came into view. These moments may have been brief — no matter — for the full spirit of life is compressed into each of them...times when the energy pulses.... It carries you into discovering new expe-rience, creating new experience...communion, connection.... Feel that core of energy that is ready to jump — to leap.... Excited, as though the energy has a life of its own.... Feel the spark of life.... Creativity. Connection. Remember the times when you felt most alive. Draw on these memories now. Breathe....

Feel this energy residing inside you now.... Like smoldering coals — breathe life into them and they leap into flame. Feel the potential; feel the power — when aroused it jumps, flashes, sings with excitement.... It resides inside, wait-ing...then it leaps at opportunity when it's incited. Imagine projecting this energy into your future. With each exhalation, the energy moves into the future. Imagine this energy infusing your future with sparkle.... As you exhale the coals glow; the sparks fly; connections are made.

Just as you scanned your past, imagine scanning your future now.... Sense what resonates with this energy.... Where are the pulls?...what arenas...what activity...what relationships...what ideas...what projects...what questions arouse this energy?... What inspires you?... What sparks excitement?...new possibilities revealed....

Is there anywhere that has gotten dull, that is thirsty for some sparkle?... Send energy there; sense it reviving....... Decide what you want to act on....... Trust the energy, let it carry you into creating/discovering a future alive! Thriving....

Partnering Discipline with Vision Makes Effort Easy (108)

This meditation addresses lack of self-discipline and follow-through. It is also good for mustering that last bit of steam needed to complete the final stage of a project; naming the project along with descriptive details will make it more effective. Parts or all of *Dynamic Center (23)*, *Inspiring Your Very Best (25)*, and *Support Sustains You (26)* will enhance it as will *Clearing Space Inside with Mental Housecleaning (11)*. You might want to use *Putting Your Will to Work (13G)* as an ending. Insert the first two paragraphs of *Create a Symbol to Tap Energy in Daily Life (13A)* at the end of the first section — then you can call upon your symbol in the midst of activity when you are vulnerable to becoming distracted. If you are not working on a specific project at this time, you may want to use only the Discipline section of this meditation along with *Create a Symbol to Tap Energy in Daily Life (13A)*.

Discipline (108A)

Bring to mind times it has taken perseverance to accomplish your goals....
Remember...times when you have had to persist, where you resisted temptation
to do something else...when you exercised stick-to-itiveness — if no times come
to mind when you were persistent, remember people you knew who were....
Bring them to mind.... Remember when perseverance was present — no matter
if it was yours or an other's.... Remember persistence, perseverance, determination.... Recall what the energy felt like.... What was it like to be in its presence?
How was it?...... Imagine how it feels to have this energy run through you....
Breathe it....

Imagine perseverance is inside you now....... Draw upon it. Embody it....
Imagine how it is to exert yourself...to put an effort into your endeavors.... It is
as though you are going uphill and making steady progress...with effort, with
exertion, making slow but steady progress. The stamina, the energy, the drive; feel
it.... Breathe it....

Imagine the context where determination thrives. Sense what feeds
it...the support...the conviction...the effort...the will....... Steady progress is
made. Step-by-step, getting closer to the goal...closer...and closer...and closer
to the goal; steady progress.... Imagine it. As though you are hiking up a hill;
it takes strength, energy, effort, perseverance, exertion.... Your efforts
strengthen you...strengthen your heart, your muscles.... Your blood fills with
oxygen as you breathe, giving you even more energy, stamina, endurance....
Remember the feel of persistence...of determination...of fortitude...of
endurance.... These qualities reside in the bedrock of being, itself.... Draw on
it.... Breathe it.... Feel it. Like the trees drawing nutrients from the ground;
with your breath draw in these energies.... Breathe them in.... Feel them make
you strong.... Feel how these qualities reside inside you...resources to be
tapped whenever you need them....

Completion (108B)

Bring to mind the particular project that you would like to move forward in your life at this time.... Bring to awareness what is important about it.... Acknowledge how much you care about this.... Envision how it will be when you have completed the project......all goals accomplished.... Imagine the difference it makes.... Feel as though this vision is already true.... Feel a sense of accomplishment...completion.

Now appreciate yourself for the efforts you make.... Imagine part of you is cheering you on.... Imagine your supporters rooting for you....... Feel yourself make steady progress. It's difficult, but you move forward step-by-step.

Then something changes; the momentum changes. Like cresting the top of the hill, your movement becomes easy when going downhill.... Notice how this is when your project takes on a momentum of its own.... Feel the gain of momentum.... Energy builds momentum and flows.... It carries itself as if it has a life of its own.... You created it and now it begins to carry you.... Feel that transition from carrying it, to it carrying you.......

It has a life of its own. It's as though it has a personality of its own.... Imagine it.... It speaks to you.... Listen to what it needs....... Tell it what you are committed to....... Feel yourself becoming especially attuned to its moods.... It flows; it has buoyancy.... As the momentum builds it is exhilarating.... It flows. It's exciting.... Feel it.... Breathe it.... Run with it.... Fly with it.... Soar with it.... Go with it!

Notice the tempo — when you can slow down, rest and relax, leave it be until the next time you breathe life into it....... Talk to it — discover the rhythm that works for you and it....... Breathe with it. Harmonize with it.... Choose how and when you will engage with it.... Imagine how this feels. Your efforts will come to fruition.

Let this vision inspire you.... Let your determination provide the stamina needed to make it up the hill.... Your vision draws you up. Discipline pushes from behind...as naturally as breath moves in and out.... Feel it.... Breathe it.... Vision uplifts you and illuminates the path to its manifestation. Discipline provides the fuel to get there....

From Procrastination to Productivity (109)

This meditation will align you with your priorities. It is especially helpful if you are initiating a new project or falling behind in one. It can be adapted for group settings in order to enhance teamwork. *Pacing (36)* and/or the Discipline section in *Partnering Discipline with Vision Makes Effort Easy (108)* will augment it as will *Clearing Space Inside with Mental Housecleaning (11)*. *Putting Your Will to Work (13G)* is a good ending to use. Replace the word "project" with the name of the actual project you are working on, and change personal pronouns if appropriate.

Bring to awareness the particular activity you would like to pay special attention to — the endeavor you want to pursue. Focus on the project that you would like to bring to the center of your life.... Witness this project. Don't do anything with it; simply witness.... Imagine as though you could share presence with it.... Tune into the nature of this undertaking.... Notice its tempo.... Imagine just what it needs.... Notice what is called for.... What quality of attention is best?... How much time would be good?... Let the project speak to you.......

Now extend your awareness to include the rest of your life.... Notice what you might need to let go of in order to really make space for this project in your life.... How can you make room for it?... What needs to be set aside for the time being?... What is likely to keep you from giving it the attention it needs?... What is likely to sidetrack you?... You choose what is at the center of your life. What needs to be arranged or rearranged to make room for your project?...... What are you willing to do?... Be deliberate.... Imagine clearing the space for it in your time...in your psyche. Breathe.... Make space.... Imagine moving it into the center.... Give it the space it deserves. Give it the attention it deserves.... Give it the time it deserves.... Offer it your efforts.... Imagine how you can do this.... Give yourself permission to truly make the effort.... Imagine doing what is needed.... Notice how it feels.... Imagine it.......

You may find that once you have the project in the center, then you really avoid it. It is as though you look for sidetracks...as though the project had a negative force field emanating from it.... Pay attention to the particular part of you who is in the driver's seat of avoidance.... Imagine her.... Characterize her.... Talk to her....... Find out what is up with her.... Ask her how she is feeling.... Is there anything she is afraid of?... What might reassure her?...

What does she need to engage?... Negotiate with her.... How can you satisfy her?... Tell her what you will do for her. Imagine doing it.... How does this feel...to you...to her?...

Sense her stance shifting.... Feel the negative force field turn around. Now the project is pulling you in.... Imagine that whatever anxieties there may have been are now transforming into excitement that fuels forward motion.... No more sidetracks. Breathe.... Feel the shift.... Feel the project drawing you in.... Open to it. Let yourself be excited by it....

Sense how the rhythm of your life changes as you bring your project into the center.... How does it feel?... Make any adjustments you need to so that it sits comfortably in the center.... Notice how the rest of your life gets cared for.... Remember the support others have for you....

Cheer yourself on.... Tell yourself how capable you are.... Muster up whatever energies you need to move forward with this project in the center. Conjure up the supportive atmosphere you need to take care of this project — to give it what it deserves....... Remember times in your life when you have been fully productive, efficient, brilliant, competent, creative.... Remember times when you have been all of these things — productive, efficient, brilliant, competent, creative.... Recall these qualities....... Invite the energies to be with you now.... Breathe these energies into your center now.... Let them fuel your forward motion.... Feel them infuse your work.... Feel them animate your work....

Breathe in productivity, determination, competence, creativity.... Imagine your center inhales and draws these qualities in.... As you exhale channel this energy to your project. And the project draws it in. Breathing with the project.......

Know that when this project is in the center, you naturally move forward, make progress, and complete it.... It feels good to do what is important to you, to put this project in the center of your life now....

On Time: Meeting a Deadline (110)

This meditation is designed to begin after you have used the first two paragraphs of *Pacing (36)*. The Discipline section of *Partnering Discipline with Vision Makes Effort Easy (108)* and the ending *Putting Your Will to Work (13G)* will enhance it. This meditation is good to use for exploration of a team project. Replace the word "project" with the name of the actual project you are working on.

As you acknowledge the grand rhythms of life, of time, focus on the particular project that needs completing. It, too, has its own time, its own place. Bring it to mind...and trust that it does indeed have its own time. Trust that this project has its own rhythm, the same way everything has its own rhythm....

Sense the inner rhythms of this project. Sense its timing. Trust that everything needed is coming together to make it happen in its own time.... Tune yourself to the needs of the project now.... Imagine listening to its heartbeat.... Trust the timing. As you breathe, let your own rhythms harmonize with the project.... Feel your whole being adjusting to the timing of the project as easily as the trees adjust to the changing of season.... Imagine it. Assume that, in fact, this adjustment is now taking place.... If you find that a shift is needed in order to make adjustments more easily, imagine making the shift.... Note what change the shift invites in your approach.... Imagine doing what is called for.... Feel yourself harmonize with the project.

Now let your imagination transport you into the future, after the project has come to full fruition. Imagine that its completion is an event in the past; that it has already come about. Don't worry about how it happened; just sense what it's like now that it has already happened.... Enter the time.... Feel it.... Imagine it in detail.... Get to know it.... Notice the difference the project has made...where it is most felt.... Sense the atmosphere, the quality of the scenes...how you're doing; how others are doing.... Get to know this time in detail....

Bring yourself to the juncture when the project has just been completed; focus on the moment of completion.... Imagine your sense of accomplishment infusing the scene.... You did it!

Imagine that you can take an about-face in this future time and see how it came to be.... Notice how everyone and everything coalesced to make it happen.... Focus on yourself; notice just what you did to bring it about.... Notice the space that was made to bring it about, the support there was for it...how it was nurtured along...what tasks were done...how the details were taken care of... how the big picture became increasingly clear...how you made it through any rough spots...if there are others you worked with, how you coordinated...how that unfolded. Witness.......

Now with your breath, breathe in the energy of the project.... Fill yourself with this energy.... Bathe every cell in your body with it.... As you exhale send the energy to your mind.... Imagine that it informs your thinking.... Let your heart absorb the energy of the project, too.... Feel your whole being become intimately attuned to it.... Sense the time that belongs to this project.... Be aware of the quality of attention it calls for.... Align your intent with what is called for....... Notice if there is anything that needs to be cleared away to make room, to make time, to give the project its due.... Imagine providing what is needed.......

Now bring yourself into the present. Notice what adjustments are needed to provide time and attention for this project to come to fruition....... Choose what you'll do; be deliberate. Imagine doing what's needed.... Imagine the support there is for this.... Tell yourself what you will do. You get the pacing just right.... Feel yourself easily meeting the deadline....... *Expect* it....

Three-Ring Circus of the Mind: Making Memory Magic (111)

Memory works by association. This meditation includes two techniques for training memory: one creates different associations for each item you want to commit to memory; the other creates one gesture that you will use every time you want to recall information. The first depends on you taking the time to detail out the associations and review them; the second works by training your body and mind to respond with recall when you hold the intention to summon up specific information at the same time as you make your gesture.

Making Memory Magic becomes effective with repeated practice. You can use either or both techniques to help retain and recall whatever you are studying. Both utilize the power of intention and suggestion. When you apply either technique it is critical that you hold in mind a clear sense of the specific information you want to recall and that you fully expect to remember it on demand.

The first technique: Making Magic offers numerous ways for you to construct an associative pattern. You will create a specific link for each item by including it inside a picture, song, rhyme, or story — this gives you a string with which to fish it out later. For this technique to work you must take the time to create an association for each specific fact that you want to remember. It is good to elaborate on your association by adding visual, auditory, or kinesthetic cues. Create only one association per item: you will confuse yourself if you create two unrelated stories for the same thing. For example you could think of something you are memorizing and envision setting it down in a specific spot in your house. Create a rhyme and imagine reciting it when you stand next to the item. Then post a label there to act as a visual cue. It is also possible to create associative links to the stories related to different items. For example you could have the final line of your rhyme call you to another room where you have envisioned placing the next item you want to recall.

The second technique: Create a gesture that you will use every time you want to recall information. Choose a gesture with metaphoric meaning: touch your thumb, index, and middle fingers together or gently bite the tip of your tongue to signify having information at the tips of your fingers or on the tip of your tongue. Follow the prompts in the meditation, being sure to repeat to yourself any suggestions that are called for. You might want to actually speak aloud in order to create an auditory association.

Making Memory Magic can be used in its entirety or in parts. Skim the meditation before using it to see how it works, then do a quick review of your study material to give yourself a good overview of what you'll be working with. To promote spontaneity you may want to begin with *Fun (33); Intelligence (18)* is also a good enhancement.

This is a time for the mind to show off its tremendous capacities. There is a special place, a magical space for the mind to perform its great feats of brilliance; its acrobatics; its genius for comprehending the widest, the deepest, and the most precise reflections of the universe. Your imagination is transporting you into its magic mind place now.... This is where the greatest acrobatics of the mind are performed; wild animals are friendly here; oddities are normal here; what may first appear as boring lights up with cheer here.

This is the magic three-ring circus of the mind. A rehearsal is about to begin. Everyone is in their dressing rooms getting ready. Imagine going to the different rooms; see what acts are in store....... Now imagine meeting up with the ringleader who is ready to brief you and provide you with the program of the show. Read it aloud. What is on the learning program for today?... Imagine reading all about it.... How are the pieces separated into chunks?... When are the intermissions?... Imagine the ringleader giving you a preview of the performance.... Maybe there are some snapshots or promotional materials that would be of interest.... Let yourself be excited about this new adventure your mind is about to embark on.... Feel your curiosity on the alert....

Be deliberate; clear your attention so you can concentrate on the acts that are about to be performed.... Breathe out distraction.... Clear the rings.... Let yourself settle in for the show. Feel yourself in a state of open anticipation, ready for the show to begin.... Tell yourself that you will give it your undivided attention.... Tell your inner critic that it can take a back row seat, because at this time comprehension, retention, and recall are on the program; there is no time for assessment — that comes later.... Just sit back and enjoy the show. Now tell your imagination about what is on the program and what you especially want to watch for in each act....... *(Be specific. Name it.)*

This is the magical place of the mind; here you get to watch and perform at the same time. You may want to go around to the different dressing rooms and meet the performers. Some of them may be aspects of yourself.... Imagine the performers limbering up now. They're concentrating, going over their parts in their mind's eye.... Notice this. Talk to them about their acts if you like.... This performance is done in your honor; you get to be in it and to watch. You get to play. You get to improvise. You're going to have a good time.

In the magic of the three-ring circus everything comes alive. Your creative self gets to be in the act and play with the script. Sometimes cartoon characters crawl right out of the pages and start to dance. Tell your creative playful self to be on the lookout for information's quirky side: jingles, rhymes, puns, and special vignettes of meaning may pop into mind. Tell your imagination to be on the lookout for what anything reminds you of.... Tell it that as soon as anything, no matter how silly, appears in awareness to let you know.... That is the time to stop and improvise; let the reminder mingle with the information and see what story gets created. They'll make a song, a dance, or a skit together. You may find that you want to try different costumes.... Bring the information to life.... Make the script have more meaning.... Ask the ringleader to capture the highlights of the scene with the camera. The snapshot freezes the moments in memory.

Sometimes in the magic place of the mind the best way to welcome new information is to bring it into old and very familiar surroundings. Here in the circus there are replicas of your current and childhood homes. You can give the new information a place inside your home. Imagine the sound it makes and the place it takes.... Some information is especially memorable because it makes itself at home in very unusual spots — like right smack in the middle of the hall, where you are sure to stumble into it...or you hear it on the radio; sometimes moving pictures place themselves on the wall; sometimes the wildest things show up in the fridge or drop from the rafters....

Other times these great improv performers link together all the information in a chain. They love to play with lists. The characters line up and create a short skit, song, or rhyme with the next in line; one plays with two, then two does something with three and three brings four into the picture.... The improv goes on down the line....... Whenever you want to return to the information, one link pulls in the next.......

Then there is the clown who makes up the dumbest ditties, so dumb you can't get them out of your mind.... They fit right into those tunes you know best.... Whether the information is placed in the house, in a chain link, or in a song, it finds a place where it belongs, an associative string.... Then later any detail can readily be fished out by simply bringing its place to mind. Tell yourself this is the case....

Whenever you come across particularly difficult information there is a fortuneteller who will be of great help. Go find her when you need her, and imagine what she has to say when she looks into the matter. Ask her a specific question and she will offer an insight on the issue. If you like, imagine doing so now.......

Sometimes you may want to give part of yourself a magic thinking cap; then that part can better think about it while you move your attention on to the new information coming in. Assume that understanding will be ready for you when you return later. Tell yourself that this is what happens whenever you use this magic thinking cap. Imagine how it will come in handy.......

(Choose one gesture that you will use to program your body to recall information you want to access later. Use this same gesture for the recall of other information.)

Tell yourself that whenever you *(name and make the gesture)*, this experience comes to awareness in full living color and stereo sound — everything detailed and in focus.

(When you read this, simultaneously make your chosen gesture and name the important information that you are flagging. Tell yourself that when you want to recall it later, all you need to do is repeat this gesture with the specific inquiry in mind to make the information quickly become apparent. As you tell yourself this, envision it working.)

All the performers are all limbered up now. The stage is ready. Turn up the lights. Everything is brighter now. Tell yourself you will have complete concentration, comprehension, retention, and recall of all the information you are about to study....... Tell yourself that whenever you *(make gesture)* you will recall it in full detail.... Tell yourself that when you bring the associative strings to mind, the information gets fished right out of memory.... Name what you are about to study.... Expect your mind to perform. Trust the brilliance of your mind.... Let yourself play with intelligence. Relax, breathe, and learn. Learning is as natural to the mind as breathing is to the lungs.

Tell yourself you will return to the magic circus of the mind soon to see how the acts play themselves out........

(Go directly to study without using your usual count-out. Throughout the study session use your gesture, naming what you'll recall later and stopping to visualize what it is doing in the circus: an improv skit or a chain. Sing it; rhyme it; put it in the familiar environment of your home. During your study let your imagination play with each item to remember. Immediately after your study session, return to the following paragraph.)

Now that you have completed this study session, tell the ringleader what you learned and all the things it inspired in you. You may want to speak all about it aloud. Tell the ringleader what the different parts reminded you of....... Be specific and detailed.... Make your own snapshots now. Review each and every place you created for all the information....... If any information is still wandering about with no spot to settle, create an associative string for it.... Place all the information in the familiar places. Let yourself joke about it. Review it all....... Use your gesture and tell yourself that whenever you use it again, the information comes right into the spotlight of awareness. Tell yourself that whenever you pull the associative string the information gets fished right out of memory. *Expect* this to be true.

Take some time to be a storyteller. Pretend that all this information has already come in handy. Recount how you used it. What happened?......

Imagine how many rehearsals are needed to really get the script down.... Imagine when you will review the performances as you go about the routine of the day. Maybe when you are in the bathroom, or stopped at a red light; choose times throughout the day when you'll review the circus acts.... Appreciate your mind for its high performance....

High Performance: Test-Taking (112)

This meditation is designed to be used with *Three-Ring Circus of the Mind (111)*. You will significantly increase your success if you record it on cassette, integrating the specific information you need to remember with the associative patterns you have created. You can then replay the tape while driving, exercising, or falling asleep. If you listen to it in the background of your awareness, it will reinforce your learning process.

Now project yourself into the exam room. Bring the ringmaster with you and any other friends you have made at the circus. Bring your pile of pictures. Imagine going through the whole exam using your pictures, your rhymes, and your gesture — all of them are with you. You have complete recall of everything. Amazing. And you know what it all means....

Envision yourself reading the questions, and each time you remember the associative string; use your gesture, and the answer is right there in the spotlight of your awareness. Recognized.... You answer each question with precision and accuracy. If an answer isn't right there give part of yourself the thinking cap and move on to the next question, knowing that when you return the answer will be there waiting for you.... When you get back you'll find the answer there; if not, then envision the expert on the issue. Ask the expert. Imagine that the expert tells you the answer. See yourself filling in the correct answer. Imagine how you will do this....

Imagine that you even enjoyed yourself in the exam. You got another chance to play with the circus characters. You performed with flying colors. Great reviews! You did it! It is true!... Imagine how you'll feel when you find out you passed with flying colors....... Imagine how you'll feel walking through the door of opportunity....

You did it! Thank your mind for being so brilliant and for providing good entertainment....

Preparing for a Job Interview (113)

Active Imagination (11), Receptive Imagination (1J), Integrity of Your Being (4), Inspiring Your Very Best (25), and/or *Personal Power (19)* will augment this meditation. For the best results use *Create a Symbol to Tap Energy in Daily Life (13A)* as an ending. Wherever possible substitute real names and titles for "company" or "job."

Appreciate your value. You are fully capable. During this meditation give yourself permission to pretend that this is one hundred percent true. You are fully capable. For now, let go of whatever shortcomings you may think you have, and focus on your ample capacities....

Bring to awareness your experience — you do know a lot. Remember what went into the development of your knowledge. Bring all of this into the forefront of awareness.... Appreciate all that you know...and all the ways that you have come to know what you know.... Remember your learning experiences. Let these times parade through your mind now.... They have empowered you.... You are knowledgeable. You are competent. You are capable.... And just as important, you are a good learner. You easily acquire whatever knowledge you need to be equal to whatever challenge you face.... Feel how all of this is true.... Acknowledge your intelligence....

Now focus on your character. Appreciate your specific strengths.... Acknowledge your special sensibilities.... Remember your passions.... Recall your talents.... Bring to mind times when these have all come alive...your strengths, your sensitivities, your passions; your talents sing and dance...and you sparkle.... This radiance is infectious.... Imagine how you can inspire others. Imagine it.... Exaggerate it.... Feel the potential.... All your capabilities, all your skills, talents, humor, sensitivities, all of them are sparkling.... Then maybe they settle into a quiet and steady glow....

Imagine the people who will be interviewing you.... Let your imagination conjure up the scene.... Imagine the room they are in.... Imagine the building.... Imagine the other people in the company. Let your imagination create all the detail.... What are people doing?... How are they interacting?... Sense the working atmosphere....

Now insert yourself into the scene. Envision it as if you were watching a movie.... Notice what you are doing.... Notice specifically how you are contributing....... What kind of rapport do you have with the people you're working with?... Notice how your contributions are making a difference....... Imagine what people say when they acknowledge what you have done.

Focus on how your unique combination of skills, talents, and temperament fits into the scene like a well-worn glove — a perfect fit...as though you and this workplace were tailor-made for each other. Pretend this is completely true.... Now imagine that you are actually inside the scene, no longer watching it but in it.... How does it feel?... Let yourself become very familiar with what it is like to have this job....... Experience how your life feels with this work.... What adjustments have you made so it fits even better?... Open to this new work.......

Now bring back to awareness the people or person who will be interviewing you.... Imagine the interview is taking place now. Imagine the room you are in.... You exude confidence.... Imagine yourself glowing or sparkling. Feel yourself fully in tune with your interviewer/s.... What are they looking for? What are they concerned about?...... What are you asked?... How do you answer?...... What else do you want them to know about you?... Imagine the interview unfolding.... As it does you begin to enjoy each other...your rapport gets stronger and stronger. It is a very dynamic scene....

Imagine them choosing you.... Imagine where you will be when you are offered the job.... Feel your excitement, your sense that this is right, your gratitude....

Speak with Eloquence (114)

This meditation is designed to follow *Courage (20)*, and it is best to conclude it with *Create a Symbol to Tap Energy in Daily Life (13A)*. It can be enhanced by combining it with *Grounded and Open (39)*, *Mustering Courage and Confidence to Express Your Truth (55)*, *Personal Power (19)*, *Active Imagination (11)*, and/or *Inspiring Your Very Best (25)*. If you want to use it for speaking up in public, just change the imaginary scene.

You have the courage to speak.... Call upon your clarity, your eloquence, your brilliance. Invite them to come forward.... You do have these qualities inside — however dormant they may be. Trust your potential. Your spirit can call these qualities forth. Experience each quality: clarity...eloquence...brilliance.... Remember times you have exhibited these qualities.... If no times come to mind, think of someone who has them.... Imagine your version of them — however you imagine it.... Experience clarity, eloquence, and brilliance.... Let your imagination conjure them up. They may come through as a knowing without form, or maybe as sensations in your body, or colors, or in your visions.... However you imagine these energies is how you tap their power. Feel the shift in your sense of self as you draw them out.... Breathe.... Invoke their powers.......

Bring to mind the topic you want to address.... Bring to mind what you have to express.... Bathe it in your clarity, eloquence, and brilliance.... Imagine your speech becomes animated by these qualities.... It comes alive.... Listen to the speech; let yourself hear what it wants expressed.... Listen deeply; let yourself know it.... Feel it.... Let yourself be inspired....

Invite all of these powers to be with you when you make your speech.... That you stand strong in your body with your strength of character...your courage...your clarity...your eloquence...your brilliance.... Imagine all the qualities you need are relaxed and alert within you.... Ready to go. Breathe them in.... Draw them into your body.... Draw them into your mind.... Draw them into your heart.... Breathe in these qualities.... Feel them inform your whole being.... Embody them.... Now bring to awareness any anxieties that you had.... Breathe through these feelings. Breathe and release them.... Breathe and experience how excitement has taken their place....

Again remember the substance of your body. Feel your bones giving you a frame to stand on. Feel your muscles giving you form, strength, flexibility.... Now project yourself into the event where you will be giving your speech.... Imagine yourself coming up to the podium...standing in front of the audience, standing in your power, standing in the fullness of your being.... Imagine looking over the audience.... You naturally tune yourself to them....... There may be someone there you especially want to speak to.... And you begin.... Imagine projecting yourself from the wholeness of being itself.... You strike exactly the right note. Energy moves through you...energy of the audience...energy of the spirit.... Energy; the whole room is charged with it...energy.... Feel it. Experience yourself expressing the truth of the matter — crystal clear.... The whole room comes alive.... People listen intently...fully grasping what you say...moved by it!... Imagine yourself inspired more than ever before.... Feel the exchange between you and everyone there...fully in tune....

Imagine what emerges as a result of all that you said.... Appreciate the fact that you did so well — honored to have had the opportunity....

Dissolve Writers' Block (115)

With word substitutions this meditation can be used for other art forms. For example, if you are composing music, replace "language" with "music" and "words and phrases" with "melody and rhythm"; or if you are a sculptor, after the word "language" insert the words "of shape and form"; other artists could replace "writing" with "dancing" or "painting". Many meditations will enhance this one; use the ones that fit your circumstance (i.e., if you need confidence, discipline, pacing, inspiration, or insight, etc.).

Witness language — language as a form of expression, words, phrases...they string together, and you say what is needed...precisely reflecting your experience in your own distinctive voice.... Like magic, what is inside you is carried by words and reflected on the outside.... You can create fantasy with words; you can create reality with words. Words are magic — give them shape and they channel energy.... You express exactly what you have in mind.... Remember how this feels...exactly what you have in mind comes through eloquently. The words dance...arrange themselves...sometimes rearrange themselves. Like art, you can paint with them. You can hear them make the music of poetry. You can feel them shape reality.... Words — they awaken the senses and create realities.... They carry information and inspire particular responses.... Words are magic.... They sing; they dance — use them like a magic wand, bringing to life everything they touch.

What atmosphere is needed for your words to come alive...for you to write?... Like growing a garden, everything needs to be done: the soil needs to be prepared; the seeds need to be planted, watered. For plants to flourish, the garden has to be weeded. Imagine laying the groundwork for your writing to grow.... What space, what time is most conducive?...... Is there any food needed for thought?... What will quicken your mind?...... What will touch your heart?... What will awaken your spirit?... Discover your voice.... Trust the expression of yourself — your ability to write, to express yourself — fluid, fluent, eloquent, concise.... Claim your voice. See yourself write.......

Bring to mind what you are writing....... What is the purpose?... For whom?...... How will they receive it?... What do they need?...... What difference will it all make?...... Imagine success....... Zero in on the detail that made this happen.......

The writing has a life of its own. Imagine that it speaks to you....... Listen intently.... The information will organize itself naturally....... Listen; the characters have much to say....... Watch the issues come into focus....... When it's finished...polished in its best form, how will it be?...... What form?...tone?...voice?

As you write you are always acutely aware of your thoughts surfacing into the light of awareness from the depths of creativity.... You clothe experience in the words that fit just right.... Clear. Concise. Eloquent.... The writing takes on a life of its own; you give it life and it grows stronger, becomes animated. You discover the life it has.... It flows.... Like a gardener, all you need to do is water, weed, and the plants grow....

Trust your process as your writing comes alive.... You know when to shape it and when to let go and watch it take off on its own. You know when to manicure and when to let it run wild.... Tune to the piece you are working. Breathe life into it.... Breathe with it.... Be with it.... Listen deeply....... Witness all the information, all the sentiments, all the details, falling into place....... You know when it is finished too....

Notice if there is anything you need to give up to make room for writing.... Is there anything you need to cultivate to support it?... What routine will create a warm and nurturing place for it to germinate?...... Imagine giving it what it needs....... Tell it what you will do....

SECTION SIX:

Creating Wellness Together

INTIMATE RELATIONS

Intimate relations ought to be one of our greatest sources of joy. For some of us, our friends, partners, and family are the center of our lives — the ground for our power in the world. For too many of us, however, these relationships have been the context for abuse. When we are intimate the wounds go deep. The meditations in this section serve to heal and to begin to establish different patterns of the heart. If you have been a victim of abuse, be sure that you get support when you are working on these issues. Be gentle with yourself and work with them at your own pace. See "abuse" in the Meditation Use Index to see which meditations will be useful to your process.

Family: A Place of Belonging (116)

You may want to use *Love (21), Calling the Ancestors (29), The Future Ones (30),* and *Home (44)* to augment this meditation.

F amily. Everyone longs for that place where we are loved unconditionally. Loved. Family is the place of love and support...the place to share life's ups and downs...the refuge in which we build up our strengths to meet the world. Family is the place of belonging...a place where you are known...a place of shared history.... Some families are far from ideal; family teaches how to create a home of love and support. Whether that teaching is from experiences that reveal how not to be or from models of loving community, family teaches how to create a home of shared care.

Family is at the center of the heart. Whether your family is one you create or the one you have been given, family is the heart of relations. Whatever forms families may take, they form the heart of community.... Family is the place of belonging...a place where you are known...a place of shared history, from one generation to the next. Tradition is kept alive through family lines.... Whatever your experience of family, your experiences have gone to the very center of your heart...to the core of your being.... Tune to the truth of this.... Family, the place of belonging; feel your place in time. There are those in generations before you...those in your generation beside you...those in generations after you. Family is the place of belonging in time.... Heritage. Legacy. Kin. Family, a place of shared history.

Witness yourself in family time: There are your ancestors who worked to nourish and sustain their children.... You were given life by your parents, birthed by your mother.... Many times family ties are not blood ties; yet still, family is made. Sometimes family is mostly made of one along with you; sometimes it is so huge it seems to extend every which way.... Acknowledge your family experience.... Revisit the journey: from infancy through childhood, sometimes accompanied by siblings...from adolescence into adulthood...from adult to being an elder.... Maybe becoming a parent, maybe a grandparent, a great-grandparent.... Witness family time.... You may not have gone through each, but these relations still form family ties....... Each phase is different, from being cared for by parents...to having adult relations with parents...with siblings...to caring for parents.... Life is cyclic. Each stage has its own gifts.... Each stage has its own challenges.... Witness what is true for you....... Imagine how the relationships change in your family as time carries you.... Feel how you change.... Imagine making the transitions from one stage to another, with dignity....... Imagine contributing your part to making family....

Imagine how you want to make family. Vision your own ideal family. Whatever form it might be, how would you make family if you could make it just as you feel it should be? Experience loving family....... A family in which hearts sing and spirits soar...everyone loves and honors one another.... Imagine how this would be....... Family...a place of love...a place of belonging...of trust. Imagine supportive relations...providing for everyone.... Everyone counts on one other, helps each other through...celebrates the highs...stays together through hard times. Family is loving, loyal, safe... in the safety everyone is free to discover their authenticity...to explore their passions...to give to community.... Imagine how you would be in family if it could be exactly how you would like it to be....... If you can imagine it you can make it so....

Family of Origin: Untangling the Patterns (117)

It is best to precede this meditation with *Family: A Place of Belonging (116)* and to enhance it with *Recollection (16)*. If you had a particularly difficult childhood, you may want to use *Protected View (12)* or parts of *Breath Is Home; Breath Heals (1G)* if tension arises. If you have more than one family of origin, then explore each, one at a time, by repeating the meditation questions. The third paragraph is designed to address the healing of childhood trauma and can be augmented with *Love (21)* or *Compassion (17)*. If you use this paragraph you may want to repeat it a few times to enhance its effects; if you don't feel the need for it, skip it. *Clearing Space Inside with Mental Housecleaning (11)* will enhance this meditation. Change personal pronouns if appropriate.

Now come back to present time. From this place in present time, look back into your family of origin.... Explore how it was for you. Witness where there are concentrations of emotional energy.... You are now going to review how your family was — the best and the worst...the lessons learned...of how to be...how not to be....

　　Go back into the past; witness what was so in your family. Remember.... What was the atmosphere in which your family lived?... What kind of energy field surrounded your family?...... Bring to awareness your family's many faces.... Witness. What was the quality of the relationships?... Remember.... How was love shared?... Where was the joy?... How were family members supported?... How were members controlled?... How were feelings expressed or hidden?... How was it for you?...... What roles were people cast in?...... If you had siblings, what was happening between you?... How were you viewed?... What were the expectations?... Did they free you or limit you?... What did you need to do?... Witness what was true for you when you were growing up....... How was it for you?... Were there ways you were neglected?... Were there subjects that were to be avoided?... Were there family secrets?... Witness what the rules were in your family....... Were there parts of your experience that you kept hidden?... Remember....... How was difficulty dealt with?... Was there shame anywhere?...abuse anywhere?... Were you ever violated?... Did you draw any conclusions about how the world worked?... Did you draw any conclusions about yourself?... What strategies did you employ to get love?...to be safe?... What did you do to make things okay?...... Witness.......

Wherever there was hurt take time to channel compassion to your child self.... Breathe....... Offer her loving attention.... She deserves it; she always deserved it.... Love heals.... Sense the ruptures mending.... Feel yourself becoming whole.... Breathe.......

Now focus on the context your family was embedded in.... Was there extended family?...... What were your community ties?...cultural ties?... What traditions did your family carry on?... Which empowered you?... Which undermined you? Recollect.......

Breathe. Bring yourself back to present time. The past is gone; this is present time. You get to choose how to carry the past. Know that you can shed the patterns that bind you and pass on the ones that strengthen you.... Know that this is true. Look over all the patterns; notice which you want to leave behind and which you want to carry on.... Note the strengths you gained; imagine how you will pass them on.... Honor the strengths; feel how they help you make family now.... Appreciate your parents for what they gave you.......

Note any negative patterns you still carry.... For any patterns that you still carry, tell yourself how things are different now.... Now you get to be free, shed the patterns that are no longer needed; breathe....... Breathe out all the old fear and anger.... Feel the relief.... Feel how it is to let it all go.... Tell yourself that the adjustments you used to make are no longer needed. Be specific.... Feel how things are different now....... Breathe the old ways out.... You can let them go now. Free yourself. Life has changed.... Feel that. Feel it in the very center of your heart.... Let your heart breathe a sigh of relief.......

You may even want to imagine what you would say to your parent/s or other members of your childhood family.... Tell them how you felt at the time and what is true for you now....... Reclaim your power. You are fully entitled....... Decide if you want to actually tell them.... If you do, imagine doing so in a manner that protects your integrity and inspires them to listen.... Imagine what is needed.......

Now look at your current family. Notice if there are any of those old patterns that you carried over. Witness....... Notice what the triggers are.... What sends you down the familiar path?...... When this happens your body tenses up...and you are off and running...in reaction.... Witness what you assume is true.... Notice if your assumption is accurate in present time. Witness.... Where is the fear?... What is the fear? Witness.... Breathe into the scene.... Make space for change to take place; life is different now. Let yourself know this deep in your heart. Tell yourself. Feel change.......

Remember your vision. Remember the feel of your ideal family.... Breathe in the vision.... Breathe out the fear.... You choose how to make family.... Notice what support you need to ask for so you are reminded that the past is history.... Now, with your current family, you create a home of love and respect together. Feel that. Reside in this knowledge. Feel how you are different now.... Feel how life is different now.......

Imagine that next time you'll remember and respond out of present time.... Imagine how that feels.... Imagine what you might say or ask members of your family to do now so that they help you remember the present is different.... Together you make a loving family....

Parenting (118)

Use *Integrity of Your Being (4)*, *Love (21)*, and *Family: A Place of Belonging (116)* with this meditation. If you are a father and/or have a son change the script accordingly. Fill in the blank with your child's name. If you have a number of children you want to focus on, make the appropriate adjustments in the script and focus on one child at a time. If you are not trying to sort out a specific child-rearing issue, skip the section Discerning What's Best; if you are, you may want to augment this section with *Crossroads (102)*, *Listening with the Heart (140)*, and/or *Ripple Effect (101)*. These may be inserted before the final paragraph of the meditation.

Tune to your child.... Invite her into your meditation now.... Sense her energy.... Feel the unique quality of her being.... Imagine sharing presence with your child.... However you imagine doing so.... Breathe, and relax into an appreciation of the sacred relationship between mother and daughter.... Appreciate the integrity of your daughter's being. She is a gift to the universe.... Appreciate the blessing she brings to your life...acknowledge the sanctity of your love — a love that never dies.... So intimate...as though (_____) is of you — part of your very flesh and bones. Yet she is not you; (_____) is a whole being unique in her own right.... In the quiet, be with this awareness; in the hustle bustle of daily life you may forget. This time is yours; take a moment to savor your relationship. It is sacred....

Bring to mind the many, many moments that have touched your heart; let them parade through awareness....... Feel them melt your heart all over again — wonderful moments.... Recall witnessing her thrill of making sense of the world...of mastering a new ability...feeling the joy of discovering the world.... Let yourself marvel at being able to experience life all over again through her eyes — a fresh look.... As she gets older, these moments accumulate into mountains of loving moments...enriching life...connecting you to what it means to be human. Love so fierce it is humbling.... Be with your experience of parenting....... *(Optional: repeat this paragraph.)*

As you exhale imagine channeling loving energy to your daughter.... Imagine this energy surrounding her.... Imagine it protecting and supporting her.... Know that this love creates a protective field in which (_____) discovers what life is all about. In this love she blooms into herself...into her life. Breathe, and love creates an energy field that surrounds her and softens any blows that might come her way. In this loving energy she grows into her true self. Feel how love protects her and invites her to discover herself....... You can't mold her into what you want; you can only help her discover who she truly is....

Notice the expectations you have for (_____) to perform — expectations of how she ought to be.... Find that place in you that believes that whatever she does is a reflection of you.... Witness which expectations are rooted ego.... Notice any feelings that need her to succeed so that you are approved of....... Notice your projections.......

Survey different interactions you've had, and witness your own motives.... Now as you inhale take back your projections.... Draw them back into yourself. Clear the air of these projections — vacuum them up....... Now breathe through them; transform them. Release them.... Breathe.... As you exhale let them go.......

You can't mold her into what you want; you can only help her discover who she truly is. Settle into honoring the person that (_____) is.... Appreciate the integrity of her being. Survey different interactions and notice if you ever withdraw your love when you are disappointed or dissatisfied....... Imagine changing how you respond.......

Breathe love and make room for her to be her own true self— whoever she chooses to be. Honor her right to choose for herself.... Imagine how you provide guidance, how you provide discipline, and honor the person she is all at the same time.... When you step forward...when you stand back....... Imagine how this feels.... What you would do.......

Discerning What's Best (118A)

If you have a dilemma about just how to handle a particular issue with (_____) bring it to mind now.... Remember the last time this issue was up and you were not quite sure of the best way to respond.... Let your heart simply share presence with this issue and with your daughter. Keep all of this in your awareness.... Breathe.... Be with it; give it soft attention.... You may want to imagine asking your daughter's true self what her experience is....... As you do, you'll find yourself knowing what is helpful.......

To go into it deeper, imagine taking one approach.... Choose one now.... Imagine it unfolds like a movie in you mind's eye.... Witness what happens...how it affects her...how it affects the rest of the family...how it affects you.... Notice where you need to let go.... Notice where boundaries would be helpful.... Notice teaching moments.... How does the rest of the family play into this? *(Repeat this paragraph for as many issues and different approaches as you are exploring.)*

Imagine what needs to be explored or communicated with other members of the family....... Imagine moving forward in the way that feels best for everyone. Imagine doing what is best for (_____)....

At Wits' End with the Children (119)

This meditation is designed to follow *Avoid Breaking Point (133)*. It is written for parents; with minor changes can be used for other relationships, such as aunt, teacher, etc. Wherever it says "your child" substitute the child's name. Change the pronouns, and "daughter" to "son" where needed. If you are working on relationships with more than one child, then repeat sections and focus on each child separately. You may want to use *Inner Witness (1H)* or *Highest, Wisest, Deepest Self (14)* to augment this meditation.

Children are who they are.... Your child has her own timing about when and how she'll grow up.... Sometimes she has a whole different idea of what to do or what not to do.... Sometimes she is right. Sometimes you have a better way.... Imagine that there are cords that connect the two of you.... Imagine that all the struggling energy pushes and pulls through these cords. When you get reactive, energy bounces back and forth between the two of you; the cords get all knotted up — entangling both of you.... Each push, each pull tightens the knots.... Witness how this happens....... Imagine the tangle of energy bouncing between you in each of the scenes....... Now imagine you breathe space into these scenes.... Imagine that as you breathe you untie the knots and cut the cords; the energy between you loosens up...and maybe releases all together.... Imagine it in each of the scenes....... Breathe openness into the scenes.... Feel them open....... Now listening happens; you listen with heart.... Feel yourself able to respond out of mindfulness....

Breathe; take the long view. Bring your witness into the scenes and observe carefully.... What happens to you?...... Just what sets you off and running down the road of reaction?... What would you have needed so you could have responded instead?... What would have made the difference?...... Imagine how the scene would have unfolded differently if you had responded instead of reacted....... Try on different responses....... How does it feel to remain mindful?... Are there others who can help shift the dynamic?... What has your daughter taught you about your own limitations?... Appreciate her for the learning she offers you....

Now tune in to your daughter.... Have compassion for her.... When you let go of your side of the tension you can see what is true for her.... Listen with your heart....... What sets her off?... Does this signal anything deeper?... Shift into your child's perspective and notice just what is happening on her end.... What's hard for her?... What's really bothering her?......

Take the long view. For each of the scenes, ask, "Will this matter next week?... Will it matter next year?"... She may have some irritating habits; imagine in what situations these same habits may prove useful.... Take the long view.... What are the lessons here?... Draw upon the deep well of love you have for your child. In the light of love what is the best approach?... What is best for your child?... How can you take care of yourself?... What support is there for each of you?... How does the rest of the family play into this?... How might you build trust?... Notice what can be done....... What boundary made or boundaries held to?... What needs to be let go of to make room for change?... Where is guidance needed?... Where are the windows, the openings, the teaching moments that might come up next round?... *(Repeat this paragraph as many times as there are scenarios to work through.)*

Healthy Family: Zeroing In on Disturbance Patterns (120)

You can start this meditation with *Family: A Place of Belonging (116)*. You may also want to use *Love (21)* and/or *Home (44)*. It can be used in conjunction with *Parenting (118)* and, with minor adjustments, can be used to focus on issues that need addressing in other kinds of relationships such as a community group or an old friendship. Use names; if you are focusing on a group, replace the word "family" with the name of your group. *Clearing Space Inside with Mental Housecleaning (11)* will augment this meditation.

Now notice how the family has been of late....... You can focus on immediate family or widen your view and include extended family.... Witness the moods, the feelings in the air.... How each of you has been.... Witness the patterns of exchange....... Pay attention to each of the different people in the family, and notice how it seems to have been for each of them?... Focus in on them one at a time. How are they doing?... Sense what is so....... Tune in to how it has been in the family as a whole....... What are the patterns? Good times...hard times...rough exchanges...love expressions.... Witness how it has been....... Are outside stresses spilling in?......

Reflect. Is anyone giving more care than they're getting?... Is anyone neglected?... Does anyone need special attention?... Is anyone being taken for granted?... Has everyone been contributing?... Is everyone taken into account when choices are made?... Who makes the choices?.... Be aware of how it has been of late. Where are the disturbance spots?... Where is there discordant energy?... Where is there dissatisfaction?... Anyone getting typecast?... Is there rivalry?... Is there cooperation?... What brings happiness?...... How are love and support expressed?... What is hard?... Anything festering?... Anyone distancing themselves?... Any negativity being held onto?... How has the family been?... Review what's been true..........

Tune in.... Has anything flared up?... Has any conflict gone underground?... Is there any silent stewing...or active rebelling? Notice.... Is anyone trying to get someone to do anything without directly asking?... Are there any currents that run counter to the family?... Anything eroding trust?...... Can you count on each other?... Is there honesty?... What raises tension?... What lowers tension?...... What inspires free expression of loving affection?... Where are the bonds being built?......

Now imagine looking through the eyes of others in the family....... Choose one person at a time, and imagine how the family is seen through their eyes.... How does it seem? How is it different?... What is needed for well-being?... *(Repeat as many times as needed to explore each person's perspective.)*

Now choose one area of dissatisfaction or discordance at a time and follow the energy patterns.... Track the energy back to its sources.... Where does it emerge from?... Follow where it's leading to....... Are different energy currents moving at cross-purposes to one another?... What will it take to turn this into healthy conflict?... What is needed to establish an atmosphere of good will?... Imagine creating a safe context for good communication.... What would that feel like? When, where might that be?...... *(Repeat paragraph as needed.)*

Imagine what you could do together to honor the family.... How might you honor particular members of the family?...... What can you do together that is special?...... How might you express your love and appreciation?... How might you strengthen the fiber of the family?......

Attracting Your Match (121)

Use *Active Imagination (11)*, *Love (21)*, and *Faith: The Beneficent Dance of Matter and Spirit (22)* to augment this meditation.

Tune to your heart. Feel your heart warm and loving....... Feel the space in your heart for love to come alive and bloom.... Tune to your loving nature.... Reside in your loving nature. Love comes as naturally to your heart as breath comes to your lungs. Feel your loving nature....

Life has many facets. Imagine the different facets of your life that you would like a partner to join you in...in loving intimacy...in companionship...in passionate ecstasy.... You have many facets of your own being; in what ways, in what places do you want loving partnership?...... Imagine how it feels to have love join you in these facets of life.... Tune to those places inside that are ready to share. Imagine what you'll share....

Imagine that the facets of yourself that you share shine out, glimmering like a diamond.... Know that as you focus on what you have inside you are ready to share. You energize these places within you. They become magnetized. They glitter with magnetic energy; they hum.... They emanate energy, drawing in your match. Imagine that.... There is a person whose energies match yours, whom you'll be drawn to and who will be drawn to you. Know that this is true. Affinity is the way of the universe.......

Imagine how it will feel when you're already in the loving relationship you desire. Don't worry with whom or when; just imagine. Generate the feelings as if it were already the case.... Imagine.... How does your heart feel?... What is it like in the different facets of your life?...... How is daily life?... Imagine....

Review relationships that didn't work out....... Remember the learning.... Embody the lessons.... Now that you know this, how will it be different?... Imagine it....... Breathe out the old patterns and any residual emotional charge.... Clear your heart.... Relax into the knowing that affinity is the way of the universe. You have changed so that next time it will be different. Expect this to be the case.

Know that you are getting ready. That you are learning the lessons you need to be ready, to honor the loving relationship that is in store for you. Your heart is open. Expect to be drawn together, you and your match. Love is the way of the universe.... Reside in your loving heart.... Clear heart draws your match near.... Trust that when the time is right, the love in your heart will join the heart of another. Together; loving together. Expect it. It is the nature of the heart to love. Trust it. Believe it. Welcome it....

A New Relationship (122)

You may want to use parts of *Making the Sacred Container of Love (123), Open Heart, Sharp Mind (42),* and *Sacred Sexuality (58)* with this meditation. Repeat any part to deepen its effect.

A new relationship, a gift from the heavens...a loving exchange of energy. Getting to know this person who is so intriguing — it is a gift. Enjoy it. Let yourself ride the energy.... Appreciate the glow, the mystery.... Savor it....

Keep yourself mindful. Be present for what is taking place. Discover; don't project.... Imagine that you could gather up all your projections and breathe them out, let them go....... Open to discovering what reality has to offer. Breathe out all the fantasies and see what transpires.... Enjoy what is there.... Accept what isn't.... Honor the process that is taking place between you.... Let yourself be present with what is real. Breathe and enjoy the moment.... This relationship could take root and endure though time.... Or maybe it is short-lived — providing gifts and lessons before you part ways. Like the springtime, enjoy it while it lasts.

Breathe. Balance. Be present. In your own wholeness, discover each other.... Keep your power.... Be authentic.... Be in your heart.... Let your hearts speak.... Listen....... Come to know what is right. When each of you is fully present it is truly a gift.... Loving energy; celebrate it....

Making the Sacred Container of Love (123)

It is best to do this meditation with your partner. If that is not possible, as you meditate simply imagine being together. *Love (21)* will augment this meditation.

As you breathe feel your life rolling through you…. Remember the breath of your partner, life rolling through your partner, as though you breathe together. Life rolling between you…. With breath sharing presence……. As you breathe together, take time to remember special moments you have shared…loving moments…when your heart smiled, maybe even quaked…moments when the connection between you was palpable. Remember…….

Feel the deep resonance you have with one another……. Breathe with it…. Feel the love moving with your breath…. Receiving the loving energy as you inhale…. Absorb it. Let it soak into you. Feel yourself being loved…. Draw it in…. Feel your love for your partner…. Breathing, feeling the love you offer…. As you exhale release love…. Breathing together loving…. Loving together breathing…. Breathing your lives together…. Weaving your lives together with love…. Love is sacred. As you breathe, reside in the blessing of your love…….

Imagine that your love has a soft glow to it…. As you breathe together there is light weaving between you……. A glowing aura weaves around you and surrounds you. Imagine it……. As you breathe together you have woven a container for your love…. You are both lifted into the light of love…. Breathing together loving…. Loving together breathing…. Breathing your lives together……. Feel yourself lifted into the light of your love…. Supported. Sense it…. Your relationship has an aura that surrounds you, holds you, supports you, carries you. Feel it…. Breathing your lives together…. *(Optional: repeat any of the preceding.)*

Loving Forever: Living Your Truths (124)

This meditation is designed to follow *Making the Sacred Container of Love (123)*; you might want to combine it with parts of *Sacred Sexuality (58)*.

Feel how each of you is entirely welcome to be your authentic self in this container of love…. Make room for this to be totally true…. With breath create an openness to the particularity of the other's ways…. Each time you exhale feel yourself open.... To love is to truly recognize your partner. See your partner for who they truly are, in all the ways they are who they are. Not loving some aspects while rejecting others; instead loving your partner whole....... Welcome the other in wholeness....

Feel your own self held in this love, regarded for who you truly are — recognized in all the ways you are who you are. All of you held in the aura of love.... Both of you held in the aura of love.... Your whole beings loved, your strengths, your weaknesses, your sensibilities, your sensitivities.... Loving in wholeness.......

In wholeness, honesty and respect are ever present — always. Acknowledge the truth of this.... It's a blessing. Safety. In your intimacy feel the sacred tenderness of your vulnerabilities....... Appreciate the blessing of being welcome to glimpse the soul of your partner....... You can nearly taste the tenderness you have for one another, so keen you are, fully tuned to each other's sensitivities....... In the presence of trust, loving blooms in the mystery of sexuality.... Your bodies celebrate life, celebrate one another. Enact the sanctity of your love. It is a blessing.... Love carries you into the depths and heights of the experience of being fully alive. Moving together, following, riding waves of loving energy.... As you breathe, feel the blessing.... Feel the magnetism of your love.... Imagine that your love reveals aspects of yourself you didn't even know were there. In relationship you feel even more connected to your own self...to life...alive!......

Your love is made strong by all you have in common; all that you share and all the ways you are different. Your differences complement each other. You fit together well. You appreciate your strengths and accept your limitations.... Notice how this is particularly true....... Witness the many ways you relate to one another.......

Now tune to the deep caring you have for your partner, that feeling of wanting the best for your partner.... Feel your desire for your partner to thrive in discovering and enacting their fullest potential.... Commit yourself to supporting your partner to thrive. Let your heart smile to imagine them soaring in life....

What is needed to truly honor your partner? Experience how your love inspires each of you to bloom in your own right....... With each other's support, you both contribute even more to the world.......

Notice for yourself what always needs to be nurtured inside, never to get lost.... In the sanctity of love, your spirits thrive as you care for your own needs separately and together.... Notice where the private worlds live.......

What is needed to protect your love...your trust?...... Imagine the place you can make for sorting out your differences...the changes you each need to make...the tolerance you develop.... Imagine how you may care for your love through all the seasons ahead...through the years ahead....... How you keep love alive...thriving....

Now as you exhale, breathe out all this wonderful sacred energy; let it surround the both of you, making a container that breathes, that is alive. Imagine it.... Your relationship is alive.... Breathe out, and your breath creates a container for your sacred love.... Supported by your love.... Carried through time.... A blessing. As you breathe you weave your lives together — together though life's highs and lows.... Your whole lives bathed in intimacy.... As your bodies carry the changes of time your love deepens.... As your lives weave through time your love may seem to lose its luster as it moves into your very bones.... Imagine that you will always remember the sanctity of your love, always reside in it through the ordinariness of daily life, in quiet, warm, tender companionship....... Reside in your commitment to weather the storms together, to grow closer through difficulty....... In time your love grows stronger, richer, deeper then you ever imagined possible. A blessing.......

Infuse Your Love with the Qualities You Want (125)

This meditation is designed to follow *Making the Sacred Container of Love (123)*. The second paragraph can be repeated; simply replace "affection" with another quality such as commitment, mutual support, patience, etc.

Experience generosity and good–will flowing between you as you breathe. Generosity. Good–will. Draw it in. Breathe it in. Feel it moving between you.... Infuse the aura between you with these energies. Draw generosity in.... Bathe in it.... Good–will. Breathe in this intent.... Listen to it sing in your heart.... Become very familiar with how this generosity and good–will feel. How it feels to be regarded with this energy....... How it is to feel this way toward your partner....

With your breath draw in the qualities you want to build into your relationship. (Affection).... Experience affection. Draw in (affection). Feel the quality of (affection) between you. Make that energy present now. Draw it in with your breath.... Feel yourselves bathed in it.... You can almost feel your skin tingle with it.... What does (affection) inspire?... As you exhale imagine that your breath weaves (affection) into the aura that surrounds you both, lifting you into the light of love. Supported.... Breathe (affection) into the aura of your love.... It is perpetually present...in the air you breathe together. Your heart smiles at the very idea of it...(affection)...your skin tingles.

Imagine that these energies are always between you. Imagine this in different settings.... These energies always have a presence — woven in the aura you share....

Assessing a Painful Relationship (126)

Minor adjustments to this meditation will make it useful for any close relationship. You might want to use parts of *Inner Witness (1H)*, *Highest, Wisest, Deepest Self (14)*, and *Protected View (12)* with it. Use *Breath Is Home; Breath Heals (1G)* if tension arises. If you want to focus on the specific patterns of distancing, you can insert any of the beginning paragraphs of *Letting Go and Moving On (127)* where noted in the middle of the meditation. *Communication Makes Healthy Conflict (135)* and/or *Crossroads (102)* also have helpful passages to insert there. *Compassion (17)* will enhance the end of the meditation. Insert your partner's name in the blanks; read the series of questions slowly to provide time for reflection; and skip the questions about children if none is involved.

Tune into what has been so between you and (_____).... Feel the quality of energy exchanged....... What is the color, the texture, the moods? Witness it....... How have you been feeling?...... How is it together?... What is the quality of energy between you and (_____)?... What has been especially difficult?... Witness if care and love are exchanged.... Do you listen to each other?... Is there joy anywhere?... If your relationship has just grown dull, what could bring back its luster?... Remember what used to be so good.... What could be re-cultivated?... What might you do together? How might you be together?...

Tune into what has been so between you and (_____).... Where are the difficulties?... Is there anything festering under the surface?... Does anything flare up time and time again?... Witness how it is for you in your relationship.... What is good?... What do you look forward to?... Where are the disappointments?... Are there lost dreams?... Is your spirit shut down?...... Are there any breaks in your heart?... Is there anything you have given up?... How do you feel about yourself when you are together?... Is there anything really important to you that you don't share?... Or experiences you have that you keep hidden?... Witness these.... Is it safe to be whole together?...

(Optional: insert the first three paragraphs of Letting Go and Moving On *(127)* *here and, if you like, use* Communication Makes Conflict Healthy *(135) or* Crossroads *(102) to augment the following section.)*

Now imagine life together.... Feel what it is like.... What can both of you do to make it good?...... Can you make amends?... Can you make a renewed commitment?......

Imagine life separate....... Are you happier?...... What about the children?... Focus on each....... What would be best?...... What feels right?...

What do you really need in life now?... What do you and (_____) need to talk about?... What can you do that honors each of you?...

What is at stake?... What is needed for your heart to smile again...for your spirits to lift again? What is needed?...

Draw in compassion — all of this is very hard on the heart....... Breathe healing energy into your heart.... Let yourself settle into knowing what is best.......

Letting Go and Moving On (127)

This meditation can be used for any relationship that has soured, be it with a partner, friend, coworker, etc. Replace the word "partner" or "other" with the name of the person. You may want to use *Protected View (12)* before beginning. *Inner Witness (1H), Highest, Wisest, Deepest Self (14), Recollection (16)*, and/or *Compassion (17)* will enhance it. Use *Breath Is Home; Breath Heals (1G)* if tension arises.

Take the time to review the unfolding of your relationship. Witness what happened. Let it pass through your mind's eye like a movie.... Witness those moments you pulled back some — or maybe your partner did, or you both did.... Remember those moments when you pulled away from one another, maybe a little, or maybe there was a whole rupture...a door closed or slammed shut.... You decided not to go there again. Remember those times that something closed down inside.... Focus on those moments...on each one. Remember them....... Breathe.... Witness and replay them.... Breathe.......

Now take them one at a time. Choose one.... Focus on what happened; replay the scene.... What was going on inside you? What were you expecting?... What were you feeling?... What was communicated?... What wasn't?... Were there any early warning signs you ignored?... Did your projections keep you from perceiving what was true?... What did you do that fed the breakdown?...... What is the lesson here?... Would you do it differently if you had it to do over again?... What are the lessons here? Choose another time and witness what happened....... *(Repeat the paragraph for each instance that you want to review.)*

Tell yourself what you have learned.... Tell yourself that now that you know this, it will be different next time.... As you inhale feel the lessons settling in. Feel your energy shift inside....

Be forgiving of yourself. You did as well as you could have....... Breathe out any energy that got trapped inside when you shut down.... Go back to each of those doors that you shut and open them; let out the feelings that got trapped there. Breathe out any disappointment...or hurt...or anger.... Let go of feeling you were wrong...or wronged.... Breathe out any righteousness.... Breathe out all these feelings; they stand in the way of change.... Feel your heart soften.

You had a difficult time of it.... Appreciate yourself for getting through.... Forgive yourself....... Forgive the other....... Give yourself permission to move on.... Breathe healing into your heart, with color or music, with love.... Breathe healing into your heart.... Be kind to yourself. Have compassion for yourself.... Have compassion for the other.......

Let go — only in letting go can you make space for change and move on. Breathe out.... Trust change. Breathe with it. Feel time carry you.... As you let go you make space for new experience to manifest. You are different now. Your experience will be different next time. Expect this to be the case. You no longer draw into your life experiences that resonate with old ways of being. Now you attract different experience. Experience change.... Open to it.... Let time carry you forward.......

Keep Yourself in the Picture While Caring for Another (128)

This meditation can help you get in touch with your own needs. It is useful for women because we have been socialized to ignore our own needs while we accurately anticipate and fulfill the needs of others. It can be used in relation to a spouse, children, an ailing friend, or family member — just replace the word "partner" with the name of the person for whom you are providing care. *In the Quiet, Greet Yourself (41)* and/or *Integrity of Your Being (4)* will enhance it. *Create a Symbol to Tap Energy in Daily Life (13A)* is a good ending, as are the other endings that speak to change.

There is a part of you that is a superb caregiver. Find that part of you that is so keenly tuned to the one/s you care for.... Orient your caring self toward your own self; orient your keen sensitivities toward your own needs. Tell yourself that you count, too.... Tell yourself that, ultimately, only by providing your own self with good attention can you provide the best for your loved one/s. Orient your keen sensitivities toward yourself now.... Notice how you are doing.......

You are so tuned to the other that you respond to their needs before you even notice what's true for you...often before your partner is even aware of their own needs. You find yourself attending to their needs before you even know your own.... Your own experience may never come into view.... Your center of attention is always on your partner. In your responsiveness you abdicate your own experience. Your partner always takes precedence.... Witness daily life; notice when this is the case...when are you continually tuned to, responding to the other...not paying attention to your own self.... Your partner takes center stage.... When do you vacate your own experience? Witness.......

Maybe you compromised, let go of your own inclinations in order to satisfy the other — often without a word of negotiation.... As you did you moved away from your own self some. Remember.... Then the next time you compromised you moved further away from your own self.... And the next time you did it again — took care of the other, compromised, and lost more ground. And again — each time you left a little of yourself behind....... Witness if this is true.... Where have you left yourself behind?... Now you may be feeling hollow, empty, like somehow along the way you left yourself behind....

Ask yourself, "What does it mean to be loyal to me?"...... With your keen sensitivity retrace your steps.... Zero in on what was true for you.... Go to those moments that you left yourself out of the picture.... Reclaim your inclinations.... Retrace your steps.... Find yourself again.... Remember what your feelings were....... Imagine what might have unfolded had you taken yourself into account...if everything wasn't on the other's terms....... Honor your own self. Imagine what it would be like to be as tuned to your own needs as you are to your partner's.... Imagine how it feels to have your thoughts, your feelings...to be fully present in decision-making.... Welcome yourself into the scene.......

Retrieve yourself.... You count, too.... What are your needs? What has gotten lost in the shuffle?...... Imagine your needs being met.... Those who care about you want you to be satisfied, too....... Imagine asking for what you want....... Let yourself receive....... As you do you can feel the substance of your being breathing.... Everyone is more satisfied; you have taken your place in the relationship. You are there in the relationship.... People get to relate to you.... Love travels both ways.......

Giving Care (129)

This meditation addresses care-giving when the other person is physically unable to care for himself or herself. It is designed to be used with *Heal Alienation (49)*. Skip the second-to-last paragraph if balancing your needs with the other person's needs is not an issue. You may want to use *Clearing the Self (13T)* as an ending.

Care is a natural reflex of the heart. Caring knits the fabric of our relationship with loved ones, with life itself.... It is an honor to have the opportunity to maintain life with dignity...to care for one in need. Feel your heart smile to be part of a family, of a community by providing for someone who needs what you offer. Care is a natural reflex of the heart.

Feel the warmth of being in the presence of the exchange of care.... It feels good to contribute your part.... You do what has to be done, contribute to making life more dignified, partake in the most intimate necessities of life. As you do, your very life is woven into the fabric of family — woven into the web of life itself. It makes the heart smile.... In vulnerability hearts open....

It is in the simple necessities of life that the sacred reveals itself....... Feel the intimacy...as though the intimacy is an invitation to touch the essence of life. Quiet, yet filled with meaning. Tender.... Care strengthens you. Feel it.... It has a way of putting everything into perspective. What matters is on top.... Appreciate the intimacy with life that caring provides, as though care is an invitation to glimpse the very soul of life itself.... Quiet. Gentle. Profound.... It makes clear what matters.

Breathe. Let yourself reside in your heart…. Bring to awareness the person/s you are giving care to. Sense how this person is doing…. Imagine as though you could simply share presence with (<u>name</u>) in your mind's eye. Breathe…. Breathe together…. Let yourself sense what is so for (<u>name</u>). Imagine that you harmonize your energy with (<u>name</u>). Know that as you do, you find yourself fully tuned to exactly what is needed……. *(If you are providing care for more than one, you might want to repeat this paragraph for each person.)*

You matter, too; take time to focus your heart on your own needs, on your own self…. Notice if there is any part of you that has been neglected…. What care do you need?… Are there boundaries that you need to establish that will enable you to care for your own self, too?… Imagine where there is support for you…. Is there anything you need to ask for?…anything you need to say "no" to?… anything that needs to be said to establish space for your own well-being?…… Imagine balancing getting your own needs met and providing care…….

Know that in community, life is cared for. The heart smiles when care is there. Care for you. Care for those dependent on you. The heart smiles in the presence of care….

Easing Another's Pain (130)

This meditation creates a way for you to be supportive when another is in great pain. It is designed to follow *Love (21)*. Using the induction *Grounded and Open (39)* is recommended; *Inner Witness (1H)* or *Highest, Wisest, Deepest Self (14)*; *Breath Is Home; Breath Heals (1G)*, and/or *Compassion (17)* will also augment it. If, when you are finishing, you find yourself with residual bodily sensations that are not your usual experience, it is important that you regain your own equilibrium: use *Cleansing After Violation (59)*. The ending *Clearing the Self (13T)* will suffice otherwise.

For easing your own pain, imagine the self as though it were another person. Change the script so that the inner Witness is fully present with your pained self, and use *Keeping the Energies Moving Through the Day (13C)* as an ending.

Invite into the light of awareness the person whom you care about; the one who is in pain at this time…who is having a hard time. Imagine bringing this person into this loving energy.... Simply be with this person.... Share in one another's presence.... Let yourselves be reassured by the presence of the other.... Let yourselves relax into the loving energy that supports All That Is, the life force energy.... Breathe together.

Imagine that you both breathe in this love.... Notice that somehow it makes it a little easier to live with the pain.... It's comforting to breathe in the love.... Imagine that as you breathe out, you transmute some of the pain.... Experience how this makes it easier to relax....... You can use this loving energy to open.... Breathe in love.... Breathe out pain.... Breathe through the pain.... As you open you can simply be with the pain. It is a little easier.... It's when one withdraws, tenses up, and pulls away that the pain gets sharper. Relaxing with love makes it a little easier.... Notice this.... Let yourselves just be with it. Let yourselves be with each other.... Your love makes it all a little easier.... Breathe in love.... Breathe out pain.... Breathe through pain.... As you open you can simply be with the pain.... Reside with it as though it is next to both of you.

When you breathe love into the pain, the painful places, it helps the pain to open, revealing what is behind, beneath, within it.... It may have an offering...as it opens, you open, and it becomes easier to simply be with it, being with what is.... Give it soft attention....

Notice if there is anything you are inclined to do as a gesture of care and concern.... Imagine doing what you're inclined to do.... Keep that loving energy moving through you, all around you.... Sense how it expands the horizons of the scene, enabling each of you to live with the pain more easily.... As you open you can simply reside with the pain.... Energy becomes looser, more fluid.... Keep breathing.... Feel love present.... In the presence of loving energy, you can let go and just be...naturally...gracefully...everything fills with dignity.... You move through time gracefully, however hard it might be.... Residing in the presence of love provides support, eases it all a bit....

As you open to love, grace naturally emerges.... As you create this atmosphere of love, grace and compassion become your closest companions.... The whole scene is infused with such a deep dignity that it's almost beyond words; it simply is....

Death of a Loved One (131)

To the question What continues after death? a Tibetan monk responded, "Close your eyes and imagine a mountain." He paused a moment, then added, "The part that was doing the imagining is what continues." This meditation works with the imagination as the meeting ground between the spirit world and the physical plane and is particularly helpful when your loved one has lost consciousness. It will help you cope with an imminent death or one that has already occurred. If the death you are dealing with has taken place suddenly, and especially if it came as a surprise, you may want to assume that the spirit of your loved one is still between the worlds and able to be communed with. (It is likely that the one who died is in as much need of closure as you are.) When you read, fill in the blanks, and replace the words "loved one" with the name of the one who is dying or has died. Adjust the meditation to fit your situation — for example, dispense with references to care-giving if your loved one has died. This meditation is designed to be used with *Inner Refuge (9)*; *Inner Witness (1H)*, *Highest, Wisest, Deepest Self (14)*, *Compassion (17)*, and/or *Calling the Ancestors (29)* will augment it. Use *Clearing the Self (13T)* as an ending.

Imagine inviting the spirit of your loved one to be with you in your sanctuary.... Welcome (_____)'s spirit.... Take time to share presence with your loved one. Imagine simply residing in each other's presence.... Being together...quietly...softly. Be in your hearts together.... Breathe.... Be together....

Imagine doing a ceremony of care. It may be a simple declaration of love; it may be an elaborate sharing of song, dance, storytelling, and commitment.... In this ceremony you may want to call upon the deep powers of compassion and dignity to be with you.... You also may want to call upon the spirits of (_____)'s ancestors to join you....... However you're inclined, do a ceremony of care together now.......

As you do this ceremony, sense an aura of gentle energy surrounding you both.... It accompanies you through this time of transition — softens the blow a bit.... Sense that this is so. Just as going into shock makes room for healing, this energy eases the death process a little.... Open to the assistance that this energy provides for the passing...for letting go...helping both of you.... Breathe.... Let yourself quietly settle into this space.... This is a liminal place.

Together with the spirit of your loved one, review what has taken place recently.... Meet what is true with soft attention....... Draw upon the powers of compassion and dignity....... If tears come, let them be.......

Now let memories of times shared pour through awareness.... Watch them together. You have been through a lot together....... As you remember you may want to comment on them to one another....... Your relationship has been a great blessing........

View your relationship in its entirety....... Are there places that need attention?...forgiveness maybe?...or acknowledgment?...or secrets finally aired? Whatever it might be, notice what is calling attention....... Imagine what you have to say....... Imagine telling (_____)'s spirit now.... Decide if and when you will tell (_____) in person....

Listen with soft awareness, for (_____)'s spirit may have something to say, too.... Listen with deep awareness — there maybe no words — only knowing. Listen....... Be in your hearts together. Sense what (_____) may want to make their passing a little more comfortable, a little easier....... Notice what (_____) may need in the different dimensions of her or his being...physically...emotionally...spiritually. Trust your knowing....... Is there anything you might do that would help (_____) come to completion? Is there anyone that (_____) wants to communicate with?

Notice if there is anything you want to tell (_____). Are there any assurances you want to offer?...... Are there particular kinds of care that would ease these last days?... Special touch?... Food?... Music?... What would make these last days a little more comfortable?...

Is there care that the caregivers need so that special attention can be provided?...... Is there anything that needs to be said to family...to friends......to care providers?...

Review your experiences in this meditation.... Come to a sense of completion in the midst of this great loss. However you can do that — for your sake, for both of your sakes, love and let go.... Breathe.... Remember compassion. Remember the love and support there is for you.... If you are inclined, you may want to do a closing ceremony, too.... Offer your good wishes; imagine each of you moving on in your separate journeys....

Give thanks....... Reclaim the space in your sanctuary, and take some time now to be with your own self. Take some time to be with your own feelings........ Breathe....... Be present with yourself.... Be gentle with yourself....... If you have any feelings that you have been pushing aside — they may be screaming, may be raging — whatever your feelings, give them some air time now.... In the safety of your sanctuary let yourself have your feelings. Give them air time. Breathe....... Be compassionate with your own self.... Tell your feelings what you will do to give them space, too..... Be tender with yourself. Breathe.... Notice what you can do for your own self — be gentle with your own self, too.......

Grief Heals (132)

This meditation is meant to be used time and again. Different paragraphs are designed to address different stages of grief. Grief has many stages; sometimes one area needs attention while another is better left alone. Repeat the paragraphs that speak to you; skip the ones that don't. Any combination of *Reside in the Quiet (3)*, *Inner Witness (1H)*, *Highest, Wisest, Deepest Self (14)*, *Compassion (17)*, *Love (21)*, and/or *Inner Refuge (9)* will enhance it.

It is as though the Earth has cracked, quaked — catastrophe has hit.... But nowhere else seems to have changed; the rest of the world goes on as though nothing happened.... For you, nothing is the same. It is as though you inhabit a different world. It is as though there is a great distance between you and regular life — as though there is a bubble between you and everything else....

Know that this bubble is here to protect you. It is cushioning your heart so it doesn't break. This bubble provides you with the space you need to be in your experience.... You needn't do anything for anyone. Let the bubble provide you with the cushion you need.... Let it provide you with the time you need to be with your feelings — or to be with the absence of feeling.... This energy field supports you wherever you are. Inside this field of energy you get to just be.... This bubble protects you.

Take a few moments to relax even more deeply into your own self. Quietly relax into the presence of your own self.... As you exhale settle into your own experience.... As you inhale draw in this protective energy.... Imagine as though you could inhale tenderness. Tenderness.... Kindness.... Compassion.... These are the energies that fill the bubble; breathe them in.......

Each time you exhale, this field of energy around you becomes even more powerfully protective...buoyant. It wraps around you like a protective blanket. Imagine that every time you exhale, you create a field of presence around yourself...space is created around you. In this space you get to have whatever experience you need to move through this time in your life.... Imagine that as you breathe out you strengthen this protective field of energy....

This loss may cause you to feel completely alone. But in this place, in this energy bubble, when you feel alone you also can feel suspended in energy that has buoyancy about it. It supports you. Feel yourself supported in this energy....

In this space you get to have whatever feelings you have, whatever feelings pass through — all the different feelings that might pass through. Breathe.... Let them be.... This is your space, space for you to be in your experience, in whatever is so for you.... Each time you breathe out, feel that you create this field of energy around you. It provides you with all the room you need to heal.... Inhale; feel compassion.... Exhale; feel protection. Breathe.... Be kind to yourself. Breathe....

Feel your own presence.... Just be with yourself in your grief, whatever form it may take.... It may have changing faces, some familiar, some not.... Meet yourself with soft attention.... Be with whatever is so for you at this moment....... Here, you have all the time you need, however much time that is. This space protects you. In this bubble your wounds heal.... Slowly, healing happens — in time you emerge healed. This bubble will remain with you as long as you need it.

Inside this bubble you have all the space you need. To mull over what is so. Death. Love. Loss. Emptiness.... Sometimes you may want to scream; many times tears well up; anger may stiffen you, or rage may scream out.... Sometimes numbness envelops you. Whatever is so for you — let it be.... Be with yourself. Grieve.... Be tender with yourself. Give yourself the time you need — you deserve it. Your loved one would want this for you. Give it to yourself.......

Here in this field of protective energy, if you like, you can relive the moments of meaning.... Feel your gratitude for the love that has been visited upon your life....... Here you can have the conversations you need to...conversations with your own heart...conversations with the spirit of your loved one. You can relive the times shared — what was said, what was left unsaid. Here you can say what you need to.......

Grieve; be tender with yourself.... Give yourself the time you need to let go. Comfort that place in your heart where your love always burns and always will. Let compassion shine into your heart where the love lives.... This love has grown even deeper in the loss. As you let go, know that the love continues to thrive.... The love is still and will always be alive.... Let go and know that the love lives on. Shine compassion into your heart — draw it in as you inhale....Your heart begins to heal.......

You may want to do something that somehow honors the love you shared — a gift to your departed loved one.... Follow the inclinations of your heart.... Imagine doing what you need to.... Decide when you will do this.

There may be some special time coming up that is particularly important, but it is different this time around...maybe a birthday, maybe an anniversary, a special time.... Decide how you want to approach it. How can this time contribute to your healing? Imagine it........

If you like, take time to look back over the past, the loss. Notice if there are any particular spots in your experience that got stuck, that keep reverberating, that you keep going over and over again. Notice how you can somehow be with this concern and move the energy.... What you can do to release it.... Maybe you need to bring in forgiveness.... Imagine yourself moving the energy........ It shifts some.... Very gradually, it shifts. Sense energy gently changing.... All you need do is honor your process, and this field of energy supports you. Be forgiving. Have compassion. Healing happens as naturally as breathing.... Breathe.

Notice that there are those whom you can connect with — people who also experience loss.... Imagine that this field of energy around you connects with similar fields enveloping others.... You can feel that someone else has that same resonance of energy — loss.... It feels reassuring to know that there are others who know what is so. Your hearts can touch....

There are family and friends in your life who want to support you. Their hearts go out to you.... Let yourself open to other's care. Imagine how you may receive their concern.... What can they do for you?... Imagine receiving support. It comes in lots of different forms.... Imagine that those who care want to know how to support you through these times. Imagine asking for what you need....

Now, bring back to awareness the rest of the world. Things still move by quite quickly. Everything goes on as though nothing has happened. All the noise, all the different people, the different events — it all seems somehow very dull — trivial in comparison to the experience you're having. Imagine what you might need to say or do...what you might need to ask for so that you can continue to be in your experience — no need to pretend otherwise.... Imagine just what you can say.... Bring particular people to mind whom you might have difficulty with. What is needed to make room for you to have your experience honored?......

Imagine moving through the activities of life with this protective field of energy around you, always protecting the space you need to grieve...protecting you.... This protective energy will stick with you as long as you need it.... Trust it; be patient with your process.... Grief heals....

GETTING ALONG

Avoid Breaking Point (133)

If you are not using this meditation in relation to parenting or conflict, skip the last sentence in the second and third paragraphs. If you are, then fill in the blank with the name of the one with whom you are having trouble. Repeating sections of the meditation will deepen its effect. You also might want to use parts of *Smoothing the Edges; Soothing Irritation (5)* at the end.

B ring to mind the times you have felt overwhelmed...times when you felt it's all just too much — way too much.... Remember times when you felt like you were being pushed past your limits and you just didn't have it in you to deal anymore.... Breathe.... Recreate the scenes.... Meet them with soft attention.... Let them pass through your mind's eye now....... What happens?... Bring up the feelings that well up inside at these times.... Breathe, and be with your feelings. Give yourself permission to have your feelings — all of them — they are your feelings.... Let go of any messages that say you shouldn't feel this way; just be with your own process.... Breathe....... Life is difficult; appreciate yourself for hanging in there.... Like the storms that pass through, know that when you are with your feelings, breathing with your feelings, they, too, pass. It's when you don't allow yourself to feel what you feel that feelings become destructive.... Let yourself experience all of your feelings...then let them go.... Breathe...full breaths moving through...feeling and releasing all the frustration...feeling and releasing all the

exasperation...feeling and releasing any anger...any feelings of powerlessness....
Breathe.... Feel and release.... Let it all go.... Breathe it out.... Imagine the
energy drops right down into the ground.... Shake out your body if you like....
Breathe.... Let it all out; you may want to make some noise. This time is yours....
Inhale; feel it.... Exhale; release it.......

Now imagine pampering yourself. You deserve it.... Notice what you need
to reclaim your well-being. What do you need — not how you want (<u>name</u>) to be
— what do you need?...

However it occurs to you, imagine taking care of that part inside that needs
attention.... Feel it receiving exactly what's needed.... Inhale; absorb healing....
Exhale; relax. Breathe.... Whatever is happening, when you breathe through your
feelings the fire dies down. You cool.... In this calm feel all your tense reactive
energy drain away.... As you breathe, settle into accepting (<u>name</u>) for who (<u>name</u>)
is.... (<u>Name</u>) is who (<u>name</u>) is....

Breathe; find that calm place inside where you can accept what is so....
Breathe.... Have compassion for yourself.... Feel the quality of kindness soothing
you.... Draw in patience.... You do what you can, and that is all you can do.... Be
patient; you do what you can and that is all you can ever do. Have compassion for
yourself.... Feel the storm pass.... Breathe....

(If you are not dealing with parenting, you may want to insert Inner Witness
(1H), Highest, Wisest, Deepest Self (14), *and/or* Witness the Issue (98) *here.
Otherwise proceed to* At Wits' End with the Children (119).*)*

Really Angry or Irritated by Another (134)

This meditation is designed to follow *Enriched by Diversity (139), Inner Witness (1H),
Breath Is Home; Breath Heals (1G), Reside in the Quiet (3),* and *Compassion (17)* will
enhance it. Change pronouns as needed and use the person's name.

Bring to mind the one you are angry with, or maybe the one you get more and
more annoyed with. Bring this person to mind now. What (<u>name</u>) has done has

gotten under your skin, or maybe it was simply outrageous. However you feel about it, bring this person to mind. Imagine their presence.... Breathe....

Note when your own energy tightens up; breathe.... Breathe through the tightness; let your breath loosen you up.... When you find yourself thinking about what bothers you about this person, let it go.... Breathe.... Just keep (<u>name</u>) in your awareness and breathe.... Breathe through tension.... Keep doing this until you feel fully relaxed and have this person in awareness at the same time.... *(Repeat as needed.)*

Remember the great diversity of humanity.... Appreciate that (<u>name</u>) is who she is.... She has her own ways about her. Accept her for who she is now....... Breathe out any thoughts of what you think she ought to be.... Let go of hard feelings; breathe them all out....

Have compassion for both of you.... Breathe in kindness....... Offer it to yourselves.... Offer it to (<u>name</u>).... Be forgiving of (<u>name</u>). Offer forgiveness....... Accept what is so.... Breathe.... In kindness clarity appears.... Listen deeply; what is the lesson here?...... Imagine what you might want to say to (<u>name</u>). Imagine that next time you are with (<u>name</u>) you have a generous heart.......

Communication Makes Conflict Healthy (135)

Integrity of Your Being (4), Call Upon Your Life-Affirming Values (24), Compassion (17), Love (21), Open Heart, Sharp Mind (42), and/or *Enriched by Diversity (139)* are all meditations that will augment this one. Fill in the blank with the name of the person you are in conflict with. If you are both using it at the same time, use the generic "friend," "coworker," "the other," etc. If the conflict you are working on does not evoke tension, skip the second paragraph. On the other hand, if you are feeling a lot of tension, interject paragraph two repeatedly to help maintain an open state.

Breathe. Be in that place where you can be true to your own self and open to another's truth at the same time. Find it: strong in character and open in heart.... Be there now.... Breathe.... Occupy your spacious awareness and compassionate heart.... Bring to awareness the person you are having trouble with.

Share presence with (_____). Appreciate that you each have your own way of doing the best you can.... Breathe.... Draw in spaciousness....

If you feel yourself tense up, breathe. Breathe out hurt.... Draw in compassion.... Breathe out fear.... Inhale spaciousness.... Breathe out anger.... Breathe through rigidity. Breathe through righteousness.... Breathe.... Feel a loosening, an opening.... Breathe in spaciousness.... Breathe in compassion.... Keep breathing till you can share presence with the other person and maintain a peaceful state at the same time — spacious awareness and compassionate heart.... If you need to, take some time in your mind's eye to be with your own feelings.... Take care of your own feelings so you can be fully present with (_____). Bring in generosity and patience — whatever qualities are needed so that you are at peace as you share presence with (_____). Assure yourself of your own safety.... Have good–will toward yourself and (_____).... Breathe....

Open yourself to change. Reside in your own humanity.... You matter...and so does (_____). Feel yourself strong in character and open at the same time. Open yourself to the learning this situation offers.... Feel your commitment to coming to resolution...to discovering and transforming your own limitations. Feel your commitment to (_____). Feel your commitment to coming to resolution.... Breathe. Reside in your own humanity. Draw in humility.... Remember resolution exists, but it is larger than what you now know. Humility invites discovery. Let yourself be humble....

Remember what took place....... How did this affect you?... How did it affect others?... Reflect on what happened, how you felt, what you thought; reflect on what happened.... What was said or wasn't said.... What was done.... What it was you expected.... Give the situation soft attention.......

Reflect.... If you find yourself distancing from (_____) or judging (_____), breathe.... Remember that everyone has their own ways about them. Breathe.... Breathe out blame and draw in respect.... Breathe.... Breathe out judgment and draw in openness. Breathe.... Transform negativity with breath.... Have faith that with commitment you'll sort it all out.... Breathe. Have compassion for each of you....

Reflect on what took place.... How did it make you feel?... Anything similar happen to you before?... Is there any fear anywhere?... Are you worried about how you're seen? Or how you'll be treated?... Are you concerned about others?... What have you done that has made the whole thing that much harder?... Or maybe there was something you should have done but didn't.... Acknowledge your mistakes....

Find that open place in your heart to understand...to appreciate that (_____) has her or his own reasons. Remember what you value about (_____)...his or her contributions...sensibilities.... Remember what you appreciate about (_____).... What is true about (_____)'s point of view?... Find openness to deeply listen and learn what is true for (_____). Reflect on how you imagine it has been for (_____). Witness what is true for (_____). How does it look through (_____)'s eyes? What would it feel like to be in (_____)'s shoes?... Imagine....

How is power situated, exchanged, or wielded?...... What is at stake?... Reflect.... What is needed to honor everybody?...... What is the ethical thing to do?... What can you do to improve the situation?... Who else might be helpful?...... What would you like to ask (_____) for?... What can you apologize for?...

Now imagine what you want to express to (_____). Imagine expressing your truth to (_____), expressing what you appreciate and what has been difficult.... Be completely honest.... Imagine expressing your dissatisfaction without blame or judgment.... Imagine expressing what you feel is at stake.... Imagine this in detail....... Apologize for your part. Tell (_____) what you are willing to do to improve the situation....

Expect that you'll find a way that works for both of you.... Know that the truth of the matter is larger than you now know. Open yourself to discovery.... Have patience for human imperfections — both yours and others'.... Imagine creating a context in which all are honored — a context in which everyone cares and is cared for....

Just Relations: A Balance of Exchange (136)

This meditation can help you become aware if there is an even give and take in your relationships. It develops sensitivity toward balance, which can help redress differences in power, and creates patterns of thinking rooted in an appreciation of our interdependence. It can help transform the scarcity mentality that fuels greed into an abundance mentality that fuels generosity. It is designed to follow *Dynamic Center (23)* and *Protecting Yourself from Being Devalued (63)*. Insert names where you can. A group can use this meditation to develop tighter bonds by working on specific dynamics with others in the group.

Like breath, magnetism both draws in and releases out. All of life is both receptive and expressive.... All energy continually renews itself in a cycle of receiving and giving.... Everything is constantly transforming in the flow of life, receiving and giving.... As you receive you replenish yourself.... As you give to others they replenish themselves.... A continual cycle, as natural as the cycles of life itself.... You offer; you receive...as natural as breathing in and breathing out...taking in and giving out...all in a balance.... Feel it.

Appreciate what nourishes your personhood.... What do you receive that feeds your body?...... What nourishes your heart......your mind......your spirit?...

Acknowledge what you give.... It is needed; what you give is received, and what you need is given. All is cared for.... Witness the continual exchange of energy....

Scan your life for imbalance. Relationships where you receive more than you give or give more than you receive.... Focus on different relations, one at a time, and reflect.......

Now choose one relationship.... Witness what happens between you.... Do you respond more than you express?... Or express more than you respond?... Do you listen well?... Are you listened to?... Witness.... Are you always doing what the other wants?... Does this person ever want your input?...or ever take your

suggestions?... Where is the balance of attention?... Focus in.... Maybe between all the relations it balances out....... Notice if there is imbalance — you don't want any aspect of your being to get bloated or drained.... Witness how it is.......
(Repeat this paragraph as needed, choosing another relationship to explore.)

Notice what you need to do to bring about balance....... Life is about balance — you breathe in as much as you breathe out — when there is more going out than coming in or more coming in than going out, disease sets in.... What is needed to maintain a state of equilibrium in your relations?... Anything need to be expressed to anyone?...... Imagine bringing balance about.......

Imagine your life moving in a state of perpetual balance.... When there is balance life resides in a natural state of grace...as natural as breath moving in and out.... Relax into knowing that you receive what you need and give what you offer...in a balance as natural as breathing in and out.... Trust it — fully secure, knowing all your needs are met.... Feel yourself appreciating what you receive and being appreciated for what you offer...continual exchange, as natural as breath cycling through animals into plants, from plants into animals.... Feel yourself part of the great cycles of life itself...in balance.......

As you relax into this trust, a generosity of spirit becomes the driving current in your life.... You know that to hold on and hoard only creates bloating and restricts the resilient, fluid, life-force energy that your magnetic center breathes....... Feel generosity of spirit; you receive what you need, and you give what is needed...in a continual free flow of energy.... Relax into the support the energy creates — a web work of supportive relations of which you are a part.... Relax into your connectedness.... Trust there is always enough.... Feel your magnetic energy drawing into your life just what you need and being appreciated for just what you offer.

Extend your awareness; imagine that your whole community shifts into honoring this balance of exchange......with one another...with the Earth...with other communities....... Imagine the details of how it would be.......

Extend this feeling to the world.... Everyone sensitive to honoring a balance of give and take....... Everyone knowing that too much or too little causes unrest....... Imagine a world where the spirit of generosity, not hoarding power but generosity, is the currency of all relations......between people and the planet...between nations....... Balance of exchange....

From Conflict to Harmony (137)

This meditation is especially good to use if there is anyone in your life with whom you are at odds. It bypasses ego and makes room for new, harmonious ways of relating. It also deepens empathy. It is designed to follow *Integrity of Your Being (4)*, and *Compassion (17)* will enhance it. Replace "this person" with the name of the person you are focusing on. If tension arises, use parts of *Breath Is Home; Breath Heals (1G)*.

Bring to mind the situation that has caused conflict of late.... Recreate the details of the scene....... Focus on a person representing the other side, a person with a different point of view.... Appreciate how this person is also part of All That Is.... This person is infused with that same life-force energy that infuses you.... Sense the tone of this person's being; without words, simply sense the tone of this person's being.... Witness the particularity of this person's life expression...different from yours.... Witness....... Imagine the experiences that have accumulated to bring this person to where they are now.... Imagine what they care about...what they are striving for.... Sense the particularity of this person's perspective.......

Now let this person fade from awareness for the moment.... Bring your attention back into your own experience.... Witness what you care about...what you are striving for.... Remember what formed your perspective....... Witness yourself in this situation....

Now bring the other back into awareness. Step outside of your experience and imagine as though the tones of each of your beings are beside one another — however you imagine this.... Imagine the exchange of energy; as if it is portrayed in colors, temperature, lines, movements, sounds, textures, vibrations....

Imagine the nature of the energy between you.... How is the resonance?... Where is the attraction?... Which areas in each of you does energy move out of...and into?... From head to head...or from lower energy centers?... Sense what is so.... Are you both communicating to and from the same level?... Witness....... Sense how the energies interact.... Where the energies may be drawn to each other or repelled.... Where they may clash or complement.... Where they may recoil or lash out.... Where are the triggers?... Just sense what takes place between you.... Witness it.

Invite the healing, harmonizing forces of the universe to roll through the situation.... Both of you are bathed in these energies.... Breathing them, feel your energies begin to harmonize, creating unique tones.... Imagine these tones wash through both of you like waves.... However you imagine this. Hear their resonance.... Feel their depth.... See their colors.... Your spirits become generous....

How can you have generosity of spirit toward the other?...... Imagine opening.... Notice what you can do that might awaken a generosity of spirit in the other.... How can your shared humanity be drawn out?... Imagine the situation transforming itself....... Notice the spots of flexibility in yourself...in the other.... Notice where the two of you can connect — coming from your different experiences.... Notice the ways you can meet each other...or be parallel...or simply live and let live.... Explore it....

Imagine acting on these insights, knowing what's right to do.... Imagine what you can give.... Imagine what you need to ask for.... Envision a new way of interacting.... What would support this taking place?... Imagine the situation transformed.......

Exploring How You Are with Others (138)

You may want to use *Inner Witness (1H)* and/or *Clarity (46)* to augment this meditation. To help make needed changes, continue with *Enriched by Diversity (139),* and end with *Listening with the Heart (140).*

Bring to mind different people whom you often interact with...people whom you frequently see in different contexts: family, friends...in the community or at work.... To examine the quality of your interactions, choose one person or setting at a time and reflect on the following questions. When you're ready, bring another scene to mind and again review the questions. Explore as many settings and relationships as you like. Witness what usually takes place.

Now choose one particular interaction to focus on.... Imagine the individual/s; recreate the scene in your imagination.... Recall the nature of what takes place between you.... Notice the atmosphere that is present. Is it...rushed...or relaxed?...calm or on edge?... Is humor present?... Is care present?... Trust?... Notice the climate....

Now focus on your own self as you spend time with the other/s. When they are speaking, how much attention are you giving them?... Are you preoccupied with anything else?... Are you anticipating what you will say...or what they are about to say?... What thoughts are running through your mind?... Just what are you doing as you listen?... How receptive are you?... Notice what is often the case. Witness....... Are you dismissing them in some way...or judging them somehow?... What is happening in your body...in your heart?... Is there anything you're grasping for?... Anything you're avoiding?... Do you shut them out in some way?... What's keeping you separate? Just what are you doing as you listen? What are you concerned about? Is there anything you need to prove...or protect?... In what ways do you connect heart to heart...or could you connect?...

Imagine simply sharing in the presence of each other...as though each moment is a fresh moment, as in fact it is.... Breathe out the ways you distance yourself from the moment; breathe it all out.... Let go of whatever pulls you out of being fully present.......

You may want to explore another interaction. If so, bring it to mind now. Witness it. *(Repeat this and the two previous paragraphs as many times as you wish.*

When you are finished exploring, if you do not use Enriched by Diversity (139) *or* Listening with the Heart (140), *end with the paragraph that follows.)*

Allow yourself to live in present time with the other/s. Honor these relations. Give yourself permission to be fully present...to share presence. Let go of what preoccupies you. Let go of what keeps you separate. Be present together....

Enriched by Diversity (139)

This meditation reminds us to keep our horizons wide. Mass media homogenizes everything and everybody into one mass culture. But everyone is not the same, and if we forget that, then the soil becomes fertile for fascism. Augment this meditation with *Compassion (17)* and *Soaring High in the Skies (8)*.

Bring to awareness the abundant diversity of nature — the great variety of landscapes: from the forests to the deserts, from the high peaks to the deep canyons, from the farmlands to the wild lands — each place distinct...each place providing home for a multitude of creatures and plants — each being different than the others....... Difference is exquisite.... Appreciate nature's multitude of expressions.... Humbling.... Every place is part of the planet, and each place has its own story. Take a deep breath, and stretch your awareness to include the great diversity of life's expressions — truly amazing! Let yourself love life.... As you inhale feel your heart awaken.......

Appreciate that people are also distinct from one another. We each have our own story, and we are all part of the whole of humanity. Every single person has their own story.... We each have dreams; we each have nightmares.... We each have reasons for how it is we are.... We each have a story.... Take a deep breath, and stretch your awareness to include the great diversity of humanity.... Relax into an appreciation of the breadth and depth of humanity.... As you inhale feel your heart awaken....

As your heart awakens it is as though you become more and more receptive — almost as though you become empty on the inside — simply keenly aware and open to whatever crosses your path…. Experience this…. Remember your own interest in people…your curiosity in people…. Recall your care for the well-being of others…. Caring is a natural reflex — all of us are part of humanity….

Let your heart breathe…. Feel it relaxing into its natural state of caring…. As you inhale feel your heart awakening…. As your heart awakens, care and compassion come forth. As you exhale, imagine breathing out the qualities of caring and kindness. Feel them begin to spread…. As you inhale your heart awakens; as you exhale kindness spreads…. Caring expands out from your heart……. Imagine the air fills with these qualities…. *(Repeat this paragraph.)*

As the Earth provides space for all of creation, imagine your own heart becoming so expansive there is ample room for all the ways people are….

Listening with the Heart: Create Listening Space (140)

This meditation is designed to be used with *Enriched by Diversity (139)*. All or parts of it are useful in family, group, and community settings. Open with *Exploring How You Are with Others (138)* for an extensive exploration of your interactions with others and for building listening skills.

When the heart creates the climate, a keen sensitivity to every nuance emerges. Life in all its complexity and all its subtlety is fully apparent in the aura of an expansive heart…. Here humanity makes itself at home. Everyone is honored in their particularity…. The authentic comes forth. Sense this…. When kindness and caring fill the air they invite story…. Imagine an atmosphere forming around you which invites story and draws out truth — a listening space…. In this space you will receive the gift of knowing another.

To deepen this receptive space listen to these words; let these words open space inside you. Focus on your breath…. Listen to your breath — listen to the air moving in and out of your body…. When you quietly listen to your breathing you become fully present…. Listen to your breath. Listen. Your breath has sound. Listen…. Breathing…. Listen to the slight sound of air moving. Listen….

The rising of the sun awakens the birds' songs. Imagine that this atmosphere enables you to listen so deeply you inspire the sharing of heart and soul.... Listening. Sharing presence...honoring another with full presence. Let yourself simply be with the other person; simply share presence.... Sharing presence is a gift. In listening space you can even hear silence....... The space between you is sacred space. Only the authentic is compatible with this space. Here truths are shared — different truths. There is ample room for everyone's truth.... Here we have the courage to be real.......

There is an honoring present, a knowing present...a respect that all stories have a life of their own, a timing of their own, and truths of their own.... Like the rose that blooms in its own time — not too fast, not too slow — it blooms in its own time; stories have their own time — each person has their own process, their own reasons, their own dreams.... Let yourself be so quiet inside that you invite story. Feel your receptivity to others....

In listening space there is no right; there is no wrong. In listening space there are no requirements. There is only a sharing of presence, of story...patience to hear the story in its wholeness, until all is said. Understanding arises, no need to agree or disagree.... No anticipating responses, no arguments, no advice, nothing to prove — simply a sharing of story, a sharing of hearts and minds. Sharing.... No rush to get to the point, no point to get to; simply sharing in present time.... In that sharing, understanding arises that appreciates what is true for the teller, what is so for the teller.... No agreement necessary, no opinions needed here; understanding simply happens. No need for explanations. No need for justifications. No need.... Just being. Just listening. Simply listening....

Imagine that as you breathe out, the qualities of kindness and caring infuse the scene...as though a bubble forms around you and the people you share with. Everyone naturally relaxes into a state of sharing presence, sharing care and curiosity. In the atmosphere of kindness, authenticity moves everyone's heart and soul. In this climate sensitivity is so keen that every nuance is perceived...messages of body and mind are received, understood.... So attuned that it is as though you read one another's hearts and minds.... So attuned to each other it's as though there is an invisible energy moving between you — an air of honoring. It has a comforting feel about it.

Feel yourself occupy listening space. Experience the quality of listening space.... Get to know it. Be intimate with it. Here everyone is honored. Know that with breath you can create this space whenever you choose to — with any-one, anywhere.... Heart listening, listening in wholeness, listening to wholeness. Listening....

Imagine creating listening space in different contexts in your life.... *(If you used* Exploring How You Are with Others (138) *before beginning this meditation, use the following paragraphs to end your meditation.)*

Now bring back to awareness the particular relationships you explored ear-lier. One at a time, project this energy into the scenes. Imagine it....... Sense a shift. Witness how it changes...how you change.......

Invite the Witness to be with you as you create listening space in your life. Invite the Witness to point out when you get carried away by your own reactions, carried away from being present, from sharing presence.... Imagine the particular relations in your life.... Imagine yourself occupying listening space when you are with each of these people in your life.... Imagine yourself settling into being fully present, softly present and keenly interested in the one you are with. Become familiar with how it feels.......

The space between you and whomever you are listening to is sacred space. Coming to know one another is a gift....

WORKING COMMUNITY

The meditations in this section will help you improve relations within your group, organization, or community and can assist in creating a culture of vision-building and action. If you use them by yourself they will help you develop insights about how to deepen your connections. *Grounded and Open (39)* makes a good induction for any of these meditations; alternatively, leaders can use it to keep themselves centered or to focus a whole group before a particularly tough discussion. *Group: Coming Into Accord (2)* provides another option for bringing people into congruence at the start of a meeting. See Tips for Leading Groups in Meditation (Part II, Page 64) for helpful suggestions on how to introduce and lead meditations in group settings.

Heart-to-Heart Energy Weave (141)

This meditation will bring more heart to life. It is good for strengthening bonds with someone you are close to or in groups. It works well for community-building in retreat settings. If you are working with a group, replace the first two paragraphs with *Group: Coming Into Accord (2)* and skip the fourth paragraph and any other sections that assume more intimacy than is appropriate. You can use this meditation to honor all or only one relationship — it is particularly good for a close friendship. If you are only working on a single friendship, skip the second paragraph, work with the third and fourth, and close with the second-to-last paragraph. *Love (21)* will augment this meditation.

In the quiet of this receptive place you can commune with loved ones.... Invite in whom you hold dear. If you don't have anyone that you love in your life right now, imagine as though you do. Invite in imaginary people. Know that in so doing you draw love into your life — for life always invites love when you open to it.... Love is as natural to the heart as gravity is to the Earth.

Invite loved ones in.... Imagine all you have affection for...friends, family.... There may be people in your life who are very important to you, though you have never quite thought of them as loved ones — invite these people in, too........ Welcome in everyone who is important to you — whom you have had appreciation for.... Welcome them.... Imagine everyone drinking in the delicious well-being that pervades this place.... Now take time to focus on one person at a time. Choose whom you would like to focus on first....

Imagine opening your heart to this person....... Feel your appreciation for this person.... Imagine telling him or her what you appreciate.... Affirm your affinity....

Savor the special ways you have of being together.... Take time to acknowledge the gift of your connection....... Now, imagine what it is you'd like to do to honor and deepen your connection...to appreciate each other.... What can you do so this relationship flourishes?... What would you like to do together?... What time...what space could you create in your life to honor your relationship?... Imagine it....... Talk about this with one another now. How might you further open your hearts to each other?... How can you care for your relationship over time?... Now do a ceremony of care, acknowledging what you share, how you support each other.......

When you're ready, focus on another person. *(Repeat the preceding paragraph/s as many times as is needed.)*

Take time to honor the rest of the people you have invited into your meditation. Appreciate each one.... Acknowledge your care.... Applaud what you share.... Affirm your affinities....... Imagine as though the affinity you have with each person forms rays of light and color, maybe music too, which moves between your heart and theirs...weaving together, creating a supportive web in which all are cared for.... They, too, have heart connections with one another.... Imagine the web of loving relations.... Community weaving.... Vibrant. Caring....

Imagine how the fabric of your relations is strengthened by what you have chosen to do to deepen your connections....... Some places in the fabric of your relations may need attention.... Take time to work on the places that need to be strengthened; maybe some places need to be untangled.......

Feel yourself moving through your lives together.... Imagine the beams of energy that weave from your heart to the hearts of others...from their hearts to yours...from their hearts to others' hearts...fabric of light, of love, of heart.... Weaving affinity from heart to heart.... Imagine it.......

Take the long view; heart connections endure through time.... Experience how you are there for each other through the coming years.... Leaning on each other. Counting on each other.... What do you need to do to honor your connections over time?...... Heart connections that carry you through time...being there for each other...being there for the long haul.... Experience bonds growing even stronger over time....

We weave community. Community supports everyone.... Experience it....... Everyone connected heart to heart in the light of love.... Everyone you have connection with has connection with others who have heart connections with others, too.... Webs of loving light extend out from heart to heart to heart to heart across the planet. Envision it....... Be healed by loving light.... Imagine a strong web of loving light supporting everyone everywhere.... The whole planet held in loving light.......

Like Geese: Freedom Is in Community² (142)

This meditation is good to use in group settings. Open with the first paragraph of *Soaring High in the Skies (8)*. Name the specific goals you are working toward. Use whatever pronouns are appropriate to your situation: if you are exploring with a team, then read "we"; otherwise, stick to "you."

Imagine flying geese. They fly gracefully through the skies in V-formation. They fly thousands of miles this way. Let your imagination follow the ways of the geese. The story of the geese is this:

The geese, they stick together; they live and fly in community. In community is the freedom of the skies.... They always fly through the sky in a V — it's clear they know exactly where they are going...and know that together is better.... The flapping of the others' wings uplifts them. In the V each flap of the wing causes an updraft for the one right behind, so they always fly in formation — it's way easier to get there together.... The ones in the back honk to encourage the one at the point who flies without any uplift. Then when the leader gets tired she drops back, and another comes forward and takes a turn at the point.... If ever one gets sick she is accompanied down to the ground by two others till she's better; then together they join up with the next flock. The geese, they stick together; they live and fly in community. In community is the freedom of the skies.... Imagine how it would be to live as the geese do.......

Imagine how it feels, when you are going somewhere, to go in community...to be uplifted, supported...to be encouraged when leading...and cared for when in need.... Imagine how it feels to stick together in community...and soar.... Imagine it; feel it....

Like the geese that fly through the sky you/we know where you/we are going. Bring to awareness those with whom you share vision, goals, or destination...with whom you share common cause.... Do you join together to get there?... If you haven't joined together, imagine how you might.... It's way easier to get there together.... You/We can uplift one another. Imagine how you/we can fly together...all with a common destination.... What would that look like...feel like?... What would you/we be doing differently?... How would you/we support one another?...

Are there ways everyone could better harmonize and organize their efforts? Only when you/we are close together can you take advantage of the uplift.... What would make getting there a bit easier?... What encouragement is needed?...... What coordination is needed?...... How can you/we fly together? Imagine it.......

How do you/we uplift each other, making travel easier?... What do you receive from others?... Appreciate that.... Are there ways you could accept support that would make the going easier?... What do you offer that makes the going smoother for others? Acknowledge your own contributions.... Are there still others you could offer?...

Some take the lead sometimes; others, other times.... How does that unfold?... How can the particular offerings of each be utilized?... Everyone has a way to uplift the others, making the going easier — each pitching in to accomplish the goals. Imagine this....... When do you take the lead?...... What are your offerings?... Imagine it....... When do you fall back and follow?......

As a community do you/we acknowledge one another's efforts? How are you/we encouraging?......

Can you/we count on each other when the going gets rough?... Do you/we need to fortify the fiber of relations, to better stick together through difficulty?... What is needed?... Imagine it....... Imagine it in detail. Focus on each person....... Focus on the whole....... Focus on particular goals. Bring them to mind one at a time.... Choose one to focus on.... Notice where the uplifts are....... Who's taking leadership?...... When will you step forward?...... When do you fall to the back to let others take you there?... How does encouragement happen?... How is care shared?...... How is it day-to-day?... How do you/we get there together? Explore all this.... How is it or how could it be? Imagine it specifically.... *(Repeat this paragraph if you like.)*

Community creates true freedom.... Notice where you/we can better cultivate community and move forward together...supporting each other to get there.... Wherever you/we are going it easier to get there together.... Imagine it.... Feel what it is like to fly together...to soar together...as graceful as the geese flying through the skies.... In community is freedom. Appreciate the blessings of one another......

Optimizing a Meeting (143)

Use as little or as much of this meditation as suits your needs. A short version can take as little as three to five minutes, and a long one can take twenty. Name agenda items and the meeting end time in the last line. It will be time well spent if you give people an opportunity to share what they have imagined — people gain valuable insights and weave their spirits together when they share. Use a round format and, if you also take time to respond to each other's comments, wait until all who want to have spoken. If the meeting gets bogged down, try using *Invite Insight (100)*. If you are exploring different options, then *Ripple Effect (101)* and/or parts of

Crossroads (102) will be helpful. If people are having trouble focusing, use the Earth section of *Grounded and Open (39)*; if people get stuck use the Sky section from the same meditation.

Many meditations can be combined with this one: some will help develop a spirit of cooperation, while others are useful for exploring issues of concern; still others will promote efficiency, creativity, or decision-making. For an induction it is best to use *Group: Coming Into Accord (2)*. You may want to augment the meditation with *Calling Upon Your Allies (27)*, *Intelligence (18)*, *Open Heart, Sharp Mind (42)*, and/or *Pacing (36)*. See Tips for Leading a Group in Meditation (Part II, Page 64) for additional help.

Let go of distraction.... Allow yourself to be fully present.

Bring to the forefront of awareness what we are commonly committed to. Contemplate it.... Be aware of each person in the room; everyone wants to further the work....... Appreciate how we are doing it together....

Take a moment to envision us putting our hearts and minds together.... Sense a cohesiveness building.... Imagine the ideal climate for working well together...creative, caring, and enjoying each other.... Focused and playful.... Efficient and relaxed.... Openly exploring when we need to and easily drawing discussion to conclusion when we need to.... Open and dynamic.... Making clear choices when needed.... Imagine this....

Everyone contributing their best...everyone sensitive to one another.... Respectful. Mindful.... Each of us knowing when to speak up, and when listening is better.... Combining our energies in ways that are truly novel.... Timing impeccable.... People's differences expanding everybody's horizons.

Bring to awareness the particular task/s we have set out to accomplish in this meeting.... Focus on them one at a time. *(Slowly name topics.)* As we each focus on them it is as though our energies begin to harmonize around each issue.

Focus on the particular challenges and notice what may be a good approach.... Notice what attention the issue is calling for.... How might we meet the challenge?

See us, feel us getting everything done brilliantly.... And in a timely manner....... Take the long view. Notice the difference this work makes....... Bask in the feeling of common accomplishment........ Imagine us completing this meeting having easily accomplished all that we have set out to do....

The Dance of Leadership (144)

This meditation is good for both individual and group exploration. It has been divided up so that it can be worked piece by piece, making it easier for groups to share insights a section at a time. (Always use the first section.) *Inner Witness (1H), Call Upon Your Life-Affirming Values (24), Calling Upon Your Allies (27), Calling the Ancestors (29), The Future Ones (30),* and/or *The Spirit of the Children (31)* will all enhance it. Fill in the blanks by naming the particular group, project, issue, etc.; wherever possible, continue to use specific names, places, times, and the questions being faced. Read the questions slowly, and maybe even repeat them.

Step Forward (144A)

What you are doing is important. Change takes leadership. Transformation takes leadership.... You are a leader. Claim your leadership.... In leading you take the long view. In leading you think with, and for, the good of the whole — you take the wide view. Believe in your own leadership abilities.... Step forward. You are a leader....

Bring to awareness (_____)....... Recall your commitment to (_____). Bring to mind your convictions about (_____). Be present with the challenge before you. Breathe.... Remember who is with you, with whom you share this care.... Remind yourself of the contributions you can make and the creative approaches you can take.... Bring all of this to awareness now.......

History Empowers (144B)

Take a long view now.... Look back over time and notice what took place to lead up to this juncture in time. Remember the history.... What happened to bring about what is true now?...... Bring to awareness the problems faced...the effort made, the work done...the obstacles that were overcome...and the ones that still have to be contended with.... Look back over the past and notice how information was shared or held...how resources and decision-making were shared or held...where the power stood or moved to.... Let all this pass through aware-ness...paint a picture of the history....... Notice if there are any gaps in your knowledge that need to be filled so you have the whole picture.... Notice who was involved...what the aspirations were...what talents and commitments were applied.... Who led before?... Who was served by the efforts?... What resources were used?... What problems were solved?... What problems were created?... Were there conflicts anywhere?... Witness the history....... What were the impor-tant moments?...... Take the long view. Let all of this pass though your mind's eye....... What are the lessons?...... What are the strengths that can be drawn from?... Take the long view. As you breathe, draw in wisdom.......

Pay attention to yourself. Remember who you were inspired by...who gave you a hand...what choices you made to step forward...what you left behind to move forward.... Breathe and feel your own history empower you to carry on....

Vision Guides (144C)

To lead, you need to know where you have come from and where you are going. History gives you wisdom; vision gives you guidance.... Now look the other way and take the long view into the future.... What is positively possible?... How could it be?... What would be ideal for everyone?.... What would honor every-one...so everyone contributes...so everyone is cared for?... How would it be?... Imagine what would inspire the spirit.... What would make hearts sing?... Envision a time when the ideal has already been brought about. Don't worry exactly when or how it happens; just envision what the ideal would be like.... Imagine it specifically.... What would people be doing?... How would people be together?... Who would be contributing what?... What would be ideal?

Project yourself into this time as though it has already come about. Feel what it is like.... Explore this time. Imagine it in detail. Let your imagination paint the picture; make up a story of how it could be....... Let your whole being become intimately familiar with this time.... As though it is already true; as though it is your daily experience now. Embody the ideal; be the change you want to make.... Breathe in the mood of the time.... Take the long view. Be a visionary.... Whatever is created is imagined first. Be visionary.... As you exhale breathe out the vision.... Imagine that it informs the air in present time.... The air glitters....

Grounded in Present Time (144D)

To lead you need to know where you have come from, where you are going, and you have to know what is so in present time.... You need to know all the currents in motion. To lead you need to be grounded in reality.... Now take the wide view.... Tune to what is true in current time.... With keen awareness scan the current reality.... Sense how people are doing....... What are they striving for?... What matters?... Observe the quality of energy between people.... Notice how each person is doing....... What do people tend to get hung up on?... Do people want change?... Do they believe it is possible?... Where do they think solutions lie?... Note the variety of points of view.... Are the compatible?... Is there anything needed to build cohesion?...... Do people trust each other?... Do they trust you?... Who do they trust?... What seems to be the case?... Scan the scene and notice what is true at this juncture in time.......

Breathe.... Move your awareness deeper...sense what is true below the surface.... What's in people's hearts?... You may want to focus on one person at a time and sense what is true....... Take the deep view.... Sense the undercurrents of energy flow...or energy blocks.... What are the crosscurrents?... Tune to what is currently so.... Witness.......

Explore Possibilities (144E)

Where are the windows of opportunity?... What would inspire people?... What positive possibilities are inviting?... How might people put their hearts and minds together?... What talents can be tapped?... Where would encouragement help?...

Scan the scene and notice these things....... Where are the spots that change can be initiated?... Who are allies?...

Bring different ideas to mind and sense how they resonate.... Try on different approaches for size.... Imagine as though people are moving forward with one, and see what happens....... Imagine; fill in the scene with different ways of going about it. Notice where the pull is.... Explore one at a time.... Choose one now.... Notice what seems to fit and what doesn't....... Imagine what can be cooked up and what seems to fall flat.... Imagine it in detail....... Notice what inspires people.... Notice what reminds people of their own capacities...inspires them to believe change can be made...to make change together.... Notice how all the voices come forth.... What might inspire each person to step forward and contribute their part?... How can people's differences make the work more effective?... Imagine all of this in detail. Tune in to the positive possibilities.... How might communication flow?... What resources are needed?... Where might they be attained?... Who are allies; who would help out? *(Repeat several times, naming the specific ideas you want to explore.)*

Moving Forward (144F)

Conjure up the mix of what is needed to set the intent...to ignite forward motion...to inspire a team spirit to make positive change.... Inspiration is infectious. Imagine it; everything takes off, doesn't need controlling. It just flies, soars!... Change is made.... Everyone's commitment and convictions weave into a strong fiber of courageous action....... Taking risks.... Mistakes are viewed as opportunities to learn.... Adjustments are made continually, feedback heard, and change made as needed....... Imagine a band of energy weaving between everyone.... Feel it.... Imagine the qualities needed: shared vision and creativity...efficiency and patience...caring and cooperation...appreciation and humor...sensitivity and respect...honesty and trust.... Feel all this in the air.... Imagine these qualities weaving people's hearts and minds together.... Notice how this could be...how these qualities can be cultivated.... Everyone committed to the work.... Weaving unity. Weaving in diversity, making the fiber strong.... Feel it....

Yourself As Leader (144G)

Now take time to focus on your own self. Breathe in all that you have discovered as you have explored leadership.... Breathe out any of your own fears and anxieties.... Breathe out any of your own ego attachments.... Trust the process.... Feel yourself carried by a vision that is larger than you. Feel yourself completely tuned to the process...understanding what is said...knowing the meaning of the silences...fully tuned to emotional nuances...anticipating what is needed...always bringing forth what will sustain the work.... Sometimes stepping forward modeling...sometimes stepping back and challenging another to step forward.... Inspiring others to take leadership....

Imagine how your approach inspires the team spirit.... You believe in people, inspiring them to believe in themselves...and contribute their best. Imagine how this is the case.... You express your values and your vulnerabilities.... You share your dilemmas and your convictions.... In the climate you create, you inspire everyone to put forward their views. You never speak for anyone...nor do you have to figure it all out. People think together.... The team spirit is brilliant.... Sense how this is true...working together, thinking together, learning together, leading together...knowing just how to navigate from here to there....

Wise, observant and visionary, like the sails that catch the winds, you can always feel what's in the air. Catching the currents, everyone moves forward together.... You take leadership, decisive and open at the same time...steering everyone toward the shared vision.... Feel your leadership capacities coming forth.... Align yourself with the process.... Knowing when to step forward, and when to step back and make room for others to come forth....

Imagine yourself in leadership.... Just what you would do?... What you would inspire?... Others with you — thinking together.... Who do you take council with?...... Who do you trust to tell you when you are doing well and when you are not?...... Take a moment and notice if there is anything or anyone that worries you.... Is there anyone you have given up on?...... What might inspire them to join in...or what needs to be done?... Imagine it.......

Leading together, always adjusting forward motion as understanding deepens.... Together you find and open up new possibilities...possibilities that haven't even been dreamed up yet...celebrating each other, celebrating your shared work.... Awesome. Moving forward together. Inspiring cooperation...inspiring initiative...inspiring change and transformation. Sharing care, together you build the visions and make them real....

Inspiration Is Infectious: Collaborative Creativity (145)

This meditation is great for setting the tone of joint creative endeavors — use it to open your meetings. It is designed to follow all but the last paragraph of *Igniting Inspiration (107)*. You may also want to use *Send an Invitation to the Solution (99)* or *Invite Insight (100)* with it. *Group: Coming Into Accord (2)* is good to use as a beginning; *Group Closing (13U)* makes a good ending.

Bring those who you collaborate with into awareness. Invite them into this inspirational magical space.... Take time to share presence. Imagine honoring the particular quality of energy that each person contributes.... Everyone has an offering. Do an imaginary ritual that honors the contribution of every person.......

Breathing together. Feel your connectedness with all life.... Breath brings the life force. Feel the charge of the life force.... This energy is always pregnant with potential.... Feel the life force carried by breath...life force — radiant, electric, powerful.... Feel a current that moves between you. Connected...curious to discover what emerges as energies combine in a great dance of creativity. Exciting. Open.

Sense an atmosphere that ignites inspiration. Imagine a field of energy that invites ingenuity surrounds everyone. In this space the creativity that may have been dormant in anyone is awakened. Inspiration is in the air.... Notice it is infectious...electric.... Sparks fly between you. Together you inspire one another. Imagine it.... Sparks meet and something entirely new comes into being. Sparks are flying and everyone gets fired up. Imagine....

The air provokes connections; ideas fly, sparking more ideas. Creating together. Discovering together. Amazement! Light in the air. Joy in the air. Breathe it in.... Fresh ways of seeing the world emerge. Creation happens. Energy dances.... The energy carries everyone.... It builds and builds, getting more and more powerful, dynamic, illuminating potentialities.... Imagine how you incite inspiration in others and how they incite inspiration in you.... It builds.... Playful. Creative........ Open to it. Let yourselves come alive and share together. Inspiration is infectious....

The energy has a life of its own.... Discover it....... Feel it.... Trust the spirit of it.... Feel it come alive...sparking off each other, spontaneous, playful, brilliant.... The collective genius has a rhythm of its own...together the creativity builds. This is where ideas are born and set free.... Everyone watches with amazement...watches where they go, where they find friends, what joins them...where they land.... Here is where ideas are born and set free....

Now project this energy into a specific shared endeavor.... You are all on a team together. As though you are keeping the ball in the air and each touch adds to the innovation. Each touch creates more intricacy, exactly as it needs to be; each touch adds to it. Imagine it.... Imagine an air that inspires everyone to contribute....

Notice what you can do to bring about this quality of collaborative creativity. Creativity ignites creativity...thinking together. Create the context and it happens as naturally as breath.... We are all creative beings. Creativity inspires creativity....

Team Spirit (146)

We often experience ourselves as being apart from rather than part of whatever groupings we are in. This meditation can be used to coalesce collective spirit or to explore it; you can substitute the word "family" or "community" for "team". Use as little or as much of the meditation as you like; the first paragraph can set the tone for any collective venture. If the team you are working with is only together for a short time, you may want to shorten it. In the opening it is good to elaborate with specifics; when you do, avoid expressing any bias. Inserting *Countdown into Deep Awareness (7)* after the second paragraph is recommended. If your group has a name, insert it often. Change the pronouns if you are exploring on your own. This meditation engages the Receptive Imagination — feel free to make up stories and to shift back and forth between the imaginary and the practical as you explore both mythic and actual scenes involving the life of your group.

Team. Bring to awareness the whole team — everyone, each of us, all of us.... Bring to awareness our activities...our common goals.... Recall our cares, our commitments, our camaraderie.... These we share as a team: goals, commitments, cares.... Each of us, all of us share these. This sharing is in the air, invisible like gravity, but always there.... Feel it.... Imagine this sharing forms a field of energy...embracing all of us, drawing each of us together and keeping us in the team.... Experience this energy field: it contains shared cares, commitments, camaraderie.... Energy weaves between us....... This energy moving between us has shape, has form.... It has a life of its own. Team spirit; experience the team as a whole.

This team has a life of its own — almost as if in another dimension it is a living being. If it were to take on the persona of an animal or a mythical character, what would it be? Or maybe it takes human form; or maybe it only has voice.... Imagine our team spirit as a living, breathing being.... Who is this Team-being?... Imagine its story.... Create it....

Greet our team spirit.... It has all the eccentricities of an independent spirit, its own personality...its own talents...its own needs.... Imagine it. Witness how it experiences life.... Its moods, its passions, what it hates, what it loves. Witness....... How is it doing?...

Imagine communicating with it....... If you have concerns bring them into the light of awareness and notice what you sense, for this spirit may not use words.......

This Team-being is remarkably resourceful. It is absolutely brilliant, for it taps the endowments of everyone — the different experiences, skills, and sensibilities of each person...all combining, synthesizing, making brilliance!... Sense the possibilities — awesome....

Much of the genius of the team's spirit is still dormant. It is eager to discover the full potential. Imagine that it invites you on a journey to dream together and witness what happens when it totally thrives.

It knows what it needs to develop — some parts may need rest, while others need exercise...maybe particular ways of sharing...or specific skills or information would be helpful.... The team spirit knows whatever is needed to realize its full potential. Witness.......

Its body is graceful and fully coordinated. It has a sense of timing that is uncanny....

Its ability to concentrate is amazing. Whatever it shines its light of awareness on dazzles.... Its intelligence is so broad and so deep it is capable of holding multiple views all at the same time.... It has a genius for problem-solving....

Everyone's passion and generosity form the lifeblood of the team. Notice what awakens these energies...how they build on one another.......

The Team-being has an immense memory. Its wisdom is informed by the generations that have gone before. The Team-being is informed by the ancestors of each team member....... It taps the forces of history to persevere. Remembering the lessons of the past, it knows the best ways to secure the future....

This Team-being travels through time, listening to the voices of the ancestors and generations to come. The vision of the Team-being is far reaching — knowing the positive probabilities... knowing the possible pitfalls.... What do those who live in the future have to say?......

Look way down the road, long after the work has spawned great success....... Is there anything to be cautious about?... Imagine the future....... What
does this mean about your current activities?......

Most of all the Team-being is extremely aware of what is currently taking
place — tuned to the whole, tuned to the detail, tuned to exactly what conditions it
meets and what it is going to take to manifest its vision.......Tuned to what is happening both within and around it. It knows exactly where attention is called for.......

The Team-being is very good about taking care of itself. Sometimes it
retreats to regroup and gather strength. Witness how it does this.... Whatever it
may need...information to be uncovered...skills to be developed...reflecting on
where it has been and where it is going...or maybe a time to meet like-minded
spirits.... Notice what the team needs now.......

This Team-being lives in a place populated by many group spirits.... Notice
particular groups....... Each group spirit has its own endowments, its own
propensities.... Some are kindred spirits.... Imagine the relations that can be
deepened or developed between group spirits....

Imagine that the Team-being tells you what structures will support its work
now.... What processes will serve its purposes now?... What does it need to
thrive?... Is there anything that it needs to do regularly to maintain good
health?... Is there any discordant energy that needs to be cleared?.... Does energy
get stuck any place...too much or too little anywhere?... Listen to what the team
spirit has to say.......

Thank the Team-being for gracing you with its visit and sharing its experience.... Tell it what you would like to do to honor it...to keep the energy flowing
between the members of the team.... When the team spirit is well nourished
everyone trusts the wisdom of the whole group.... The Team-being carries everyone through. And everyone contributes to success....

Appreciate everyone on the team.... Appreciate the particular offerings of
each member to the whole.... And what the whole offers each.... The spirit speaks

differently through each of us. Witness this....... Everyone is so tuned that it is as though communication is nearly telepathic.......

Thank the team.... Imagine what offering you might make as a gesture of good will....

When Competition Hurts: Dissolving the Competitive Edge (147)

Competition has wounded our culture. Most of us are haunted by a feeling that we have to prove ourselves in order to be accepted. When we let go of the patterns competition has created, we can reclaim our sense of belonging and be better able to build mutually supportive relationships. To optimize transformation it is best to follow this meditation with *Fellowship (148); inserting Recollection (16)* after the first paragraph will enhance it. *Clearing Space Inside with Mental Housecleaning (11)* will augment this meditation.

The competitive edge is often there contaminating the scene — putting everyone on edge. For some it's the constant vying for special praise and prestige; for others it's getting out of the way for fear of being exposed as somehow not making the grade. Everyone is guarded, stiff — on edge.... Witness the ways this competitive edge forms a wedge between you and genuine experience...keeping you from relaxing and appreciating your own self...keeping you from relaxing and appreciating others.... The competitive edge wreaks havoc on the heart.

Competition comes in many guises. Witness the forms it takes in your life. Notice when you compare yourself to others...always ranking who is the best; you may decide you don't measure up, or maybe you find someone else to put down.... Some above, some below; by the time the ranking is done you find yourself all alone, left to fend for yourself. Always judging: judging yourself...judging others...others judging you.... When competition rules there are only winners and losers, and even the winners are left alone, fending for themselves....

Competition. Witness what activates it in your life...how it forms a wedge between you and your experience....... Notice the thinking patterns competition has carved in your psyche.... Thoughts that tell you that you are somehow not quite good enough.... Notice the thinking patterns competition has carved in your psyche, keeping you from being your natural self and keeping you from appreciating others for who they really are.... Do you have feelings of envy or rivalry?... Do you ever feel like you are superior in some way...or feel ashamed for not making the grade?... How does competition move through your psyche? Notice it....... What calls it into play?...... Does it compel you?... Are the edges so sharp they cut? Witness it.... What does it feed on?...

Competition wreaks havoc on the heart, pitting people against one another.... Bring to mind different contexts in life, work, school, community, family life — notice where competition is injecting alienation into the scenes....... What forms does it take in the different contexts?... What provokes it?... Witness how it infects the mood...constrains the interactions.... Witness it.... It is insidious...and sometimes quite devious...oftentimes pettiness accompanies it. Witness the faces of competition in your life...how it makes you feel about your own self...how it makes you feel about others...no one is ever quite good enough.... It never lets you relax and appreciate life. Witness....

Look back over your past. What has competition cost you?... Times it caused you to feel bad about yourself....Were you ever mocked? Were you ever teased?... Were you compelled to hide parts of yourself for fear of put-downs?... What disqualified you?... Any aspects of yourself that never could fit in?... How has competition shamed you?... What has competition cost you?... Maybe there are parts you were compelled to overuse to stay ahead, while other parts got neglected.... Has competition ever bloated you with false pride?... Has it kept you guarded — feeling you had to watch your back?... Where has competition driven its cutting edge into your life?...

Witness how it has come between you and authenticity...how it has come between you and others with whom you could have made heart connections.... Witness how competition has infected your life...your relationship to your own self...your relationships to kindred spirits.... Witness how competition has cut through your life....... What thinking patterns has it carved in your psyche?... How does it drive you?... Witness; where does it live inside you? Notice how it dictates where you go...forcing you onto narrow roads.... What does it keep out of view?...

Now for a moment, set aside all of this. Breathe.... Clear your awareness. Give yourself permission to take another route — a wider road, one with a variety of scenery, one that offers a diversity of experience. Breathe.... Fellowship has an entirely different temperament.... Evoke it....

Fellowship (148)

This meditation is designed to be used on its own or with *When Competition Hurts (147)*. If you are using it on its own, skip the last half. Insert *Recollection (16)* after the first paragraph to enhance it. Where noted, you might want to use at least the first two paragraphs of *Create a Symbol to Tap Energy in Daily Life (13A)*.

Take a moment to create a welcoming space in your psyche for the spirit of fellowship.... When the spirit of fellowship is present, discordant energies shift and move into a harmony. There is a mood of companionship, of conviviality.... There are no winners and losers; there is only mutuality. We're never pitted against each other; instead we are with each other in fellowship.

Breathe.... Evoke the spirit of fellowship. Scan your past and remember feelings of fellowship, companionship, camaraderie, and mutuality.... Remember relationships in your life that were filled with these qualities.... Times graced by someone's generosity.... Recall the mood in the air.... Bring these experiences to mind.... Remember when you have done a project with others and cooperation made a beautiful dance. Working well together, everyone pitching in — glad to be contributing to the effort.... Re-experience the climate in these scenes.... Fellowship was in the air.... It has many forms, fellowship — experience it.... Times people put aside their own concerns and stepped forward to help...cooperation and generosity infused the scene.... A time of crisis and everyone lives and breathes their shared humanity.... Fellowship makes community; it makes the heart smile....

Breathe.... Draw from these times.... Invite the feelings to remain with you — like an afterglow.... Savor the humanity we all share.... As you breathe imagine that it grows. Mutuality, goodness, good will in the air.... Breathe.... As you inhale feel warmth.... As you exhale feel the energy spread.... It is infectious.... Everyone breathes it.... Imagine that all of these feelings swirl together: fellowship...mutuality...companionship...care...conviviality...love... good–will...generosity...cooperation.... Imagine all these feelings swirling together and forming a beam of healing power. This power could take many forms: music, color, light, vibrations, knowing — whatever forms these energies take as they coalesce, notice their synergy.... Awesome. Breathe....

This is heart energy...powerful healing energy. Feel it.... As you breathe, feel it inform your whole being.... This energy makes the heart smile.... Know that it has great healing powers. Sense every cell in your body infused with it — smiling.... Now take time to direct this energy into those places that have been wounded by the competitive edge. As you exhale, shine the energy into those places that have been left in isolation.... Let the healing power move through and heal the wounds.... As you exhale aim the healing wherever it's needed.... Feel healing....

Imagine how everyone responds to one another in this atmosphere of mutuality. As if the sun emerges from behind the clouds on a cool day, spreading warmth.... People smile and enjoy one another.... Spontaneity emerges.... It's safe.... The edges dissolve in the warmth of shared humanity. Trust emerges....

It is a given that everyone belongs....... Everyone contributes.... In all the openness there is space to really be together, to discover each other, to discover new ways of being...to think together — no longer required to know before speaking up. Now exchanges are full of exploration. Everyone thinks together...a multitude of possibilities opens up...only together can the best route be figured out. Differences of experience, differences of opinion widen the context. Contributions build on one another instead of competing. In the old ways differences caused tension; now they open opportunities.... The question is never who is right but what is best. Mistakes are taken in stride, learned from; then we move on together, stronger than before. Imagine it.......

Work together; share together. Laugh together and care together. Enjoy life, and be there for one another when the need arises.... Fellowship. Feel it. Breathe it. Imagine it spreads through your whole life.... Kinship with everyone....

(Optional: use at least the first couple of paragraphs of Create a Symbol to Tap Energy in Daily Life (13A) *here, and then go on with the rest of the meditation after using* When Competition Hurts (147). *If you are not using* When Competition Hurts, *use* Create a Symbol to Tap Energy in Daily Life (13A) *to end the meditation.)*

All the scenes you brought to mind earlier, all those feelings provoked by the competitive edge...shine this healing power of fellowship into them.... Imagine the scenes change....... Imagine icy rivalry melting into mutuality.... Appreciation of yourself...appreciation of others awakens spontaneously.... Imagine it.... Feel it.......

Shine the energy into all those thoughts that tell you that you are not quite good enough.... Shine energy into all those thoughts that say others are not good enough.... Let healing melt the edges.......

Imagine healing pours down all those grooves that competition cut through your psyche...healing soaks into your deepest beliefs.... Let the healing move through and open new roads in your psyche. Notice how your feelings change.... Feel how your thoughts change.... Imagine it. Sense it. Change happens.... Energy shifts. Breathe with it.... You no longer have to suppress yourself to fit in.

Go back to those parts of yourself that you had to keep hidden away or parts of yourself that got neglected in the fray.... Go back and shine the healing

powers of fellowship into them.... Breathe life into them.... Make yourself whole again.... They have something very creative and enriching to contribute.... Each of these aspects of your being has developed great strength of character which would be welcomed by all. Notice what these aspects of yourself can offer.......
You may want to talk to these parts; tell them how things are different now.... Find out what they need to feel safe so they can contribute....... Reclaim your pride.... Appreciate your whole self.

Welcome yourself for who you are in all your strengths and weaknesses.... Feel your heat open.... We are all good — more than good enough.... Everyone belongs in fellowship.... Relax into authenticity.... Welcome wholeness....

Breaking Down the Barriers:
The World Opening to You and You Opening to the World (149)

This meditation, each section of which can be used on its own, is useful for groups who are seeking to work on issues of oppression and diversity; it will help ferret out the ways in which people may unwittingly be perpetuating monoculture. Most people have social power in some ways but not in others. Listen to the first part of the meditation from those parts of you that have been locked out; listen to the end from the parts of you that occupies a place on the inside.

It is important to create settings that invite everyone's contribution. It is a truism that the more privilege we have the more isolated we become. If we stay inside our comfort zones, associating only with people who share our assumptions, we never get the experience necessary to break down prejudice, recognize institutional injustice, and move to eliminate it.

Usually it is the view from the outside that enables us to see situations in a new light and to make positive change. Often the perspectives most needed to move us forward are the very ones that have been left out. We need to step back, notice who is and who is not in the room, and recognize whose views are being paid attention to. When we realize who is missing or not being taken seriously, we can begin to make the necessary changes toward becoming more genuinely inclusive.

This meditation is designed to follow *Enriched by Diversity (139)*. *Recollection (16)* will enhance it. If tension arises use *Breath Is Home; Breath Heals (1G)* as needed. You may want to use *Spreading Through the World (13R)*, *Spirit of Change (13D)*, or *Communicate Change (13I)* as endings. After the meditation, you may want to have people who share a common history (or identity) talk with each other before you open discussion to the whole group. See Tips for Leading Groups in Meditation (Part II, Page 64).

When You Are Not Seen for Who You Are (149A)

Recall the ways people assume you are the same as them, but you really aren't...or there is such a preoccupation with your difference it's impossible to have a casual connection...or plain and simple, they just don't trust you....... Bring to mind the ways you are continually reminded of this....... Let the myriad of incidents pass through awareness now.... How you are not seen for who you are.... Breathe....

Focus in on the ways you have left your own experience behind knowing it wouldn't be understood anyway; maybe it gets minimized or exoticized in some way...or downright denied....... You know that if you want to be taken seriously you need to leave part of you at the door and act just like them...put on a mask and pass.... You've learned that you have to fit in to be treated respectfully.... Bring to mind when and how you do this....... What ways of being, what experience, which aspects of your identity do you check at the door?... What masks do you put on?... How do you constrict yourself in order to fit in?... When do you find that you have to act differently than what comes naturally...just to be safe...just to be taken seriously, to make it more likely you'll be treated respectfully?... What are you obliged to leave out; what are you obliged to pretend if you want to be recognized?......

Dividing oneself up hurts. Breathe out the pain there has been; invite yourself to be whole again....... Imagine how it would be in different scenes if you could act naturally, comfortably, be your own self...be your full self......be recognized for who you really are.... Breathe.......

The parts left behind are the same parts that make a way out of no way. These parts know how to get through; they're wise, they know.... They're survivors; they're needed by everyone now.... What you left at the door are ways of being that will shed light and find the best ways to make change.... They know a different way...how everyone can do things differently....

What if the aspects of you that you had to leave at the door were invited in and were seen as indispensable for getting through?... This part knows what it means to get through.... You know what is inside and what is outside the bounds.... You know where to break the barriers down.... You know ways of being that don't erect barriers.... Bring your knowledge in.......

Imagine that the part of you that has been the cause of rejection is the very part that is at the table, offering the knowledge you have gained, offering what is needed on your terms.... Imagine sharing in your way.... Imagine that whatever you usually leave at the door is at the table. You have no mask on; you are your regular self. Your experience informs everyone.... It is seen as important.... No need to keep quiet; what is needed is your experience.... The scenes are infused with respect and interest in your contributions.... Imagine that your passion is with you instead of locked away.......

Imagine how the scene shifts.... Imagine it specifically...what you offer...how you are now treated different than before. Imagine it....... What would change?...... How would things be done differently?... How would this feel?... What difference would it make...to you?...to others?... Witness.......

What can be done to make this vision possible in the different contexts in your life?...... Do you have allies who may be of help?...... What could you ask of them?...... Imagine how things might unfold differently....... The constricting assumptions are broken.... People open, broaden their view.... Imagine how this might happen.......

Breaking the Constraints of "Normal"(149B)

Scan your life now; notice who you interact with, who is in your world....... Notice this at work, in the community.... Witness who is in your life now.... Broaden your view.... Does everyone have the same options you do?... Notice who is there but not contributing in the different contexts of your life or who is being ignored even if they do....... Notice who is not there.......

Those who are different in some way offer a fresh look at our world and exactly what we are inside of. "Normal" is seen in a new light.... The definition of what's possible expands — the world opens up and comes alive.

Recollect times when you discovered a way of being in the world you didn't even know was possible.... You met someone who was different in some way, who had different ways of being, who had different ways of seeing...or maybe you read or watched something that revealed people who had different assumptions, different approaches.... At first you might have thought they were less capable, only to find out they were more resourceful.... Your horizons expanded. Remember....... You discovered life on the other side of the lines of possibility.... Limits were broken, horizons extended; the world became a richer more vibrant place.... You had to take a second look and reevaluate just what was so, just what was possible. Your world grew bigger...opened up further — more room to be alive!

Remember when you had to redefine just what normal was. Recollect those times you discovered a different way of being in the world. Stereotypes shattered. Limits dissolved.... The world opened up.... Recall when this happened.......

Imagine the particular ways of being that narrow your world. Imagine shedding the norms that homogenize.... Ideas that say "look the same, or if that can't be, at least act the same"...ideas that assume some people are incapable.... Breathe out the ideas that make normal a very narrow place to live.... Breathe out the stereotypes.... Welcome difference.... It frees us all from living in the box....

There still may be ways you narrow your experience.... Who takes you outside your comfort zone?...... Who do you exclude because they don't fall within the bounds of what you think is okay?...someone who looks different?...acts different?...who somehow isn't how you think they're supposed to be....... Look at your daily life and notice who you diminish in your own mind in some way....... Are there people you see regularly who you don't take notice of?... Are there people you make sure to avoid?... people who are labeled? Maybe you were taught they were not okay in some way.... You know better now.... Let go; breathe out these narrow ideas.... Or maybe there are people you don't bother to pay attention to, thinking they have little to contribute anyway......

Open to the world of difference. Let yourself be enriched by it.... Replace prejudice and ignorance with curiosity and openness to discover the depth and breadth of humanity.... Be humble; there is no such thing as normal....... People have contributions that open the world up.... Feel a welcoming spirit begin to stir in your heart.... Feel your mind opening with interest.... Feel yourself glad to have the opportunity to get to know people different than yourself....

Who in particular do you run across in daily life that takes you outside your comfort zone....... Imagine opening to a particular person you have distanced yourself from....... Appreciate the opportunity for your horizons to expand.... Feel yourself opening your heart and mind when you are with this person. Imagine it....... Your horizons expand.... Imagine how you might be the next time you see this person....... Give yourself permission to move outside your comfort zone...to expand your comfort zone....... Imagine breaking bread together. Imagine laughing....

Shedding the Veneer (150)

Most of us, especially women, are socialized to be nice at all costs; after years of behaving "nicely," habituated patterns set in and squeeze out authenticity. This meditation is designed to make room for us to bring our full selves back into our interactions. It is designed to follow *Integrity of Your Being (4)*. *Clearing Space Inside with Mental Housecleaning (11)* will augment this meditation.

Take time to review the interactions that usually take place in your life in an average week.... Review the different settings in which you find yourself...work...community...public settings.... Witness your interactions...who you see, what takes place.... Notice when your authentic self recedes.... It might feel like somehow something is between you and the world; the real you disappears, as though a protective coating comes between you and who you are relating to.... In the different settings in your life, note when the real you recedes. Witness it.... There is stiffness about it...awkwardness...or your center of attention is simply somewhere else. You go through the motions but you aren't really there.... Freshness is gone. It's as though you're gone. You react by rote — filling in the blanks of expectation. Witness when the real you recedes in the different interactions of daily life at work and in the community.......

When you cut the world off from who you really are, you cut yourself off from the world. When your real self comes forth you experience the world in wholeness. Authentic.... Bring back the waves of energy.... Breathe this energy.... Send the waves through yourself and your life.... Breathe.... Waves of energy dissolve the veneer that formed the wall between you and the world.... Waves of your essence roll through you. Breathe...waves washing away pretense, revealing truth.... Waves of breath dissolving the walls...dissolving what stands between your real self and the world.... Reclaim your wholeness. Vibrant. Breathe. Feel your real self.... Feel the deepest tones of your being vibrate.

Remember you belong.... Invite your whole self into your interactions.... Risk being real.... Imagine honesty blooms.... Reclaim wholeness...your whole experience....

Go back over the particular scenes when the veneer hid your truth away.... Breathe into these times. Take one scene and imagine how you can be real.... How your truth improves the scene. Feel what this would be like....... Imagine your honesty somehow improves the scene. Everyone welcomes authenticity.... As you express it, you evoke it. Interactions become genuine...fused with meaning....... Honesty blooms.... When you're authentic, you make authentic connections. Your relationships occupy the genuine.... Expect this to be true....

Each time you speak truth you strengthen your convictions; you vitalize your integrity and infuse all your relations with authenticity....... Your relations come to stand on solid ground. Experience this....... The fiber of your relationships gets so strong, the integrity of your being so vital, that you speak truth even against the prevailing winds.... You speak truth.... You stand in the ground of your being.... In wholeness you speak truth.... The scene comes alive and denial dissolves.... Experience the power of truth....

Claiming Integrity: Living True to Your Values (151)

Without integrity we are relegated to being alienated from our deepest selves and from our ability to open to the world. Being true to our integrity is not a static process but a dynamic one; it requires us to deeply and continually listen to what is happening inside and to discover what is true around us. When we rededicate ourselves to our core values, we rediscover our authentic selves and have a compass for decision-making that helps us to know what to do when we are tempted by, or come up against, unprincipled activity. This meditation is designed to follow all but the last two paragraphs of *Call Upon Your Life-Affirming Values (24)* and can be used for the past, present, and/or future. Wherever possible name the circumstances you are exploring. If you are only exploring the present or the future, then skip the first section and begin at "Present" or "Future"; for these parts, *Ripple Effect (101)* will be useful for deepening your investigation.

Sometimes we find that we have compromised our values — for whatever reason, put aside our convictions. Maybe at the time there didn't seem as if there were a choice in the matter, or you were even forced to compromise. For whatever reason, when you compromised your integrity your values vacated the scene, and some cynicism moved in.... You shut yourself down some; you shut life out some.... You ignored that part of you that cares, giving up on the world a little bit, giving up on your own self a bit.... Each time you compromised your integrity, you diminished yourself...your life...the world...and cynicism set in. You diminished your soul. You deserve more.

Your values are at the core of what is important in life. When you think about it now, wherever you put aside your convictions, you find that you shudder a little inside.... There may be shame there; there may be guilt there.... Now you can heal.... Now you can go back and reclaim those parts left behind — reclaim your wholeness, your integrity...reinstate your values, regain full respect for your own self, for life itself. Now you can heal. You can care again....

Bring to mind those particular times when you fell short of your own standards. You may want to look into the distant past, or more recent times.... Bring to mind those times that just don't sit quite right....... Times that sit a bit uncomfortably in memory...times you may have hurt someone or caused harm in some way?... Have you promoted yourself at someone else's expense?... Maybe you knew someone was being wronged and you turned the other way.... Maybe you got caught in the currents of peer pressure and went along when you knew it was wrong, or maybe you thought it was just easier or more expedient.... Maybe there were lots of small incidents that when they're added up just don't come out right...or commitments you neglected.... Bring these times to mind.... Let the different scenes pass through awareness.... One may be calling your attention.... Choose one scene to focus on now.... When you are ready you can focus on the others.

Remember.... What happened?... What did you do?... Just what doesn't sit right?... Are there particular choices you made that bypassed your convictions?... Remember.... Recall what was up for you. What did you choose to ignore at the time?... Was there something you weren't quite honest about with your own self?...with anyone else?... Recall what took place.... Remember the details....... What did you shut down inside yourself at the time?... Are there ways you abdicated your power? Reclaim these parts you left behind. Be whole again.......

Don't judge yourself harshly.... You did what you did, but now you can make amends, shift the energy, and reclaim your integrity. Honesty takes courage.... Have compassion for yourself....

Notice what you need to do to reclaim your integrity...to let that part of you that you shut down at the time, to let that part of you out now.... Welcome that part back into the light of awareness. Let your honesty open up now.... What does that part of you have to say?... What can be done to set things right?......

What do you need to do to make yourself whole again...to honor life?... Notice what is needed to bring it all back into congruency.... There may be

someone that needs to be spoken to...or something that has to be changed....
There may be amends that need to be made...or something to be done to secure
that the next time will unfold differently. Just what is needed to stand by your
convictions?......

No matter what happened, people always appreciate witnessing acts of
integrity.... Truth always shines. Imagine acting with integrity. Imagine doing
what you need to.... Make commitments to yourself, especially that part of yourself that got shut out. Tell yourself what you are willing to do.......

Feel yourself regaining self-respect. The energy shifts inside.... No need for
avoidance. Feel yourself whole again. Feel the shadow lift from your heart....
Breathe.... Feel openness happen....

If you like, bring back to awareness another scene that needs to be
worked with. *(Repeat from "Choose one scene to focus on now" as many times as
you like.)*

When you live ethically you live life fully for there is nothing that doesn't
count. Everything and everyone is of value.... You needn't expend energy ignoring anything. You are whole; you live life fully alive! Appreciate yourself; take
pride in your integrity. It matters.... You need it; the world needs it....

Present (151A)

Notice how your life lines up with your principles in the present time....
Breathe.... Let yourself simply be present with what arises in awareness as you survey your life.... Breathe.... Be present with what is so for you.... As you breathe
know that your honesty opens up, offering you what is true.... Witness.... Are
there any circumstances that don't sit right?... Anything that has been ignored?...
Anything that is calling for a deeper look?...... Anything going on that you feel is
wrong?... How are people being treated?... Are you compromising your integrity
anywhere?... Notice what comes to mind as you reflect on these questions....
Witness it. In all honesty let yourself witness.

How are you treating others?... Are you ignoring anyone's needs?... Are you being honest? Are you promoting yourself at someone else's expense?... What is the truth of the matter?... Do you need to do things differently? What is at stake?... Are there issues you need to raise with anyone?

Are there ways you spend your time and attention that aren't quite in harmony with what you care most about?... Are you honoring what is most important to you?... Is there anything getting neglected?...

Witness.... Notice if anything needs to be adjusted, changed, expressed.... What is needed to be true to your values?... Imagine standing by your convictions.... Make commitments to yourself. Tell yourself what you are willing to do.... Imagine acting with integrity. Imagine it in detail.... In the act you inspire respect. Whatever has been going on, people always appreciate witnessing acts of integrity.... When truth shines hearts open. Remember what is important.... Stand by your convictions. They are there for you to lean on.

Future (151B)

Breathe.... Let yourself be present with what arises in the light of awareness as you survey the future.... Breathe.... As you breathe know that your honesty opens up and offers you what is true. When honesty is present the heart breathes. Let your heart breathe.... Witness.

Choose a particular situation whose possibilities you would like to explore, its probabilities. As though you could peer right into the future and see how it might unfold.... Bring the situation to mind. Imagine the details of the circumstances. Who is involved?... What is everyone up to?... You may want to focus on different people one at a time....... Sense what is so for the others involved.... What are people striving for?...... Where are people coming from?... Bring all this to mind.... What are your leanings?... Imagine.... Watch the interactions.... What happens?... How are people being treated?... What is the impact of what is taking place?... Is the Earth being honored?... Imagine how things may unfold.... What is likely to occur? Imagine it.... Imagine the different possibilities....

If there are choices you are facing, take one option at a time and imagine how it might unfold.... Take some time to explore all the possible unfolding.... Use your imagination to fill in the details of the possibilities.... *(Name specific options and reread the questions in the preceding paragraph.)*

What does your heart feel about the matter?... Do you have a gut feeling about it?... What are you aware of?... How does it line up with your principles?... Notice where special care is needed to assure everything remains true to principle.... Is there anything that needs to be said?... What is the right thing to do?...

Imagine doing what is needed.... When you stand in truth the heart sings.... You align yourself with the movement of the universe; you are not at cross-purposes with the way of things.... Truth shines, opens everyone to humanity.... Imagine that acting with integrity inspires others to do the same....

Stand for What You Believe in the Face of Adversity (152)

To augment this meditation, open with all or part of *Call Upon Your Life-Affirming Values (24), Calling the Ancestors (29), The Spirit of the Children (31),* and/or *Grounded and Open (39).* The latter three can be inserted where they are mentioned in the text of the meditation. End with *Create a Symbol to Tap Energy in Daily Life (13A).* If you are feeling shy you may want to add parts of *Claim Your Space (60), Protected View (12),* and/or *Breath Is Home; Breath Heals (1G)* to your meditation. Change personal pronouns if appropriate.

Feel yourself standing in your convictions, gaining power from them. Grounded in what you believe in. Like the trees whose roots stretch deep into the ground and draw nutrients from the Earth, imagine yourself rooted in your convictions, drawing power from them....... Power moves up into you as the sap moves through the trees. Your convictions are the lifeblood of your integrity....

Like the roots that enable the trees to weather the storms, your convictions will get you through. Know that this is true.... Know that you are not alone — all of those who stand by their principles stand with you now. It is true. Feel it....

Like the roots that draw nutrients out of the soil, imagine that as you stand on your convictions you draw up courage.... Breathe.... Draw it in.... You have the conviction to stand your ground. Draw courage from those who have gone before.... Draw courage for those who will come after.... What you do makes a difference for all of them. Let them give you courage to stand your ground. *(Use sections of* Calling the Ancestors (29) *and* The Spirit of the Children (31) *if you want to augment this section.)*

Remember what is at stake.... Recall why it matters.... Appreciate yourself for standing for what counts...insuring that what counts is taken into account.... As you persist you will prevail....

Take time to be with the part of you that might be scared; notice what she needs.... Bring in your allies. Know you are not alone.... In fact the great powers of all of humanity are behind you.... *(Augment this section with* Calling Upon Your Allies (27)*).*

Dare to tell the truth.... Reside in your humanity, in wholeness with what is true, with what is sacred. Truth nourishes the soul.... Residing in your humanity you can open to different perspectives...honor differences and make the choices that honor the whole of humanity. There may be controversy in it.... The truth will shine through.

Stand by your convictions even when the winds are blowing the other way. Know that by standing up against what is wrong, what is the worst in people, you bring out the best in people.... Feel yourself not righteous but courageous...no blame, no shame; only a reminder of what matters.... Flexible, fluid in your power.... Imagine yourself bold.... Claim your voice.... Tell your truth.... Imagine as though you have a bullhorn and you broadcast the truth to the world.

Imagine it. Be bold!... What you stand for is important.... Breathe.... Notice what you need to gather strength.... Remember the support you have.... Imagine what you need...who you need to stand with you.

Imagine yourself with people who say and do things that go against your values.... Imagine standing up for what you believe in.... You are so clear you reflect back to them the truth of what they are doing. Like a mirror, you bounce it back.... People take into account what you say.... And then they can choose to change....

The trees weather the storms. Rooted in your convictions, stand your ground.... Trust the way of the universe. In openness life affirmation comes forth.... As you persist you will prevail. Truth speaks to humanity....

Creating Shared Intent for Perilous Times (153)

> *"When a boat is in dangerous waters, one centered person with strong intention can prevent it from capsizing"*
> — *Thich Nhat Hanh*

This meditation prepares people to be able to remain centered and unified in the midst of chaotic and potentially violent circumstances. It was written in collaboration with Ruby Phillips to help Seattle demonstrators protest the meeting of the World Trade Organization in 1999. Drawing on people's own sense of the sacred, the meditation weaves their spirits into a web of power so they can hold strong and offer a powerful presence, increasing both their effectiveness and safety. By using symbols, it empowers people to re-access their meditation experience in the midst of stressful circumstances. (See Creating a Symbol for Calling Up Energy, Part II, Page 39.) If people practice this meditation as a group a few times and participants also occasionally take a moment to focus on their symbols, it increases the likelihood that they will spontaneously call upon their symbols when confronted with danger.

This meditation is also very useful for opening a meeting or a controversial discussion because it amplifies group cohesion. The first and last few paragraphs make a shortened version that can be completed in less than five minutes — or in less than one minute once people have created symbols. No induction, ending, or count out is needed with this meditation. See *Tips for Leading Groups in Meditation* (Part II, Page 64).

Bring your awareness into your body. Notice your body breathing.... Feel breath rolling through your body.... Feel the rise and fall of your breath.... Relaxed and full....

Breath carries life. All that is alive breathes. Appreciate the simple miracle of breath.... Breath renews life.... As you breathe, feel your breath renew you now.... Every cell of your body bathed by breath.

Feel your feet.... Feel the Earth.... Feel yourself supported by the Earth. Feel the stability of the Earth.... Grow roots down into the ground; draw strength from the Earth.

What you breathe out, the plants breathe in.... Breath weaves life together. Breath carries life.... Imagine as though the Earth itself is breathing with you.... As though the Earth and sky breathe, as though All That Is is alive....

Remember the sacred.......

Life is sacred.... Remember the beauty and uniqueness of human beings living in different places on the Earth.... All people on the Earth are sacred....... Remember the life of the forests.... Remember the life of the seas....... Feel the power of the forests...the animals...the seas...and deep in the Earth......life everywhere.......

Now notice that all of us here are breathing.... Remember that we are all here to take a stand for life, for all living beings on the Earth. We are here together; together we are powerful.... Breathe the power of life.... Imagine that our breathing finds harmonic rhythms.... Notice how the quality of energy here is changing as we focus on our common purpose.... Bathe in this energy....

Breathing our unity, breathing our common purpose...breathing the power of our shared intention...breathing with the Earth, breathing with each other, breathing the sacred.....

Now create a symbol or a gesture that represents this energy — whatever feels right to you. (Or bring to mind your symbol/gesture, if you already have one.)....... Know that when you call it to mind, you evoke our shared intent. Know that every time you evoke it, its power increases. Tell yourself this now....

As you breathe out, send this power to where it is needed...to work well with one another, to stand with all life.... Imagine bathing the situation with this energy.......

Tell yourself you'll remember to call upon this energy. Tell yourself this now.... Expect it to be true. Envision the success of our shared intent....... Expect it to be true.......

(Optional) Imagine a chaotic situation....... Project yourself into it.... Call up your symbol. Evoke our shared intention.... Feel your feet; feel the Earth.... Breathe.... Breath creates space.... Draw upon the energy around you and imagine channeling it into our shared intention.... Feel everyone stand their ground.... You might want to imagine roots stretching deep into the Earth, breathing with the Earth, drawing strength from the Earth...weathering the storm.

(Optional) Take some time to focus on the issues that we will be addressing in this meeting, and imagine that we remain focused and come up with our best collaborative thinking. *(Slowly name the issues here.)*

Begin to move your attention to an outer focus.... Bring the power of this shared intention with you....... Slowly, coming back to an outer focus of attention....

When you are ready, open your eyes....

Web of Inclusion: A Gathering (154)

This meditation will help bring people into accord at the beginning of a gathering and to make the transition back to their own lives smoother. Use the sections that fit your needs. Before beginning it is good to invite people to look around the room and silently appreciate all who are present. If you would like to set a more intimate tone or augment the meditation, use parts of *Heart-to-Heart Energy Weave (141)*, *Calling the Ancestors (29)*, and *Spirit of Place (38)*. See Tips for Leading Groups in Meditation (Part II, Page 64) for suggestions that will help you to introduce and lead the meditation.

Opening (154A)

As we sit together, feel the whole room pulsating with energy. Take a moment and appreciate those who made it possible for us to come together.

Extend your awareness to the time that you chose to come here. Remember how you felt...what you wanted...what you thought might transpire here...what felt important about gathering and spending our time together...what we might create together. Remember what brought you here...what you care about.... Remember....

Now extend your awareness to include all of us sitting here in this room together. Each of us cares. Each of us has reason to share.... Feel all of this present in our hearts and minds. Breathing together.... Conscious of what is important. How we want to be together....

As we breathe together, imagine a positive energy beginning to glow in the room — a gladness to share together. Imagine as though with each exhalation of breath the room gets brighter with this light — glows more. Our energies begin to build something together. Imagine our time together unfolding in this positive light....

Imagine what would be the very best that could be created in the time we share.... We do all that we have set out to...and more! Sense it unfolding in the very best way...all attuned to one another......inspiring each other.... Now stretch your imagination even further and imagine that the time we share surpasses your best expectations. The time we share is exhilarating, marvelous, amazing!... It opens the heart, sharpens the mind, and uplifts the spirit. Imagine it.... Breathe life into this vision. Feel the room come alive with vision....

Create an openness inside to receive the offerings of our time together. As you inhale draw on the powers we create together.... Open yourself to discover what we will bring into being.

Imagine what you would like to share...how that might unfold.... Imagine how you might share what your offer.... Acknowledge that each of us has contributions to make; each of us has gifts to offer...and each of us welcomes these offerings. The exchange is as natural as the plants breathing in what we breathe out. Exchange. Gifts...offerings...energy weaving....

Imagine luminous lines of energy exchange moving between our minds, our hearts, our spirits...that each exchange creates a bright line of energy moving from person to person. Web weaving. Energy weaving. Sharing.... The web we weave is bright.... It holds all of us up.... It supports us all.... Feel it.... Trust it....

Closing (154B)

As we sit together feel the whole room pulsating with energy. All that we have created together is alive in the room. Recall your arrival, and follow your experience through all that we've shared together. Each day, remember the special moments of meaning....... Connections: ideas connecting, learning happening.... Hearts connecting, caring awakened.... Spirits connecting, laughter bubbling...all the connections that happened. Recall them.... Learning...caring...laughing...crying...sharing. Breathe; let all this settle in....

Breathing together, present together.... Imagine luminous lines of energy between yourself and each person you connected with — lines of energy for all the connections you made.... Lots and lots of luminous lines of energy, maybe sprays of energy between us...lines of energy connecting mind to mind...heart to heart...a line of energy for every connection. Vibrant, colorful; imagine it...glowing...alive...luminous....

Notice that everyone here has made connections as well. Everyone has glowing lines of energy moving between them and others here. Imagine you can see all the luminous energy lines...webs of energy woven, glowing energy crisscrossing the room...webs woven, glowing.... We have all spun this web together. It encompasses us all.

Imagine breathing life into our luminous web of connectedness. Every time you exhale the lines glow even brighter....

This energy transcends the limits of space and time. Imagine each and all of us leaving here — some by foot, some by car, by train, by bus, by plane, some alone, some with others; imagine each and all of us leaving this place and returning to our homes. When we leave these lines stretch out...get very long. We remain connected and the web gets very, very big....

We return home and include others in our experience; we share.... Imagine what and with whom you'll share....... More lines of connection are made.... The web is woven stronger.... All of us leave and extend the web, build the web...pulsating energy, getting brighter with each connection made, weaving the web of life together, the web that supports everyone. Feel yourself supported....

We each tend the web to keep it strong.... Imagine what you do to maintain it.... On these lines of connection energy continues to move. Heart connections grow stronger.... Ideas move along the lines, gathering momentum, illuminating what is so wherever they go.... Relationships glow and hearts are gladdened; minds expand and spirits are lifted, all in the web of inclusion. It encompasses us all and all our relations — the whole globe held in a luminous web of energy...lifelines...heart lines.... Our breath keeps it alive; our care keeps energy moving — weaving the web of our lives...together....

The World: How It Is (155)

You may want to continue from this meditation to *The World: How It Could Be (156) and People Make History (157).* You can augment it with *Reside in the Quiet (3), Calling the Ancestors (29), The Future Ones (30),* and/or *The Spirit of the Children (31).* Include especially long silences.

Tune to the state of the planet. However you imagine doing so, in the quiet, be with the planet....... The Earth that provides home for all beings, the Earth is wailing...storming...quaking. Species disappear; soil is lost, land paved over, and toxins strewn everywhere — even the sky is dying.... The Earth cries.... For the first time in history it is not clear that the Earth will be able to provide for the generations to come.... Yet everywhere there are children excited to be alive.... Everywhere people care.... There are communities working for common cause....

Open to your feelings of care and concern.... Open your heart to the grief you carry for the state the world is in.... The world is the container of our lives — of all life. Open to your feelings of care and concern...all the peoples and all the critters and all the places that live under continual assault.... Open to your feelings of care and concern.... Breathe.... Acknowledge the truth of the times. You needn't be numb; to feel is to be alive...to honor life.... The truth sets us free.... Life is resilient, always resilient.... Grass grows up through concrete.... Breathe.... In the quiet, be with the planet.......

Tune to the state of humanity.... Imagine as though humanity has a spirit; tune to how the spirit of humanity is doing...how it is feeling....... There are people everywhere whose right to self-determination is being trampled; sometimes their lands are taken, and sometimes their lives are taken. There are people all over the globe who are disregarded and then massacred for standing up.

Witness: Despotic governments kill in the name of power then roll out the red carpet for the corporations while the children go hungry. The corporations know no boundaries as they scour the entire Earth to feed their insatiable appetites. They chew up people and places, then spit them out, spent, and move on searching for another profitable venue elsewhere. They always leave devastation in their wake.... Fast food restaurants spring up everywhere. Majestic landscapes are lost to make way for more malls. The rich keep getting richer, and everyone else pays the bill and gets poorer. Our children and our children's children and the great forests and the seas — what about them? Progress has become intoxicated; it's careening full speed down a road toward total destruction. It is time to be sober. These are sobering times.......

There are people everywhere who stand up for what is right...caring for people...caring for place. Remember those who have stood for what is important...who have made a difference.... Breathe.... Draw on their courage.......

(Repeat the opening paragraph.) Remember what you care about...maybe a place...maybe people who are having a hard time of it.... Maybe you have tried to put it out of your mind, feeling there was nothing you could do about it.... Focus on what especially grieves you.... Breathe.... Witness.... Open to the truth.... We can, we will make a difference. People created the situation; people can change it. People make history.... Everywhere people care.... With conviction and vision we can work miracles.... Feel yourself part of the world; take joy in being alive and contributing your part to healing.... What you do matters....

The World: How It Could Be (156)

Envision a world that is organized around care and concern...a society that revolves around the heart...not power, the heart....... Imagine a time when we could take it for granted that all life would be revered.... Justice would reign....... What if all our intelligence were dedicated to developing the heart instead of wealth?... Everyone would have health care.... Everyone would have a home...no poverty anywhere.... Imagine it.... Everyone included in making the decisions that affect them...everyone contributing their gifts. Every single person seen as important and celebrated....... Diversity cultivated.... Cooperation is a way of life. Care rules.... Trust is a given. Imagine it.... How would this feel?......

What would it be like to know you belonged? Imagine always being able to take it for granted that you belonged...that there would be a place for you and for your children and for your children's children.... Imagine it....... Envision a time when we live in harmony with the cycles of nature. The Earth is honored — whatever is taken is returned — nothing is taken out of the life cycle.

What would it feel like to live in a time where security was a given?... People treat one another fairly. Trust is assumed; justice reigns.... Imagine the world at peace.... Violence and coercion are social crimes. Shared care is the norm.... Create this time in your mind's eye.......

Project yourself far enough into the future that it is conceivable that this time really has come about. What would it feel like?... If you knew your livelihood was secure, what would you do to contribute your best?... How would it be to live in this world?... Let your imagination paint this time.... Feel what it would be like day-to-day....

What would be celebrated? What would we do together?... How would we share resources?... How would those in need be cared for?... How would the arts weave though life?... What sorts of communities would there be?... Imagine it.... How would it be when everyone understands that everyone is interdependent?... What would you be doing?... How would it feel?...

If you can imagine it, it's entirely possible.... In fact there are people every-where working to bring it about.... Breathe in and draw on this vision.... Bring it into present time.... Feel the vision provide sustenance to your commitment, to your convictions....... This vision makes you strong...dedicated to healing the future...partaking in changing the course of history....

People Make History (157)

This meditation is designed to open with the third and fourth paragraphs of *Grounded and Open (39)*. You might want to use *Calling the Ancestors (29), The Future Ones (30),* and/or *The Spirit of the Children (31)*.

Now life itself is struggling to continue spiraling. The times call for all wisdom accumulated in all of history.... People make history. People made history before.... People make history now.... You can contribute to the making of his-tory.... People have always struggled for change. People have always worked to make the world a better place for their children. People make history.... Think of people who worked to make the world a better place — some famous, most not.... They worked to secure a better life for the next generation....

People who make history always have courage, commitment, and vision.... They're never alone; they join with others who share their cares....

Feel common cause. Imagine who shares your cares. Imagine joining in a community of common cause...to contribute your part, to offer your gifts...to claim your legacy and answer the call of the generations that have gone before: your parents, your parents' parents, and theirs....... Feel yourself part of securing the future for the generations to come: your children, your children's children, and theirs...that they are blessed with a healthy life...that life is always secure and thrives....

Commit yourself to what you truly care about.... You can make a difference. The world teeters on such a precarious point that small contributions could be all that it takes to tip the balance and secure the future.... Breathe; relax. You need not know all the answers.... Trust that in joining together, we'll figure it out as we go.... Imagine contributing to healing the future....

Imagine living the change you want to make....... Vision and conviction are the fuel and fiber of action....... Together we can make it better.... Together we heal present time. Together we heal future time....

Life is sacred. Vision is sacred. Envision that this energy surrounds all the Earth.... The Earth and all who live upon her are sacred. Together we secure the future....

APPENDIX

The Principles of Applied Meditation

Inner dimensions operate in a different fashion than our ordinary world; it is good to periodically review the information that follows so that it remains in the forefront of awareness when you do your meditation work. Otherwise you are likely to employ your usual way of judging and dismiss the very experience you should be paying special attention to.

Keep in Mind:

- Applied Meditation works with the Witness to be aware of the quality of energy that's present; the Active Imagination is used to help achieve goals; and the Receptive Imagination is used to gain insight. Usually all three modes operate simultaneously.

- Meditation is synergistically more powerful in group settings and causes groups to be more cohesive.

- Meditation utilizes a very familiar state of consciousness where imagination is most prominent.

- In addition to being the source of creativity, the imagination is the medium of psychic/intuitive information and the stuff of which probabilities are made.

- Meditation work takes place in the realm of the sacred.

- Affinity is the way of the universe. In the dimension of probabilities, like energies attract one another.

- The subjective world and the objective world mirror each other — change in one causes change in the other.

- Healing energy is always accessible in the inner dimensions.

- Healing happens naturally when you let go and trust life-force energies.

- All behavior stems from the imagination, whether or not it is to our liking. Nothing is done unless it is imagined first.

- For any problem, if you do not have a positive vision to strive for, then the problem itself is perpetuated because there is nothing else in your imagination to replace it — it becomes the source of your behavior by default.

- What you believe determines how limited or expansive your expectations are. Beliefs are the conclusions you have drawn from past experience. In the presence of the Witness you can discover outdated limiting beliefs and then move to transform them with the process of Mental Housecleaning.

- When you can imagine what it would actually be like, it is possible.

- The act of "making it up" provides a context for intuitive information to make itself known.

THE CHARACTER OF INNER CONSCIOUSNESS

- Thinking and imagining are not the same. The imagination is dominant when you are in a relaxed state of awareness and rational processing has receded into the background.

- The inner consciousness lives in the perpetual here and now. It is literal, suggestible, and does not comprehend negatives.

- The inner consciousness communicates through rhythm, repetition, rhyme, ritual, sensation, symbol, pun, metaphor, memory, and childlike make-believe.

- Inner consciousness lives in the realms of universality, and therefore its insights often feel cliched.

- Intent, expectations, and questions determine the angle of the light of awareness and therefore control both what comes into view and what is drawn into experience.

- The rational mind tends to discount the workings of inner consciousness. Discounting does not impact the effectiveness of the work; in fact the presence of a discounting voice usually means that you are doing effective inner work.

- Inner consciousness is fluid and prone to wander; whenever it does, notice if there is anything significant about where it has taken you. If not, bring it back to where you were last working and continue where you left off.

ALWAYS STRIVE TO:

- have fullness of breath.

- regularly meditate on your own, in group settings, and with or without meditation scripts.

- keep a journal of your meditation work.

- credit your inner dimensions when credit is due.

- have the Witness present at all times.

- follow your own inclinations of what feels right for you.

- notice and set your imagination to work coloring in and fleshing out the details of your first impressions, gut feelings, and the vague hunches that you find in the back of your awareness.

- never dismiss your experience just because it feels like you "made it up." In this work it is your imagination that is the purveyor of your truth. If, when you are asking a question, the answer is not already there, don't wait for it to come — make it up.

- be optimistic and open. If you have no positive vision in relation to a particular dissatisfaction, find one and work with it to bring about change.

- notice constriction and breathe through it, making space for the presence of the Witness so that you can recognize what is taking place.

- move all that you imagine into a state of well-being, balance, peace, and wholeness.

- trust the harmonizing forces intrinsic to life and know that you access them when you meditate.

- express your gratitude for the gifts you receive from inner dimensions.

THE WITNESS:

- is a state of being, not a character that resides within. It is a verb not a noun.

- emerges with full breath and should be present in all meditation work.

- brings a sense of wholeness.

- has no attachments, reasons, or justifications. It simply knows. The information it offers can be ignored but not argued with. Any perspective that has a drive behind it is not being offered by the Witness. The Witness is not invested in having its perspective heeded.

- provides spacious awareness, where freedom lives, making response instead of reaction possible.

In the presence of the Witness you can:

- recognize what feels right (balanced) or where well-being may be found.

- perceive intuitive information and catch sudden insight. (Aha!)

- recognize energy that is at cross-purposes with intent.

- know the meaning of metaphor and recognize puns and their specific significance.

- discern the potential outcome of any action under consideration.

- discover the internal congruence/collusion with external limitations.

- see the underlying expectations, intentions, and assumptions that limit or open energy flow.

- notice impulses to do things differently.

- note when there is no vision toward which to strive.

- recognize points of reference that can form a basis for making change.

- notice if a projection you are working with is, in fact, what you really want.

- surround problems with spacious awareness, making room for the Receptive Imagination to do its work.

- identify what is conceivable, plausible, and possible and detect whether expectation or wishful thinking is operative.

- know when to employ the Active, or the Receptive Imagination.

THE ACTIVE IMAGINATION

- Work with your Active Imagination to align yourself with and energize your aspirations, dreams, and goals.

- For any specific concern ask yourself how you would like it to be and imagine how that would feel, look, taste, smell, and be like — as if it were already true. Give it three-dimensional detail and project what you want.

- Do not concern yourself with why, how, if, when, or where the projection may come to pass; just assume it has.

- Embody the projection and pretend that it is already true. Experience how that feels in your body and what your life would be like if it were the reality. Be sure that, in fact, it is what you want.

- Notice the impact of your projections on others. When projecting do so with the attitude that it will only come to pass if it is in everyone's best interest. Always respect the choices of others.

- Maintain a humble attitude that acknowledges you may not know what is best.

- Make the projection believable by telling yourself that, incrementally, this new experience is manifesting itself, or project it into a time in the future when it is conceivable that it will already have happened.

- Cultivate faith; remember past successes and acknowledge when change comes about.

- Create an affirmation and/or symbol that represents your projection.

- Have your last image/thought in meditation be positive and open.

- After working with the projection forget about it. Suspend judgment and assume the projection is working in its own way and its own time.

- Expect change; assume it is happening under the surface. If you watch for signs of success, it encourages the emergence of your projection.

- Invite your Receptive Imagination into the process whenever you feel constriction or can't find a positive vision for which to strive.

- Invite the Witness to discern if your vision is truly in your, and others', best interest.

THE RECEPTIVE IMAGINATION

- Work with the Receptive Imagination when you have no vision for which to strive.

- Story-making provides a context for insight to reveal itself. Use your creativity. Make up stories like children do.

- Imagine as though all thought forms have an intelligence of their own.

- Personify the constriction/problem — make up a character that represents it. Dialogue with the character. Ask it questions like, "What are you protecting?" or "What are you worried will happen?" "What do you want?" "What can you offer?"

- Work with whatever comes spontaneously into awareness or make it up; don't wait for it to happen. Give detail to the first image, thought, and/or sensation of which you are aware.

- Never concern yourself with whether or not what you are aware of is "correct." When your rational mind does this, simply let it take a back row seat in your imagination.

- Remember that what is "made up" and what "comes to" you both emerge from the same source.

- When you formulate a question notice what you sense to be true at the same time as you formulate it. Since inner consciousness lives in the perpetual here and now, answers often present themselves simultaneously to your process of clarifying the question. Sometimes you will feel that you already knew the answer.

- Inner consciousness resides in the realm of universality, so the answers it offers often feel corny. What matters is whether or not the information is useful.

- Pay attention to exactly how the imagination depicts any concern; metaphorically this represents the current state of reality.

- Negotiate with the character representing the problem; imagine what it can offer, and tell it what you are willing to do.

- When you agree to do something take manageable steps and renegotiate with your inner self if you find that you are not keeping your agreements.

- Whenever constriction arises breathe and invite the spacious awareness of the Witness. Endeavor to move the imaginary scene into a state of openness. This makes room for the Receptive Imagination to do its work. It will point to a strategy that you can use in your life.

- Invite your Active Imagination to project how it is to embody the newly received insight.

Beliefs: Surveying Your Subjective Landscape

Your beliefs underlie all of your expectations and motivations and dictate the effectiveness of the Active Imagination. The assessment surveys that follow are designed to help pinpoint the beliefs that undermine your work and to reveal those that can be used to empower your work. (See Self-Defeating Beliefs, Part II, Page 44.) Once identified, limiting beliefs can be transformed, and when you remember your strengths you can transfer your sense of capability in one area to another that you want to improve.

Use as many surveys as you like; they are designed to be used repeatedly, singly and together. Your purpose here is not to gain new insights but to see what has gone unnoticed. Read using the soft awareness of the Witness, and pay keen attention to the first thought that comes to mind. This is not a time to analyze why but to notice what pops up. What comes up will provide rich resources for you to work with in your meditations.

Some questions may have more meaning to you than others. Their purpose is to evoke your first response, so don't belabor any; if a question doesn't inspire an immediate response, skip it and go on to the next. With each response ask yourself if that is okay or if you would prefer it to be otherwise. Don't worry if you believe if it is possible to be different; simply notice if you would choose change if you could. If your experience is satisfactory, leave things be. If you want to make a change, look up a word in the Meditation Use Index that describes the experience you would like to transform — isolated, worried, etc.

The surveys can be used by individuals or groups, but they will yield the best results if you work through them with other people. In a group setting, pair up and take turns reading to each other. Whether you are working on your own or in a group, it is good to start off with the short meditations *Reside in the Quiet (3)* and *In the Quiet, Greet Yourself (41)* before reading the surveys. (There is no need to use a count-out.) This method enhances your capacity to focus in on the spontaneous responses that point to current beliefs. Pause briefly after you read each statement in order to allow enough time for a response to come into full view — one or two complete breaths ought to do it.

BELIEFS

Working at a fast pace, fill in the first blank using a word from the list, and then finish the sentence with what is true for you. Keep repeating and finishing the sentence, using a different word each round. Feel free to add to or delete from the list.

In regard to _____, I am _____ because _____.

age	empathy	intimacy	sense of humor
ambition	faith	joy	sensitivity
appearance	family	leadership	sexuality
approval	generosity	love	spirituality
authority	gratitude	loyalty	spontaneity
commitment	greed	money	the future
community	happiness	nature	the world
compassion	health	personality	time
conflict	heart	politics	trust
creativity	honesty	relaxation	work
discipline	inspiration	responsibility	
ego	integrity	security	
emotion	intelligence	self-esteem	

CLIMATE

The mood I am in most of the time is:

I really savor:

Most of my attention is focused in the (past, present, or future):

The regrets that haunt me are:

I worry about:

I characterize my predominant disposition as:

I'm impatient when:

I handle time:

I feel gratitude when:

My sense of humor comes out when:

I feel really isolated when:

The best thing about my life is:

Usually when I awaken I meet the day with a feeling of:

My perpetual challenges are:

I am inspired by:

I often get defensive when:

I am always preoccupied with:

My curiosity is awakened when:

I find meaning in:

I fully enjoy others when:

I shut down when:

POSITIVE SUBJECTIVE RESOURCES

Positive points of reference are invaluable when you are in the midst of doing transformation work. As you answer the questions that follow, note where the greatest concentration of positive energies is and use it as a source from which to draw in your meditations.

To be alive is truly a blessing because:

I love:

One of my greatest strengths is:

I feel fully supported when:

People turn to me for _____ because:

I always have faith in:

I always know I can count on:

I am grateful for:

The person who really inspires me is _____ because:

I am really generous when:

I am really proud of:

What I like best is:

I take great pleasure in:

I feel radiant and fully alive when:

I feel the sacred when:

I am motivated by:

I have felt the power of healing when:

What really gets me into a playful mood is:

I'm really good at:

I smile when I remember:

I discovered I was capable beyond expectations when:

I am in my element when:

I always look forward to:

I feel appreciated when:

What I really care about is:

I feel fully content when:

My life is most meaningful when:

I feel I make a difference when:

My shared love with _____ is such a:

One of the very best moments of my life was when: _____

Another was when:

One of my best sources of replenishment is:

REVEALING NEGATIVE SELF-CONCEPTS

I am just too:

Shame comes up for me when:

I'm always afraid people will reject me because:

Sometimes I feel people don't want to be with me because:

I try to reshape myself when:

I crave the approval of:

I keep _____under cover because if I were to reveal it then:

Sometimes I feel like I just don't quite make the mark because:

I have to look out for myself when it comes to:

When people express their appreciation to me I can't accept it because:

Sometimes I feel like a martyr because:

I get intimidated when:

I give my power away when:

I'm afraid people will find out that I'm really just:

I'm really bad at:

I often argue with myself about:

I discount myself when:

I can be irresponsible when it comes to:

I can be overly responsible when it comes to:

I get embarrassed when:

I feel jealous when:

I am hard on myself regarding:

I have always wished I could:

SOCIAL CONDITIONING

Our culture depends on relations of domination in order to function; we have all acquired attitudes that keep us separated from each other and that collude with injustice. The following survey is designed to reveal the beliefs that hinder your ability to live and act with full appreciation of yourself and others. Many of the questions are rooted in stereotypes; the point is to discover if part of you holds any to be true.

Notice that part of yourself that agrees with the following and under what circumstances it is true for you.

Showing vulnerability will bring disrespect.

It is always best to strive to be totally independent.

I look for flaws in others.

I am always comparing myself with others.

Affluence is a sign of virtue, poverty a sign of inadequacy.

If I am not careful, I will be taken advantage of.

I feel like I have to prove myself.

People naturally tend toward violence.

What I own is a reflection of who I am.

Humor is a sign of lack of commitment.

I often take charge of situations because I am more capable.
I have to show that I am in control.
Showing affection is a sign of weakness.
I always prefer to interact with good-looking people.
Certain kinds of work are beneath my dignity.
There are some people that I would be ashamed to be associated with.
I strive to stand out as special.
The suffering of other people is none of my business.
People choose their station in life; if they want a better life, all they
have to do is work for it.
I pretend that I know even when I don't.

There is some work I could never learn how to do; it is simply
beyond my ability.
I pretend that I don't know even when I do.
I often feel like I should apologize for myself.
I am not important in the scheme of things.
Sexuality is shameful.
I am more comfortable on the sidelines.
I usually leave the decisions to others.
I am too emotional.
When I get treated badly it is because I deserve it.

Complete the sentence or answer the question for the following.

What parts of who I am, my experience, or my heritage do I minimize in public?
I never directly ask for what I want because:
I feel I am going against the grain when:
People would reject me if they knew:
What I have to say is not as important because:
People like me are not very good at:
Sometimes I feel that I stick out like a sore thumb because:
I feel ashamed of my _____. (Fill in the blank. Feel free to add to the list.)

appearance	gender identity	lack of resources	sexual orientation
disability	heritage	past	job

Notice the first thought that comes to mind when you read the following statements.

(Feel free to add other examples to the list, such as ethnicity, religions, kinds of work, etc.)

Women tend to be:

Men tend to be:

Children tend to be:

Asian people tend to be:

Black people tend to be:

Latino/a people tend to be:

Native American people tend to be:

White people tend to be:

Immigrants tend to be:

Lesbians tend to be:

Gays tend to be:

Transgendered people tend to be:

People with disabilities tend to be:

Poor people tend to be:

Rich people tend to be:

Old people tend to be:

Fat people tend to be:

CONSTRAINTS ON THE QUALITY OF LIFE

What has been bothering me lately is:

My life would be better if:

I've always wanted to _____ but:

I feel victimized when:

I can make things worse by:

What is really unfair is:

I am really guarded about:

I have an aversion to:

I get tense when:

I expect to be unhappy when:

Others cannot count on me when it comes to:

I don't speak my truth when:

In my relationships it would be better if:

I drag my feet when:

I hate:

I wish I could do more of:

I get compulsive when:

I worry about:

I get taken advantage of when:

I feel rebellious when:

I have to put my needs aside when:

I'm really tired of dealing with:

One thing I can never trust in people is:

One thing in life I simply have to endure is:

Cul-de-Sacs of the Mind:
Symptoms of an Unhealthy Subjective Climate

All the conditions that follow are riddled with beliefs that bring unsatisfactory experiences and are not likely to be congruent with what you want. They are cul-de-sacs of the mind. These attitudes invariably coexist with one another. When you are caught in them they lock you into a self-perpetuating, closed system, which blocks your ability to learn the very lessons you need in order to shift out of them. The tension they bring squeezes out learning, joy, compassion, generosity, humor, curiosity, creativity, and healing energy. They create a context in which negativity grows and in which pettiness, anxiety, and reactive energy fester.

The simple act of witnessing the presence of any of these conditions is the first step on the road to a more open, life-affirming experience. Viewing changes your vantage point — because you move from the inside to the outside of the problem you broaden your context.

THE CONDITIONS

- **Reactionary**
  There is no space between stimulus and response; your energy constricts, and you are on automatic pilot, trying to protect yourself from experiencing a pain that once again seems to be an immediate threat. You shut down and move into action. Your own thoughts are so loud that they blot out full comprehension of the current situation. See the meditation *From Reaction to Response: Turning Buttons into Pearls (87).*

- **Negative Expectations and Cynicism**
  Your expectations lead you down a path you would rather not be on, but you are convinced that there are no alternative paths. You frame situations inside the limitations and disappointments of the past.

- **Wishful Thinking**
  You expect that you will never get what you want. Your focus of attention is on your longing, yet you believe that you will never really get to enjoy the experience others have. You are absorbed in dissatisfaction and envy of others.

- **Victim Mentality**
  You believe that important circumstances will always be completely outside your control. You sometimes derive satisfaction from feeling righteous and from getting

sympathy from others. You might have a subtle investment in the perpetuation of the problem, especially if you meet ideas for resolution with "Yes, but...." Notice when everything is framed in terms of "them." Be on the lookout for thoughts that include words like "can't," "hopeless," or "helpless."

- **Stuck with What You Have Got**

  You are unhappy, yet you can't imagine that anything else is possible. A heavy sense of resignation — "This is life. It has always been this way and it always will be." — often accompanies this condition.

- **Circular Thinking**

  You find yourself thinking the same thing over and over again, creating a closed system in which there is no opening for insight to come and shift the situation. You focus on all the reasons why the problem exists — understanding the problem so thoroughly that it is inconceivable it could be any other way.

Two attributes that further narrow the context and make any situation more difficult accompany these conditions.

- **Dualistic, Either/Or, Binary, or One-Sided Thinking**

  You think there is only one correct approach. You find yourself shutting down and ignoring anything that contradicts your point of view. This kind of thinking makes it impossible to view anything from a holistic perspective, cuts you off from appreciating what other perspectives might contribute, and sets up a win/lose dynamic; dogmatism sets in and control patterns prevail. Watch for words like "never," "only," "always," "entirely," totally," "impossible," "absolutely," and "completely."

- **Comparative Value Judgment**

  This mentality replaces the intrinsic integrity of you and others with a pecking order. The synergy of being in community can't be experienced since you are perpetually preoccupied with judging who is better. (The subtext of this mentality is that no one is ever quite good enough.) This mentality brings on isolation, alienation, and distrust. You can never simply be present because you feel that if you relax you will be taken advantage of. See the meditation *When Competition Hurts: Dissolving the Competitive Edge (147)*.

In the presence of the Witness you will be able to detect if any of these conditions are present in your subjective landscape — if they are, you know it is time to shift. Do Mental Housecleaning (Part II, Page 43) and the meditation *Clearing Space Inside with Mental Housecleaning (11)*. If you have a positive vision, cultivate it; if not, engage the story-making capacities of your imagination to gain insight and discover one. All of the meditations in Getting Unstuck: Emotional Resilience (Part III, Page 202) can be used to transform your experience, as can *The Transformative Power of Breath (45)*.

Affirmations

Please follow the instructions in Part II, Page 40 on how to use affirmations. Inner consciousness is especially responsive to repetition: feel free to adjust any affirmation until it describes precisely the experience you want to cultivate, and then stick to the same wording.

GENERAL WELL-BEING

I cultivate a joyous heart.

I am grateful.

I love life. I love my life.

I am happy.

The Earth sustains me; the sky inspires me.

The universe supports me.

My life is full of laughter.

I am relaxed.

I am glad.

I am humble.

I am curious.

I am always learning.

I am fully resilient (or, the whole of my body, mind, heart, and spirit are fully resilient).

My needs are always met; there is enough for everyone.

I experience the sacred in all that is: in all people, in all places, in all life.

I have a generous spirit and a happy heart.

I am grounded.

I am responsible.

I maintain a healthy inner life (or, attitude toward_____).

I believe in myself.

I am courageous.

I transform fear into faith.

I am more and more keenly tuned to my intuition every day.

I am at peace with myself.

I am open.

I am an excellent _____ (artist, friend, mother, healer, etc.)

I witness what is so at all times — both inside and out.

I am present. I fully accept and occupy my experience.

I successfully pursue my dreams.

The future welcomes me.

I open to life's lessons.

I am receptive in my power.

I am centered.

I maintain balance amidst change.

May the best manifest.

May all be well.

May my meditation practice increase well-being in the world.

HEALTH

I honor my whole self with good care.

I am healthy. My _____ is healthy.

My immune system is strong and correctly determines what my body needs protection from.

My _____is healing and getting healthier every day.

I am emotionally and physically resilient.

I go to sleep easily, sleep soundly through the night, and awake refreshed, alert, and full of energy.

I honor the sanctity of my body and treat my body with good care.

I easily maintain healthy habits.

I meditate regularly; my inner life is deep and satisfying.

I exercise regularly.

I take time to rest and replenish my body whenever I need to.

I honor my body with healthy eating habits.

I have a relaxed relationship with food.

I continue to enjoy and easily maintain my sobriety (or, my resolve to _____).

I love my body.

TIME AND ROUTINE

Mindful, I live in the present moment.

I have a relaxed relationship with time.

I pace myself throughout the day, successfully accomplishing my responsibilities.

I make transitions easily.

I keep my environment clean, comfortable, and beautiful.

I have all the time I need.

I am mindful; I use my time wisely.

I am patient.

I have faith in the future.

ACTIVITIES

I open to the guidance, vision, and courage I need to be equal to the challenge ahead.

I am clear about what is most important and act accordingly.

I always recognize insight.

I am visionary and pragmatic.

I am creative.

I am intelligent.

I am talented.

I am successful.

I am decisive.

My understanding is always expanding.

I am always getting better at _____.

I learn from mistakes.

I am productive.

I am always fully present and focused on what is most important.

I engage my heart and spirit in all that I do.

I establish and protect my boundaries, and I balance my work and personal life.

I do excellent work and I enjoy doing it.

I contribute my best.

I see all situations as they truly are.

I am enthusiastic.

I work efficiently, completing all tasks and projects in a timely manner.

I have complete comprehension, retention, and recall of all that I study.

I easily fulfill all my commitments on time.

I have a relaxed relationship with money.

I successfully organize my financial life, knowing what I can afford.

I recognize opportunities as they present themselves.

I am prosperous, patient, and productive.

RELATIONSHIPS

I am loving and kind toward myself and others.

I live in a web of mutually loving and supportive relations.

I am cooperative.

I give and receive the support that is needed.

I am fully honest with myself and others.

I build community in my life.

I am independent.

I respect the choices of others.

I listen with an open heart.

All of my relationships are loving and mutually supportive.

I say "no" when I need to.

I ask for support when I need it.

I am sensitive and respectful of others.

I am clear and express my truth in a timely manner.

I respond to conflict gracefully, truthfully, and easily.

I remember that conflict is an opportunity to learn; I welcome reconciliation.

I am enriched by differences.

I am ethical.

My intimate relations are deeply satisfying.

I reside in the love we share.

Our love always illuminates the path that is right.

I honor _____'s process.

My family life is rich and satisfying.

I am relaxed about each person in my family and trust that they will each take care of themselves.

My family is harmonious and cooperative, with mutually supportive relations.

My partner and I cooperatively and amiably agree on an approach to parenting that is helpful to each person in the family.

I have the wisdom to empower my children to successfully take responsibility for their lives.

I know when to let go, when to teach, and when to intervene with my children.

GROUP

We act in accord with our mission.

Our vision inspires and guides us.

I am fully attuned to our vision and contribute my part in bringing it about.

We pace our work together well.

We easily meet the deadlines.

We are each fully attuned to one another and work well together.

Everyone contributes to success.

We each create a joyous, respectful, and open working atmosphere.

We are patient.

We are inspired.

We have a good sense of timing.

We are open and honest with each other.

We learn from mistakes.

We easily work through tension and learn together.

We depend on each other.

We are generous toward one another and the rest of the world.

We help each other know what is needed to bring balance into the world.

THE WORLD

My compassion for all beings grows deeper each day.

I care about the world and contribute my best toward its well-being.

I always appreciate the sacred in All That Is.

I contribute to making peace and justice.

I am mindful of the impact of my actions and only do what is beneficial for all.

My leadership empowers others.

I have the wisdom to know when to step forward and offer leadership, and when to step back and receive leadership.

I live in a manner that honors the Earth and all who live upon it.

I am aware of the impact of all my actions and act in accord with the greater good.

I remember that people make history.

What I do makes a difference.

May we each receive the support we need so that we are able to offer our best to securing the world for the generations to come.

Notes

Part I

1 See David Bohm, *Wholeness and the Implicate Order* (Routledge & Kegan Paul, 1980). Also see my Web site <www.toolsforchange.org> for a more comprehensive set of references to material covered in the remainder of *Meditations on Everything Under the Sun*.

2 Work having to do with imagination and the body/mind connection in medicine is a burgeoning field. See O. Carl Simonton, Stephanie Matthews-Simonton, and James Creighton, *Getting Well Again* (Bantam, 1992); Jeanne Achterberg, *Imagery and Healing: Shamanism and Modern Medicine* (Shambala, 1985); Herbert Benson, *Timeless Healing* (Scribner, 1996); Joan Borysenko, *Minding the Body, Mending the Mind* (Addison-Wesley, 1993); and Martin L. Rossman, *Guided Imagery for Self-Healing* (New World Library, 2000).

   Work having to do with mindfulness and health is being brought into the mainstream. See Jon Kabot-Zinn, *Full Catastrophe Living: Using the Wisdom of Your Body and Mind to Face Stress, Pain and Illness* (Delacorte Press, 1990).

   The use of imagery and the body/mind connection is also being taken up by athletes. For example see B. S. Rushall and L.G. Lippman, "The Role of Imagery in Physical Performance," *International Journal for Sport Psychology*, 29, 57 – 72 and "Imagery in Sports," *Coaching Science Abstracts*, vol.6(2): October, 2000. Also see Ken Baum and Richard Trubo, *The Mental Edge: Maximize Your Sports Potential with the Mind/Body Connection* (Perigee, 1999).

3 Some strands within Western scientific tradition have recognized a larger perspective: Newton was as skilled in alchemy as he was in physics. Many physicists in the twentieth century understand the implications of quantum mechanics and relativity theory as pointing to an animate universe. See Minas C. Kafatos and Robert Nadeau, *The Conscious Universe* (Springer-Verlag, 1990); and Amit Goswami, *The Self-Aware Universe* (Putnam's Sons, 1993).

   Biology has supported several holistic schools of thought, and many biologists have worked from a whole-organism frame of reference. The whole discipline of ecology was born out of a desire to investigate the multiple interactions of living beings. For example see Fritjof Capra, *The Web of Life* (Anchor Books, 1996). Today, we can celebrate the living systems theory that is emerging as one that takes a non-dualistic approach. See Joanna Macy, *World as Lover,*

World as Self, (Parallax Press, 1991) and *Mutual Causality in Buddhism and General Systems Theory* (State University of New York Press, 1991); and Joanna Macy with Molly Young Brown, *Coming Back to Life: Practices to Reconnect Our Lives, Our World*, (New Society, 1998).

4 Vine Deloria, Jr. reminds us that indigenous people have always understood the connection between spirit and matter in ways that Western European culture has suppressed. See Vine Deloria, *Spirit and Reason* (Fulcrum Publishers, 1999).

   There are those who are working within Western traditions to mend the schism between spirit and matter. See Matthew Fox, *A Spirituality Named Compassion: Uniting Mystical Awareness with Social Justice* (Inner Traditions, 1999). For work in reviving Earth-based spirituality, see Starhawk, *The Spiral Dance: A Rebirth of the Ancient Religion of the Great Goddess* (HarperSanFrancisco, 1999) and *Dreaming the Dark: Magic, Sex, and Politics* (Beacon Press, 1997). In their own ways all three of these authors explore the spirit/matter schism and offer ways to heal its impact on the Earth and its inhabitants.

5 I strive to make sense of my experience — to understand why prayer works at one time and doesn't seem to at another; to understand causality. I stand in awe of the mystery. My striving is utterly clumsy in the face of the sacred, yet what I have come to understand is of great help to me in my life. I make no claim to being scientific or objective. I am neither a scholar nor an initiate of any religious tradition. I share solely my personal observations and conclusions.

   The question is not if the perspectives herein can be proven; the question is whether or not you find them helpful as you navigate through your inner dimensions to discover and develop the powers that reside in your psyche. You need not agree with my views on the nature of consciousness to make use of the meditations — use what works and leave the rest.

6 See Gary Zukav, *The Dancing Wu Li Masters* (Morrow, 1979); Michael Talbot, *The Holographic Universe* (HarperCollins, 1991); and Norman Friedman, *Bridging Science and Spirit* (Living Lake Books, 1994).

7 This particular meditative exercise, in which you focus on being more than your body, mind, and feelings is adapted from a psychological methodology called Psychosynthesis. See Roberto

Assagioli, *Psychosynthesis* (Hobbs, Dorman, 1965). Assagioli was a pioneer in the therapeutic use of imagery; his work synthesized spiritual and psychological perspectives.

8 It is sobering when we realize how much the mass media images that flood our consciousness fuel violence, eating disorders, restrictive gender coding, and mindless consumption. In his book, *Four Arguments for the Elimination of Television* (Morrow, 1978), Jerry Mander quotes the comments of researcher Eric Peper: "The horror of television is that information goes in, but we don't react to it. It goes right into our memory pool and perhaps we react to it later, but we don't know what we're reacting to....later on, you're doing things without knowing why you're doing them or where they came from" (211).

The average child spends 6 ½ hours per day watching television. For an overview of the issue of television and its effects see the American Psychological Association's summary of research on the impact of violent images on children: <www.apa.org/pubinfo/violence.html> and <www.mediaandthefamily.com/research/fact/

9 In my book *Working Inside Out* (Wingbow Press, 1984), I explore suggestibility and ways of changing deep-seated patterns and levels of consciousness in detail. See my Web site <www.toolsforchange.org> for information about the forthcoming revised edition.

10 The placebo effect brings about positive outcomes. In his book, *Timeless Healing*, Herbert Benson argues that there is a corresponding "nocebo" effect, in which negative expectations bring about negative effects. Benson says, "Just as our bodies can remember wellness, they can project sickness and even death" (39). Also see Larry Dossey, *Be Careful What You Pray For* (HarperSanFrancisco, 1997).

11 For a detailed description of the continuum of change, see Chapter Eight *Working Inside Out*.

12 I had the opportunity to join in a women's consciousness-raising group that was exploring techniques developed by Jose Silva. See <www.silvamethod.com> for more information.

13 See Benjamin B. Wolman, ed., *Handbook of Parapsychology* (Van Nostrand Reinhold, 1977), p. 193.

14 We can applaud the work of Caroline Myss, PhD, who has brought her work as a medical intuitive into the mainstream: see *Anatomy of the Spirit* (Harmony Books, 1996). Also see Mona Lisa Schulz, MD, PhD, *Awakening Intuition* (Harmony Books, 1998).

15 Do not assume that by using this example I subscribe to the notion that those with cancer are somehow to blame for their condition. The "you create your own reality" philosophy compounds people's problems by adding the burden of guilt. My intent is to depict how a real-life situation can benefit from Applied Meditation practice.

Part II

1 Recordings of the meditations in this book are available through Tools for Change. To order, see our Web site <www.toolsforchange.org>, email us at <meditation@toolsforchange.org>, or write to: Tools for Change, P.O. Box 14141, San Francisco, CA 94114.

2 The gap between rich and poor continues to grow. On average a CEO now receives a salary that is 475 times that of a worker; the corresponding figure for 1980 was 42 times. See <www.unitedforafaireconomy.org> for more information.

3 For comprehensive surveys of scientific studies that address the impact of prayer on healing, see Larry Dossey, MD, *Healing Words* (HarperSanFrancisco, 1993); *Prayer Is Good Medicine* (HarperSanFrancisco, 1996); and *Reinventing Medicine* (HarperSanFrancisco, 1999). One of the most widely publicized of these studies was conducted by Dr. Randolph Byrd at the coronary care unit at San Francisco General Hospital. In a double-blind study half the patients had people praying for them; half did not. Results showed that patients who were prayed for fared better than those who were not. For an on-line write-up about Dr. Byrd's study, see "The Proof That Prayer Works" (February 25, 2001) at <www.holisticonline.com>. This Web site also provides an overview of the latest research on prayer and the use of imagery.

4 See chapter six, "Energy Circles: Concentrating Consciousness," *Working Inside Out* for a full description of how to work with Energy Circles — a form of collective meditation by which people support one another and channel energy where it is needed.

5 See Note 1.

6 If you would like help in starting or finding Applied Meditation groups in your area, see our Web site <www.toolsforchange.org> or email us at <meditation@toolsforchange.org>.

7 See note 6.

8 See Notes 1, 4, and 6.

Part III

1 Please see Chapter Six of *Working Inside Out* for an explanation on using this technique. Or visit my Web site at <www.toolsforchange.org> for more information.

2 This meditation was inspired by a presentation "Lessons from the Geese," which was transcribed from a speech given by Angeles Arrien at The 1991 Organizational Development Network.

Meditations Listed by ID Numbers and Page Locations

Meditations Use Index

Note: *Numbers refer to Meditation ID numbers.*

Tools ❖ for ❖ Change

Tools for Change is a multi-cultural organization working with individuals to promote healing and leadership development; and with organizations to create sustainable democratic structures in which everyone can contribute their best. In our work, we call on spirit, heart, history, collectivity and vision. We offer long-term consultation, large group meeting design and facilitation, as well as training in power, diversity and vision-building. For those engaged in making social and ecological justice, we host gatherings to inspire dialogue, open the imagination, deepen relationships and empower people's work.

Available from *Tools for Change:*
- o RECORDINGS of the meditations found in this book, organized topically, including: Healing, Healthy Relationships, Leadership and more.
- o CUSTOM RECORDED MEDITATIONS made to fit your specific individual or group needs.
- o *WORKING INSIDE OUT:* APPLIED MEDITATION TAPES for intuitive problem solving on personal, interpersonal and community levels.
- o ADDITIONAL PUBLICATIONS *The Subjective Side of Politics, Breaking Old Patterns: Weaving New Ties, From Leadership to Empowerment* and forthcoming publications on facilitating Circles.

Contact **Tools for Change** *to find others in your region to work with:*
- o APPLIED MEDITATION SUPPORT GROUPS:. Get together on a regular basis to meditate. We offer information to help start and sustain groups.
- o CIRCLES FOR CHANGE: study the integration of politics and spirituality. *Tools for Change* will provide you study guides and other support materials as well as ways to share your experiences with other groups.
- o APPLIED MEDITATION TRAINING: *Basic* – explore imagination, intuition and mindfulness; *Advanced* – Hone your practice; *Leadership* – design and lead meditations for individual problem solving and group settings.

Let us know how you are using *Meditations On Everything Under the Sun* — what difference it has made; where you use it; what adaptations and you have made; what has left you wanting; and what would support your journey.

Bring *Tools for Change* to your area — contact us for our schedule.

For more information: www.toolsforchange.org
Write: info@toolsforchange.org or PO Box 14141, San Francisco CA 94114
Call: 1 800-99TOOLS

About the Author

M ARGO ADAIR has been developing and teaching Applied Meditation for Intuitive Problem Solving since 1975. She maintains a private practice, working with people individually and facilitating support groups. She is the author of *Working Inside Out* (Wingbow, 1985) and founder of *Tools for Change* which offers consulting and training services across North America. Along with a culturally and geographically diverse team, Adair has worked with organizations and groups committed to ecological and social justice. Coauthor of *Breaking Old Patterns Weaving New Ties: Alliance Building and The Subjective Side of Politics* (both published by *Tools for Change*), her work weaves together political, psychological and spiritual perspectives for personal, interpersonal and planetary healing. She lives in both Seattle and San Francisco.

If you have enjoyed *Meditations On Everything Under The Sun*,
you might also enjoy other

BOOKS TO BUILD A NEW SOCIETY

Our books provide positive solutions for people who want to
make a difference. We specialize in:

Sustainable Living • Ecological Design and Planning
Natural Building & Appropriate Technology • New Forestry
Environment and Justice • Conscientious Commerce
Progressive Leadership • Resistance and Community • Nonviolence
Educational and Parenting Resources

New Society Publishers

ENVIRONMENTAL BENEFITS STATEMENT

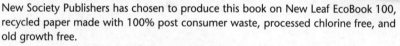

New Society Publishers has chosen to produce this book on New Leaf EcoBook 100,
recycled paper made with 100% post consumer waste, processed chlorine free, and
old growth free.

For every 5,000 books printed, New Society saves the following resources:[1]

50	Trees
4,484	Pounds of Solid Waste
4,934	Gallons of Water
6,435	Kilowatt Hours of Electricity
8,151	Pounds of Greenhouse Gases
35	Pounds of HAPs, VOCs, and AOX Combined
12	Cubic Yards of Landfill Space

[1]Environmental benefits are calculated based on research done by the Environmental Defense Fund and
other members of the Paper Task Force who study the environmental impacts of the paper industry.
For more information on this environmental benefits statement, or to inquire about environmentally
friendly papers, please contact New Leaf Paper – info@newleafpaper.com Tel: 888 • 989 • 5323.

For a full list of NSP's titles, please call **1-800-567-6772** *or check out our web site at:*

www.newsociety.com

NEW SOCIETY PUBLISHERS